Conversations on Photography

KEHRER

Index

Foreword
Antonio Cataldo

During the autumn of 2018, we started conversations with performance artist Marthe Ramm Fortun. Her relation to photography is manifold and grew during her time at New York University, where she taught analogue photography in the school's darkroom. The subject of our discussions was the failure of history to adequately and equally report artistic positions, especially within small-sized institutions such as Fotogalleriet, which I had come to direct some months earlier. Work on the archive to uncover close to half a century of work had started prior to my arrival at the institution. When studying it, I became preoccupied by the way in which certain stories are repeated so often that they become legend, and how this, supported by academic writing, is the mechanism through which history is formed and then cemented as hard truth. Some bodies are granted an existence for posterity, while others become invisible.[1] Central questions around the construction of paradigms and artistic positioning in art and photographic history cannot be solved via a univocal answer. There are multifaceted reasons behind the founding and labelling of artistic movements, through which art history seals social attitudes to class, provenance and gender, propagating canonical views on art by universalising and popularising them.[2] Living at the height of an economic system called globalisation, where the alienation of labour goes hand in hand with the alienation of knowledge, communicating and preserving a multiplicity of histories within the day-to-day operation of an institution is a Borgesian task.[3] Institutional duty, however, calls for an attempt to be made.

Struggles for emancipation have been the motor guiding photography as a medium outside its prescribed role of mirroring nature first, the page later, and its final inscription as an art form in its own right.[4] While being based in Scandinavia, however, a region at the forefront of feminist, equality, and welfare issues, Fotogalleriet takes a surprisingly, almost unconscious and certainly unspoken conservative approach to its own history, which it has not sought to 'trouble'.[5] If the way in which what happened in the past is retold erects the pillars for the present, then failure to question this past undermines the possibility to build a different future. In this respect, it is important to analyse how patterns have

Antonio Cataldo has been the Artistic Director of Fotogalleriet since 2018.

[1]
In the creation and perpetration of history, there is a movement between collective and individual memory, as well as a social framework of definition. 'The family, the neighborhood, the peer group, the generation, the nation, the culture are … larger groups that individuals incorporate into their identity by referring to them as "we". Each "we" is constructed through shared practices and discourses that mark certain boundaries and define the principles of inclusion and exclusion. To be part of a collective group such as the nation one has to share and adopt the group's history, which exceeds the boundaries of one's individual life span.' Aleida Assmann, 'Transformations between History and Memory', *Social Research*, vol. 75, no. 1, *Collective Memory and Collective Identity* (Spring 2008), 49–72. It is important here also to keep in mind anticolonial practices pushing for greater attention to methods foregrounding an intersectional engagement with gender, class, sexuality, nation, disability and other axes of identity that shape knowledge production, in particular addressing the renewed gap brought about by new technology. See: Elizabeth Povinelli, 'The Woman on the Other Side of the Wall: Archiving the Otherwise in Postcolonial Digital Archives', *differences.* 22 (1), 2011, 146–71. See also: Roopika Risam, 'Decolonizing The Digital Humanities in Theory And Practice' (2018). https://digitalcommons.salemstate.edu/english_facpub/7 (accessed 11 May 2020).

[2]
Manuel João Ramos, 'Drawing the lines. The limitations of intercultural ekphrasis', in Ana Afonso et al., *Working Images. Visual Research and Representation in Ethnography* (London: Routledge, 2004), 147–56.

Antonio Cataldo

been institutionalised as historical 'facts', and why difference has not been inscribed in schoolbooks, in the vocabulary, in institutions. Forms of foreclosure are in the very words and concepts that inform thinking.

In an institution devoted to still and moving images, image production and its ethics are ever important. They have also come to dominate the outside world. Whether on smartphone screens or advertisement hoardings in the urban landscape, it is the rhetoric of images, not of words, that is now the guiding principle.[6] As subjects looking for individual and collective sovereignty, our senses are ruled by images. Therefore it is necessary to maintain a constant understanding that these visual images are not randomly produced, but more often than not subtly aimed at commerce, with the intention to captivate us and stimulate our desire to purchase material and immaterial products. These are one-direction images: we have no power to affect them. If we are to wake from the daydream through which we attempt to 'profile' our eternal happiness through social media, we should ask instead how we see and how representations mirror society, and we should question why we must conform rather than create our own relation to the world of images. I believe that art guides our aesthetic experience in a different way, which deepens the ability of a body to become vulnerable to what surrounds it, to let itself be taken over by sensations, and to note the disparity between forms of reality fluctuating under an apparent stability.[7]

In order to address these issues, Ramm Fortun embarked on the task of navigating Fotogalleriet's extensive archive both literally and poetically. She delved into the available material and conceived a number of performances both within and outside our premises, bringing in the physical location surrounding the institution, which is usually taken for granted. She studied the institution's life beyond its working hours as an exhibition space, seeing its living architecture as an agent within a breathing neighbourhood, rather than an artificial space uprooted from its environment. She used the interior of Fotogalleriet as an intimate room, licking its ceiling, smashing the archive against its walls (the physical limitations of the art space for thinking), tearing apart celebratory pages and trembling on a structure resembling a hospital bed in the middle of the exhibition room. Outside – in the park facing the street, populated by different categories of Oslo's

Foreword

3
Forms of knowledge alienation have been studied through cognitive capitalism, defining the accumulation of immaterial capital in the dissemination of knowledge, and the driving role of the knowledge economy today. See: Yann Moulier Boutang, *Cognitive Capitalism* (Cambridge: Polity Press, 2011), 50. Melvin Seeman, 'Alienation and Knowledge-Seeking: A Note on Attitude and Action', *Social Problems* 20, no. 1 (1972): 3–17.

4
Nancy Van House, et al., 'The Social Uses of Personal Photography: Methods for Projecting Future Imaging Applications', 2004. http://www.sims.berkeley.edu/~vanhouse/pubs.htm (accessed 12 May 2020).

5
I refer here to the concept of 'trouble' as formulated by Judith Butler. Power operates in the production of a binary gender frame, and the internal stability of those terms. Judith Butler, *Gender Trouble: Feminism and the Subversion of Identity* (New York: Routledge, 1990), viii. What happens if we apply these constructions of power to art institution? What happens to their subject and their ontology? Rather than basing itself on the structure of an experimental kunsthalle for photography, Fotogalleriet cemented its form to mirror a small museum during the last decade. For instance, artist Shirana Shahbazi calls it 'Museum Fotogalleriet' in her biography. See: http://www.peterkilchmann.com/exhibitions/past/shirana-shahbazi (accessed 16 May 2020). The problem with museums is that they are powerful institutions that are often unchallenged by their publics. Art museums in particular position themselves as the protectors of a collective aesthetic past, and as curators of the contemporary moment. Often museums catalogue and display a collection of artworks and artifacts that represent the ideals of a privileged cadre of gatekeepers who have cultural

inhabitants at different times of the day and night – she shook the blossoming tree in the park and ate its unripened flowers, at midnight, welcoming a hoard of unusual art visitors while mumbling a chant, an unspoken request. She hugged people to campaign for the tacit plea. She quivered with them.[8]

When the white cube reveals its resemblance in this way to other institutions such as the hospital, the prison, the school and the factory, it too seems to shiver – it becomes less secure, less safe. The relation between cure and curating is not random here, since certain forms of curating have 'purified' and simplified the normalising institutional apparatus grounding the concept of the white cube.[9] Ramm Fortun's use of the ceiling in her performance – which could be translated into a glass ceiling, where you imagine you have open access to what's above, but in fact it's an illusion, harder than a concrete wall – was inspired by a manuscript by Henny Lie that she found in the archives. Lie is an artist who was extremely active during the first years of Fotogalleriet and its establishment as a landmark institution in a cityscape that lacked a critical discussion around photographic art. She planned a playful and witty book, which never found a publisher – perhaps due to this very glass ceiling. Ramm Fortun decided to let the book speak for itself, as a document without a body for posterity.

Ramm Fortun's performance was an experiment to find a method to shake history and how we think we know it. She sought to give the archive a vindicatory power, providing a core to the poetics of those artistic proposals whose potency resides in their vitality and the virus they carry with them.[10] In this case, to quote the archive means to access its living effects, the ideas inscribed in the institution's memory. These hints at inherited traumas can be actualised in new ideas, instead of creating a sterile scholarly archive inscribed in our representational memory and reproduced to authorise other writing.[11] History is written by power, yes, but it is also unwritten by the many who seek recognition for other forms of truth, and other forms of being. It is how we fight to attain equality and a more porous, diverse and rich storytelling with multiple outputs concerning multiple realities.[12] Ramm Fortun's notes for her yet unfinished performance cycle are reproduced here in order to undermine any claim to the linearity of history, and to weaken any attempt to read this book as a conclusive statement on the institution or the subject matter.

Antonio Cataldo

and economic power. Social inequality and hierarchies organised by gender, sexuality, social class and other identitarian forms are evident in the context of museum collections. See: Mary Kosut, 'Gender in the Museum', in: Renee C. Hoogland, *Gender: Nature* (New York: MacMillian, 2016).

6
In 'Rhetoric of the Image', Roland Barthes examines the messages that images contain, and the role they play in creating an ideological worldview. He focuses on commercials since they contain a highly condensed image that aims for maximum efficiency in conveying its message. Roland Barthes, *Image. Music. Text* (New York: Hill and Wang, 1977), 32–51. Harun Farocki speaks about 'ruling' images: 'computer images can really become ruling images, and I think they already belong to the ruling class'. Harun Farocki: 'Computer Animation Rules', IKKM Lectures, video recorded, delivered on 25 June 2014. hdl.handle.net/11346/0S9T (accessed 15 May 2020).

7
Suely Rolnik, *Archive Mania: 100 Notes, 100 Thoughts: Documenta Series 022* (Berlin: Hatje Cantz, 2011).

8
Marthe Ramm Fortun's intervention started within the exhibition *Women in Three Acts* curated by Kati Simon, which opened on 14 March 2019. A second performance, *LOOK AROUND IN JOY*, was held at the stroke of midnight on 27 April 2019. A third one is forthcoming.

9
Felix Ensslin, 'The Subject of Curating – Notes on the Path towards a Cultural Clinic of the Present', *OnCurating.org*, no. 26, October 2015, *Curating Degree Zero Archive: Curatorial Research*, 17–31.

10
Rolnik 2011 (see note 7), 11.

11
Ibid.

12
Lucy M. Salmon, 'Why Is History Rewritten?', *The North American Review*, vol.

Institutions themselves are often born out of frustration, and this is no less true for Fotogalleriet. Indeed, when I said this in a public presentation, one of the institution's founders told me I had given words to the very feeling that had prompted Fotogalleriet's foundation.[13] As the first *fotohalle* in the Nordic Countries, Fotogalleriet responded to a lack of critical discussions around photography as a free art form unveiling subjective positions. I often return to this recent moment in history – the launch of Fotogalleriet in 1977 – during my public speeches, because there is an empowering emancipatory satisfaction in literally creating a space to re-access the role that artistic practices have in shaping democratic processes – and this is even more true today. To fill a gap in the system, to initiate a kunsthalle for photography, was to mark out a guiding principle not to preserve the medium, but rather to mediate the critical ideas it generates, and to show-case contemporary production in a location where permanent collections and museum facilities were few.[14]

* * *

The book you hold in your hands is the result of a dialogue with individuals who have shaped a critical photographic discourse during the last half of a century in the Nordic Countries and beyond. These conversations were held between 2018 and 2020, and all the practitioners have contributed to Fotogalleriet's programming, as well as participating in important international exhibition venues around the world. Each conversation unravels a story from photographic history – something that was missing or unacknowledged. In opposition to academia, which privileges a self-referential way of writing history, the conversation form leaves spaces open; it is less assertive, and threatens the canonical idea of the singular artist as a genius. Therefore, the oral conversation, here transcribed and edited for readability, becomes politically motivated and, in the spirit of Fotogalleriet, calls for an experimental approach refusing singular forms of categorisation.

The conversations collected in this book are not classic interviews. There is no univocal principle connecting them, and there is no single tendency towards definite answers. Institutions' histories are complex. Artistic work and artists' long-term research are complex. Intricate networks of story-telling and platforming are needed in order to honour these

195, no. 675 (Feb. 1912), 225–37. Alfred Schutz 'On Multiple Realities', in: Maurice Natanson (ed.), *Collected Papers I. Phaenomenologica* (Collection Publiée Sous le Patronage des Centres d'Archives-Husserl, vol. II, Springer: Dordrecht, 1962), 207–59.

13
Presentation for a professional meeting organised by the Henie Onstad Kunstsenter on 12 June 2019.

14
Here, I'm referring to a larger history of kunsthalles as spaces emerging in Europe to present temporary exhibitions of art and science before the evolution of the modern museum (1793) and of the grand exposition (1851). The first kunsthalle, the Kunstverein Nuremberg, was founded in 1792 as a Kunstsozietät, an association of art enthusiasts and artists, dedicated to the mediation of contemporary art and for debating societal issues raised by artists. https://kunstvereinnuernberg.de/en/kunstverein (accessed 8 March 2020). See also: Gerald Matt, *Kunst und Geld, Das Museum, ein Unternehmen* [Art and Money, The Museum, a Company] (Vienna: Verlag Österreich, 2001), 46.

complexities. In this assemblage, we did not aim to highlight artistic successes, but to unveil the strategies and motives behind their unique productions, as well as the effect of world events taking place at the time their work was being shown. In addition, we aimed to discover why certain images are still meaningful to this day, and how that meaning can change – to put it in Walter Benjamin's words, how history is driven 'irresistibly into the future'.

* * *

During the past five decades, we have witnessed a plethora of paradigmatic shifts within the medium specificity of photography, with its constant technological flux generating a multiplicity of discourses. But we cannot consider this a straightforward evolution. Quite the opposite,[15] it is a roller coaster that is today at one of its peaks, with a cluster of institutions showing a renewed interest in the medium and demonstrating that photography is as important today as it was half a century ago. The role images have come to play in our everyday lives is not unprecedented: it is part of modernity and of living in the information age.[16]

During the 1970s, when Fotogalleriet launched its programmes, a historical transition was taking place within the field.[17] Traditional practices were not only being questioned but also undermined. That photography managed to profile itself as a tool for self-expression equal to other art forms was amplified by the teaching in art schools of the subject in its own right.[18] One of the first institutions to do so was Trent Polytechnic in Nottingham, UK. The photographer Paul Hill led a course there called 'Social Documentation'. In this way, he became the mentor of two of the acknowledged founders of Fotogalleriet, Dag Alveng and Tom Sandberg (1953–2014), who took the course at Trent Polytechnic due to a lack of similar programmes in Oslo. In 1977, Hill was invited to be the subject of the first Fotogalleriet exhibition, together with Raymond Moore. In 1979, Hill also co-authored with Thomas Cooper, *Dialogues with Photography*,[19] among the first published records of interviews with photographers, done by artists for artists.[20] He continues to be an active voice in the field today, practising, lecturing and giving workshops, as well as advocating for further development of the space and language of the medium. We invited him to discuss his story

9.　　　　Antonio Cataldo

15
See: Rosalind E. Krauss, 'Reinventing the Medium', *Critical Inquiry*, vol. 25, no. 2, 289–305. See also: 'Photography in Flux – Reinventing the Medium', a seminar held on 15 March 2012, moderated by curator, writer and *Art in America* contributing editor Marvin Heiferman, with Matthew Witkovsky, Roe Ethridge, Jane Hait and Vince Aletti.

16
The discourse around the technologisation of the image, liberating it from its 'parasitical' dependence on religion ritual, and thus allowing it to lose its 'aura', is key for Walter Benjamin. Walter Benjamin, 'The Work of Art in the Age of Mechanical Reproduction', in: Hannah Arendt (ed.), *Illuminations*, (New York: Schocken Books, 1969), 31–41. In the mid-1960s, Marshall McLuhan argued that the Western world, after five centuries, was exiting print culture into something new. He prophesied that electronic media would create an increasingly interconnected world. See: Marshall McLuhan, *The Gutenberg Galaxy: The Making of Typographic Man* (Toronto: University of Toronto Press, 1962). Such theories popularised the idea of the end of machine-age technology, opening up for an information-technology era. See: Edward A. Shanken, 'Art in the Information Age: Technology and Conceptual Art', in: Michael Corris (ed.), *Conceptual Art: Theory, Myth and Practice* (Cambridge: Cambridge University Press, 2004).

17
In his essay for the 25th anniversary of the Fotomuseum Winterthur, art historian and photography curator Florian Ebner retraces the inception of independent places for photography in Europe. The first fotohalle was established in Germany in 1975. See: Florian Ebner, 'Smell Elvis's Brilliantine, Feels the Whoosh of Reality, Encounter the Faces of Power', in: Nadine Wietlisbach et al. (eds.), *25 Years! Fotomuseum*

with Aaron Schuman, an artist and an educator in his own right. Schuman has been pivotal to Fotogalleriet in recent years, mentoring upcoming practitioners in Norway, such as Terje Abusdal, the winner of prestigious photographic prizes including Fotogalleriet's Nordic Photobook Award in 2017.

Dag Alveng has unquestionably been a central voice within the photographic field in the region, yet almost no trace of his relation to Fotogalleriet has been left in the institution's archives. The Henie Onstad Kunstsenter, a central collaborator and supporter of Fotogalleriet's work in its establishment and foundation, held a retrospective of Alveng's work in 2018, curated by Susanne Østby Sæther.[21] She spoke to Alveng especially for this publication, unveiling his seminal conceptual approach to art-making, specifically within the sphere of photography, a yet to be fully recognised position at the time.

A year prior to Alveng's debut exhibition at Fotogalleriet, in 1978, the institution hosted one of the first solo exhibitions of the prolific artist Marianne Heske. Her name is inscribed in the tradition of conceptual art, but her allegiance to the world of photography is less well known. Her inclusion in Fotogalleriet's programme in 1978 proves its vision of photography as an experimental field where boundaries were open and porous. For her contribution in this book, artist, writer and professor Lotte Konow Lund engaged in a journey spanning Heske's lifetime work, her notes and her time in Paris in the 1970s and 80s, revealing the mutual influence between Heske and the Fluxus artists with whom she shared time and space in the French capital.

On the other end of the spectrum of photography's preoccupation during those pivotal years, we find records of Ellisif Ranveig Wessel, born Müller (1866–1949), known as a writer, trade unionist and politician and less known as a groundbreaking photographer. Artist Eline Mugaas brought her to my attention when I shared with her my preoccupation about decisive positions being silenced by time. Mugaas is known for building her own art genealogy and historiography. Her relentless research as a photographer reaches far beyond the known, always looking for escapist forms of knowledge – the non-given.[22] Believing that academic research alone is a patriarchal way of validating knowledge, she contributes to this publication with a visual conversation with Wessel, possibly the only one to reconnect with the artist's work. Wessel's exhibition at Fotogalleriet in 1978 was amongst a number of

Winterthur: Shared Histories, Shared Stories: Fast Forward (Leipzig: Spector Books, 2018), 213–23.

18
In Norway, photographer, critic and professor Robert Meyer had advocated for the use of photography as a free tool of self-expression, 'free photography', in the 1960s. Freedom, he says, always needs to be seen in relation to defined structures and within a certain context. Robert Meyer in conversation with the author, unpublished interview, 15 August 2019. See also: Paul Hill, 'How British Photography Found Its Voice', http://www.hillon-photography.co.uk/writings/how_british_photography_found_its_voice.pdf (accessed 10 February 2020).

19
As described in the interview for this book, *Dialogue with Photography* was published in 1979 by Farrar Straus & Giroux, who had already printed Susan Sontag's *On Photography* (1977) and other text-based books about photography. In *On Photography*, Sontag expresses her views on the history and present-day role of photography in capitalist societies. She makes a harsh critique of documentary photography as an act dictating: 'what is worth looking at and what we have a right to observe'. Susan Sontag, *On Photography* (New York: Farrar Straus & Giroux, 1977), 11.

20
David Campany, *So Present, so Invisible. Conversations on photography* (Rome: Contrasto, 2018), 6.

landmark programmes at the turn of the decade looking into socially engaged photography within and outside the arts, bringing together unrecognised local and famous international figures such as Diane Arbus, Lewis W. Hine and Christer Strömholm, who had started to access the realm of the white cube.

In studying the archives, we came across conflicting documents about the foundational years – important records because they weaken the possibility of flattening history univocally and uni-directionally – showing a multiplicity of engagements fundamental in shaping the institutional long-term vision, and gaining external support from both the artistic and the extended community.[23] My colleague and editorial coordinator of this publication, Karen Fosse Rosness, started a conversation with Gry Martinsen to pick her brain about such troves. Martinsen was part of the working group that launched Fotogalleriet, as well one of the signatories, together with Anna Thurmann-Nilsen, of *Daily life at Fotogalleriet*, a memorandum reporting the rules of conduct and general procedures, together with recording visitors, financial and other notes during the first two years of the institution's existence.[24] In 1968, Gry and her life-partner, photographer Tom Martinsen (1943–2007), had met Ann Christine Eek at the School of Photography (Fotoskolan) in Stockholm, and they invited her in 1978 to exhibit *Arbeta – inte slita ut sig* (Work – Don't Wear Yourself Out), a work that was central in the formation of Scandinavia's feminist history.[25] In conversation with Moderna Museet's curator Anna Tellgren, Eek clarifies her research and position at the time, when she was moving from Sweden to Norway in an attempt to escape the already overdetermined categories within the field of photography.

If Ellisif Wessel was privileged enough to document the Indigenous Sør-Varanger area of Norway at the turn of the twentieth century – leaving unique records of the region behind – I was lucky enough to have a number of conversations with Bente Geving about her work as a Sámi artist, including touching upon her thoughts about the historical images Wessel took of the Sámi people. Geving's own take on her Sámi family in the area is equally unique. They belonged to the generation that bridged Sámi shame under the Norwegianisation process with Sámi pride after the Alta Uprising in 1979. Geving reconnected with them late in their lives, when only the last traces of their Sáminess remained.[26] She builds on

II.

Antonio Cataldo

21
In the statute of Fotogalleriet from 1979, Henie Onstad Kunstsenter appears as one of the founders. This is repeated in subsequent editions and revisions, but has dropped out of knowledge.

22
Eline Mugaas shared some of these opinions in the conversation 'Publishing from a Feminist Perspective' with Delphine Bedel, moderated by Tine Semb on Thursday, 22 November 2018 as part of Fotogalleriet's series 'Let's Talk About Images'.

23
In the first number of the *Nordisk Fotohistorisk Journal*, Robert Meyer mentions Tom Sandberg and Dag Alveng as Fotogalleriet initiators, who were subsequently followed by others, including Jamie Parslow, Tom Martinsen, Anne Thurman-Nielsen, and Vidar Askland. He also mentions Gry Martinsen as taking on the daily managment of the institution. *Nordisk Fotohistorisk Journal*, vol.1 no.1. July 1977. Knut Evensen, in: 'Fotografiet får sitt galleri' [Photography Gets its own Gallery], *(Dagbladet*, 25 July 1977) reports a group of founders consisting of photographer and medicine student Dag Alveng, photographer and editor Vidar Askland, journalist and bookshop manager Bjørn Høyum, children's pedagogue, author, translator and journalist Gry Martinsen, photographer Tom Martinsen, social worker and photographer Anne Thurman-Nielsen, photographer Jamie Parslow, photographer and editor Tom Sandberg, in addition to more loosely connected members of the group Øyvind Hagen, Frode Holand and Per Berntsen. Gry Martinsen and Jamie Parslow speak on behalf on the working group in: Sissel Keyn, 'Kunstens realister for sitting eget galleri' [Art Realists Found Their Own Gallery], *VG*, 13 August 1977. Jamie Parslow, Anne Thurman-Nielsen and Tom Martinsen are mentioned as three of the founders of Fotogalleriet in: 'Oslos første

this trauma in a non-nostalgic way by chronicling the sense of a community's resistance to colonial processes via its smallest nucleus, the relation between three sisters: Anna, Inga and Ellen.

Wessel's images can be found in several museum collections today, the largest located at the Grenselandmuseet in Kirkenes, which tells the story of the people, groups, constructions, natural and cultural landscapes in Sør-Varanger, a society forced to transition from its traditional livelihood to industrial growth. The results of this attempt at cultural-historical self-preservation are some of the last visual traces remaining of Finnmark county, systematically bombed and burned during World War II. Geving's image production, almost in contraposition to Wessel's socio-documentarian perspective, questions the sterile positioning of images in the space of a museum, and argues for the need for the situatedness of artefacts (including images) whose context enables a sensorial reconnection to peoples and their cultural belonging, instead of risking an appropriation dictated by the forces of scientific research.[27] Through these discussions, Geving was able to trace a photograph of her grandmother as a child, taken by Wessel during her wanderings in Sápmi. I found this proof that their paths had actually crossed and that they may even have been in conversation – which for months had only been speculation – deeply affecting. We are reproducing the image in this book as a testimony to the truth of Geving's belief that history should never be spelt with a capital H, and should always be seen as plural histories.

The 1980s, when Geving visited Sør-Varanger, was a time when the Sámi people were embarking on a movement of renewed reconnection to their forbidden and forgotten traditions. After the peak of the Indigenous uprising of 1979 in Alta, reparations were made by the state of Norway in the form of financial support for the establishment of Sámediggi, the Sámi Parliament of Norway, and other related programmes. In 1997, King Harald V issued an official apology on behalf of the government to the Sámi and Kven people.[28]

The recognition of injustices perpetrated on the northernmost populations goes hand-in-hand with studying the formation of the nationalist ideas on which the Norwegianisation process had been based. Photography was an instrumental tool for building the ideals of a people in search of its own identity. We asked choreographer, artist and producer

fast fotogalleri' [Oslo's First Photogallery], *Aftensposten*, 21 January 1978.

24
Dagliv i Fotogalleriet [Daily Life at Fotogalleriet] is a notebook in Fotogalleriet's archives. The newspaper article to which I refer is by Sissel Keyn, 'Kunstens realister får sitt eget galleri' [Art Realists Get Their Own Gallery], *VG*, 13 August 1977.

25
See: 'Work – Don't Wear Yourself Out – A Life in Black and White Photography', a conversation between the photographer Ann Christine Eek and curator Anna Tellgren, published in this book, 91.

26
Norwegianisation was an official policy carried out by the Norwegian government directed at the Sámi and later the Kven people of northern Norway to assimilate non-Norwegian-speaking native populations into an ethnically and culturally uniform Norwegian population. The practice has roots in missionary programmes of the 1700s, but formally began as official government policy in the late 1800s. The practices were motivated by Norwegian nationalism and also by religious differences between the Sámi and the Norwegian populations (the Sámi practised animism and polytheism, while the Lutheran Church of Norway was the official state religion). The Norwegianisation policy was discontinued as late as the 1980s. See: Henry Minde, 'Fornorskinga av samene – hvorfor, hvordan og hvilke følger?' [Sámi Norwegianisation – why, how and what follows?], in *Samisk skolehistorie 1* [Sámi School History. vol. 1] (Kárášjohka: Davvi Girji, 2005).

27
Sigrid Lien, 'The Aesthetics of the Bear Hunt: Contemporary Photography in the Ecology of a Sámi Museum', in: Elizabeth Edwards et al. (eds.), *Uncertain Images: Museums and the Work of Photographs* (New York: Routledge, 2014), 95–112.

Foreword

Helle Siljeholm, who is working on developing poetic aggregations of human bodies in relation to nature and culture – in the form of mountain-climbing structures – to discuss these ideas with artist and educator Robert Meyer, a central local figure, and the first chairman of Fotogalleriet. They unveil radical ideas about research into national collections and photographic work made in order to construct an iconic Norway as a *terra nullius*, a majestic land dominated by nature, following a nationalism in need of images to support the ideal behind the newly established, independent nation state.

Hanne Hammer Stein, curator and associate professor at the UiT, further complicates such positions through her focus on the work of Kåre Kivijärvi (1938–1991), a Kven photographer who first crossed the realm of visual arts from documentarian practices in 1971.[29] According to Hammer Stien, Kivijärvi creates a 'deterritorialised' and 'conflicted' image of the region, opposing a dehumanised representation of the north coming from that romantic tradition that Meyer describes in his research into the nationalist project.

The north continues to be the cradle of legends and make believe. It is a territory often identified with the Vikings – not necessarily the Norse people inhabiting primarily southern Scandinavia from the late eighth to late eleventh centuries, but a more abstract one-dimensional concept of warriors, invaders, predators and sanguineous barbarians and explorers. Artist and relentless agitator Lill-Ann Chepstow-Lusty, who moved from England to Norway in 1981, embraces these popularised stories, taking them to their logical conclusion. Her project *Absolut Viking* (2000–02) is a unique documentation of the way Vikings are perceived internationally, recorded at Viking festivals around the world. Chepstow-Lusty's personal and institutional obsessions have made her a key voice of dissent from conformist traditions. She has spearheaded a number of projects against normalising institutions, including *Gay Kids*, a schoolbook for children of all ages (and an exhibition) retracing gay, lesbian and bisexual childhoods, and deconstructing the institutionalised claim of gendered bodies by looking into people's photographic archives.[30] In conversation with art historian Liv Brissach, Chepstow-Lusty retraces the stepping stones of her work, including her important contribution to feminist art and curating. At the age of twenty, before being exiled by her parents to Oslo, she contributed to the ground-breaking ICA exhibition *Women's Images of*

[28] This struggle for emancipation of the Sámi peoples is longstanding and ongoing. See: Urban Wråkberg and Karin Granqvist, 'Decolonizing technoscience in northern Scandinavia: The role of scholarship in Sámi emancipation and the indigenization of Western science', in: *Journal of Historical Geography*, vol. 44, 2014, 81–92. See also: Henry Minde, 'Assimilation of the Sami – Implementation and Consequences', in: *Acta Borealia*, vol. 20, 121–46.

[29] Kivijärvi was the first photographer to be accepted within the Autumn Exhibition (Høstutstilling), the Norwegian salon of acceptance into the visual art world, in 1971.

[30] *Gay Kids* was published on 6 November 2008 and an exhibition of the book's photographic material was on display outside the Museum of Cultural History in Oslo from January to July 2009. Rolf Martin Angeltvedt, et al. (eds.), *Gay kids. kule barn som også finnes* (Oslo: Abstrakt forlag, 2008).

Antonio Cataldo

Men (1980) in London, and one of her works even became the cover of the book. To give a picture of how needed that exhibition was, the queue to enter reached from the ICA in the Mall to Trafalgar Square.

Gender became a contested category during the 1980s following important laws decriminalising homosexuality in a number of countries all over the world, but also unfortunately by the AIDS outbreak. Fin Serck-Hanssen's portraits of AIDS sufferers have become iconic, giving a face to the epidemic – not simply portraying victims, but people. Colombian researcher Michael Forero, co-founder of Museo Q, conducted a conversation with Serck-Hanssen over a period of two months to delve into issues of homosexuality, collective memory, architecture and how to 'queer' exhibition spaces. Forero quotes Professor Jonathan Katz, who maintains that 'historically, queer art has drawn power from oppression and from the inventiveness, ingenuity and originality it encouraged as a strategy of survival'.[31]

With the advent of the Internet, still and moving images began to intersect and blur into one another. Victor Burgin, who participated in a seminar at Fotogalleriet in 2005 titled 'On Time', had recently published the book *The Remembered Film* (2004), where he wrote about the cinematic heterotopia – an in-between space (material and imaginary) in which we encounter heterogeneous fragments of film that can no longer be confined to the physical space of the movie theatre. The Internet comes to play a major role in such a reconfiguration of mainstream cinema: 'video mashups' and 'machinima', as Burgin calls these new experiences.[32] These ideas resonate with Amar Kanwar's statement about his first solo exhibition in Norway, *Portraits*, presented at Fotogalleriet in 2005. Kanwar writes in his introduction to the slim exhibition catalogue:

> The project is conceived in a manner presentable in many forms – as a series of small films or fragments that can be exhibited in varied combinations or as a single long film that integrates its many parts. It can also be seen as a series of films and events closely linked to collaborative educational processes and experimenting with different media, forms of expression and exhibition.[33]

31
Jonathan Katz. 'Hide/Seek: Difference and Desire in American Portraiture', in: Jonathan D. Katz and David C. Ward (eds.), *Hide/Seek: Difference and Desire in American Portraiture* (Washington, DC: Smithsonian Books, 2010), 10-57 (56). Companion volume to the exhibition of the same name which opened at the National Portrait Gallery, Smithsonian Institution, October 2010.

32
Victor Burgin, *The Remembered Film* (London: Reaktion Books, 2004), 7: 'the cinematic heterotopia [is] a hybrid material and imaginary space in which we encounter a heterogeneous variety of fragments of cinema beyond the confines of the movie theatre. The internet, of course, is a major contributor to this space, and I spoke about two current internet practices which draw upon and reconfigure mainstream cinema: "video mashups" and "machinima". The remixed Hollywood film trailer seems the most popular mashup genre, often used to lampoon box-office hits. Other mashups satirize prominent politicians, or provide new image-track accompaniments to popular songs. In contrast to video mashups, which cannibalize contents from outside the software used to produce them, "machinima" is a form of "film" production shot entirely with virtual cameras in such virtual worlds as those of "massively multiplayer online role-playing games" and Second Life.' Ryan Bishop and Sean Cubitt, 'Camera as Object and Process: An Interview with Victor Burgin', *Theory, Culture & Society*, vol. 30 (7/8), 2013, 199–219.

33
Amar Kanwar. Portraits, exh. cat. (Oslo: Fotogalleriet, 2005), n.p.

We have perhaps so fully digested the effects of these new technological displacements on artworks and the exhibition space itself, that we have forgotten them. The white cube has become a more malleable space, offering a less sedimentary situatedness to the artworks, opening to a more nomadic approach.[34]

Portraits included several short films addressing a search for solidarity in support of democratic movements worldwide. The films were recorded in the US, India and South East Asia, as well as including exiled voices in Oslo, and interrogated several issues relating to equality and its simulation in the drive towards national projects. Kanwar also participated in the 'On Time' seminar with Burgin, together with British curator and writer Susan Bright.

Matias Faldbakken, a celebrated author and hermetic artist, held his launching exhibition at Fotogalleriet under the directorship of Eivind Furnesvik in 2003.[35] He debuted as a writer in the fall of 2001 under the pseudonym Abo Rasul with the novel *The Cocka Hola Company – Skandinavisk misantropi* (The Cocka Hola Company –Scandinavian Misanthropy), a contemporary satire about the porn industry. Under the same pseudonym, he also wrote *Macht und rebel. Skandinavisk misantropi 2* (Macht und rebel. Scandinavian Misanthropy 2) (2002). For his first institutional solo exhibition, he presented a work titled *Getaway* (2003), where he appropriated footage recorded from the handlebars of a motorbike travelling at excessive speed, its rider pushing the journey into a near-death experience. Far from the artist's current production, *Getaway* captures new-media technology's race to catch up with high-speed real life, as well as playing with the obsession with life-death gaming, while borrowing its means of representation from art-historical linear perspective. Faldbakken and Furnesvik engage in an erratic conversation, recalling memories from their experience of presenting the work. They chose to leave their dialogue unedited here. Reading it makes you feel as if you're in the room with them, so don't be surprised if you want to ask a question or two at the end.

Susan Bright returned to Norway in 2007, having been asked to curate an exhibition at Fotogalleriet coinciding with another anniversary: Fotogalleriet turning thirty. As she recounts to artist and editor Nina Strand in this book, 'I consider the curatorial space a site of collective learning, for the artist, the audience and myself. This needs to be based

34
In recent years, Amar Kanwar has come to use the exhibition space, as a site for collecting evidence more than displaying it. Between 2012 to 2016, his work *The Sovereign Forest* was installed at the Samadrusti campus in Bhubaneswar. Here, he invited visitors to work on an archive of evidence to document villagers' struggles against mining companies. This resulted in a collection of images, newspaper clippings, land records and maps describing local resistance. 'If we were to use poetry, which is inadmissible evidence, we could actually get an insight into the nature of the crime, the scale of the crime, its meaning and implications, from a totally different perspective', states Kanwar. Violence, he argues, 'cannot always be comprehended through facts or forensics. It requires a language that can encompass deeper ideas.' Alexandra Chaves, 'How artist and filmmaker Amar Kanwar presents new ways of understanding justice', *The National*, 27 January 2020.

35
'Both my art practice and my writing have been about negation and negativistic strategies: hate, misanthropy and so on. My books are deliberately easy to read and entertaining whereas my art is more hermetic and mute [...] I use my art more as a tool for doing silent, negativistic gestures without any intention of convincing, impressing or communicating with an audience.' Matias Faldbakken interviewed by Luigi Fassi, 'A Million Ways To Say No', *Mousse*, March 2009, 12.

Antonio Cataldo

on relations of partnership, solidarity and sharing.' During
her preparatory research, she confesses that she was tempted to construct an exhibition around the idea of landscape,
finding such romanticism seductive. It was in this search that
she encountered Ane Hjort Guttu's *Smalvollen*, a multi-site,
sculpto-photographic work that became the centrepiece of the
exhibition. Bright and Strand talk about the idea of 'sculptural photography', as well as discussing sociological photography, and the more recent trend of 'diary photography', adopted by a number of contemporary artists challenging ideas
of everyday life documentation, in relation to their self and
others, including the work of the young and upcoming Maria
Pasenau.

Discussing *Smalvollen* with Professor Mike Sperlinger,
Hjort Guttu describes how she became disillusioned with
photography's romanticising representation of disorder and
potential to turn everything into a certain idea of beauty,
submitting to modernity's technocratic mission and ideals,
and therefore making art appear as a depoliticised sphere.
Touching upon the shift from still to moving images that has
come to characterise her work, she explains her artistic motto
of 'practising poetry' – in Surrealist terms – meaning finding
continuous ways of transgressing one's own limitations.

Maria Pasenau has recently made a new claim on sculptural
photography. For her first solo exhibition at Fotogalleriet in
2019, she produced a new series of photographic works including *self portrait with graveyardlog 1994–2019*, where she freezes
her being in a specific moment in time thanks to the use of
3D scan technology. A comprehensive process of posing for
countless hours to get an exact copy of herself sitting naked
on a stump in an office results in a full-size 3D image by way
of printing, gluing and sanding. In comparison to a regular
photograph, we get the highest possible concentration of data
about a body in all of its dimensions. Pasenau discusses with
writer Bjørn Hatterud using photography to overcome fears,
specifically those of creating alternative representations, and
to be audacious and bold in taking contact with people beyond
social boundaries and artifice. She has foregrounded and continued a feminist tradition that refuses to conform to norms of
education, and dissents from the steps dictated by society.[36]

UiT researcher and former Fotogalleriet Artistic Director
Stephanie von Spreter speaks about forms of care, including
motherhood and curatorship, with Iranian-born photographer

36
Jennifer Chapman. *Politics,
Feminism and the Reformation
of Gender* (London: Rout-
ledge, 1993).

Foreword

Shirana Shahbazi, whose work was presented at Fotogalleriet in November 2017. Capitalistic and masculine tropes of success and achievement, Shahbazi argues, perpetrate the idea of the artist as a genius, silencing the essential private sphere: 'You're defined as an individual who only exists in and through his (not her) art.' Through a discussion of her photography while travelling, we come closer to *Tehran North* (2015) and other projects by Shahbazi, where images become complex and universal, and can no longer be applied solely to one place.

Space has larger connotations than the physical and material dimensions of architecture, landscape and the natural and the artificial world. Such categories are bypassed in the digital age, where we not only move between different forms of reality, but are also finally acknowledging the importance of the multiplicity of beings co-inhabiting space and time with us.[37] For artist and professor Susanne M. Winterling, the problem has become which lives can survive climate change and how we can overcome violence and trauma. In conversation with Sara R. Yazdani, she proposes that 'the artist's poetry', a different rhythm, can help. In her work *ants and ashes*, Winterling reimagines textures, politics and affective forces, in the same way as Kafka did when meditating on the world while watching a spinning toy.

Artist Bjarne Bare and Catherine Opie, who was his professor at UCLA in 2016, discuss issues of space in a different way: as a method to measure our relation to a community in order to define a new language. Though photography has been much about space, Opie suggests that 'we don't know how to deal with space these days', because we are constantly navigating between the screen world and the physical world. Contrary to the claim that there are too many images overwhelming us today – something that people were already complaining about in the 1920s – she declares that to create history, we need to create language, and in order to create language we need to create more images – the missing ones – so that minor, other, unacknowledged histories will become forever part of language. This is also the unspoken plea of Ramm Fortun.

Silja Leifsdottir developed an important master's thesis converging with a curated exhibition at Fotogalleriet, *What Remains* (2017), where she shows that in forty years of history with more than 800 artists exhibited at the institution only

37
In her 1984 essay 'A Cyborg Manifesto', Donna J. Haraway envisioned the neutrality of cyberspace as a means of liberation from binary gender. 'By the late twentieth century, our time, a mythic time, we are all chimeras, theorized and fabricated hybrids of machine and organism – in short, cyborgs.' One could argue that she prefigured digital spaces, and the neutrality of the Internet, opening up the possibility for the spread of feminist ideas, the erasure of national borders and the formation of new forms of gender and protest. Donna J. Haraway, *A Cyborg Manifesto. Science, Technology, and Socialist-Feminism in the Late Twentieth Century* (Minneapolis: University of Minnesota Press, 2016).

Antonio Cataldo

twenty-six percent were women up to the 1990s. This exhibition celebrated both Fotogalleriet's fortieth anniversary and the *Voyager Golden Records* – phonograph recordings of sounds and images representing human life, which were sent out into space by the *Voyager* spacecraft, intended as a greeting to extraterrestrial life and future descendants. *What Remains* was an attempt to send a new message to posterity: 'I have chosen to invite six artists who in each their own way illustrate the challenge of representing the contemporary to an unknown audience' – Liv Bugge, Kristina Bengtsson, Toril Johannessen, Ditte Knus Tønnesen and Tori Wrånes Featuring Clare Milledge.[38] The interconnected publication included work by over 100 photographers and artists, bringing together a multiplicity of voices into an irreducible constellation. Such an endeavor was facilitated by Martina Petrelli. She worked at Fotogalleriet between 2016 and 2018, developing a unique archival system for a non-collecting, medium-sized institution, paving the way for a methodology to come, and drawing from work she had initiated during her studies and at other art institutions. She continues to imagine archives, both physical and conceptual, as tools for structuring our vision not only of a possible past but of possible futures.

Space, physical or imagined, is what we share momentarily, or repeatedly, and where conversations can take place, predicting or mounting a different future, whether a revolution, political asylum or just a safe-haven for a few minutes or a few hours. Because of this potential of the encounter to make space and claim a different citizenship or space of belonging, we decided to close this publication with our eyes directed towards the present. Berlin-based artists Ellinor Aurora Aasgaard & Zayne Armstrong, whose work about unorthodox and precarious communities we brought into the space of Fotogalleriet during the autumn of 2020 share a conversation that is more of a short story.[39] In their artwork they address different forms of precarity in different communities they inhabit dictated by the current financial market, a new culture that since the 1990s has appropriated the term 'free' to disempower workers and their labour, not only widening the gap between rich and poor but also creating a new socially exposed class. Armstrong and Aasgaard appropriate the soap-opera format, an open-ended, infinite structure allowing for the creation, production and distribution of images that does not always have to follow logics of linearity and make

---

[38] 'Fotografier for en ukjent fremtid' [Photographs for an Unknown Future], 9 February 2017, https://ofks-foto.no/2017/02/09/fotografier-for-en-ukjent-fremtid/ (accessed 25 June 2020).

[39] At the time of writing this introduction, we are coming out of a six-week lockdown in Norway due to the Covid-19 pandemic, which has transformed the world as we used to know it. Borders have been closed and international travel is temporarily halted.

sense immediately, therefore allowing for a more organic documentation of communities and common lives otherwise remaining undocumented. Here, Armstrong, with the support of Aasgaard, Ziyad Hawwas and Nicholas Korodi, draws from preparatory interviews leading up to the new work, to pen a short story. The process of typing up handwritten notes quickly turns into a whole writing process in itself, where foggy memory, illegible notes and other unforeseen perspectives produce a text that naturally embraces fiction. We eagerly awaited their new images, foregrounding new thinking, and where the visual comes before the cognitive.

During the past two years, we have been undertaking discussions with the Indian-born artist and writer Nikhil Vettukattil about the lack of blackness in Fotogalleriet's programming, and the lack of 'creolisation' in the photographic discourse. This morphed into a reflection on the intersection of class, gender and race. We spoke about structures and funding and how funding determines the production of ideas. This is mirrored in the recent Black Lives Matter movement, as theorised by American academic and activist Keeanga-Yamahtta Taylor,[40] who believes that the BLM movement will only be able to achieve its demands, including requests for defunding the police, through theorisation by a number of individuals. This is an important point that attributes real transformative power to knowledge, informing society at large despite systemic inequalities. We worked out a radical proposal with Vettukattil that will demand financial support in order to address these ideas properly. Through this process, we came to see how many projects have remained unrealised during the past forty-plus years at the institution, or having been realised, failed to make it into the archives, remaining simply in people's memories. This tangibly demonstrates the serendipitous nature of archives, remarked upon by Foucault in his anthology of prison archives, *The Life of Infamous Men*,[41] where traces of certain people remain for posterity only circumstantially through their encounter with the institution (the law, the hospital, the clinic, the prison, and by extension, we could say the white cube), rather than because their lives were willingly or consciously recorded due to their membership of the aristocracy or the bourgeoisie. These discussions pointing to the failure of archives and to what escapes the net of history, as well as paying homage to the revolutionary potential of the informal, the unsaid and

[40] 'How do you change things?', Keeanga-Yamahtta Taylor talks to Adam Shatz about the intellectual and historical background to the Black Lives Matter movement, and why she is optimistic that the current protests might bring change. *London Review of Books*' podcast, 30 June 2020, https://www.lrb.co.uk/contributors/keeanga-ya-mahtta-taylor (accessed 13 July 2020).

[41] Michel Foucault, 'The Life of Infamous Men', in: Meaghan Morris and Paul Patton (eds.), *Michel Foucault. Power, Truth Strategy* (Sydney: Feral Publications, 1979), 76-91.

Antonio Cataldo

the unregistered, which history reveals to posterity in other forms such as oral knowledge, are Vettukattil's contribution to this book.

With this publication, we are not attempting to give a perspective on a single organisation, but rather on the way in which the institution moves like a living being to create and record history, with all the traps that entails. It therefore speaks about a region and networks of alliances, as well as where history finishes and art begins. It is an invitation to come closer to certain artists and certain positions, to join a new assembly. The performances yet to come by Ramm Fortun are a call for that 'in-betweenness', where history is being lived and waits for remediation. For novel politics to take place, demands must appear in the visual field, the dominant aesthetic domain, to emancipate unrecognised forms of living.

Marthe Ramm Fortun's performance took place as part of the exhibition Women In Three Acts *on Saturday 27 April 2019 at 23:59. This is a translated, unedited version of her performance script.*

What if it is too late to be THE NEXT GENERATION OF CONTEMPORARY ARTISTS?
Or too early to be of HER generation, if a belonging is coined after incurred death?

Martha Wilson kept her C-prints under the bed until her solo show at Mitchell Algus Gallery in 2009, an exhibition entitled *Staging Self.* There has been nothing discreet about Wilson's life as an activist, archivist and preserver of the avant-garde, as well as hovering amongst the may-or-may-not-bes being Guerrilla Girls.
Choices from the top shelf.

The exhibition *Positions – Norwegian photographers in the 1970s–1980s, where do they stand now?* featured the following artists: FINN SERCK-HANSSEN. JIM BENGTSON. PER BERNTSEN. MARIT ANNA EVANGER. LEIF GABRIELSEN. HALVARD KJÆRVIK. ØYSTEIN KLAKEGG. SIGGEN STINESSEN. DAG ALVENG. ESPEN TVEIT. JAMIE PARSLOW. TOM SANDBERG. JENS HAUGE. HENNY LIE. TOM MARTINSEN.

POSITIONS – NORWEGIAN PHOTOGRAPHERS IN THE 1970s-1980s – WHERE DO THEY STAND NOW?

Narratives from the top shelf!

Henny Lie and Marit Anna Evanger are not mentioned with a single word, two women among fifteen established Norwegian photographers. Henny Lie had her last solo exhibition in 1996, Marit Anna Evanger does not figure in the archive of Fotogalleriet after 1994, but in a series of interviews in connection with the award of a five-year work grant in 2016 the artist talks about an active and unconventional practice in which photography is combined with independent theatre.

Editor's note:
Marthe Ramm Fortun held two performances so far at Fotogalleriet; the first on 14 March 2019 and the second at the stroke of midnight on 27 April 2019. These notes come from the second performance titled *LOOK AROUND IN JOY*, a title she borrowed from a seminal show Henny Lie participated in at the Fotografiska Museet in Stockholm in 1981: *Se dig om i glädje: sex fotografer, sex temperament.* 'Se dig om i glädje' can be translated as 'look around in delight'.

Whose responsibility is it to analyse and historicise being an artist outside the norm if not one's own professional environment? ANSWER OWED!

FLASHES OF MEMORIES AND OBJECTS.

Henny, you gave me a ladder!
In a letter in the archive you write that you taped a flashlamp to the ceiling and lay down on photographic paper, let the light capture what you called 'Ur-forms'[42] in a photogram. It also caught your contours. But I have no need to indulge in biographical speculation to get close to your conceptual backbone. In the catalogue for the exhibition *Look Around in Delight* at Fotografiska[43] in Stockholm, Leif Wigh describes an artist who was inspired by experimental film and photography in New York in the 60s, after a stay at the Parsons School of Art and Design. JONAS MEKAS! You had Diane Arbus as one of your most important ideals, without this being explicitly visible in your works. Why should it be? Bathed in pictures of your own time. With colour pictures as building blocks, Wigh wrote.

Henny Lie wrote a 180-page book that was never published: *IN PURSUIT OF THE UR-FORMS*. I see Sandra Vaka Olsen. Amy Granat. Jonas Mekas. But these are assumptions, a sensed affinity, not knowledge. Such intuitive connections do not write art history. They do not know who Henny Lie is. I ought to have told the students at the Academy of Art[44] about Henny Lie. I did not know her works before I was roped in to say something about the lack of female exhibitors in the archives of Fotogalleriet. Personally intensify the vacuum by owing an answer!

Can one disappear when one has never been present?

Mail from Karen: 'Just got a message from the National Library saying that they need more time to look for the book. In other words, I can't go and fetch it yet. This happens to practically all the literature I attempt to dig up linked to these artists!'

     Marthe Ramm Fortun

[42]
Editor's note: In Norwegian 'urformene'. The prefix 'ur' in Norwegian stands for 'original' or 'primary'.

[43]
Editor's note: This refers to the photography department of the Moderna Museet in Sweden, not the independent institution, also located in Stockholm.

[44]
Editor's note: Ramm Fortun is a professor at the Academy of Fine Art in Oslo, and was interim dean for a year.

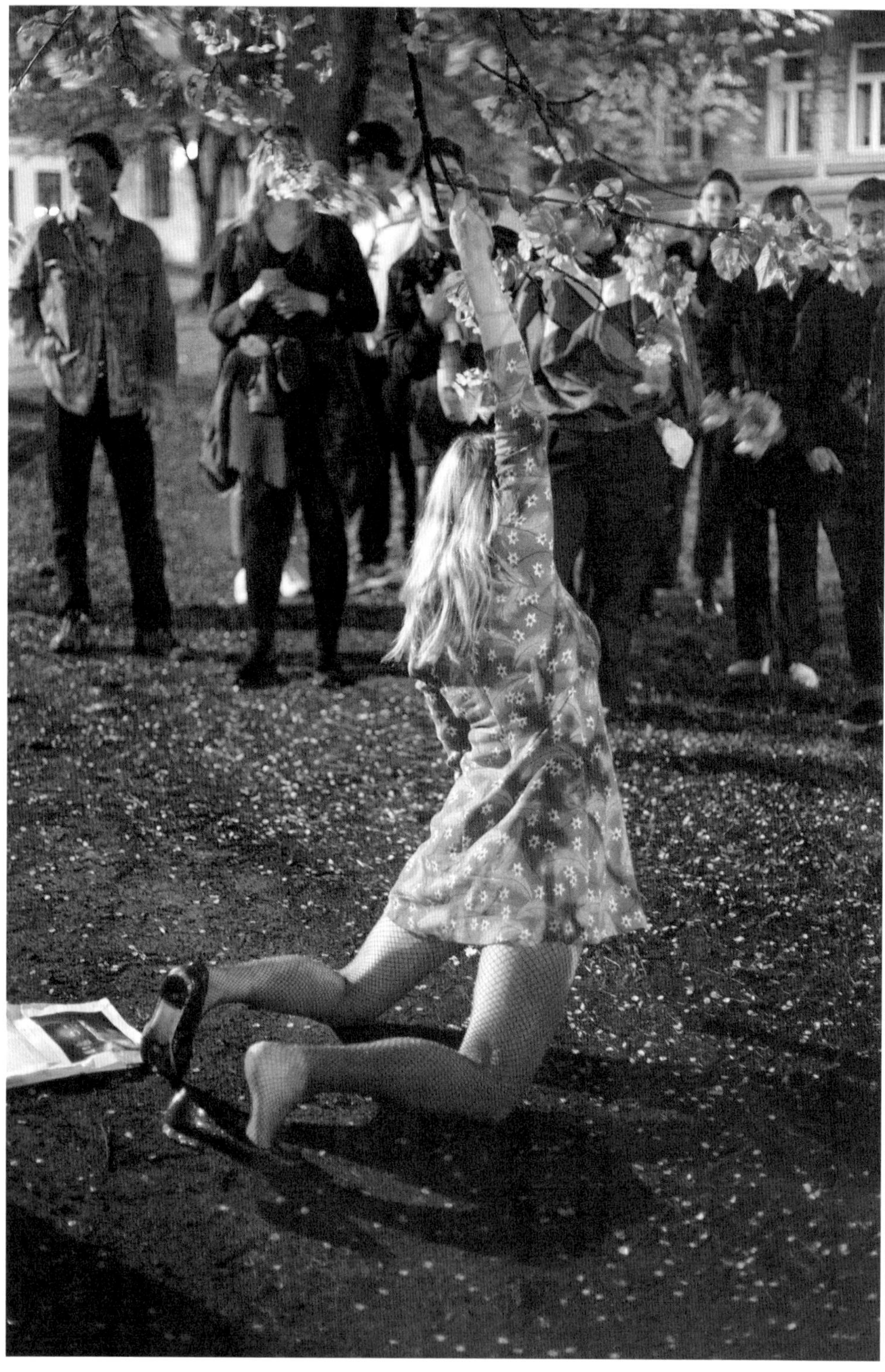

Look Around in Joy

Is deliberate withdrawal a reason to discharge artists from history? The following is stated about Henny Lie: 'This biography is for the time being brief or inadequate, and you can help Wikipedia by expanding it. (See style manual)' – perhaps with Dag Alveng's recitation-like presentations, one could say copious source material, in the archive. Marit Anna Evanger has no Wikipedia site. Nor have I. Once, as part of a project about archives, all the students in a group with Einar Granum wrote a Wikipedia site for each other. They were there for a few hours before the administrator excised them, because the source material was regarded as unmerited. A so-called mature student started to cry when she saw her own name.

In 1993, Jonas Ekeberg, current editor of KUNSKRITIKK and then newly appointed head reviewer of *Aftenposten*, wrote the criticism 'OUT OF POSITION' about the exhibition *Positions*: 'As a point of departure, this exhibition has all the odds against it. The format is almost threadbare; a group of photographers without any marked common denominator exhibits one to three pictures each. This is the same form that has been used for both the photographic spring exhibition and the photographers' grant exhibition, a format that one has tried to get away from over the past few years. The exhibition presents photographers who have partially worked tradition-ally. This naturally involves challenges for the individual artist, but in this context, one has a lurking feeling of stasis.'

In the text, Leif Gabrielsen, Jim Bengtson and Dag Al-veng come off quite badly, while Fin Serck-Hanssen and Tom Sandberg get reasonably positive mention. Ekeberg says about the exhibition: 'The title *Positions 1* becomes unintentionally ironical. Photography, or art in general, has precisely to do with adopting positions, finding a place to stand and taking a stance.' The fact that there are only two women among the fifteen artists selected to present the country's first generation of photographic artists escapes the analyst's notice.

But as early as 1991, the idea of 'photographic uses' in a feminist context was coined by Abigail Solomon-Godeau. In the book *Photography at the Dock: Essays on Photographic Histo-ry, Institutions, and Practices*, published in 1991, Solomon-Go-deau writes: 'The history of photography is not the history of remarkable men, much less a succession of remarkable pic-tures, but the history of photographic uses.'

          Marthe Ramm Fortun

A perceptive and presentable analysis of Henny Lie's works and conceptual background was written in a catalogue for the exhibition LOOK AROUND IN DELIGHT. There's no reason her work shouldn't be read up against this text, launching Lie into the renaissance of analogue techniques NOW, closer to sculpture and painting. She is no Charlotte Wankel, but not a Jack Smith or Cady Noland either, in deadly opposition to the world of art. Smith died in a caravan; Lie stopped painting when all her things were destroyed in a fire. There was a paradigm shift, a decision from the supreme court in connection with an insurance case is one of the few documents about her to be found on the Internet. Look around in delight! But I have not discovered Henny Lie. We are contemporaries, just as Jonas Mekas sings to us from the other side, and Sandra Vaka Olsen paints with light and sun lotion. Sings under water.

May I never again be asked to shed light on lopsidedness and under-representation in the archives! In file after file lies the basis for reading the complexity, and the few accessible documents are more than enough to include the artist in a critical discourse. In file after file there are nuances that since their coming into existence have opposed the truth alleged by the market. Pictures. Incidents. Locations. A flashlamp taped to the ceiling so the body of the work will not be lost. A contact copy in the archive, an unpublished manuscript. The content of the archive makes impossible the market refrain: 'She wasn't good enough. She didn't want it badly enough.' The body of the work slips from us in omissions in teaching, in collections and in the absence of a critique of the premises of the art work. LOOK AROUND IN DELIGHT! When fragments of papyrus were found on the rubbish tip, Sappho's collected poetry had to be re-read. In the refuse the basis was found for the claim that Sappho was an undisputedly great literary figure. Hunger drives one to search among the refuse. The language of omissions is sparse.

In 1991, or early on today, Solomon-Godeau gave us the concept 'photographic uses'. So use it!

*Paul Hill was amongst the first artists to exhibit at Fotogalleriet in
1977, in a joint exhibition with the works of Raymond Moore. He was
invited by Fotogalleriet to hold a workshop at Henie Onstad Kunstsenter
outside of Oslo in 1978. Aaron Schuman is an American artist, writer
and curator based in the UK.*

Aaron Schuman It's my understanding that you began your
career as a photojournalist, working for local
newspapers in the Midlands. Can we discuss the
shift that occurred within your practice when it
began to transition from traditional photojournalism to what you've referred to in the past as
the 'more personal photographic statement' or
'psychological document' – that shift from being a
journalist to being an artist?

Paul Hill Well, initially I started out as a print reporter – writing
for local newspapers for about six years – before I went
into photography full time in 1965. This shift you mention is very interesting, but like all these things, it didn't
happen overnight. As a freelance photographer with
a wife and family, I did whatever work came my way
locally in the Midlands. As time progressed, I began to
shoot for several national newspapers – *The Guardian*,
The Observer and so on. It sounds strange now, but in
those days very few newspapers included bylines with
the photographs, but *The Guardian* and *The Observer*
did, and as a consequence my name was seen by the
lecturers at several local colleges and polytechnics,
who asked me to come and give a talk to their students
about what I did. I was then invited to not only give a
one-off talk, but also to lead some classes, so I began to
do a bit of vocational teaching.

At that particular time – the early 1970s – there
were very few photography courses and certainly no
'art photography' courses; photography was very often
included as part of graphic design courses, and 'personal
work' wasn't actively encouraged, or included within
their curricula. But around that same time, there was a
new photography course being set up in Nottingham at
Trent Polytechnic. A guy called Bill Jay – who'd been
the editor of the influential magazine, *Creative Camera,* and whom I'd worked for when he was the picture

The Bridge

editor of *The Daily Telegraph Magazine* – was asked to teach the history of photography there one day a week. He put my name forward to the course-leader, Bill Gaskins, who invited me to teach a class on what was then called 'social documentation'. I was still working as a freelance photojournalist, although I had also had a few small exhibitions by then.

A S   Where were you exhibiting your photographs?

P H   I was living in Wolverhampton at the time – in fact, the same city where Oscar Rejlander had lived and worked in the nineteenth century – and a friend of mine who was an art history lecturer at Wolverhampton Poly-technic suggested to the young curator of the Wolver-hampton Art Gallery that he should give me a show, as they'd never had a one-man photographic exhibition before. So the curator made contact and invited me to have an exhibition, which I did in 1971.

In that same year, The Photographers' Gallery opened in London, and I knew its founder, Sue Davies, through Bill Jay. I'd done some photographs for her of what would become the new gallery space, and had given some money to their set-up fund. So once the show in Wolverhampton closed, I told her that it was available, and she asked me to exhibit it at The Photographers' Gallery, which I did in 1972.

A S   As a freelance photojournalist, was exhibiting your work in museums and galleries something that you'd ever even considered or aspired to?

P H   Not really. I'd thought about it a little bit because I'd seen a Henri Cartier-Bresson show at the Ikon Gallery in Birmingham, and the *Bill Brandt: Shadow of Light* exhibition at the Hayward Gallery in London in 1970. I was a big admirer of both of those photographers, and they were great inspirations to me at the time. But I hadn't really thought that much about having exhibitions myself.

   Paul Hill in Conversation with Aaron Schuman

A S Did this shift – from seeing your work within the
context of the newspaper to that of the gallery –
have any effect on your photographic approach or
practice?

P H Yes, definitely. At that particular time, my work was
'personal' in a sense, but it was very influenced by
traditional documentary practice – mostly 'slices of life'
pictures around Wolverhampton and the Midlands.
But when the invitation came to show my work at the
Wolverhampton Art Gallery, alongside the pictures
that I'd done for newspapers and magazines, I made
new pictures specifically for the exhibition; I decided to
make it more of a personal project, centred on the area.
They were still in the social-documentary tradition –
and the images were printed in quite a dark, high-con-
trast style, which was current at that time – but I added
some *objet trouvé* images as well.
I should also say that working as a lecturer at Trent
Polytechnic several years later made me much more
aware of the greater potential of the gallery within
photography. As I said before, this was a new and quite
innovative photography course, so there was a lot of
freedom for experimentation – in fact, right at the start
of the course, in the students' first year, they were re-
quired to take a class called 'Experimentation'. So students were experimenting early on, not only visually but
contextually as well, rather than aiming for technical
perfection or being taught how to do things specifically
for the commercial or editorial industries.

A S In fact, I think the course at Trent was specifically called 'Creative Photography' – rather than
simply 'Photography' – correct?

P H Yes, the course was called 'Creative Photography',
which sounds extraordinary now but it certainly helped
to distinguish us from other courses. Our aim was
to educate what at that time we referred to as 'visual
thinkers', and with Bill Jay contributing to it, as well
as other lecturers who had backgrounds in fine art, we
became a trail-blazer course, at least within Britain.

What happened was that Bill Gaskins had been given a Kodak Bursary to go over to the States, so he'd seen how photography was being taught within art departments there, and he brought that experience to Trent and applied it to our course. Bill also became the first chairman of the photography subcommittee of Arts Council England – which I joined later – that greatly influenced the development of creative photography throughout the UK in subsequent years. So all of these things were evolving and intertwining together – new courses, new exhibitions spaces, new financial support mechanisms, and a burgeoning photographic culture and community – and everyone seemed to know each other. It was a relatively small group of people, but we all had a shared mission to make photography a seriously regarded medium that could be studied as an art form as well as a vocational subject.

A S   Alongside your teaching within academia, in the mid-1970s you began to develop a series of independent photography workshops, which you hosted at your own home. What were your intentions for these workshops, which were delivered outside of a traditional educational institution?

P H   Well, when I started teaching at Trent Polytechnic on a full-time basis in 1974, I was given the job of overseeing the first-year students, and I would often use similar 'workshop' tactics to help bond the students together at the beginning of the year. I was very aware of the creative potential and educational possibilities of an intensive, immersive environment where everyone is working and living together for several days on end.

Then I was asked to run a photography workshop that was specifically aimed at photography lecturers, hopefully to support and inspire them in their own careers. We brought in people like David Hurn and Raymond Moore, who would talk not only about their practice, but about their educational approach as well. This was quite successful, so in 1976 I began to run workshops more regularly, outside of the polytechnic. And then in 1978, when I left Trent Polytechnic, I ran the workshops on a more full-time basis, alongside doing some part-time teaching here and there.

    Paul Hill in Conversation with Aaron Schuman

When I'd first got the teaching job in Nottingham, my family and I had moved to a rural location in Derbyshire, where we bought two run-down cottages. With the help of my brother and some students we did them up, built a workshop space and a darkroom, and created a place where we could accommodate visiting photographers; we actually called it The Photographers' Place.

The whole idea of the workshops, apart from creating an immersive teaching experience, was to be able to invite well-known photographers – within this small emerging area of fine-art photography (we called it 'independent photography' back then) – to come and stay with us. Once we did up the cottages, I could write to them and say, 'I've got this cottage out in Derbyshire – come out and visit, run a workshop, and you can stay as long as you like with no distractions.'

For example, in 1976, when I was just starting the workshops, I'd heard via the Arts Council committee that the New-York based photographer Ralph Gibson had been given a grant to make some work in England and was coming over soon. He already had a lot of experience in running workshops, in both the States and in Arles, where the now famous photography festival had been going since 1969; so I invited him to do a workshop in Derbyshire. He, Thomas Cooper and I ran the workshop together over one Easter weekend, and it went really, really well.

Of course, it was a niche market, but it was pretty successful, so we organised some more. We'd get about fifteen participants who were fans of these well-known photographers, and they could meet and talk with them, as well as with each other. Mostly, the conversations revolved around ideas rather than technique, and the participants would often bring their work and have it reviewed by some of their favourite photographers. Furthermore, alongside the participants, we'd have students who would get involved by assisting me and gaining some professional experience as well. Actually, the photographer Paul Graham – who was studying microbiology at the University of Bristol back then – has been quoted as saying, 'The only photographic education I ever had was a Paul Hill workshop.'

A S   You mentioned Thomas Cooper. In 1979, you and
       Cooper co-authored the very influential book,
       Dialogue with Photography – a compilation of
       interviews that you both conducted with some of
       the most important photographers of the twenti-
       eth century. How did that project originally come
       about?

P H   It was a self-initiated project. In the mid-70s, Tom
       and I were both teaching at Trent Polytechnic, and
       we thought it would be a good idea to gather together
       some material for the students. We were having a lot of
       discussions about the differences between the European
       and American aesthetic, which was more distinct then,
       and so we thought we'd investigate this, and meet some
       interesting people in the process. We started thinking
       about where we might find both European and Amer-
       ican photographers quite easily, and we realised that
       Paris wasn't that far away – Man Ray, Henri Cartier
       Bresson, Jacques Henri Lartigue, Brassaï, Paul Strand
       and many others all lived there.
           We'd both met the Curator of Photographs at the
       Bibliothèque Nationale in Paris, Jean-Claude Lemagny,
       through an exhibition that we'd had at the Arnolfini in
       Bristol, so we wrote to him and asked for the contact
       details of these photographers, and he sent them to us.
       Then we contacted the photographers, arranged inter-
       views, and went to Paris – actually, just for one week-
       end, if you can believe it.
           Both Henri Cartier Bresson and Man Ray didn't
       initially reply to us, but we knew where Man Ray lived,
       so we decided to go to the bar below his apartment and
       ring him from there. When he answered the phone,
       we said, 'Hello, we've come all the way from England,
       we're big admirers of your work, and we'd just like to
       come by and meet you.' At first, he said that he didn't
       do interviews, but then he started talking about him-
       self, telling stories, and we said, 'We're just around the
       corner – can we come over?' Once we got into his flat,
       he opened up, we switched the tape recorder on, and
       off he went. We didn't get to talk with Henri Cartier
       Bresson on that trip (we did a few years later, however)
       but otherwise, it was a very successful weekend!

                                      Paul Hill in Conversation with Aaron Schuman

Of course, when we got back home, I quickly realised that this was material publishable beyond just giving it to our students, so we got the Paul Strand interview typed up (by one of our students, who'd worked as a stenographer), and sold it – to either the *British Journal of Photography* or the *Royal Photographic Society Journal* – I can't remember which one. In the meantime, Tom had gone to Switzerland with a girlfriend, and while he was there he met up with Allan Porter, the editor of *Camera*, which was a very good trilingual photography magazine published in Lucerne at the time. Allan said, 'Every time you do an interview, send the text to me, and I'll publish it' – which was great, and that arrangement lasted for about two years. Then the polytechnic gave us some research money to go to the SPE [Society for Photographic Education] Conference in America, where we met with Ansel Adams, Imogen Cunningham, Elliot Porter, Wynn Bullock and so on. Then Tom eventually went back to the States again, and ended up doing a few more interviews there. So, over the course of several years, we were compiling this collection of interviews very gradually, publishing them individually in *Camera*, and getting a cheque every once and a while.

Finally, once we had a good number of them, we thought that maybe we could collect all of them together and publish them as a book. Since Tom was still in the States, he went over to Aperture and proposed it to them, but they weren't interested. Then he went to Farrar Straus & Giroux, who'd published Susan Sontag's *On Photography* and other text-based books about photography. Actually, Tom went to see Nancy Meiselas – Susan Meiselas's sister – who was working as an editor there. She loved it, and became our editor, gave us an advance, and said that we just needed to get a few more interviews and we could go to press. So that's what we did, and finally the book, co-published with Thames & Hudson, came out in 1979 – and it's still in print forty years later!

In 1979 both the exhibition and the book, *Three Perspectives on Photography*, came out, which I co-authored with Angela Kelly and John Tagg. For me, and for a lot of people I imagine, the 1970s was the most important decade for British photography in the twentieth century. So much happened – there was such energy and focus, a community and a culture was established, and we all felt like we were going in the same direction. Maybe each of us was located on a different part of the photographic spectrum, but we were all pushing the same way. It was a fascinating period.

AS   I understand that two of the founders of Fotogalleriet – Tom Sandberg and Dag Alveng – were students of yours. How would two aspiring Norwegian photographers have found out about a small, very new photography course at a polytechnic in the English Midlands?

PH   Perhaps they were familiar with my work and that of the other lecturers through seeing it in various European photography magazines. Also, I remember them explaining to me that there were no photography courses in Norway at the time, but you could get a grant from the government to study your particular specialist subject abroad. So through that route, people like Tom and Dag came over to England to study. Also, in my recollection at least, Norwegians at that time were real Anglophiles; people in Sweden tended to go to American institutions, but the Norwegians used to come to Britain. And additionally, I was starting to run the workshops by that time, so they may have seen those written about somewhere. In fact, Tom Sandberg eventually assisted on the workshops while he was a student – I've got lots of pictures of him when he was a lad.

AS   When the current Director of Fotogalleriet, Antonio Cataldo, invited me to interview you for this book, he explained in an email, 'Paul Hill was a professor of Dag Alveng and Tom Sandberg – two of the forefathers of Fotogalleriet – and therefore, in many ways, could be seen as a seminal inspiration and influence on the development of contemporary art photography within Norway.'

          Paul Hill in Conversation with Aaron Schuman

Significant exhibition in a promising gallery
By Knut Evensen

A group of young idealists have managed to create a photographic gallery, and, not least, a photographic environment
in two modest basement rooms in Oscarsgate 50A in Oslo.
Fotogalleriet is the official name, and it is run according
to non-commercial principles.

The opening show consists of black&white prints by the two
English photographers/photo-teachers Paul Hill and Ray Moore.
They are both well-known names in international photography,
and are central persons in the English debate about photography as a medium.

Common to the two exhibitors is a distinct sense of the symbolism
~~and~~ and drama in our everyday environment; in situations
that happen by accident or on purpose, in constellations
between humans, nature, and material. The situations are
caught by means of visual aerials (antennas) directed towards
the decisive moment, the now. The constellations are caught
by means of the same aerials, but also by well considered
distortion of perspective, alteration of proportions, and
concious choice of angle and framing.

A big car park forms a geometrical pattern, consisting of
fences, parking spaces, direction arrows, cars, and people.
Both these photographers are able to treat this subject
so that one not only sees it as a visual novelty, but as
drama, that most people are blind for.

The difference between Moore and Hill, ~~the way~~ as I see it, is
that Moore to a little degree controls his subject, while
Hill to a large extent constructs (not in a negative sense)
his pictures from a concept, like in "Legs over High Tor",
where formal contrast and treatment of proportions are so
exciting, that the picture becomes a "real winner".

Dagbladet, Oslo, 23/9-77   (Norwegian newspaper review)

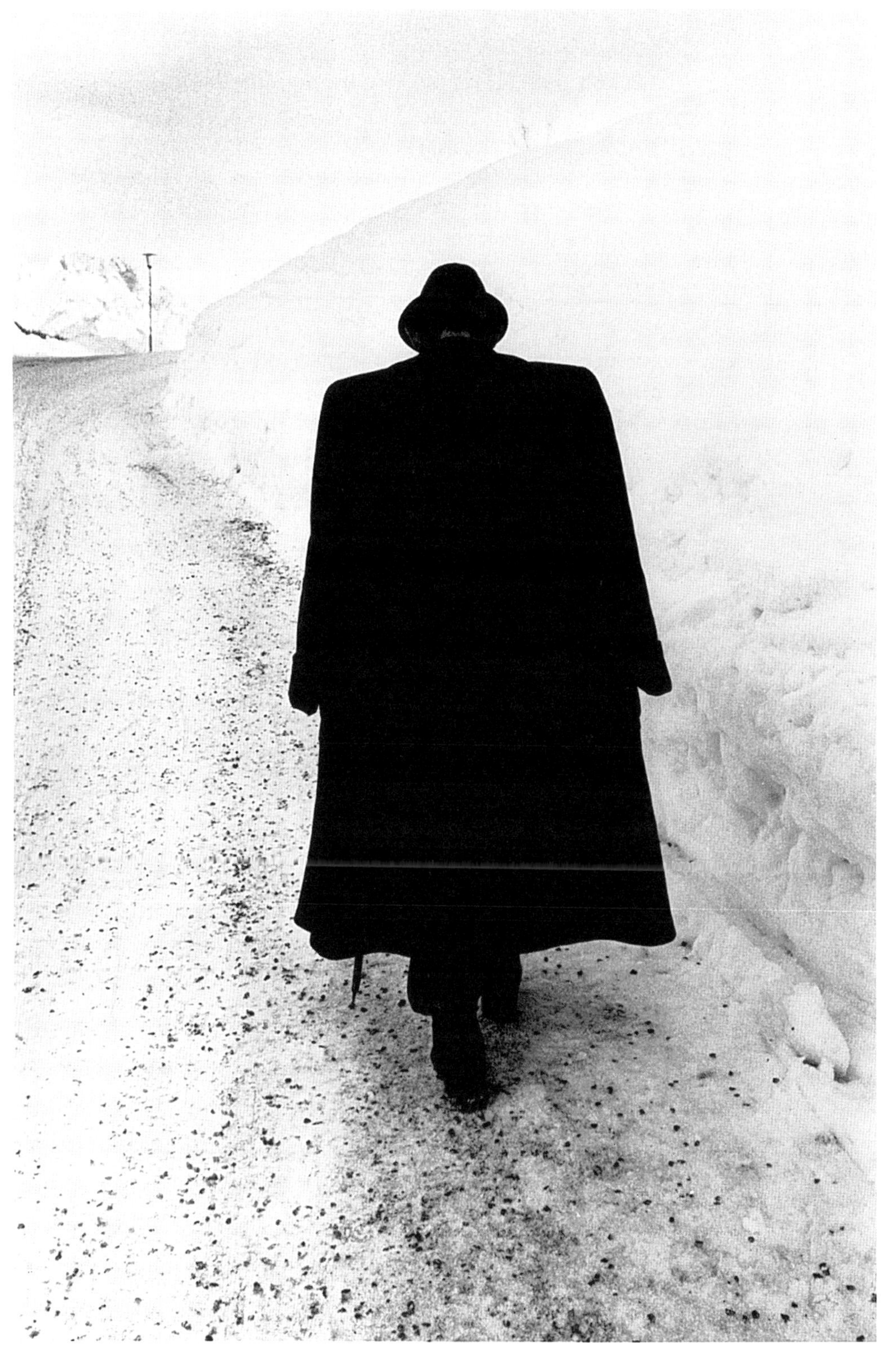

   Paul Hill in Conversation with Aaron Schuman

P H

Well, I don't know about that! But I imagine that their experiences over in England – at the polytechnic, at my workshops, and studying with members of the burgeoning British photography scene – influenced them in some way, and made them want to replicate it in Oslo, which they subsequently did very successfully through Fotogalleriet. I guess they went back to Norway inspired, and wanted to do something interesting in their own country – set up an exhibition space, run workshops and so on. And once they got Fotogalleriet set up, they invited Raymond Moore and me to be the two featured photographers in its first exhibition – in 1977 – as we'd both been their teachers. I then went to visit them for the first time in Oslo in the spring of 1978, and did a few talks, a workshop, and some portfolio reviews at Fotogalleriet.

A S

What are your own memories of that first visit to Fotogalleriet in 1978?

P H

I remember the workshop being in a basement, and that there were some good participants. It was very busy and lively, although everything closed at ten at night, due to various licensing laws and restrictions at the time in the city.

The visit was sponsored by the British Council, and I'd also been invited afterwards to give a talk in Stockholm. By that time I'd obviously gotten to know Tom well – he was very quiet and nice, but at the same time very ambitious and driven, and he really wanted to meet some of the curators I was working with in Stockholm, so I invited him to come and join me there. He secretly stayed on the sofa in my hotel room (courtesy of the British Council), and had to surreptitiously come and go via the hotel's back door. So in a sense, I smuggled him into the photography scene in Sweden as my 'assistant'!

The British Council was quite active in Scandinavia back then, and its representatives in Norway were very supportive – the Council paid for my travel, accommodation, subsistence and so on, but there wasn't any artist fee attached. And since I was a freelancer, I had to think about earning a little bit of money as well, so Fotogalleriet also offered me a small fee to do the talks, workshop and portfolio reviews.

A S   During those workshop and portfolio reviews you gave in Oslo in 1978, do you remember noticing anything particularly distinctive about Norwegian photography at the time? Did you discover that it was drawing inspiration from anything in particular?

P H   I think that in the same way that those British photographers who were interested in more personal, creative, self-expressive photography – the 'independent photographers' that I mentioned earlier – were drawing inspiration from America at the time, the Norwegians were also picking up on this American influence through their visits and studies in Britain. In a sense, we were the bridge: America to Norway, via England.

Also, during that same era in Britain, we had people like Victor Burgin starting up the photography course at Polytechnic of Central London, which had a very conceptual and theoretical approach, and was gaining some traction within the photography world. And David Hurn, of Magnum, had also started up a new Documentary Photography course in Wales. So I imagine that the Norwegian students were also influenced by all of the different movements and schools of thought in Britain in the 1970s.

But as I explained, there weren't really any photography courses like ours anywhere else in Europe at the time, so where else could they go? They either had to go to America or come to us. In terms of the course at Trent, I always said that the students would be our best advert – and that proved true, certainly in the case of Fotogalleriet and its connection with the course at Trent.

A S   As I said, the current Director of Fotogalleriet – and I imagine many of its founders – credits you with having been one of the primary inspirations for the gallery and organisation, but this wasn't

   Paul Hill in Conversation with Aaron Schuman

common knowledge until very recently. In fact, it was only when Antonio Cataldo discovered *Dialogue with Photography* via David Campany's 2018 book, *So Present, So Invisible: Conversations on Photography*, that he himself became fully aware of your fundamental importance in its creation. Had you ever thought of Fotogalleriet as a small part of your legacy yourself?

PH I've always found it rewarding to pass on how important photography is – through my work, as well as through talks, teaching, exhibitions, workshops and books – and to try to inspire others to pursue ideas and experiences for themselves, photographically and otherwise. Actually the 3rd edition of *Approaching Photography* is soon coming out. For me at least, it's much more rewarding than just being a gallery artist. Of course, in the 1970s, if you tried to charge even ten pounds for a print people would look at you strangely, so that wasn't a possibility anyway. But like I said, even when they were students, Tom and Dag already had something special about them, and I'm absolutely thrilled by what they went on to do – with Fotogalleriet, as well as with their own photographic careers. They realised, like we did in the UK, that you have to create a supportive environment as well as make your own work.

A Field of Norwegian Photographic Art Takes Shape
Dag Alveng in Conversation with
Susanne Østby Sæther

Dag Alveng is regarded as a pioneer of Norwegian photographic art, and he was amongst those who took the initiative in establishing Fotogalleriet in 1977. He has followed the development of Norwegian art photography since the early 1970s up to the present day, and contributed to shaping the field. In this conversation, Alveng talks to curator Susanne Østby Sæther about the path he took to photographic art, how important it was for photographers in the 1970s to have their own exhibition venue, interdisciplinary exchanges of ideas among artists, and the gradual incorporation of photography into contemporary art. They met on 5 November 2019 in Alveng's studio.

Susanne Østby Sæther You returned to Norway in 1976 after having studied photography at Trent Polytechnic in the UK, where Tom Sandberg and Per Berntsen had also studied.

Dag Alveng Yes, and it's important to explain why I chose Trent. I was extremely interested in artistic photography and there were very few people in Norway who were interested in photography as a form of expression at the time. While I was studying medicine, I was sent the Swiss periodical *Camera*, which was published by Allan Porter. I used to feed on this every month, like some kind of mental nutrition. In an effort to find out what I wanted to do with my life, I travelled down to Switzerland to meet Allan Porter and show him my pictures. I asked him: 'Maestro, I'm a young man from Norway – what ought I to do now?' He answered: 'Young man, go to Nottingham, to Trent Polytechnic. That's a good place to study photography in Europe right now.' So I took the train from Switzerland to Nottingham, where I met Thomas Joshua Cooper, who was a professor at Trent Polytechnic, and we agreed that I could start. I took leave from my medical studies and started studying photography at Trent in autumn 1975. There I also met Tom Sandberg and Per Bernstsen. I discovered that there was a fantastic tradition, that photography as a form of expression had a history. There were a lot of interesting artists studying at Trent, and fantastic books in the library, too. I remember my teacher showed me the latest book by Lewis Baltz, *The New Industrial Parks Near Irvine, California* (1974), which had just arrived by post. The school had a direct link to the most important photographic artists at the time.

                A Field of Norwegian Photographic Art Takes Shape

SØS   What would you say were the most significant
       impulses or the most important elements adding
       to your understanding of photography that you
       came home with after your stay in England?

DA   I had teaching in the history of photography, film and
                            art, such as Dadaism and Conceptualism, and I got to
                            know about a tendency that has become very important
                            in Norway called New Topographics. I had initially
                            been interested in the history of art and used to draw
                            when at upper secondary school, but I acquired a vast
                            amount of knowledge at the school in a short space of
                            time. I arrived with a somewhat romantic view of art,
                            so for me this was an extremely sharp learning curve.
                            Those to the fore in Norway at the time were pupils of
                            Christer Strömholm, people such as Tom Martinsen,
                            Fritz Solvang and Anders Petersen. The prevailing view
                            in Norway was more pictorial, with photography com-
                            petitions and the idea of a snapshot. I distanced myself
                            from this.

SØS   Did you have any allies or like-minded people in
       Norway before you left for England?

DA   Yes, I had some contact with a group of what you could
                            call radical young photographers, such as Tore Røyne-
                            land, who called themselves Fotogruppa Vaterland.
                            They were politically active and I used to hang out at
                            Club 7 and mix with that environment. It was Foto-
                            gruppa Vaterland who drew my attention to *Camera*.
                            Without them, I wouldn't have found it.

SØS   For a while, Fotogruppa Vaterland had its rooms
       at Henie Onstad Kunstsenter.

DA   Yes, indeed. And Henie Onstad Kunstsenter was ter-
                            ribly important when I came back from England, but
                            before I left I didn't have any contact with it, apart from
                            looking at exhibitions and going to concerts there.
                            The Henie Onstad Kunstsenter opened in 1968 and,
                            at the time, it was the only art institution in Norway
                            that exhibited photography. The first director at the art

                    Dag Alveng in Conversation with Susanne Østby Sæther

centre, Ole Henrik Moe, and Per Hovdenakk, whose title was 'Editor', were both open to and interested in new art practices. I got on especially well with Per Hovdenakk, and his door was always open to me. It was always inspiring to meet him – he was a good conversation partner and his view and understanding of art was of great importance to me. During the 1970s and 1980s, Høvikodden[46] became a natural meeting place for those of us who gradually established and grouped ourselves around Fotogalleriet. At Henie Onstad, we organised lectures, etc., including one by Ralph Gibson, who talked about 'The Limits of Photography' – barefoot. I don't think we had to pay any rent for the rooms. Fotogalleriet was in Oscarsgate then, but we often held events at Høvikodden.

S Ø S   Robert Meyer has aptly remarked that you of the so-called 'England Generation' didn't come to a ready laid table in Norway. There were few grants around and few chances to exhibit, as well as little interest in artistic photography. Along with Tom Sandberg, you took the initiative in 1977 to establish Fotogalleriet, which began as a private gallery.

Fotogalleriet soon became an arena both for the showing of important international photographic art and for discussion and debate. It became a springboard for campaigning for the recognition of photography as an art form – even if not directly in terms of policy. Can you say something about the various stages in the process towards establishing Fotogalleriet, and what you regarded as the most important function an exhibition venue should have?

D A   The Norwegian Association for Fine Art Photographers was established in 1974. Tom, Per Berntsen and I returned to Oslo around 1976, and by then FFF[47] had already been established. But we felt that FFF was bogged down in reportage photography, and that photography existed that was much stronger than what the organisation represented. We were young, with impulses from abroad, and perhaps not born diplomats. At the

46
The site of the Henie Onstad Kunstsenter.

47
Forbundet Frie Fotografer (Norwegian Association of Fine Art Photographers).

    A Field of Norwegian Photographic Art Takes Shape

same time, we embraced the controversial photographer Robert Meyer, as he did us. When Tom and I came back from England, we felt that we were coming with something new and had golden treasures in our hands that no one here knew existed. In actual fact, we came back to a kind of vacuum. Personally, I'd developed a great deal as an artist, but there was considerable resistance to the photographic language I used. Just to take an example: I photographed a light switch, and believed that it could be an important motif, but that sort of imagery met with great resistance. As I said, we knew that photography of fantastic high quality existed that no one in Norway had ever seen. So it was natural for us to believe that Norway simply had to see this.

The initiative for Fotogalleriet got under way with Tom and me becoming like two peas in a pod and one of us saying to the other 'I'm going to start a gallery.' We agreed to do it together. It turned out that Tom was a disorganised person, so we needed a kind of book-keeper, someone who was a bit more down to earth. Eventually, we arrived at Bjørn Høyum. His photobookshop in Tanum on Karl Johan street became a sort of central office for us; we could always meet or deliver things there.

When we decided to start up an exhibition venue, we had to find premises. I remember extremely well how one evening I was visiting some friends of mine, and a guy called Chris Roggema said that he had a place we could rent. The evening grew late. I remember walking through Oslo at 5.00 am through the newly fallen snow and looking through the windows of Oscarsgate 50, which subsequently became our first venue. It was a very special feeling. Tom, Bjørn and I were formally responsible, because we were starting a company, but there were a great many people who contributed. Tom and I gathered together all those who wanted to be part of the project and formed a working collective. There were both photographers and people interested in photography. Everyone contributed and we shared the rent, held plenum meetings where we divided up the assignments for the exhibitions, and made lists of those prepared to function as gallery attendants.

     Dag Alveng in Conversation with Susanne Østby Sæther

It seemed natural to us to let our teachers, Paul Hill
and Raymond Moore, be the first to exhibit. It wasn't
a problem to find people willing to exhibit, as long as
we took care of transportation to Norway. No matter
whether it was Diane Arbus or Alfred Stieglitz, there
were few or no formal demands regarding transportation or other structural conditions. It wasn't until we
were going to exhibit Robert Mapplethorpe that there
was a requirement that we were to sell the pictures.
Mapplethorpe's gallery, Robert Miller, wanted a guar-
antee that 1/6 of the pictures would be sold. I had no
idea how we'd be able to sell pictures for Kr. 40,000
back then, but it would have been a good investment if
someone had bought a Mapplethorpe at the time.

søs How did you finance your exhibitions, including
transport and other expenses?

DA We established 'Friends of Fotogalleriet', which among
others included our own parents and Håkon Bleken.
Membership cost Kr. 100 a year. We also got some support from the American Embassy, and lighting equipment from Leif Preus. And then we scraped money
together from various places. We travelled to Sweden to
pick up the work of Diane Arbus, and placed the pictures in the boot of the car, and Robert Meyer drove to
Paris in his car to fetch Alfred Stieglitz. Robert Meyer
also personally financed the catalogue we did for the
Stieglitz exhibition. I remember I was at the customs
house to pick up a small wooden crate with the pictures
for the Edward Weston exhibition, which was one of
the exhibitions financed by the American Embassy.

søs Bearing in mind the amount of administration,
logistics and especially the expenses involved in
producing exhibitions nowadays, it's amazing that
it was possible.

DA We got the Diane Arbus show from Camera Obscura,
an exhibition venue for photography in Stockholm,
which started a month after us. We were the first Scandinavian exhibition space dedicated to photography.
Camera Obscura had a bit more money than we had,

 A Field of Norwegian Photographic Art Takes Shape

so we got already framed pictures with passe-partouts from them. Generally speaking, framing was a problem, but we managed to find enough money for that too. I don't think anyone had all that many personal expenses. We shared the rent and refurbishing – we refurbished the whole lot. And then we got a little money from here and there. If one looks back at Norway in the 1970s, I think the recognition of photography and the way forward to where we are now started then. There were many musicians and film people who were also drawn to this environment and who helped to give it dynamism.

s ø s I'm interested in the extent to which you predicted or actively worked for Fotogalleriet becoming a meeting place and a driving force in the work for the recognition of photography. Did this take place by itself, as a consequence of the exhibition programme, or was it something you actively sought to bring about?

d a We sought to reach an audience by sending out invitations to openings in the form of postcards. We also held workshops, including one with Paul Hill, one of the teachers from Trent Polytechnic. It took place at Fotogalleriet (1978), but we also made use of other arenas. As mentioned, we organised a workshop with Ralph Gibson at Høvikodden (around 1977) and one with Lewis Baltz in Lofoten (1985). Sally Euclaire gave a lecture after the publication of her book *New Color. New Work*, which came out in 1981. Christer Strömholm was in Oslo on several occasions in the late 1970s and the early 1980s, and stayed at my place. We had a number of conversations while he laid naked in the bath tub. Christer was a very natural choice for an exhibition and he was one of the photographers whose work we did two exhibitions of.

We had a very clearly formulated aim with Fotogalleriet – we wanted to show the best of international photography and the most exciting Norwegian up-and-coming artists. We got the final result we aimed for, which was that we've shown the established masters, and the coming generation of Norwegian photographers had their debut exhibition with us.

   Dag Alveng in Conversation with Susanne Østby Sæther

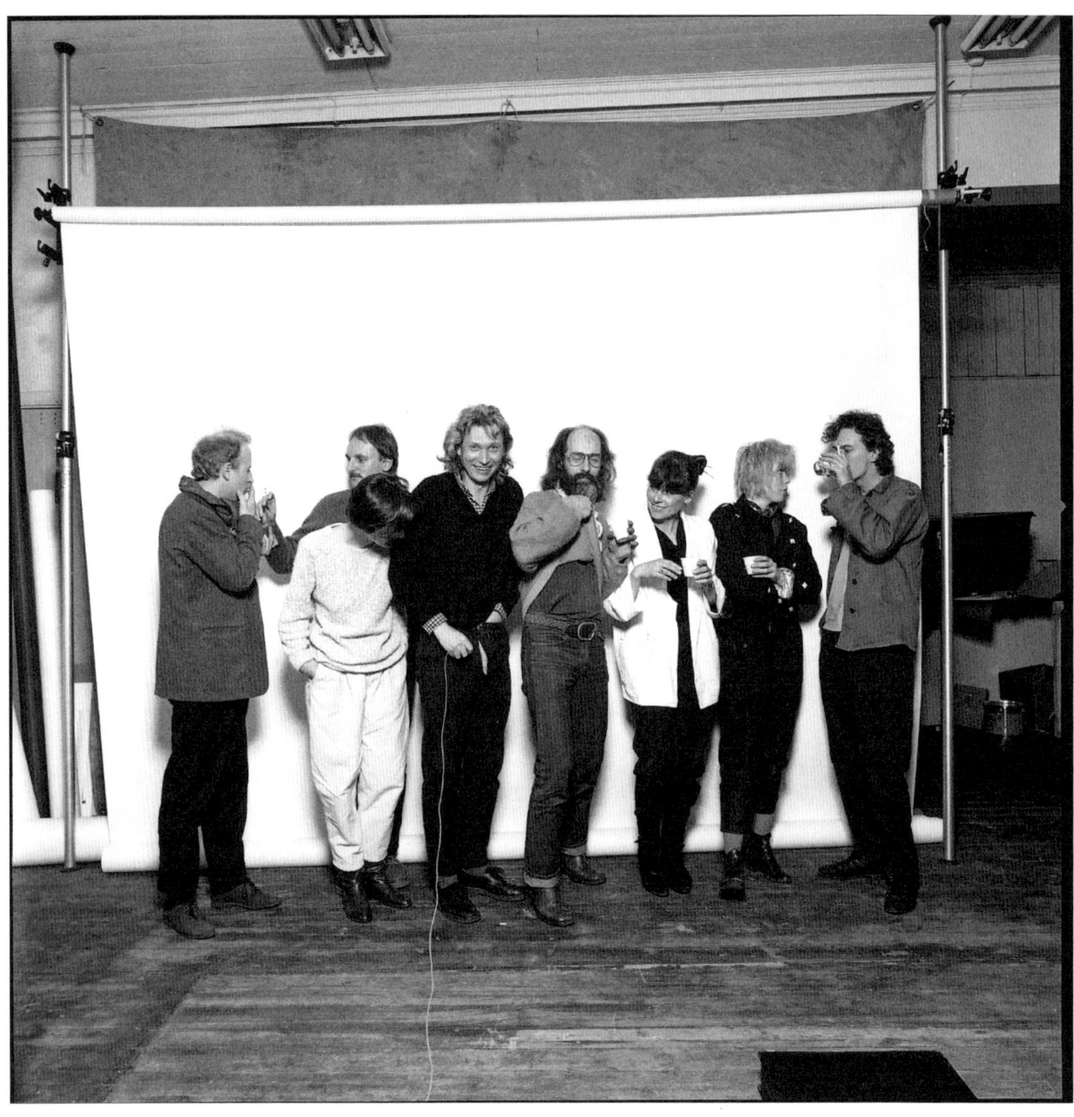

   A Field of Norwegian Photographic Art Takes Shape

s ø s Who made the decisions about which artists to
show?

D A On the whole, decisions about the exhibition programme were taken in plenum by the working collective, a loosely organised group of photographers, artists
and photography enthusiasts who wanted to contribute
to the running of Fotogalleriet. Most of these people were our friends and acquaintances. The working
collective met regularly where work assignments and
responsibility for various exhibitions were decided on.
Arne Walderhaug was a really key figure in this group,
and later he became general manager of Fotogalleriet.

s ø s And in 1979 you also had your debut exhibition
Vegger (Walls) there.

D A Yes. Our aim was of course not just, or even first and
foremost, to show our own photographs, so I waited
for a couple of years before putting on my own exhibition. By then we'd already made our mark by showing
extremely good photography. We felt as if we were the
new wine and were well to the fore. People knew that I
was a practising artist with a new view of photography,
and that I was a key figure in the running of the exhibition venue, so perhaps they had high expectations of my
debut exhibition at Fotogalleriet. For *Vegger* I chose to
show photographs of the walls in the exhibition space,
i.e. 'invisible photographs', as I've also called them.

s ø s Can you describe your pictures shown and the
underlying idea?

D A Yes, they were 1:1 photographs that hung on the wall
and covered precisely the field on the wall that was
portrayed. My idea was that people should come in
and believe there were empty frames on the walls and
I think I succeeded in this.

s ø s The *Vegger* exhibition has since become inscribed
in the history of Norwegian art as one of the first
examples of Conceptual photography in Norway,

  Dag Alveng in Conversation with Susanne Østby Sæther

but when it opened, it received – on the whole – a
rather negative critique from the daily press. The
exhibition was lampooned and you had a pretty
hard time of it. Would you say that at the opening
there was also widespread scepticism about these
'invisible photographs' among the visitors?

D A   Yes. People were either for or against. Things got pretty
heated at the opening and almost resulted in fisticuffs.
Per Hovdenakk, the Editor at Høvikodden, was perhaps
the only one who was not avidly for or against. He was
internationally oriented and had probably seen similar
things before. Back then in Norway, people expected art
photography to be well-printed, beautiful pictures. And
then they came to Fotogalleriet and saw these direct,
unprocessed depictions of an apparently utterly trivial
motif, and the ordinary public felt provoked by this.

S Ø S   So Fotogalleriet in general – and the *Vegger* exhibition in particular – attracted visitors who were
not already part of the artistic environment?

D A   Yes. My German teacher came along, for example. It's
interesting that even today everyone can remember if
they saw the exhibition or not, and if they were for or
against it. To me, this was simply a Conceptual idea,
and it was important to get across that I was working
along with other Conceptual artists. I did a number
of collaborative projects with Bente Stokke and Sissel
Tolaas – both of them are key Norwegian artists in
Conceptual and process art. The sculptor Bård Breivik was a friend, and I was a member of the Poetical
Theatre, which was a Fluxus-inspired group of artists
from various disciplines and countries. Also Marianne
Heske, who's considered a pioneer of Norwegian Conceptual art, exhibited at Fotogalleriet. I was part of the
larger art environment in Norway, and shared some of
its interests in ideas and processes of material transformation, while the photo environment was still working
using the Golden Section, 'snapshots' and pictorialism.

S Ø S   The 'invisible photographs' in *Vegger* would have had
a considerably larger resonance in the contemporary

    A Field of Norwegian Photographic Art Takes Shape

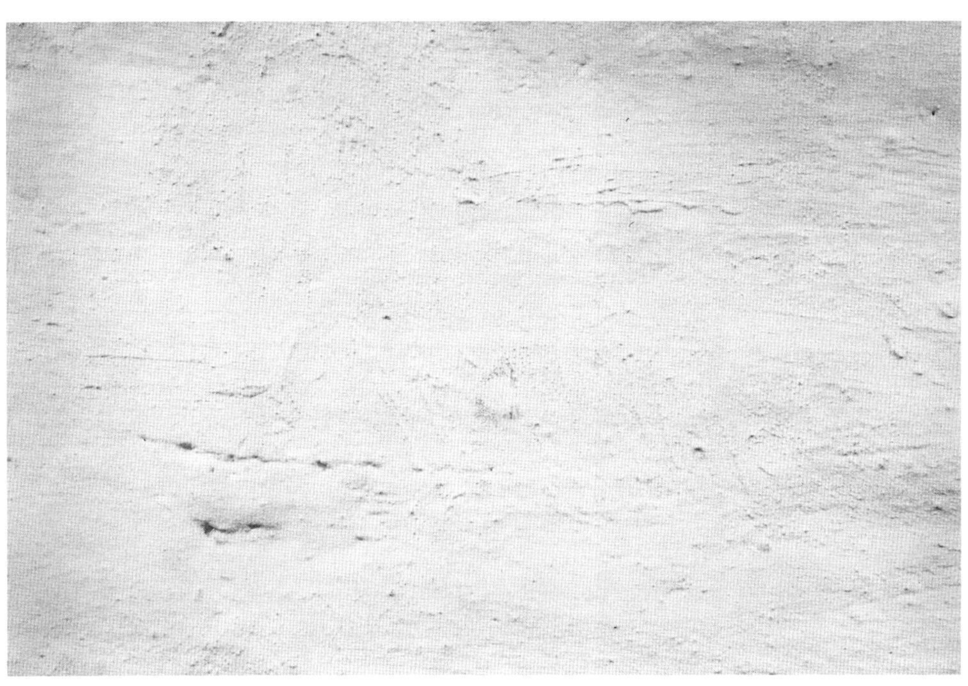

   Dag Alveng in Conversation with Susanne Østby Sæther

art environment than in the rest of the photographic milieu. To depict a motif directly and artlessly on a 1:1 scale is something a number of international Conceptual artists – who are not mainly photographers – have done, such as Joseph Kosuth, who you yourself mentioned earlier, and Victor Burgin. To what extent were you inspired by their projects?

DA   I was profoundly inspired by international Conceptual art. Joseph Kosuth's *One and Three Chairs* (1965) was an important work for me. I gained an interest in Conceptual artists such as Kosuth and Burgin while studying in England. These artists weren't shown in Norway at the time, but I saw, for example, an exhibition of works by Kosuth at the Pompidou Centre in Paris. Also, proto-conceptualists such as Marcel Duchamp and, for instance, the Fluxus movement were extremely important. These were trends that I was – and still am – greatly inspired by.

SØS   Generally speaking within the history of art and photography, Conceptual art is regarded as a way into contemporary art for photography. To work conceptually became a way for photographers to be taken seriously as artists, in the same way that the Conceptual artists to a great extent made use of photography. But did you feel that this also applied in Norway: that Conceptual art became a way into the contemporary art field for photography?

DA   I think I was pretty much on my own. Tom wasn't a conceptual artist. Marianne Heske, who exhibited at Fotogalleriet, was, and so was Bente Stokke, who used photography as a documentation of her processional works, but I was pretty much on my own as someone who'd studied photography but had an interest in Conceptual art. Artists who work with photography are normally either educated at art academies or photo schools. You can often see what kind of educational background artists have had – it's part of their expression. Robert Rauschenberg used photography, but his work is characterised by an art education, while Cindy Sherman was educated as a photographer. You can also often see if artists working

    A Field of Norwegian Photographic Art Takes Shape

with photography have worked commercially as
photographers. For example, Philip-Lorca diCorcia has
had many advertising jobs, and this has given him a
photographic vocabulary that he has used actively in a
art context. Photographic artists come from different
starting points, and mine was a study of photography.
It was photography that gripped me.

s ø s   In many ways, your Conceptual tendency connected you more strongly to contemporary art, but
you were perhaps somewhat alone in that tradition as a photographer in Norway.

D A   Yes, I think that's so.

s ø s   Did you collaborate with anyone apart from
Bente Stokke and Sissel Tolaas?

D A   I also collaborated with Haugen and Maning, an advertising agency that was interested in what we were doing
at Fotogalleriet. Per Maning in particular, a graphic
designer, was interested in art and photography, and
has since then become a recognised artist and photographer. Gradually, I collaborated a lot with Haugen and
Maning. They hired me as a photographer for cam-
paigns, and they organised exhibitions and published
exhibition catalogues. This included being involved in,
and making the catalogue for, the exhibition *KOKS* at
Trondhjems Kunstforening in 1983, where I took part
with the a process-oriented photography project. As
I've mentioned, I also had contact with Bård Breivik
and other artists from the Bergen environment. When
Bård and several other Bergen-based artists exhibited at
Høvikodden, I was extremely impressed by the loosely
organised group LYN, which, in addition to Breivik,
consisted of Stein Rønning, Gerhard Stoltz, Bjørn
Krzywinski, Birger Larsen and Arvid Pettersen. They
shared both workshop and studio. They also ran Galleri
1 in Bergen, where I exhibited and met these artists. It
was a fantastic time, with plenty of energy in the field
of art. I worked like a madman, and one New Year's
Eve was developing film when the clock struck twelve.

                    Dag Alveng in Conversation with Susanne Østby Sæther

S Ø S Today, the situation is a completely different one, where photography is well established and institutionalised within the field of art. Photography is recognised as an independent form of artistic expression. Also with regard to educational opportunities, exhibition venues and financial support the situation is completely different.

D A Especially since now there are many people fully employed, such as yourself, studying and working with photography as art.

S Ø S Yes, professionalism has entered all aspects, including the production of exhibitions, registration and conservation as well as mediation.

D A Fotogalleriet's director Antonio Cataldo said something very true: that we started Fotogalleriet out of pure frustration with the lack of understanding about what we were doing. Now though, the situation has completely changed, and the level of frustration is no longer the same.

S Ø S As you see things now, is it still important to have a dedicated exhibition venue for a camera-based mode of expression?

D A I've seen photography flourish, and especially in New York there was a period when over half of the galleries showed only photography. It's most welcome that photography is now being shown to such an extent, both nationally and internationally, but I see a lot of very bad photography. Today, photography is our language, with Instagram and selfies, and images have become an everyday form of communication, as we're always sending images to each other. There's an enormous consumption of images, and one could call photography the folk art of our time. I would say that it's no longer necessary to have exhibition venues dedicated to photography, but that such venues have a right to exist as long as they show what's really good – both the classic oldies and new forms of expression.

   A Field of Norwegian Photographic Art Takes Shape

55.

The large photographs that Marianne Heske exhibited at Fotogalleriet in December 1978 are shown at the back of the book *Arbeider & Notater* (Works & Notes). It is a small, pocket-sized book, which when it was printed in a new edition in 2012 was given a bright orange book band with the title translated into English. Under the band, thousands of small larvae seem to be crawling, but on closer inspection they turn out to be tiny human faces. The recurring theme of the book is the mask and the human need to categorise, define and suppress other people, based on superficial criteria. The text in the book moves between French, German, Norwegian and English, 'a natural result of my existence over the past few years', Heske writes in a postscript to the artistic statement with which she opens the book.

The black and white photographs shown at Fotogalleriet in 1978 are of individuals standing or walking, either alone or with others in the background. Some are in towns, others in nature. All the pictures are collages, where the heads of the humans depicted have been replaced by those of dolls. On the dolls' skulls is a grid filled in with numbers from 1 to 35. On each picture, a form has been printed with certain character traits that correspond to the numbers. The characteristics are divided into *Emotional* and *Intellectual*. In a strip under each photograph is the caption *Phrenology Analysis*, the name of a place, and a date.

Phrenology[48] is a long-ago debunked pseudo-discipline that identifies human characteristics by analysing the surface of the skull. Historically speaking, humans have always found ways to justify prejudices and substantiate racism. Heske has used phrenology, the mask, the marionette and other forms to show the strong human need to label both the world and other human beings.

Heske was working conceptually when she visualised her ideas about human beings and society, a fact emphasised by the press release sent out by Fotogalleriet in connection with the exhibition in 1978:

> Marianne Heske is known as a Conceptual artist. Conceptual art can perhaps be described as art where the expression (the picture, sculpture, act, etc) represents thoughts or an idea (concept), unlike a more traditional work of a more directly emotional nature. But the boundaries are fluid and it is often a case of both/and. At any rate, this is the first time that Fotogalleriet has shown photographs with a conceptual feel.

48

Phrenology is the study of the conformation of the sku[ll] as indicative of mental faculties and traits of character, especially according to the h[y]potheses of Franz Joseph G[all] (1758–1828), a German docto[r] and such nineteenth-centur[y] adherents as Johann Kaspar Spurzheim (1776–1832) and George Combe (1788–1858). Phrenology enjoyed great popular appeal well into the twentieth century but has be[en] wholly discredited by scienti[fic] research. (*Encyclopaedia Britannica*).

The First One

Lotte Konow Lund *You worked with videos as early as 1975. Was there an environment for video, Conceptual or what was called 'contemporary media' in Norway back then?*

Marianne Heske At the time, I was living in Paris. But no, there was nothing at all.

L K L Can you remember what you yourself thought when you made your first video works?

M H I was already exhibiting graphic art and material works in Paris when I started with videos, and basically it was the same mode of thought. It's a different medium and expression, but the underlying philosophy is the same. It was a way of manifesting thoughts that came from America, of course, as everything did then. Video carries sound waves and light waves just as much as our human gaze does – we see what we film at the same time as we talk and look. It's the first medium that can do that: register sound waves and light waves in the same way as the human eye. And therefore I thought of using this spontaneity all the time. If I think a thought, I can capture it in pictures and sound. Photographic film, on the other hand, you have to get developed, copied, cut – physically. Video works directly from my thought and soul.

L K L It is 1:1?

M H Yes, precisely. 1:1.

L K L Did transferring something so directly from your thoughts mean that you became more visible to yourself – or, to put it another way, is it a tool for seeing ourselves, seeing what we otherwise are unable to see?

MH What became visible was that which is innate in all humans, which some people are more aware of than others. Artists are probably more aware. And composers and writers.

  Marianne Heske in Conversation with Lotte Konow Lund

LKL   Did art schools have video equipment back then?

MH   They had 'Portapaks', as we called them, or reel-to-reel
                            tapes. At the time, in 1975, I was studying at Beaux Arts
                            in Paris in 1975 and after that at Jan van Eyck in Brus-
                            sels. You had to book the equipment in advance at both
                            places.

LKL   Was that because it was really expensive?

MH   Yes, and also because it was physically big. The tape
                            was on heavy rolls that you had to thread onto the
                            machine. You could see the magnetism in the tape,
                            in a way, which absorbed sound and image and light.
                            First it was Open Reel, ¼ inch and ½ inch. Then came
                            U-matic with enormous cassettes. Then U-matic Low
                            Band, U-matic High Band, which was too expensive
                            for us and was used more for TV and things like that.
                            Low Band was for low-end people like us. I've got them
                            all at home. Then there was a problem with the various
                            formats. In the US there would be one format, France
                            and Europe another, and Germany and Scandinavia a
                            third. Three formats. Madness!

LKL   Did you learn how to edit?

MH   No, we did that in the studio alongside a technician.
                            Why should I learn how to sit and press all the buttons?

LKL   No, why should you?

MH   Plus the fact that practically everything I do is unedi-
                            ted. I plan everything in advance. And I make time
                            itself part of the work. 'Time-based media' is what
                            video art was called at that time, and there were a great
                            many artists who used time as the main element in
                            their works. For example, they'd sit for hours in front of
                            a video camera, like Marina Abramović.

LKL   When did you move back to Norway?

MH   1980.

                    The First One

L K L   You must have stood out here at the time. The
art audiences must have regarded you as pretty
outrageous.

MH   Yes. And didn't I get to feel it! I knew, of course, when
I moved the small wooden barn [*The Gjerdeløa Project*]
from Tafjord to the Georges Pompidou Centre in Paris
that it would raise hell back in Norway. I was called
'Madam Artist' with capitals and inverted commas, etc.
But it was calculated. I knew nobody in Norway would
understand about the barn. I was well aware that no
one would care for the videos. And when I returned in
the 1980s, I stopped working with the dolls, since no
one got the message anyway, so there wasn't any point
in carrying on.

L K L   Did your first videos connect to the dolls?

MH   Everything's connected for me. Everything's connected
to everything else. I don't know anything, but everything is possible.

L K L   How did the dolls appear on the scene?

MH   The dolls appeared on the scene as an image of the
programmed individual. I found a box of 100 dolls that
I bought in Paris in 1971, at a flea market. I just love flea
markets. There's such a great atmosphere there, of lived
lives. Even back then, it had to do with fake news. In
Works & Notes I used a quotation from Cocteau: 'What
I recount are lies that are true.' And have you noticed
the statement I made there? It says: THE OBJECT –
THE CONCEPT – THE OBSERVER. What I ask,
time and time again, is this: what is illusion – or what
writers call fiction – and what is reality?

L K L   But you're not talking about Marshall McLuhan's
assertion that 'The medium is the message' – content means nothing, it's form that creates reality?

MH   No, that's something quite different.

    Marianne Heske in Conversation with Lotte Konow Lund

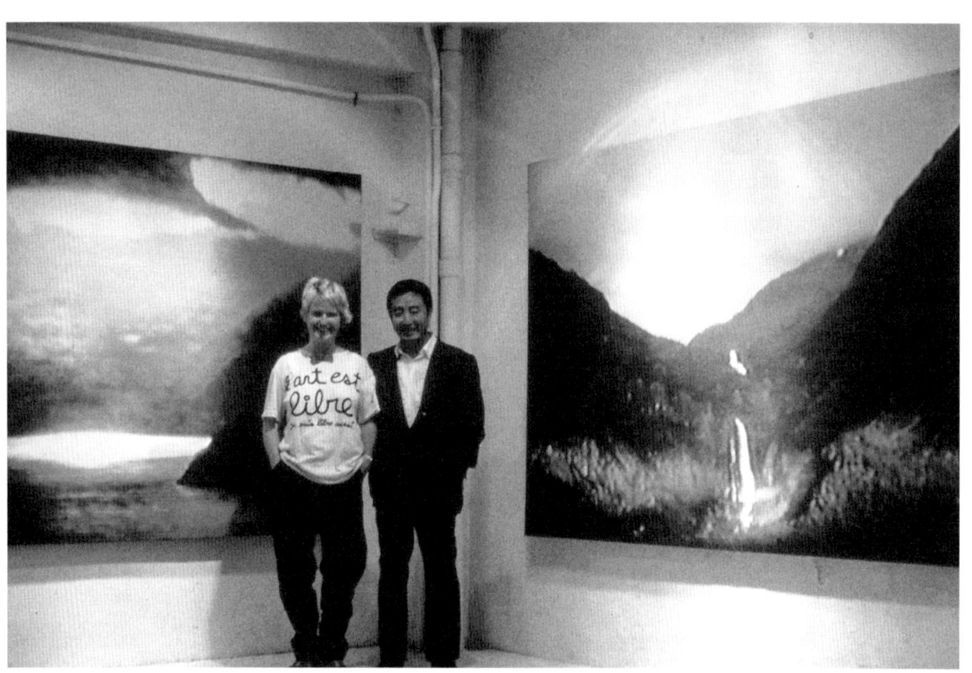

60.   The First One

L K L   But was what you saw in this huge analogue box
of dolls a question of reality?

MH   Yes. But I'd already worked on the same theme at the
Academy of Art and Design in Bergen.

L K L   Did you work with dolls there too?

MH   No, I worked with graphic art and etchings of people
who all looked the same. Lots of teeny-weeny people
together. You can also find them in *Works & Notes*.

L K L   They're the ones on the cover, aren't they? But
your fascination with dolls has to do with ...

MH   Has to do with us. We're programmed. All of us are
programmed.

L K L   How long have we been that?

MH   We've always been that.

L K L   Always?

MH   Yes. We've always constructed conventions that we
think are real. Both the barn and the dolls have to do
with Norway. Here, we don't have the marionette tradition that exists in China, Japan, Italy and France. There
they have a marionette theatre that reflects society and
can criticise those in power, right? But that tradition
doesn't exist in Scandinavia. Despite this, you can of
course see political puppet-regimes here. For that reason, I made these marionettes movable and alive with
video. In that way they became real.

L K L   When you're written about, your comprehensive,
international education is often mentioned: Bergen Academy of Art and Design, École Nationale
Supériore des Beaux Arts in Paris, Royal College
of Art in London and Jan van Eyck Academie in
Brussels. That makes a total of eleven years, with
most of them outside Norway. Was it due to your

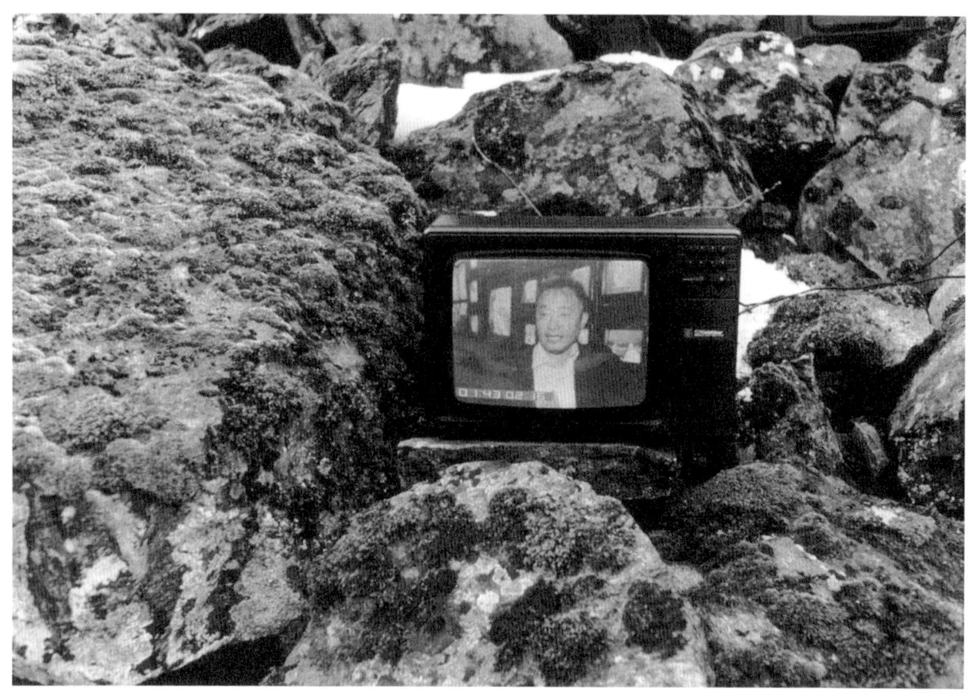

      The First One

living abroad so long during your formative years
that you started working conceptually so early?

MH   I discovered Conceptual art when I was on a trip to
Poland with my father in 1967 and met artists there who
were in advance of those back here in Norway. But I
was definitely working conceptually while attending
the Academy of Art and Design in Bergen. I made my
debut in the Autumn Exhibition with an aquatint and
a line engraving entitled *Impromptus*, after Schubert, in
1969.

LKL What's your interpretation of Conceptual art, and
has it changed for you?

MH   Let me put it this way: in Norwegian we call
Conceptual art 'the art of ideas' don't we?

LKL Yes.

MH   In English 'concept' means condition, right?

LKL Hmm … Idea? Conception? Is that the same as
condition?

MH   Maybe it's my personal interpretation that the concepts
are the conditions we have around us the whole time
that don't actually mean anything. Who decides the
conditions? That's why I move these houses around the
place. They're so full of conditions and pre-assumptions.
And the conditions are what I want to dissolve, so that
they become something completely different.

LKL So, if I understand you correctly, it's classic Duchamp: to do something with something, such
as move it, or dissolve it, no matter whether it's a
hay barn or a line, changes the premises for that
which surrounds us, and draws our attention to
how we position all our self-imposed systems to
which we believe we have to adopt a stance?

MH   Nicely put. It's also in the book *Works & Notes*. Have
you got to that list? I worked a great deal on it. 'The

          Marianne Heske in Conversation with Lotte Konow Lund

observer and the perceiver', it says in the book, and there you can see the whole thing about conditions. *Works & Notes* isn't just a book; it's also the catalogue of my solo exhibition and video installation at Bonnefantenmuseum in Maastricht in 1978.

L K L What's the list of names that's at the back of the book?

MH It's a thank you to all the people I'd met in my life until then. Now the list is much longer.

L K L When you had the hay barn make a journey to Paris, you had an object and a space, both highly symbolic bearers of identity, meet for the first time. Norwegian National Romanticism on a visit to the centre of Europe, or Norwegian poverty on a tour to get close to the French Revolution. It's the same sort of approach as when, some years ago, you took a condemned house and placed it in front of the Norwegian parliament building in Oslo and called it the House of Commons. Is there a lot of politics in your actions?

MH It all depends on who's looking and what they see.

L K L Why?

MH If you take the House of Commons, for example, some people will only see the political aspect, others the architectural. And yet others will be interested in the historical. So it's all in the eye of the beholder. To move something adds something, but what you're also saying is that what was there before no longer has the same meaning.

L K L Or that it can acquire more meanings and readings.

MH Precisely, but this can also be highly complicated. Just think: there are five million people in Norway; in China there are 1.9 billion, more or less. So we have

The First One

five million conceptions about things, but they have 1.9
billion – you can multiply it a great many times when
there are more people involved, so the pressure on conceptions is much greater.

L K L   And with the Internet, the amount becomes more
visible and more concrete.

MH   Yes, but it's unable to challenge you in the same way.
The Internet is a closed system, and can only give you a
certain response.

L K L   That's true. When you travel, or even just walk
through a library, you can't help coming across
things you've never encountered before, but with
the Internet, we're becoming increasingly aware
that we're being manipulated to believe that we
discover things on our own, while we're just going
round in circles in our own tracks. We can sense
the falseness, the fact that everything we do, our
own actions, is staged so that someone can earn
money out of us.

MH   Yes, well, that's the Internet for you. And the Internet
is something that someone has programmed. And that's
what people are up to all the time. We've been coded
and are remote-controlled. There's nothing one can do
about it, except just let it be, really.

L K L   When was the first time you showed photography?

MH   It was photographs of people holding dolls' heads –
they're also shown in *Works & Notes*. They're various
people whom I met while travelling in Europe. It
became an installation, which I showed at the ICA in
London, in 1975. I thought the National Museum in
Oslo would buy them at some point, but they haven't so
far.

L K L   How did you view photography back then?

   Marianne Heske in Conversation with Lotte Konow Lund

MH   I use photography to freeze moments, either as art or as documentation of projects and of people. I exhibited photographs as photographic art at Galleri 1 in Bergen in 1974, and integrated photography into my assemblages very early on indeed. When I was studying in London, I showed a photo installation with 100 slides plus sound at the ICA. When I exhibited photographs at Fotogalleriet in 1978, it was montages that I'd photographed and copied onto canvas that was covered with photo emulsion – this was long before data arrived on the scene. The photo canvases had a format of approximately 2 x 1.6 metres. They're shown at the back of *Works & Notes.*

LKL   *Works & Notes* is full of photographs. There's a great picture of you right at the beginning, kneeling, while you hold a doll's head above your head and there's a semicircle of cows standing behind you. It's as if they're conferring with each other about what a human being could be. Underneath it says in capital letters: JE NE SAIS RIEN – TOUT ME SEMBLE.

MH   That means 'I know nothing – everything is possible', but also 'I can imagine all sorts of things'.

LKL   What is the work in that photograph? Is it the action, the doll's head or the photograph? Or doesn't it matter?

MH   The whole atmosphere is surrealistic. It is a mixture of Dutch cows, role play and absurdity.

At that time, I was living in Maastricht and working in a gallery in Brussels. Which, of course, is in the heart of Europe. It was a fantastic time. It only took an hour to drive to Brussels, to Amsterdam, to Antwerp or to Düsseldorf. I felt more at home in Europe than in London. The British are more like this: 'Painting, painting, painting, painting …' And so I went back and applied for a state grant in the Netherlands. Which I got. I used to do lots of applications back then. And it was a very accommodating grant. So I stayed in the Netherlands for three years. And there I found artists

      The First One

from all over the world – Israel, Egypt, Britain and
South Africa … At the time, I was also working in
a gallery in Brussels called Gallerie le contemporare.
Marcel Broodthaers worked there, and he was pretty
conceptual. Is he well known in Norway?

L K L   Yes, you could say that. He was known both as
a poet and an artist. I recall being told about his
debut work of 1964, where he cast his last collection of poems, *Pense-Bête*, in plaster. Was it in
Brussels that you became known?

MH   No. It was via the gallery I worked at in Paris, which
was called Galerie Jean & Jacques Donguy, in the
Bastille area and was the Fluxus gallery at the time. I
exhibited with Alison Knowles, who was married to
Dick Higgins, and the dancer Merce Cunningham. I
became one of their gang and lived at Alison Knowles's
in Spring Street in Soho when I was in New York,
which I was quite a bit for a while.

L K L   The very first of your works I ever saw were the
large photo paintings, when I was quite young.

MH   Video painting – it was Nam June Paik who called
them that, and he was inspired by my technique. I
showed them at the Biennale in Venice, at the Nordic
pavilion, in 1986.

L K L   How did you arrive at that expression?

MH   You may well ask. It was pure intuition. The light
waves in a video harmonise with the stripes in an inkjet
machine.

L K L   They're tremendously heavy, those paintings.

MH   Yes, they are. One of them, which is 5 metres high and
4 metres wide, hangs at Skaugum.[49] King Harald was
given it for his fiftieth birthday – he's eighty now, isn't
he? So it must have been thirty years ago.

[49]
The official residence of
Crown Prince Haakon of
Norway and his wife Crown
Princess Mette-Marit, located
in Asker municipality, 19 km
southwest of Oslo.

   Marianne Heske in Conversation with Lotte Konow Lund

L K L   But when you call them video paintings … I see
them as a continuation of our urge to link art to
nature, as part of nation-building and national
identity. I see them as a continuation of Munch in
a new medium. I also feel there's an affinity with
Weidemann's paintings from the 1980s, but it may
just be the colours.

MH   They're based on organic forms, and it is Munch and
Weidemann and Van Gogh and all of these – they
painted nature as well. But to me, it's just as much what
happens *between* humans and nature. I'm very much
interested in the human mind.

L K L   And while we're talking about this 'between', can
we go a back to Fluxus and New York? You'd
become a friend of Nam June Paik.

MH   Yes, we were together a lot. I have lots of pictures of
him, me and Alison. Of the whole gang too. And all of
us lived in Soho. It was because I'd moved the barn to
the Pompidou Centre that I was adopted by the Fluxus
artists. They were all crazy about that project.

L K L   Did you feel at home with the Fluxus artists?

MH   Oh yes, right at home!

L K L   Was Yoko Ono a part of it?

MH   Yes, but she lived up on Park Avenue, she didn't live in
Soho. So we didn't see her as often.

L K L   And how did you get along with these people?
They were extremely playful and perhaps not so
interested in making rules for Conceptual art as
many others were back then.

MH   Well, I'm actually very playful myself – you can also
see that in *Works & Notes*, and in the earlier video
works, as in *A Video Point of View,* or *Elastic Band or
Tape Measure.* It's all a lot of nonsense, really.

L K L   To me, both *A Video Point of View* and *Elastic Band or Tape Measure* are highly thought-out and extremely serious, like the other works you were involved in at that time. I'd like to see more art made today about art, language, conversation, dialogue – a mixture of seriousness and humour – as you did back then.

MH   And that was what the Fluxus artists did too. They thought and worked a lot before the final work came out. Take the reading aloud they did, for example, down at the Chelsea Hotel in New York, which just came about, like happenings – it was incredibly good. Yoko Ono used to come there occasionally. I was present a couple of times. They knew exactly what they were doing.

L K L   This is important art history. Do you think about the fact that you were part of it today?

MH   Yes, but there's no point me saying things like that in Norway. Here, it falls on deaf ears.

L K L   I think a lot of people here are interested in it.

MH   Are they? Well, that wasn't always the case.

L K L   Did your meeting with the Fluxus artists influence how you viewed materials and media?

MH   No. I've always done my own thing. Take Alison Knowlcs, for example: she was busy with seeds and food and stuff like that. But it strengthened my own art – that's how I would put it. If I'd lived in Norway, I wouldn't have been strengthened in that way at all. Everyone who works with art needs inspiration and reinforcement. Well, everybody in general does, too. But I have a large Fluxus catalogue from an exhibition in Cologne that I was part of, where I'm included in the Fluxus artists at the time.

L K L   And would you call yourself a Fluxus artist?

   Marianne Heske in Conversation with Lotte Konow Lund

MH   I never call myself anything.

LKL But you are a Conceptual artist?

MH   I'm nothing whatsoever. That's what my art is! There is
            no definition. As Jacques Braque once said, definition is
            restrictive by definition.

LKL But today, it's your way of working that's become
     the template. Today, those who work within a
     traditional genre are thought of as narrow.

MH   That's wrong. One mustn't be at the expense of the
            other – everything must exist at the same time. It's the
            quality that's the important thing, no matter what form
            or expression it takes.

LKL I recall Lotte Sandberg once wrote in a review
     about you that it's not enough to be first.

MH   I agree with that: it's not enough to be first.

LKL But what is artistic quality? Is it possible to define
     it?

MH   We don't have to define anything, not even quality.
            In these corona times we're unable to define anything,
            since the virus is completely organic and wild. Quality
            is something innate that will never become dated. My
            photos with people holding dolls' heads, which were ta-
            ken fifty years ago, will never become untrendy. Quality
            has to do with materials, message and aesthetics. When
            I moved the barn to Paris, for example, I was interested
            in how it would function architecturally, but also in re-
            lation to history, age and how the contrast between the
            barn and the Pompidou Centre would work – every-
            thing has to interact. Quality is serious stuff, you know.

Fire Friske Egg.
Postkort fra Sør-Varanger
Ellisif Wessel 15. mai 1889 – 5. mai 1928
Fotografert av Eline Mugaas 26. mai 2020

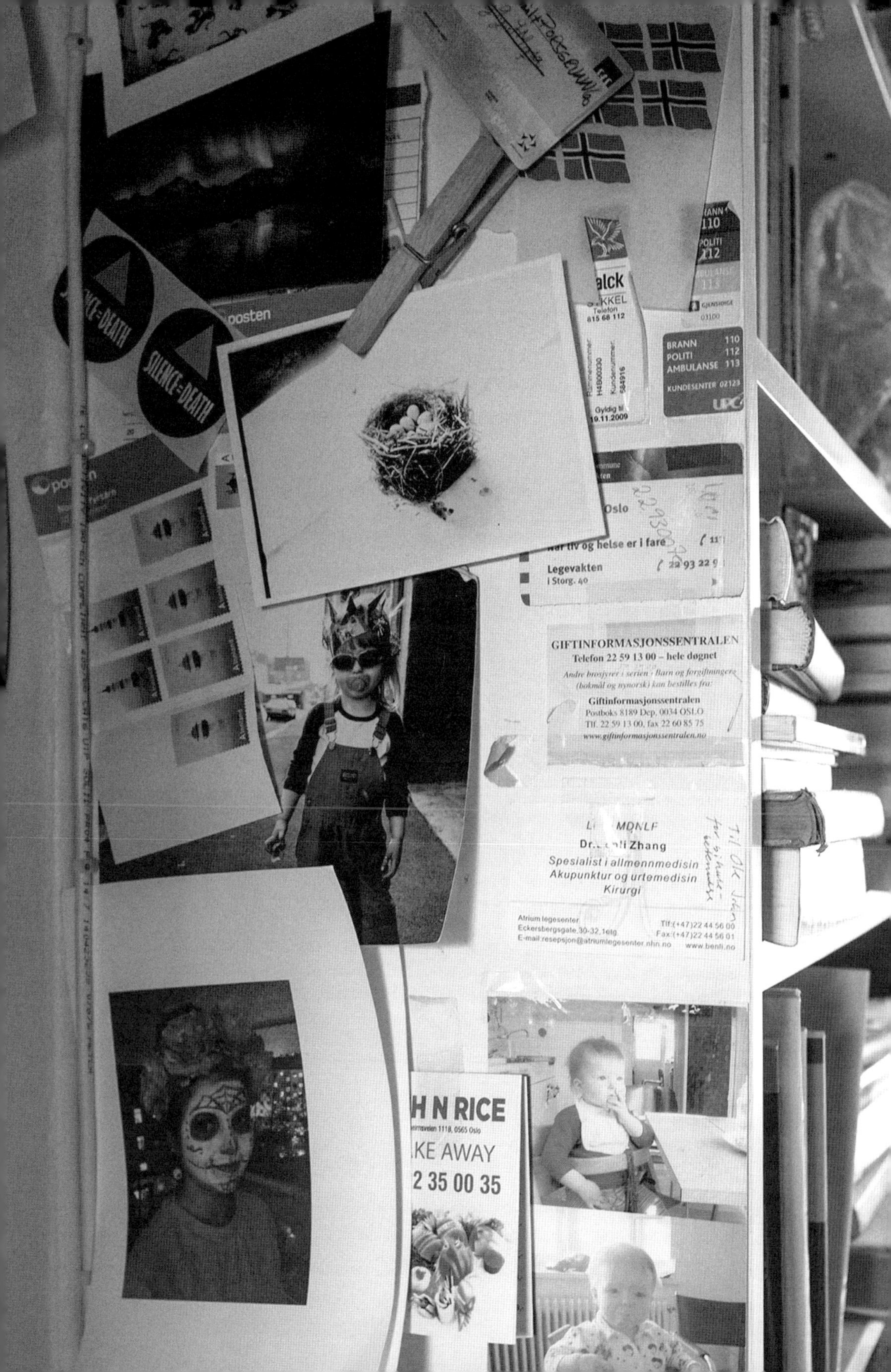
SILENCE = DEATH
SILENCE = DEATH
posten
alck
SYKKEL
Telefon
815 68 112
Rammenummer
H4B000390
Kundenummer
584916
Gyldig til
19.11.2009
BRANN 110
POLITI 112
AMBULANSE 113
KUNDESENTER 02123
UPC
Oslo
Når liv og helse er i fare
Legevakten
i Storg. 40
22 93 22 9
GIFTINFORMASJONSSENTRALEN
Telefon 22 59 13 00 – hele døgnet
Andre brosjyrer i serien · Barn og forgiftninger
(bokmål og nynorsk) kan bestilles fra:
Giftinformasjonssentralen
Postboks 8189 Dep, 0034 OSLO
Tlf. 22 59 13 00, fax 22 60 85 75
www.giftinformasjonssentralen.no
MDNLF
Dr. Benli Zhang
Spesialist i allmennmedisin
Akupunktur og urtemedisin
Kirurgi
Atrium legesenter
Eckersbergsgate 30-32, 1 etg.
E-mail:resepsjon@atriumlegesenter.nhn.no
Tlf:(+47)22 44 56 00
Fax:(+47)22 44 56 01
www.benli.no
H N RICE
heimsveien 1118, 0565 Oslo
KE AWAY
2 35 00 35

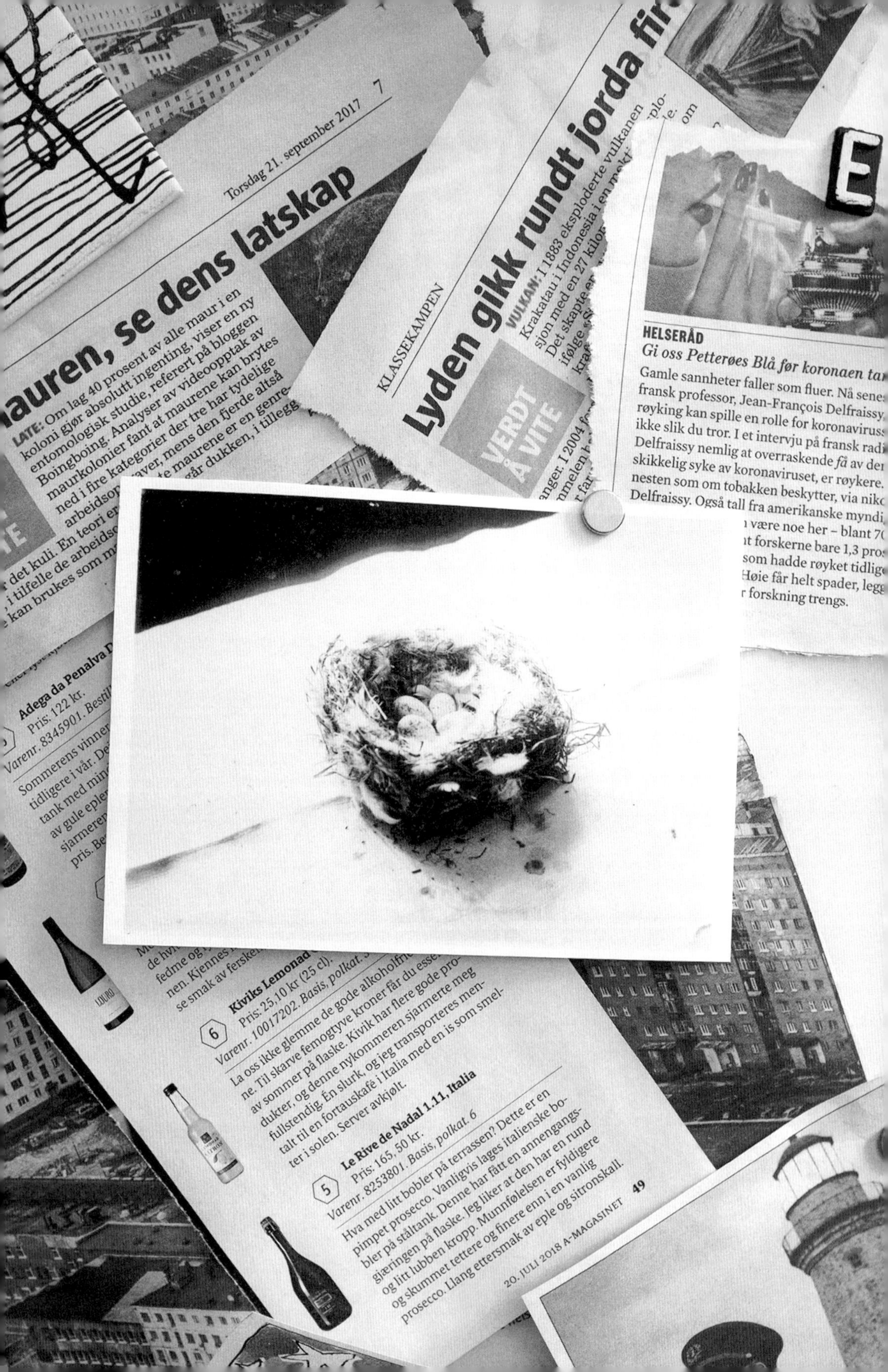

...auren, se dens latskap
LATE: Om lag 40 prosent av alle maur i en koloni gjør absolutt ingenting, viser en ny entomologisk studie, referert på bloggen Boingboing. Analyser av videoopptak av maurkolonier fant at maurene kan brytes ned i fire kategorier der tre har tydelige arbeidsoppgaver, mens den fjerde altså ...te maurene er en genre... ...går dukken, i tillegg
...det kuli. En teori er...
...i tilfelle de arbeids...
...kan brukes som m...

Torsdag 21. september 2017   7

KLASSEKAMPEN

Lyden gikk rundt jorda fi...
VERDT Å VITE
VULKAN: I 1883 eksploderte vulkanen Krakatau i Indonesia i en mekt... sjon med en 27 kilo... Det skapte en... ifølge «... kraf...
...anger: I 2004 f... ...melen... ...r far...

HELSERÅD
Gi oss Petterøes Blå før koronaen ta...
Gamle sannheter faller som fluer. Nå sene... fransk professor, Jean-François Delfraissy røyking kan spille en rolle for koronaviruss... ikke slik du tror. I et intervju på fransk radi... Delfraissy nemlig at overraskende få av de... skikkelig syke av koronaviruset, er røykere. nesten som om tobakken beskytter, via niko... Delfraissy. Også tall fra amerikanske myndi... ...være noe her – blant 70... ...t forskerne bare 1,3 pros... ...som hadde røyket tidlig... ...Høie får helt spader, legg... ...r forskning trengs.

Adega da Penalva D...
Pris: 122 kr.
Varenr. 8345901. Bestil...
Sommerens vinner...
tidligere i vår. De...
tank med min...
av gule eple...
sjarmeren...
pris. Be...

...de hv...
fedme og...
nen. Kjennes...
se smak av fersk...

Kiviks Lemonad...
6   Pris: 25,10 kr (25 cl).
Varenr. 10017202. Basis, polkat. ...
La oss ikke glemme de gode alkoholfri... ne. Til skarve femogtyve kroner får du esse... av sommer på flaske. Kivik har flere gode pro- dukter, og denne nykommeren sjarmerte meg fullstendig. Én slurk, og jeg transporteres men- talt til en fortauskafé i Italia med en is som smel- ter i solen. Server avkjølt.

Le Rive de Nadal 1.11, Italia
5   Pris: 165, 50 kr.
Varenr. 8253801. Basis, polkat. 6
Hva med litt bobler på terrassen? Dette er en pimpet prosecco. Vanligvis lages italienske bo- bler på ståltank. Denne har fått en annengangs- gjæringen på flaske. Jeg liker at den har en rund og litt lubben kropp. Munnfølelsen er fyldigere og skummet tettere og finere enn i en vanlig prosecco. Llang ettersmak av eple og sitronskal...

20. JULI 2018 A-MAGASINET   49

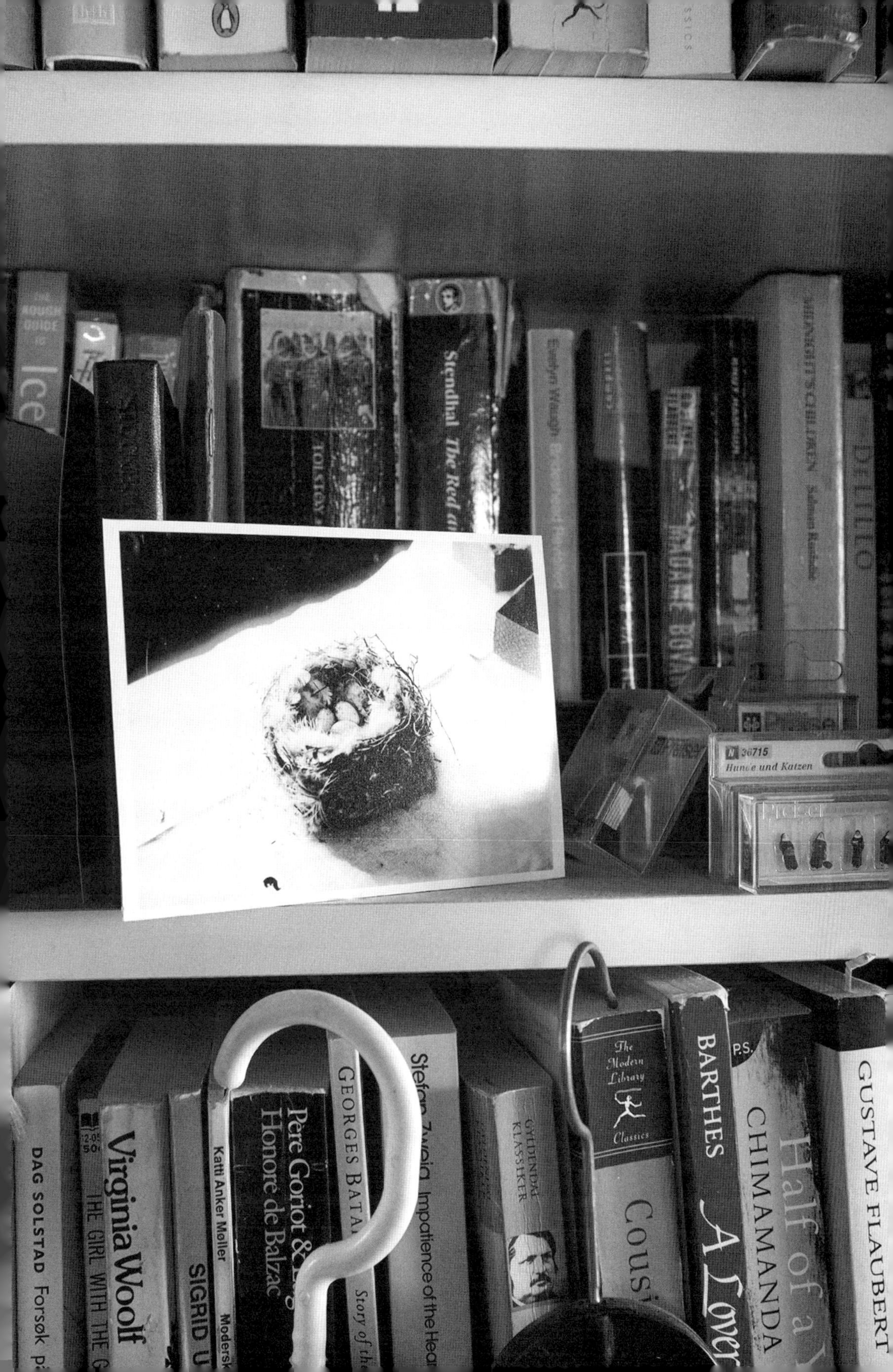

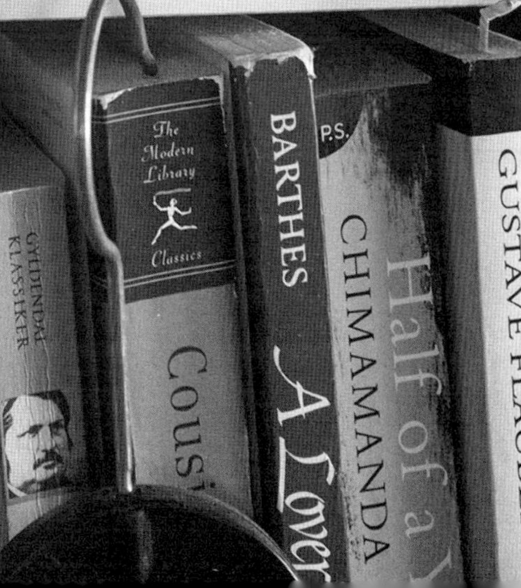

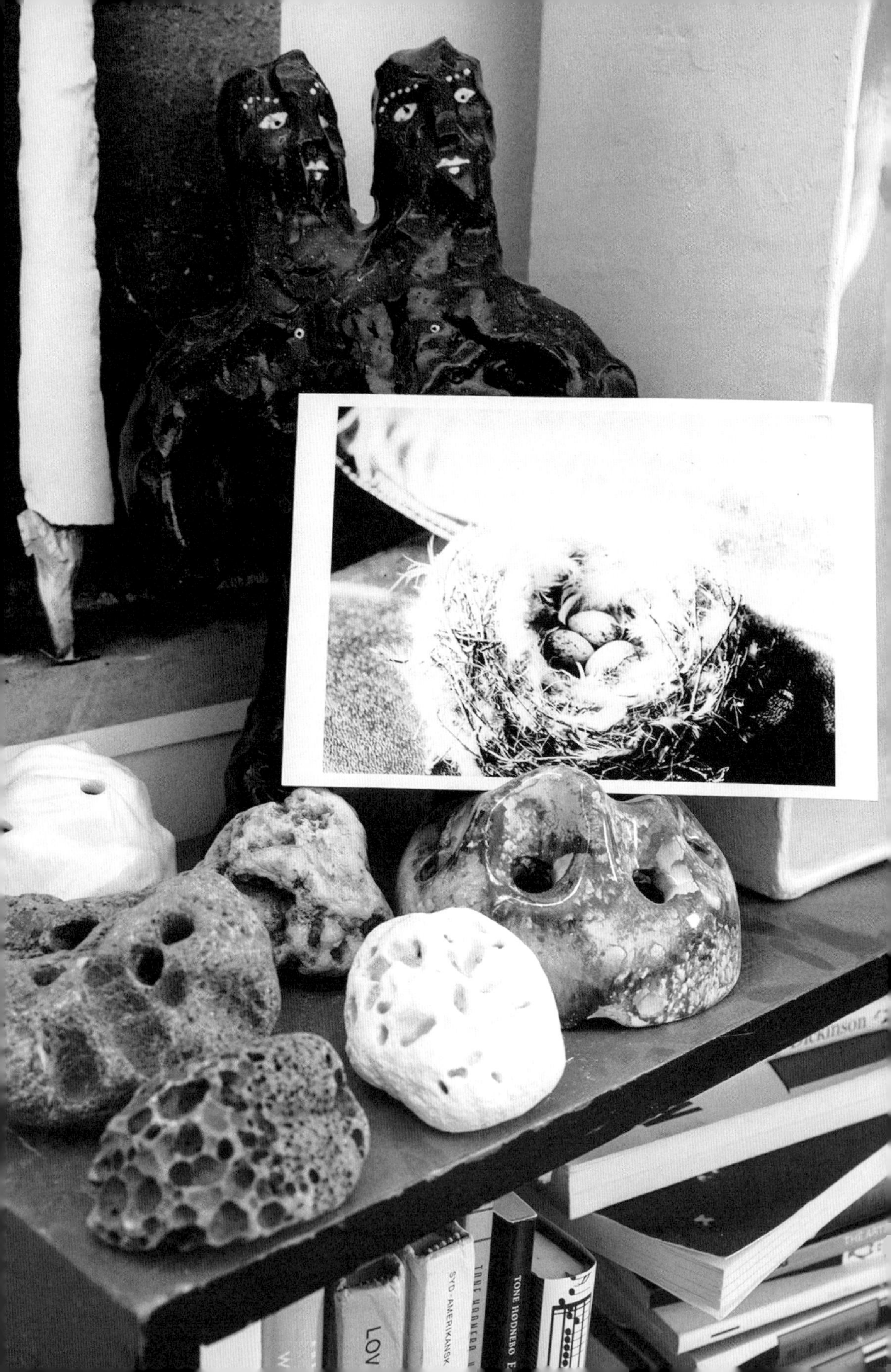

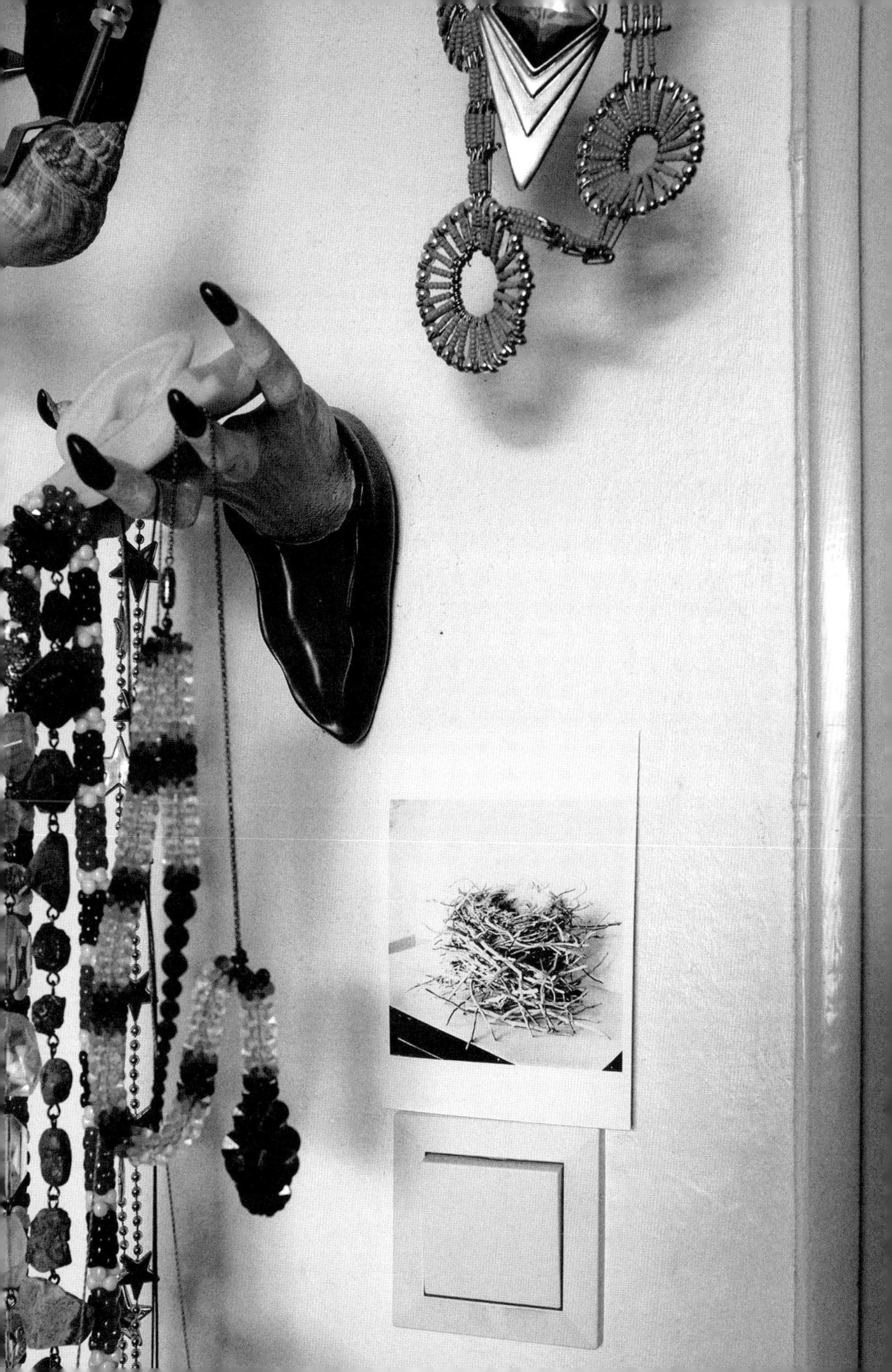

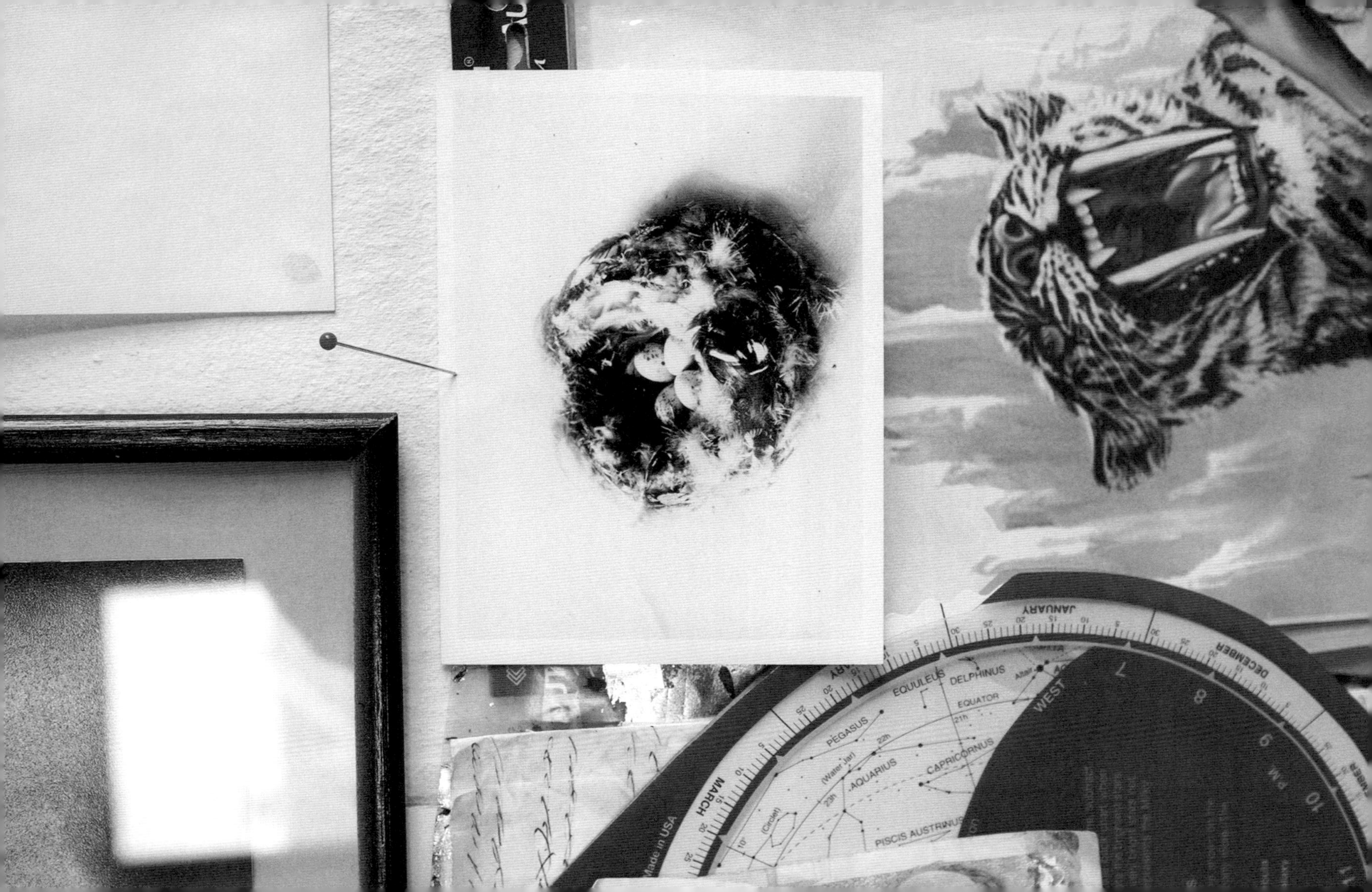
JANUARY
DECEMBER
EQUULEUS
DELPHINUS
EQUATOR
WEST
PEGASUS
(Water Jar)
AQUARIUS
CAPRICORNUS
MARCH
(Circlet)
PISCIS AUSTRINUS
Made in USA
7
8
P.M
9
10

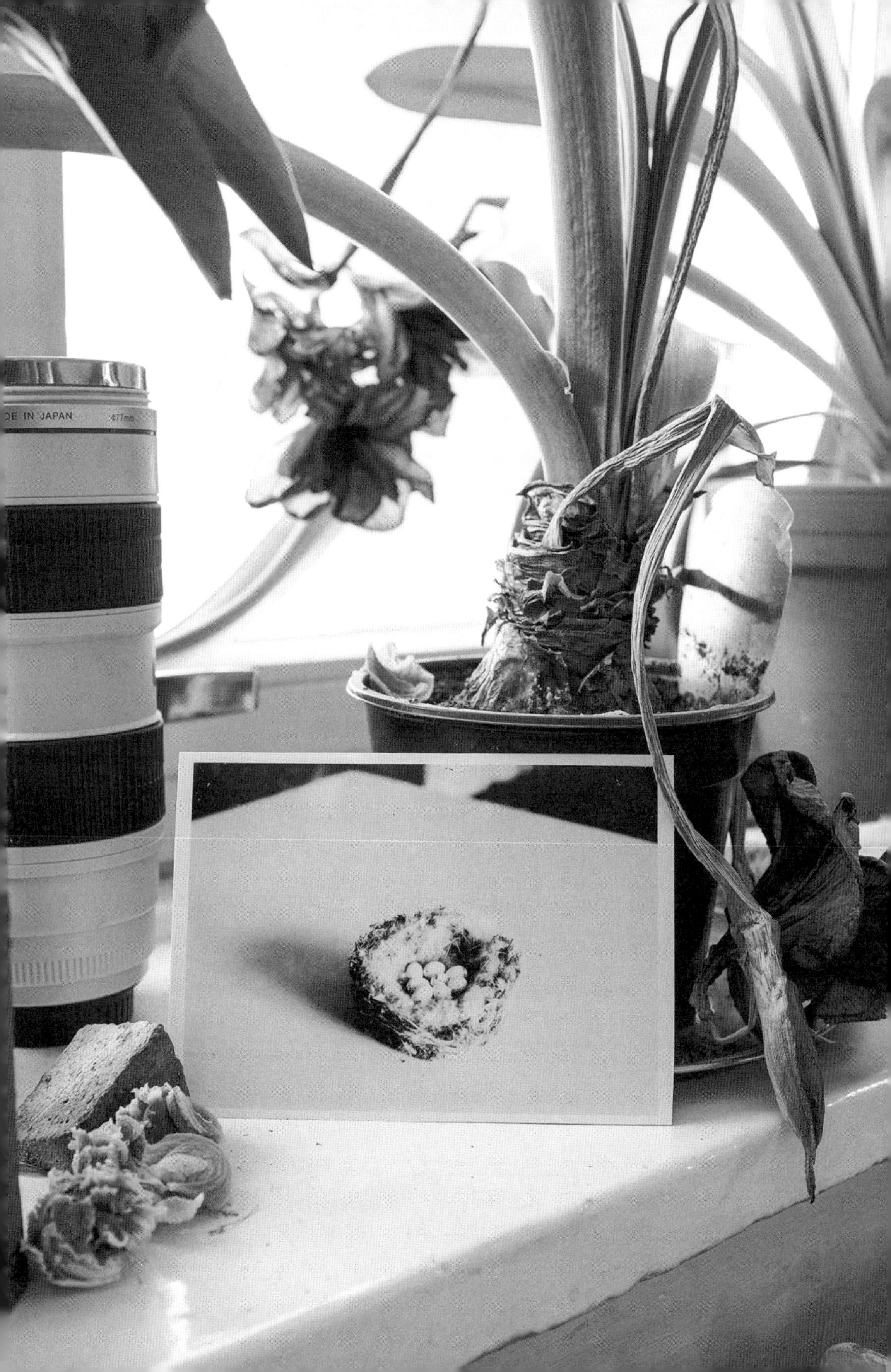

The Beginning
Gry Martinsen in Conversation with
Karen Fosse Rosness

Karen Fosse Rosness, and Gry Martinsen met on 26 September 2019 in Skøyen in Oslo.

Karen Fosse Rosness In the earliest archive material we have
at the institution we found a document with
Fotogalleriet's statutes, the minutes from the first
meeting, along with a press release stating that
the gallery was to open its doors for the first time
in 1977. At the bottom there are a number of sig-
natures, including yours. Perhaps you could start
by telling us something about the beginning?

Gry Martinsen
I got the idea of an exhibition venue for photography after a trip to London in 1974, when I visited The
Photographers' Gallery, which was in a side street not
far from Covent Garden. They had an exhibition room
for photographs, a café and a library, and an institution
like this was something completely new back then. I
thought it was really cool, and immediately felt that this
was something I wanted to try to get started in Oslo.
My husband, the photographer Tom Martinsen, and
I had just returned to Oslo after three years in Stockholm. There, Tom had studied photography at Foto-
och Dokumentarskolan, which was run by the Swedish photographer Christer Strömholm, at Stockholm
University. So when I returned to Oslo from London
and enthusiastically told Tom about this experience,
we got in touch with Tom Sandberg and Dag Alveng,
who were also back in Oslo after having studied photography in England. I think they also knew about The
Photographers' Gallery, and the idea of opening an
exhibition venue for photography in Oslo grew out of
this.

KFR Was there already a milieu for photography in
Oslo? How did you and Tom get to know Sandberg and Alveng?

GM
When we came to Oslo in 1972, the photographic environment was in its infancy, and Tom Sandberg, Dag
Alveng, Jamie Parslow and several other young photographers arrived there at the same time. Tom started
as a press photographer on *Dagbladet* and was eager to

　　　　　　　The Beginning

succeed in finding other photographers who regarded photography as visual art. We often went to Club 7 – all young people interested in culture used to go there – contacts were established, and one contact led to another.

K F R How did your interest in photography begin, the interest that took you to The Photographers' Gallery?

G M I got to hear about the Photographers' Gallery via the photography milieu around Christer Strömholm. I've always been interested in pictures, and I found Tom's interest in photography infectious. At the Academy of Photography, which is what the school used to be called back then, teaching was organised in such a way that the students took photos all day long. In the evening it was time for darkroom work, and after that the day's pictures were spread out across a large table and everyone took part in discussing them. They gave each other critical feedback and focused on aspects that had impressed them. I often joined in that evening session, and by participating in the conversations and discussions about the students' photographs, my view of pictures broadened.

K F R With a more theoretical approach to photography and pictures, as you describe it, did you feel that you were able to contribute something else to the discussions?

G M Yes, absolutely. I didn't take pictures, but I became quite good at analysing them and expressing what I felt about them. I was often asked if I attended the school or had studied somewhere else. I think people found my quiet confidence about my own statements reassuring, and I had a certain understanding of photography. I was an optician at the time and worked as such in Stockholm. After a while, I got involved with an organisation called Ungdomskontakten (Contact with Youth). I used to go out as a night-worker, helping drug addicts, alcoholics and the homeless. I had a book published, *Produkter* (Products, Cappelen, 1972), which deals with these meetings with them.

  Gry Martinsen in Conversation with Karen Fosse Rosness

I think that these experiences gave me a certain weight in my discussions about art. Both Tom and I are from Tønsberg, south of Oslo, a small, assimilable town. The years 1968 to 1972, which we spent in Stockholm, made a deep impression on us. The environment we lived in there, both the cultural life and the social life among artists, photographers, drug-addicts and the homeless, was a boundary-shifting experience for me. I became more flexible after the years in Stockholm than I had been previously.

There were many different ideas about how an exhibition venue ought to be run and what it ought to be like, but I felt quite at home among the 'lads' when we discussed exhibitions and why we wanted various artists in the gallery. I felt and still feel that more voices and various kinds of experiences create more energy and creativity than when everyone is in the same bubble. We all shared a wish to display photographs that could make people think and show them that photographs were more than just wedding photos and postcards.

KFR How did you set about implementing this?

GM Sandberg and Alveng were active and dynamic with regard to realising the project. They'd heard of a basement room in Oscarsgate, which we went and inspected and decided to rent. We couldn't afford to buy some of the things we needed to open an exhibition venue, so we got into contact with Leif Preus, who was already a known name in photography circles at the time. He'd established his own small exhibition venue in Langgata in Horten. The Preus Museum, which is now a national museum of photography, hadn't yet been established. But we went and talked to Preus and aired our ideas with him and asked him to help us realise our project. Among other things, we asked him if he could perhaps sponsor us with spotlights for the rooms. Preus believed in the idea and in us, so he agreed. We mounted the spotlights and painted the walls as a collective voluntary effort. When Fotogalleriet was ready, we opened at weekends. All of us took turns to be attendants.

The Beginning

K F R Fotogalleriet became a foundation in 1979, which among other things made it possible to apply for the necessary financial support. You say that you didn't have any money to invest initially in the project, so how did you make ends meet?

G M We had something called 'Friends of Fotogalleriet', which was an arrangement where friends of ours could donate money to running expenses. These friends helped a bit, but not much – just about enough to pay the rent. Those involved were from the environment around us, our friends and others who were interested in pictures and photography.

K F R That testifies to a high level of involvement, and to the fact that there was a need for what you wanted to bring about. What do you remember now as having been the greatest driving force?

G M The greatest driving force was an interest in art and especially photography – and in starting up something that hadn't been there before. There was a lot of activity and many discussions about the place of photography as art because of Fotogalleriet, and the whole photography scene was chock full of people who were ardent fans of photography and who had strong opinions. Alveng and Sandberg did a great job that was of crucial importance to ensuring that the exhibition venue existed as long as it did, and they were profoundly interested in the cause of photography as artists.

At the same time, the struggle was going on for photographers to gain entry to the Autumn Exhibition. Kåre Kivijärvi was the first to exhibit there, and in 1979 Tom, my husband, was also accepted. I remember that we were tremendously proud. All photographic artists felt misunderstood or unappreciated at that time. That the Autumn Exhibition opened up for photographers meant a certain degree of recognition for us. At *Dagbladet*, Tom fought his own fight to get photographers and their work respected in the same way as the journalists. A number of photographers worked freelance, some at the theatres during productions, where they partially earned their living.

  Gry Martinsen in Conversation with Karen Fosse Rosness

Some people also campaigned for the Norwegian Association for Fine Art Photographers to be on an equal footing with other artist organisations with state funding. They wanted to give photographers the same chance to gain scholarships and grants as other visual artists. Others wanted to be non-organised and to continue with the independence that Fotogalleriet had. But I was never very involved in that particular debate, not being a photographer myself.

KFR Why was it important for Fotogalleriet to be non-organised and independent?

GM It was important for Fotogalleriet that others shouldn't assess what was good and bad visual art.

KFR Can you say a bit more about how you all used to work on promoting photography as art via Fotogalleriet?

GM We wanted people to see and understand photos, to view photography as something more than wedding photos, and for the photographer to be respected for his or her work. That was the great aim. Purely artistically, it was among other things important that the pictures hadn't been 'arranged' – that a photo had been taken at the very same moment the photographer saw the motif. The pictures were in black and white, and the light was important. It was still an age of analogue pictures and working in darkrooms. Before this, photography was connected with wedding photos, babies on fur rugs and reportage and press photos. Photographers who took pictures and insisted that the picture should command the same attention as a painting, graphic art and drawing was something new. It took time, but the struggle got results. Photography now is accepted as art in Norway, and we've got the concept 'art photography'.

KFR Who was the intended public you wished to communicate with? Was there active mediation with various groups?

     The Beginning

I've always been socially interested, so I wanted contacts to be made with schools and a school class to take pictures of their everyday lives, to get young people to come to the gallery and to actively create pictures. But that didn't fit into the vision that Alveng and Sandberg had. To them, it seemed too unserious and it didn't coincide with their concept of art – and this developed into a discussion of what the task of Fotogalleriet was. But I feel it would have been smart to actively attempt to include other groups in society, which would have created a more live environment around the exhibition venue. My opinion is that one could do both without any clash being involved. One reason why it didn't work for them may be that because photography wasn't recognised as art at that time, they were afraid that neither Fotogalleriet nor photography would be taken seriously if they opened up for amateurs. And that was probably a correct assessment at the time.

However, we did hold lectures about the various exhibitions. I can't remember who it was who gave the lectures, but there were many interested people who crept down into the basement room to hear them.

K F R You came, of course, with inspiration from abroad. Many of you had studied in Stockholm and England. How do you recall the situation was, internationally speaking?

G M Photography was recognised both as a tool for social reporting and as art in the US, England, Sweden and Denmark. The Swedes and Danes had come a lot further than Norway at the time. Particularly in Copenhagen, there was considerable openness around photography. In Sweden, Christer Strömholm was an important driving force, through exhibitions, for example, and especially through his book Post Restante.

K F R Fotogalleriet exhibited many international and national artists, and something that's clear, particularly during the first two years, 1977–79, despite the fact that this was a male-dominated environment, is that Fotogalleriet had more solo

      Gry Martinsen in Conversation with Karen Fosse Rosness

exhibitions with women artists than men, which
is a rare tendency, even today. Was this done
deliberately on your part, in order to redress the
imbalance of gender within the field of art?

GM   Yes, you could say that. We wanted to bring to the fore
the women who worked creatively with photography
and who deserved to be seen on an equal footing with
the 'lads'. It was neither possible nor desirable to exclude
women from exhibiting. The time was ripe for it, and it
was part of the spirit of the age.

KFR   Would you say that there was a feminist awareness in the environment?

GM   Yes, definitely. Generally speaking, there was a hard
struggle taking place in society for free abortion, equal
pay for equal work. Girls went on 'thug courses' to
learn self-defence. In the photography environment it
was of course difficult to hold one's own in the discussions because there were more men than women who
were photographers. But the men also had to fight to
be taken seriously. Everyone had to contend with this
struggle, irrespective of gender. I remember Ann Christine Eek, who studied photography at the same time as
Tom. She'd fought for several years for a rightful place
and to become visible. She was at the picture agency
SAFTRA in Stockholm at the time, and, as far as I
know, she was the only woman photographer there.
She's the one I recall as being the strongest feminist
at the time within photography.

KFR   Are there any exhibitions from the first years that
you recall particularly well?

GM   I remember our joy and pride when we were able to
present pictures by Edward Weston at Fotogalleriet.
There were many works hung on the walls by important photographers from other countries in the first
period. It was important to be able to show works taken
by known photographers, since it enhanced the aim of
the gallery to promote photography as art.

It was fun simply to start Fotogalleriet: the feeling one has of having an idea that really grips you and then realising that idea. We who started Fotogalleriet got to know each other well and formed something that became important for the environment in the whole of Oslo. It's this creative process that I remember best, and how we did voluntary work, took turns to be attendants there on Saturdays and Sundays alongside our everyday jobs. We did so because we felt it was interesting and important. We were really enthusiastic about it.

     Gry Martinsen in Conversation with Karen Fosse Rosness

Work – Don't Wear Yourself Out –
A Life in Black and White Photography
Ann Christine Eek in Conversation with
Anna Tellgren

Ann Christine Eek, whose exhibition Arbeta – inte slita ut sig *showed at Fotogalleriet in 1978 and curator at Moderna Museet Anna Tellgren, met in Stockholm on 18 August 2019.*

Anna Tellgren When did you move to Oslo and why? What caused you to leave Stockholm?

Ann Christine Eek I'd been working extremely intensely for a number of years. I had some quite sizeable assignments for illustrating schoolbooks, but this work gradually started to seem so predictable – it was almost as if I knew the conditions for a given situation. I could have done a drawing of what the photograph would look like before taking it. I'd grown tired of my own way of photographing – I was stuck. Today, I'd probably say that I was pedagogically or politically correct. I discovered that I was worrying about all sorts of things I needn't be concerned with. So, in autumn 1978, feeling somewhat jaded, I sat down and looked through all my negatives. At the time, I had about half a million of them.

AT That's a lot. You must have been very productive during that period.

ACE But I didn't feel I could see myself in them. At the same time, that year, I was also involved in the picture agency SAFTRA as CEO. We had this basic idea that one ought to do all sorts of things collectively. But you can't take care of finances collectively.

I spent a lot of time that autumn sorting out SAFTRA's financial situation, but as Christmas approached, I was fed up with everything. I had some friends in Norway who said to me 'Well, why don't you come here for a while?' So I travelled to Oslo in February 1979. I was there for a week and something happened. I started to play with form and with light and landscape. When I got back to Stockholm after that week, the situation there was becoming completely intolerable. It felt as if I'd been some sort of mother figure for the SAFTRA crowd, but that no one ever stood by me.

 Work – Don't Wear Yourself Out

A T   Were you the only woman in SAFTRA?

A C E   Yes, for a very long time. Angelica Julner was there
                   from the beginning, but she left quite early on. More
                   women eventually came in – Cecilia Borggård and
                   some others.

A T   When was the SAFTRA group founded?

A C E   SAFTRA was started in 1967 by Anders Petersen and
                   Kenneth Gustavsson, and two years later there were
                   around ten photographers. After that, some journalists
                   and film people joined as well. I shared a writing desk
                   with Anders Petersen for ten years – and we're still
                   good friends.
                       I remained in Stockholm for about another month,
                   but one of my friends invited me to live in her flat in
                   Oslo, so I returned there around Easter 1979. I had a
                   five-year work grant, and a project waiting – I was to
                   have an exhibition at Fotograficentrum (the Photogra-
                   phy Centre) in Örebro in December 1979. So that was
                   what I busied myself with, and I started to photograph
                   landscapes once more. Another friend brought me to
                   Stavanger and I photographed the landscape there. A
                   lot happened to me during this period, but what really
                   set me off was Esaias Baitel. He's a Jewish photogra-
                   pher, born in Sweden, but now living in Israel. He was
                   living in Paris then, and came into contact with SAF-
                   TRA via Neil Goldstein, I think. Esaias said: 'Do you
                   know what? I actually think you should simply leave all
                   of this behind you.'

A T   I see. So you simply moved?

A C E   I didn't move officially, just travelled across to Oslo and
                   stayed there for a year. After the *Minnesbilder* [Recol-
                   lections] exhibition in 1980 at Galleri Camera Obscura
                   in Stockholm, I met Per, whom I married.

A T   And then you stayed for good? Because you met a
       Norwegian man?

                                     Ann Christine Eek in Conversation with Anna Tellgren

A C E   Yes, I remained in Oslo. Officially, I moved in September 1980.

A T Do you regard yourself as a Swedish or a Norwegian photographer today? Or are you a Nordic photographer?

A C E   I probably ought to call myself a Nordic photographer. The strange thing is that I don't seem to exist anywhere.

A T That's interesting. You're somewhere in between and don't belong to ether the Swedish or Norwegian history of photography. Is that what you mean?

A C E   Yes. But I had, for example, a huge retrospective exhibition in 2004 at the Preus Museum of Photography [Horten, Norway] and at Dalarnas Museum [Falun, Sweden] in 2008, and I've been active in both countries.

A T Let's talk a little about Fotogalleriet, which started in 1977. You had an exhibition there as early as the following year, didn't you?

A C E   Yes, it was called *Arbeta – inte slita ut sig* [Work – Don't Wear Yourself Out].

A T And how did that come about? Who contacted you?

A C E   Tom Martinsen and his wife Gry, who started the space with Dag Alveng and Tom Sandberg. I got to know Martinsen in 1968 when I was at Fotoskolan [the School of Photography] in Stockholm. He later became one of the most prominent press photographers in Norway.

        He and his wife knew that I'd done the book *Arbeta – inte slita ut sig* and were highly enthusiastic about the material.

A T And you travelled with that exhibition?

A C E   The book came out in November 1974 and then we had
a small exhibition at Bokhandeln Oktober in Stockholm, which was actually the first exhibition. Then
there was a large exhibition at Kulturhuset called *Kvinnfolk* [Women]. I think I contacted them about exhibiting my photographs of women, and they were included
in the *Kvinnfolk* exhibition in February 1975 as large
prints mounted on cardboard. That exhibition was later
shown at Malmö Konsthall in autumn 1975. In addition,
we made an exhibition of sets of ten posters, based on
this material.

A T So it travelled as a poster exhibition?

A C E   Yes. We sold each set of posters for 100 SEK. I think
it went off quite well, actually. There were many study
groups across the country that bought them.

A T But that wasn't what you displayed at Fotogalleriet?

A C E   The posters were included, but there were also silver
gelatine prints.

A T It was more of a classical photo exhibition?

A C E   Yes, a classical photo exhibition. It was actually the first
time I exhibited photographs that had been matted and
framed. Before that, tacks in the corners were what held
the prints to the wall.

A T Yes, I recall that. Back then it was common to
mount them on cardboard. Do you remember
anything about how you worked on the installation? Were you the one who made the display?

A C E   I think I was the one who did it, but I'm not sure.

A T And was there a private opening? The exhibition
took place during March 1978. Did you have guided tours and discussions at the exhibition?

            Ann Christine Eek in Conversation with Anna Tellgren

A C E   There was a vernissage, but I don't recall any guided tours. I was only there for a few days.

A T Weren't you living permanently in Oslo at the time?

A C E   No, I was still living in Stockholm then.

A T Today, do you regard *Arbeta – inte slita ut sig* as a feminist project? It's been seen as part of a feminist history.

A C E   The writers of the book's text were Kajsa Ohrlander and Ann Mårtens. Ann Mårtens later said 'All of us were communists.' But I replied, 'No, I've never been a communist', even though I did sell photographs to *Gnistan* and other left-wing newspapers. But I've never been politically organised.

A T The late 1960s and 1970s were characterised by a wave of political Leftism among students, writers and artists. Photography also became a part of this, and the documentary tradition was strong, particularly in Sweden.

A C E   And that was also one of the reasons why I left Stockholm – because I was working so intensely on *Arbeta – inte slita ut sig* and with the women portrayed in the book. We had a lot of contact and I talked a great deal with them. So when I'd completed the project, they were still there inside my head for several years afterwards.

A T You needed to see something else, do something else?

A C E   Yes, to liberate myself a bit. In addition, I was part of an environment where I met an incredible number of people all the time. I was tired of this life, quite simply.

A T If one looks back at *Arbeta – inte slita ut sig*, it seems to fit into the documentary ideology.

ACE   Yes, it does. One of the photographers who made the greatest impression on me was W. Eugene Smith. In the early 1960s, I saw his 'Country Doctor', his large reportage for LIFE magazine.

AT   Yes, it's still absolutely amazing.

ACE   Yes it is. Also 'Nurse Midwife'. Smith spent a great deal of time with her, and their close relationship resulted in these incredible photographs.

AT   Was it your idea, or were you commissioned to photograph women at work?

ACE   It was my own project. I had a female friend in London who, along with another young woman, had started to photograph women in London in the early 1970s. I thought this was important and it was, of course, at the same time as Group 8 was active.

AT   It was in the spirit of the age. I'm thinking, for example, of other photographers such as Monica Englund, who was also working at the time on various projects, including ones concentrating on birth and pregnancy. Were you in contact with Agneta Ekman?

ACE   I knew Agneta Ekman from the School of Photography and met her later when I had the exhibition at Camera Obscura in 1980.

AT   It really was something important and new, what you were doing – focusing on and documenting women's everyday working lives.

ACE   I thought it was terrible how male photographers exploited women in every possible way, and the photographs you could see in the daily press and weeklies were so superficial. My method consisted in digging out these women in various ways and then going off to meet them, often after work or at home, and explain who I was – my background, why I wanted to do what I was doing. And then we devised a plan as to how I

      Ann Christine Eek in Conversation with Anna Tellgren

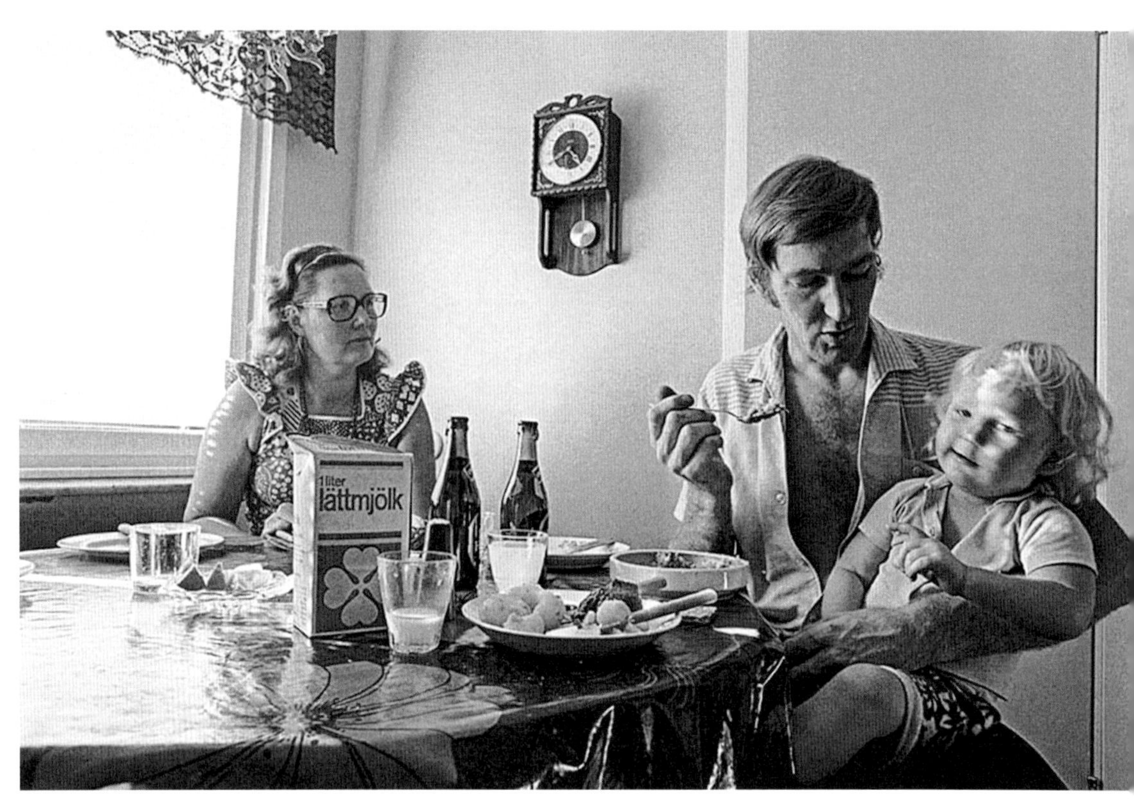

98.   Work – Don't Wear Yourself Out

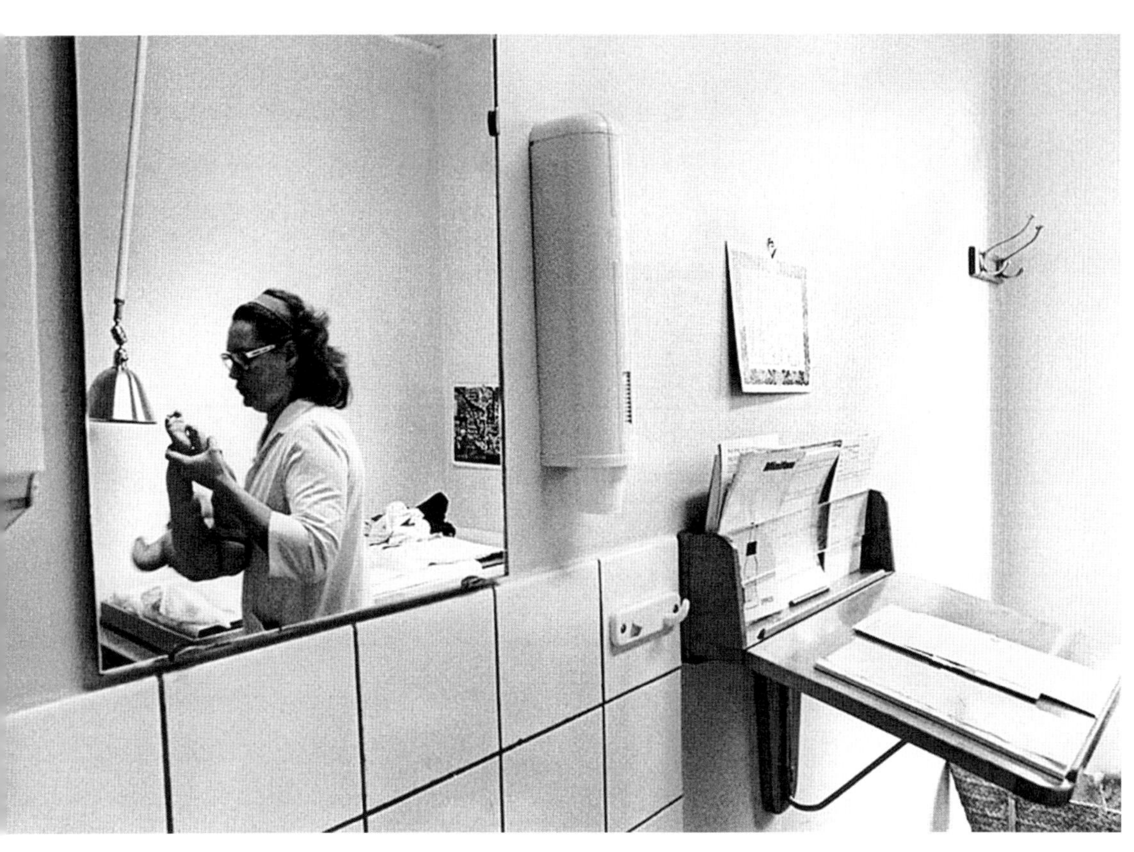

Ann Christine Eek in Conversation with Anna Tellgren

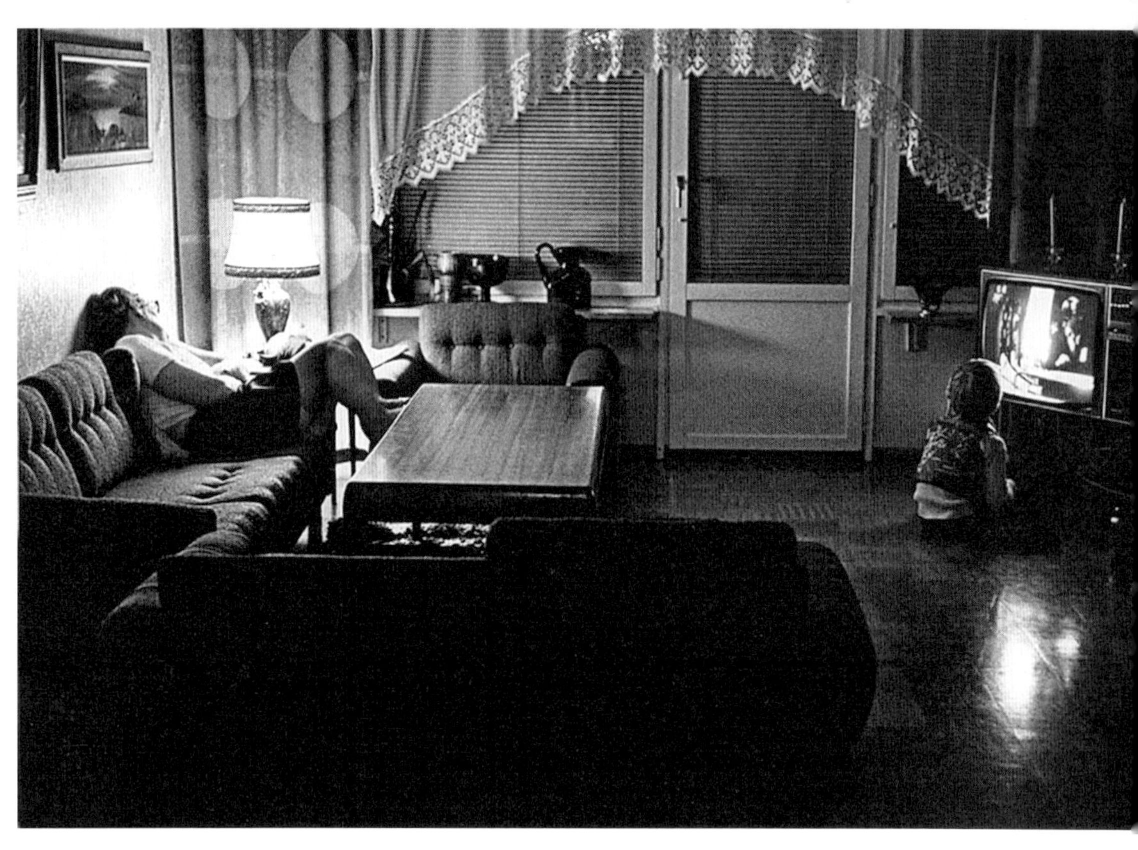

   Work – Don't Wear Yourself Out

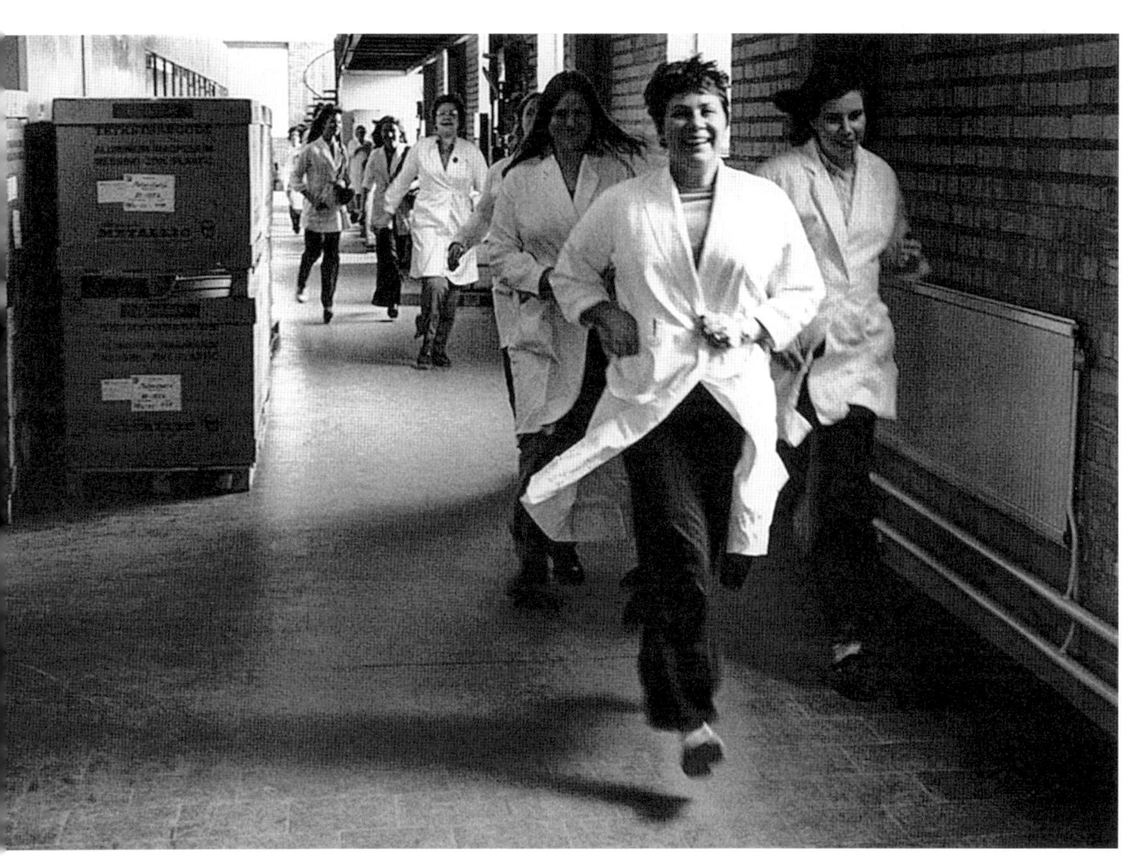

Ann Christine Eek in Conversation with Anna Tellgren

could take the photographs. What I wanted to do was follow them round the clock, to show what their unvarnished reality actually looked like.

A T   And you made notes while you were meeting them?

A C E   I've got some old black notebooks, but I don't think I actually noted down all that much then.

A T   The photographs were your method of expression?

A C E   Yes, I worked with images. I began on my own at first, but then I felt that I needed to have some kind of theoretical basis for it. Kajsa Ohrlander had written two books; one was called *22-hour Workday [22 timers arbetsdag,* 1971]. I thought she had some extremely important views, so I contacted her, and she thought it sounded like a great idea. A little later, Ann Mårtens joined us too.

A T   It sounds as if your collaboration was creative and great fun.

A C E   I was often the one who met the women first, and photographed them, and Kajsa and Ann went to their homes afterwards and interviewed them, often based on my photographs.

A T   Let's go back to Fotogalleriet. When you established yourself in Oslo, did you keep up with the programme? Were you there at the exhibitions?

A C E   I got to know quite a lot of people in that environment, those at Fotogalleriet to start off with, but also those in FFF (Norwegian Association for Fine Art Photographers), where I was on the executive committee for a while. I had quite a bit to do with Dag Alveng and Tom Sandberg, as well as Jim Bengston, Jamie Parslow, Johan Sandborg and Arne Walderhaug. Those are the ones I remember most. And it was there that I met Per Torgersen, whom I later married. Both he and I

    Work – Don't Wear Yourself Out

perhaps had a bit more 'gravitas' when we talked about photographs, because we'd both studied art history. He wrote about photo exhibitions and books on photography in what was then called *Arbeiderbladet*, and was active for almost thirty years writing about exhibitions. I also wrote about exhibitions until 1993, when I stopped for personal reasons.

AT   So, one could say, then, that it was an important place for all of you?

ACE   It was until I gave birth to my first child in 1981. We all used to meet on Thursday evenings and look at exhibitions, and afterwards we often went to a restaurant, drank beer and talked.

AT   So it was a sort of community, perhaps, of photographers? If you compare SAFTRA and the people involved there – was it the same sort of socialising?

ACE   At SAFTRA we were much more engaged in day-to-day politics and we used to discuss political issues a great deal. We talked about how our photography functioned in relation to society. So our talks were quite ideological most of the time, even though we perhaps weren't all that good at expressing ourselves to start with. But what first felt extremely liberating when I came to Oslo was that there weren't any political discussions whatsoever – we just talked about photography, less about topical political matters.

AT   Was it based on images, photographs that you were showing, or was it more of a general discussion?

ACE   We were photographing the whole time and took an awful lot of pictures. It was in the period around 1979, when I had quite a bit of contact with Tom Sandberg, and we talked a great deal about photography, about light and composition.

AT   You discussed theory and method?

   Ann Christine Eek in Conversation with Anna Tellgren

A C E   It made me understand that we had a 'use-and-dis-
               card' mentality regarding our photographs. Early on,
               I stopped using the entire photographic paper when
               printing, and began to leave white edges, to make it
               possible to hold the picture without getting thumb
               prints all over it. Then the type of paper started to
               become important, and I made larger prints. To exhibit
               framed photographs wasn't snobbish – it was to protect
               the print. Looking back, how many thousands of hours
               have been spent in the darkroom? And how many
               prints have been ruined by editors sitting there with
               their red pens?

A T   You're a skilful printer: you've worked a lot and
      a long time on it. Did you like working in the
      darkroom?

A C E   Yes, I thought it was great. We had a darkroom at
               home for several years. But with children, I started to
               feel that all those chemicals were a bit too dangerous.

A T   You didn't have any more exhibitions at
      Fotogalleriet, apart from taking part in the the
      Spring Exhibition on several occasions and in
      New Norwegian Photography 2 in 1980?

A C E   It was FFF who organised the Spring Exhibitions. I
               took part in the the Spring Exhibition in 1980 and then
               there was one more in 1982, when they refused some of
               the photographs – for biased reasons, in my opinion –
               so I withdrew my pictures. I left FFF the same year.
               I started to work at the Ethnographic Museum, and
               simply didn't have enough time.

A T   You moved on in your life. Let's talk about an-
      other project that's been important for you and is
      represented in the Moderna Museet Collection.
      I'm thinking of your work in the former Yugosla-
      via. You worked on the project from 1975 right up
      until 2009 – is that correct?

ACE   It's still on-going! It all started when I travelled to Albania with a journalist. We'd even been to the Albanian Embassy and tried to get permission to photograph, but it was like talking to a wall. I was a member of something called the Swedish-Albanian Friends Association, and there was a Norwegian association with a similar name. We were a group of about forty, Swedes and Norwegians, who made bus tours from Durrës on the coast for a fortnight in July 1975.

AT   Were you interested in this part of Europe, or was it just by chance it happened to be Albania?

ACE   I think quite a lot of people became curious about Albania via others who'd been there. But when we went there, there was no representative from the travel agency, the trip down took a terribly long time, and we got no food on our way. I went off in search of the local representative, who turned out to be a Norwegian social anthropologist. She was doing fieldwork in Kosovo.

AT   Was that Berit Backer?

ACE   Yes it was. It turned out that her father had been a photographer, so she was interested in photography. We got on exceptionally well and decided to carry out a project in the village of Isniq in Kosovo, where she was doing fieldwork. So, at the beginning of 1976 we started to plan things.

AT   And then you continued to collaborate?

ACE   We worked together for periods of time until she was murdered in 1993.

AT   That's a terrible story. Very sad.

ACE   A refugee from Kosovo murdered her. I've written about the events and it's even included in the book I'm working on now. After her death, I felt I ought to try to resume our work on Albanians.

                 Ann Christine Eek in Conversation with Anna Tellgren

A T   Is the project you're working on now connected to
the photographs from Albania?

A C E   No, it's the documentation that Berit and I made in
1976, in Isniq. The book is almost finished. When Berit
and I presented our exhibition in 1991 at the Ethnographic Museum in Oslo, we came into contact with
the vice-director of the institute of popular culture in
Tirana. She invited me to Albania, so I travelled there
in 1992 – it was a bit less dangerous then. Since then,
I've been to Albania and Kosovo fifteen times, but
mainly to northern Albania, more than to the southern
part, and to Kosovo.

A T   We have around forty of your photographs from
the village of Isniq in the collection – a series
we've shown several times at the museum. In your
book, will you be including all the material from
your first trips to the most recent?

A C E   No. I had thought of writing chronologically, from the
first trip in 1975, but discovered that the material from
1976 is so comprehensive, and important, that I had
to focus on this early material, which is unique. Tira
Books will publish *Albanian Village, Isniq - Kosovo 1976*
in 2020. Then we'll have to see what I'll do with the rest
of the photographs later on.

A T   Something I find interesting about your various
projects is that you quite clearly have a documentary profile, yet at the same time you've always
worked on more artistic projects. I'm thinking of
your landscape photographs and more personal, intimate portraits. You've always alternated
between these different ways of working and
expressing yourself as a photographer.

A C E   It's always been important for me to create photography
that's visual, that makes use of light and form. I haven't
expressed it in this way, but that's what's important.

AT   That they're strong photographs, quite simply?

ACE   That they're powerful, expressive photographs that at
                       the same time tell a story. As early as at the School of
                       Photography we used to discuss the fact that one is
                       often only able to use a single photograph to tell a story.
                       And that means it has to be visually powerful.

AT   If one really likes analogue and black and white
       photography – as I do – it's marvellous that you're
       so faithful to the black and white medium.

ACE   I have digital cameras now, but I convert to black and
                       white. Apart from one project. I come from Dalarna,
                       and I love the scenery there. So, I might just do a book
                       in colour at some point.

AT   I'd like just to ask you one final question, and it's
       got to do with what we started by talking about
       – the Nordic dimension. How do you view con-
       temporary Nordic photography? How would you
       characterise what's taking place now?

ACE   I can't really claim to have all that much of an overview.
                       When I was at the School of Photography, there weren't
                       all that many women taking photographs, and most of
                       them disappeared. So it's fantastic how I've been able to
                       combine having children with working as a photogra-
                       pher.

AT   Yes, you're a pioneer, you really are. Is that what
       you can see now – that there are more powerful
       female photographers?

ACE   I wouldn't say I think they're powerful. There are lots
                       of female photographers, but they're ideological in
                       various ways. It's more a discussion about theory than
                       working with photographs.

                                    Ann Christine Eek in Conversation with Anna Tellgren

A T   What I think you have in mind here is what happened in the early 1990s, when so-called photo-based art had its breakthrough, which led to many representatives from an older generation of the classic black and white photography ending up in the background. Today, though, one can see that these various traditions have come together and exist alongside each other in a different way.

A C E   It varies so much. Some make their mark, and do 'great' work, with photographs that I think aren't particularly interesting, and then there are others who work more traditionally – Monica Englund and Joanna Helander, for example.

A T   But isn't it true that present-day photographers are working a bit more like you and Monica do? With the new digital technology, there are so many possibilities and challenges for contemporary photographers. In your job at the Ethnographic Museum, you worked just as much with historical collections of photography and historical images.

A C E   I developed the technique of working with a large-format camera via my work as a museum photographer, and I even used that technique in my landscape photographs. I also got the opportunity to do a certain amount of historical research into photography, in connection with the photographs of Roald Amundsen and Carl Lumholtz.

A T   I feel we could go on talking for a very long time about photography and its history and all those you've met during your long career as a photographer, but we must stop here. Thank you, Ann Christine.

A C E   Thank you!

        Work – Don't Wear Yourself Out

Memories Return When Least Expected
Bente Geving in Conversation with Antonio Cataldo

Bente Geving is a Norwegian Sámi photographer and artist, born in the northern town of Kirkenes, but raised in the southern city of Asker. After living for many years in Maastricht, Berlin and Hamburg, she exhibited the project Anna, Inga and Ellen *at Fotogalleriet in 1988. The exhibition was a result of her investigation of her Sámi identity and roots, and time spent with her family in Kirkenes. Geving's work is represented in several collections including the Preus Museum – the National Museum, the Northern Norway Art Museum, the Sámi Art Collection and the Berlinische Galerie, and numerous private collections.*

Artistic Director of Fotogalleriet Antonio Cataldo and Geving met on 29 May 2019 in Enebakk, a community an hour away from Oslo where she currently resides, to speak about how her photography helped her to get closer to her Sáminess.

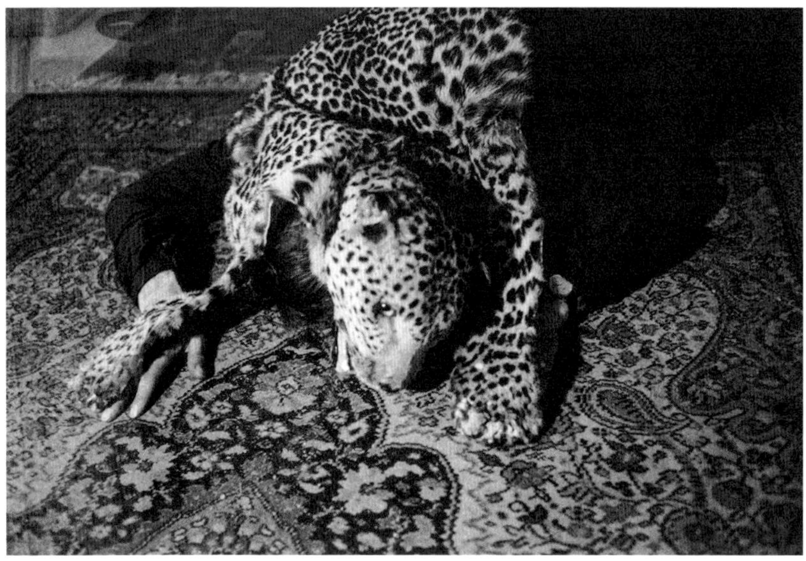

Antonio Cataldo Can you describe this picture?

Bente Geving   It's a mysterious photo of a man hiding under a leopard's skin. I was participating in Anders Petersen's workshop. We were given a task to make portrait of a stranger. And this man was an artist. I remember one of his sculptures: a man with an animal's head.

A C   Where did you first meet Anders Petersen?

                          Memories Return When Least Expected

B G   In his workshop in Malmö, 1983.

A C   He exhibited at Fotogalleriet in 1980, and he's
been quite a reference for Scandinavian photography.

B G   Yes. The first photography exhibition I ever saw was
Cafe Lehmitz at Oslo Kunstforening. I was eighteen or
nineteen years old. That was long before Fotogalleriet –
around 1970, it must have been. My interest in photography came through that exhibition. *Cafe Lehmitz* went
directly in to me; I was really touched by that exhibition.

A C   So then you went on to study art. Was it art in
general or photography?

B G   It wasn't possible to study photography as art in Norway at that time. But I went to Westerdals School of
Communication in 1972, and there we had a photography course where I learned to work in the darkroom.
In 1973, I had a summer job at Philips Design Center in
Eindhoven, and then I met a Czech man on the boat
on the way to Kristiansand, and he had a Nikkormat
camera. That was the first time I looked through a
SLR-camera, and I immediately felt I'd found something that was special to me. I was at an age when I
was trying to find out what I was going to do in life.
After that experience, I bought a Nikkormat with an 85
mm lens. It was so exciting, and I photographed everything around me: the grass, the sky, doors, the roof and
friends. I still have my first film, which was a diapos-
itive film. At that time, Fotogalleriet didn't exist, nor
any exhibition space for photography.
On the last day of Petersen's workshop, he told us
to go out and photograph ourselves. I was looking at a
shop window, and wondering how to make a photo of
myself. Then I heard a baby cry, and I felt a reaction
inside myself like a reflex, and I immediately thought
of my sons. My two sons were home with my parents
and I missed them terribly. I still breast-fed the smallest
one sometimes, and felt it in my breasts. When I turned
around, I saw a couple with a baby wagon, and went to

talk to them. Una and Peter were their names. I told
them I was in this workshop and asked if I could follow
them and photograph them, and they invited me home.

A C   So you photographed this couple from the street?

B G   Yes. In the workshop, I learned to follow and trust my
body's intuitions and to use that as a 'helper' to decide
what I was going to follow or not follow, what I wanted
to photograph or just walk past. It was special that a cry
on the street could lead me to take a photograph like
this, and that this photo is now in the Robert Meyer
Collection, at the National Museum, Oslo. You know,
pictures live their own life, or have their own story in a
way.

A C   What do you think that document says to other
people? What do you think the photograph in
itself becomes? Is it for you a trace of something,
or is it something else?

B G   I think that if I remain honest to myself, then the
pictures will also touch other people.

A C   Were you already a practicing photographer at the
time?

B G   I was already taking pictures, and my first exhibition
was in Maastricht at Bella Ciao Photogallery in 1982.
But before moving to the Netherlands, I lived in Haus-
mannsgate in Oslo, on the first floor, under Gro Jarto's
apartment. She was friends with Ann Christine Eek,
and she'd seen my café photo series that I took in Liege
(1979). Eek asked me if I'd like to work with her in the
dark room and learn something more about developing, and we borrowed the dark room of Robert Meyer.
That way, I came onto the photography scene in Oslo.
I'd already been to Fotogalleriet and seen Dag Alveng's
exhibition *Vegger* (1977).

A C   When you saw Alveng's exhibition, what did you
think of it? I mean, it was very different from
Anders Petersen's works, being more Conceptual.

     Memories Return When Least Expected

B G

It was very different from Petersen, but I was very open. It wasn't the way I wanted to work, but it was interesting. At that time, I was married to Viggo Andersen, one of the few Conceptual artists in Norway. Through Viggo, and also through discussions with his architect colleagues in the Czech exile milieu in Oslo, I came into the art world and I started to see art in a different way. Ole Henrik Moe at Henie Onstad Kunstsenter invited Viggo to take part in the Youth Artist Biennale in Paris 1977, and we travelled with our son Lars, who was only three months old. Later, we spent two years in Maastricht, where he went to the Jan van Eyck Academie. Our second son Terje was born there. There I had a real art 'wake-up' when I saw my first Fluxus exhibition. I was very taken by the humour and the playfulness. Then in Ravenna in 1982 I was deeply touched by the mosaics and the atmosphere there. Photography was how I connected to these very different art forms. At that time, photography wasn't looked at as art, and not accepted as an art, even by many artists.

A C

You seem closer to Petersen in your practice. What do you think you took from him? What did he give you?

B G

In this workshop, he taught me how to trust in myself – how to look through the camera from my own angle. In 1983, I got divorced, and I was alone with two children. Petersen liked my images, and he said that if I had to steal film to continue, I should do that, and that convinced me that I should be a photographer. I didn't have a job, and when I arrived home I went to NAV [Norwegian Labour and Welfare Administration] and told them I was a photographer: 'That's what I am, and that's what I'm going to do.'

A C

So Petersen really gave you courage?

B G

Yes, he gave me courage and the confidence to follow my intuition. One task he gave us was to photograph something that we feared. I thought that I should photograph Petersen himself. But when I walked onto the street, I met the photographer Garry Winogrand,

Bente Geving in Conversation with Antonio Cataldo

and I was quite nervous when I asked him if I could
take a portrait of him. He said 'I'm going to eat, will
you come with me?', so I went with him and took a few
portraits of him while he was eating. He told me that
he had a real fear of flying, that he was afraid the plane
would crash, so he always took with him a pair of socks
that his daughter had knitted. And I photographed him
with these socks.

A C   Because the socks gave him some kind of relief or
safety?

B G   Yes, they meant luck. It was a very special meeting, and
I took many portraits of him. Unfortunately, he never
got to see them. Eventually, I exhibited in the Spring
Exhibition in 1988 with this image of a woman I also
met on the street, standing with her keys. For these I
made textile frames, sometimes with very strong, lime
green colours.

A C   Were they colours that you associated with something? Why did you start bringing textile on to
the frames?

B G   It started as an experiment, I think, and because I had
some textiles that I liked, which were the right colour
to match the pictures. Then I used a gleaming, light
green textile. I associated the colour or the pattern with
the motif in the black and white photos.

A C   That's something that comes back later on in
your work. You bring this interior material, which
belongs to the intimate sphere, into the 'purified'
space of exhibition. The white cube is very clean
and anaesthetised, so the black and white photograph – in its first years of entering the museum
space – should be as 'pure' as possible. But then
you introduced this element that kind of dis-
turbed that.

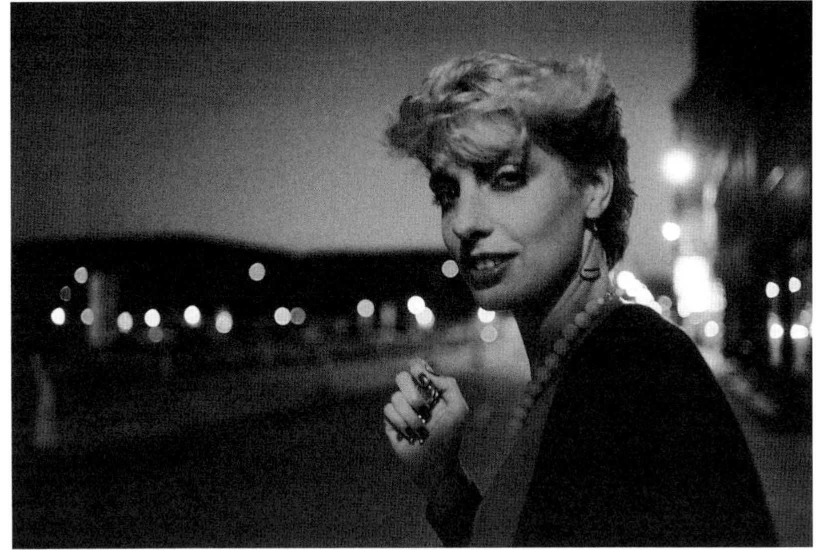

B G   Yes, it can be disturbing. And it's kind of a little protest, maybe? To make something more – yes – maybe disturbing is the right word. Or more a supplement to the motif.

A C   Do you think it's a feminist act in that sense?

B G   No, I don't think it is a feminist act. It was more an act of finding my own language as an artist. And I imagined that there were no rules in making art. My mother was a seamstress. She was very good with textiles, but I never was, and as a daughter it could be difficult. I was photographing and playing music. In retrospect, I can see that it was perhaps a way to connect with my own tradition. So in that sense it was in fact a feminist act. Then in 1988, I had my first solo exhibition in Norway, at Fotogalleriet, called *Anna, Inga and Ellen*.

A C   Why does it say 'photo, yoik and psalm song' on the poster for that exhibition? Did someone *yoik* for the opening?

B G   It was the headline in the Sør-Varanger paper, for which I gave an interview. But yes, I included a soundtrack of Anders Skum from Kautokeino performing *yoik*. One evening in Kirkenes, I went out with my cousin and met Skum. I asked him if he could *yoik* and

        Bente Geving in Conversation with Antonio Cataldo

he said yes – although *yoik* was forbidden, it had survived in his family. He made me a tape that evening, which he gave me. On the tape he also *yoiked* me, and that was a way to find out about my history. You could say this project really started my quest to find out about my Sámi identity.

Anders Petersen said to me, 'Now Bente, you have to do a project that's really close to your heart.' Right away, I thought of my children, who were the closest to me, but it didn't feel right to make an art project of them. Then I decided to go north to photograph my Sámi grandmother Ellen and her two sisters Anna and Inga.

In 1986 I moved to Berlin, and then it felt even more important to go up north. The Cold War was so close. I was living in Kreuzberg 36, and the darkroom I was working in was just by the Spree, the river that was the border to East Berlin. We were surrounded by the wall, and my children were playing just beside the wall. It influenced me greatly. These signs by the Spree said it was forbidden to go down to the shore because you could be shot. It was depressing. And children had drowned there because nobody dared to swim out and save them. That was terrible. I never heard stories like this in Sør-Varanger. Norway has a 200-km-long border with Russia. Although there's no wall in Sør-Varanger, you were forbidden to walk over or fish in the part of the river that belongs to Russia. You could be shot. So suddenly I saw this connection between Kirkenes and Berlin. Kirkenes is different today because of the neighbour passport, which allows people who live 30 km on either side of the border to pass without a visa. But during the Cold War, it was very difficult to cross that border. It was like being closed in. So to come to Berlin made me understand much more of my past. I lived in Berlin until 1995, and it was good to travel from Berlin to Kirkenes.

A C   Because when you went to the north, you experienced the same borders that you were experiencing in Berlin. You're really close to the border in Kirkenes. It's very present.

                    Memories Return When Least Expected

B G   In Kirkenes, as in Berlin, you're close to Europe and to European history. I grew up with my mother's stories about the war, when she and her family had to evacuate. That was one of the last stories that she remembered.

A C   And it was in 1985 that you went to photograph Anna, Inga and Ellen in Kirkenes?

B G   Yes, I got a grant from the Norwegian Photographic Fund to go north and photograph my family members in 1985. Then I went back again to do more photographs in 1988. I was very proud to have got that grant. It was an acceptance for my work as a photographic artist.

Ellen was my grandmother, Anna was her younger and Inga her older sister. They talked Sámi together and they had a strong Sámi identity. They'd lived a Sámi life – which means speaking the language, eating the food and wearing the clothes. Their mother couldn't speak Norwegian. When my mother, Margit Ellinor, grew up, she was taught by society that she had to be a Norwegian and forget about her Sámi roots. She grew up during the time of race research, when they tried to prove that the Sámi people were primitive and childish. Norwegian politics against the Sámi culture were very strong, and it was done without dignity. You weren't allowed to speak Sámi at school, and all you learned was about the Norwegian culture. Near the coast, this politics was even stronger than in Karasjok. There were more Sámis living there.

A C   And are Anna, Inga and Ellen wearing Sámi clothes in your pictures?

B G   No, they wore ordinary dresses, but Anna and Inga had Sámi clothes that they used for special occasions and celebrations. Their parents always wore Sámi *kofte* or *pesk*, which are clothes made of reindeer skin. My great grandmother sewed all the clothes. I never saw my mother wearing Sámi clothes. When she was an adult, she wanted to get a national dress, but she bought a Finnmarksbunad, instead of traditional Sámi clothes. My mother never denied that she was Sámi – she had an inner loyalty and cut off friends who talked badly about the Sámis – but it was only when she got Alz-

   Bente Geving in Conversation with Antonio Cataldo

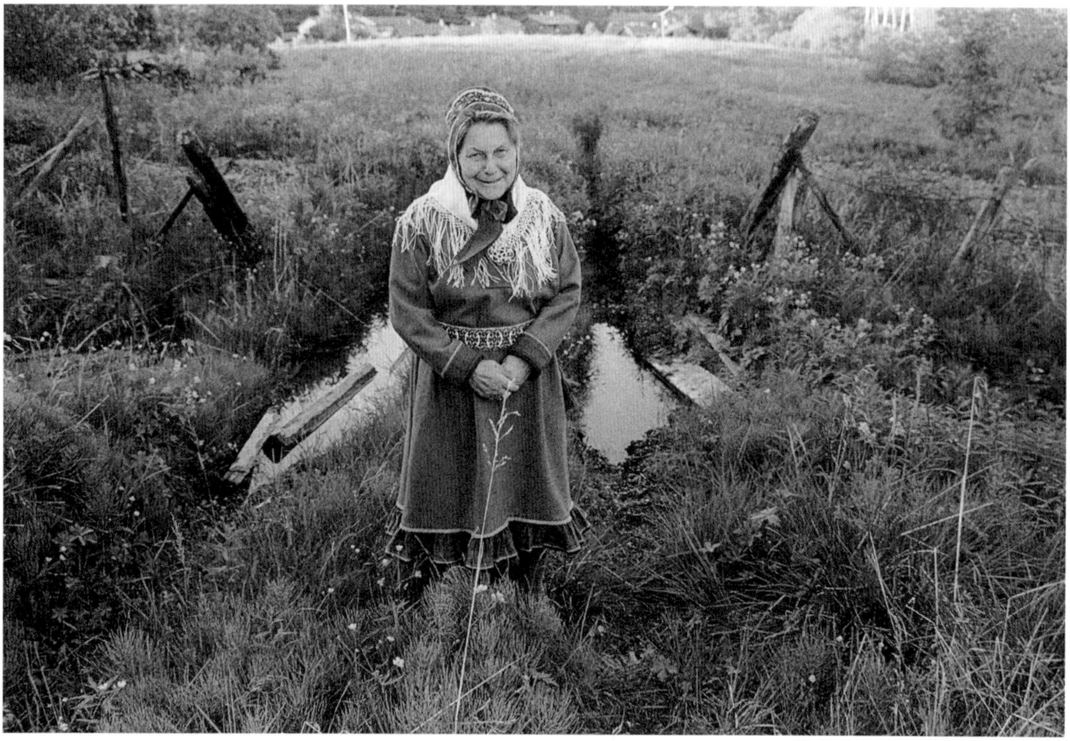

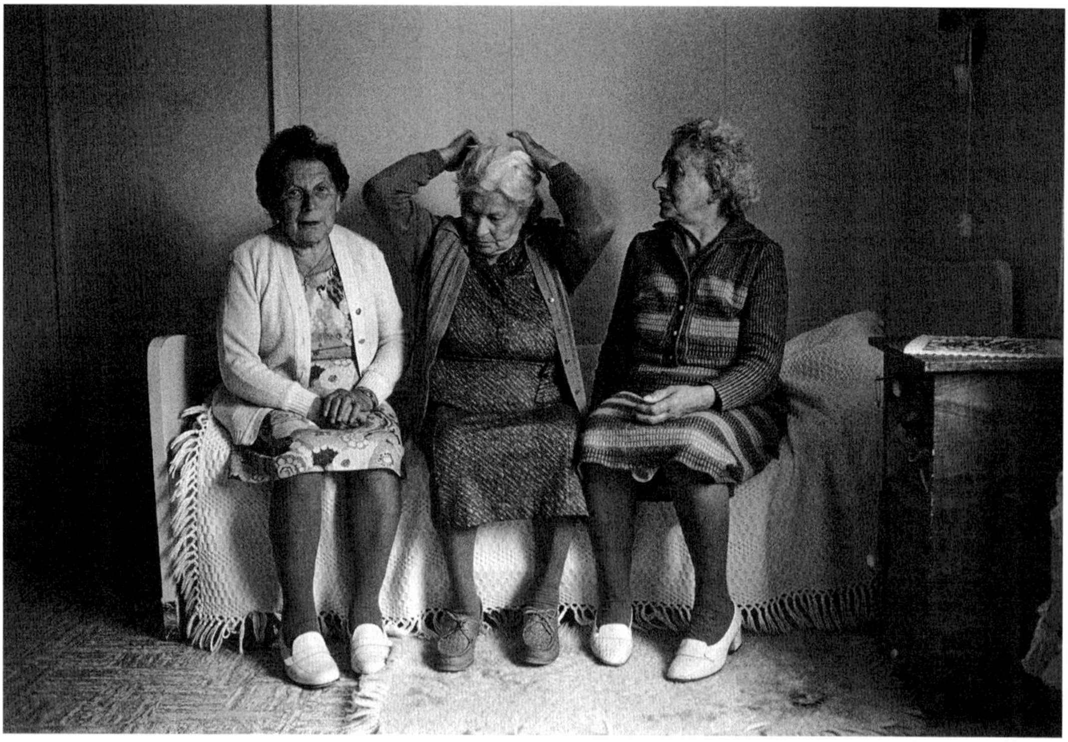

   Memories Return When Least Expected

heimers that she started to bring Sámi things into the
living room, and told people that she was Sámi.

A C Yes, this is something very beautiful that you
wrote in an email to me: that memories come
back when you don't want them to, or when you
don't expect them to.

B G Yes. What you displace and try to forget in your life,
you'll remember when you start to forget. I think that
an image will always be there, in your body and in your
mind. And when you start to forget, like my mother
did, it comes out. My grandmother forgot the Norwegian language when she became demented; she only
talked Sámi then. The trouble was that nobody talked
Sámi in the retirement home where she lived.

A C And do you think photography is about that as
well: remembering something you're trying to
forget?

B G Yes, it can be. It's an interesting thought. I made a
series with some photographs I forgot I'd taken. I had a
difficult period in my life with no possibility to work in
a darkroom, so the films where never developed. When
I developed them after many years, I'd forgotten where
and when they were from. I picked out images that I
was attracted to, and made the series called *Memory*,
which I exhibited together with my series of colour
photos about my mother, *Margit Ellinor*, in *Forgotten
Images* at the Preus Museum 2005.
    When I'm working with an idea or a new project, I
never know what it's going to be. So what comes out of
it is often unexpected. Before I decide to use it, I have
to let the photographs stand and rest, and see after a
period of time if they have something or not. I mostly work with series now, unlike in my first exhibition
when I worked with single pictures. I can think 'That's
a nice image', but then it means nothing more to me. It
has to be combined with something else, like another
image, or fit into a series.

  Bente Geving in Conversation with Antonio Cataldo

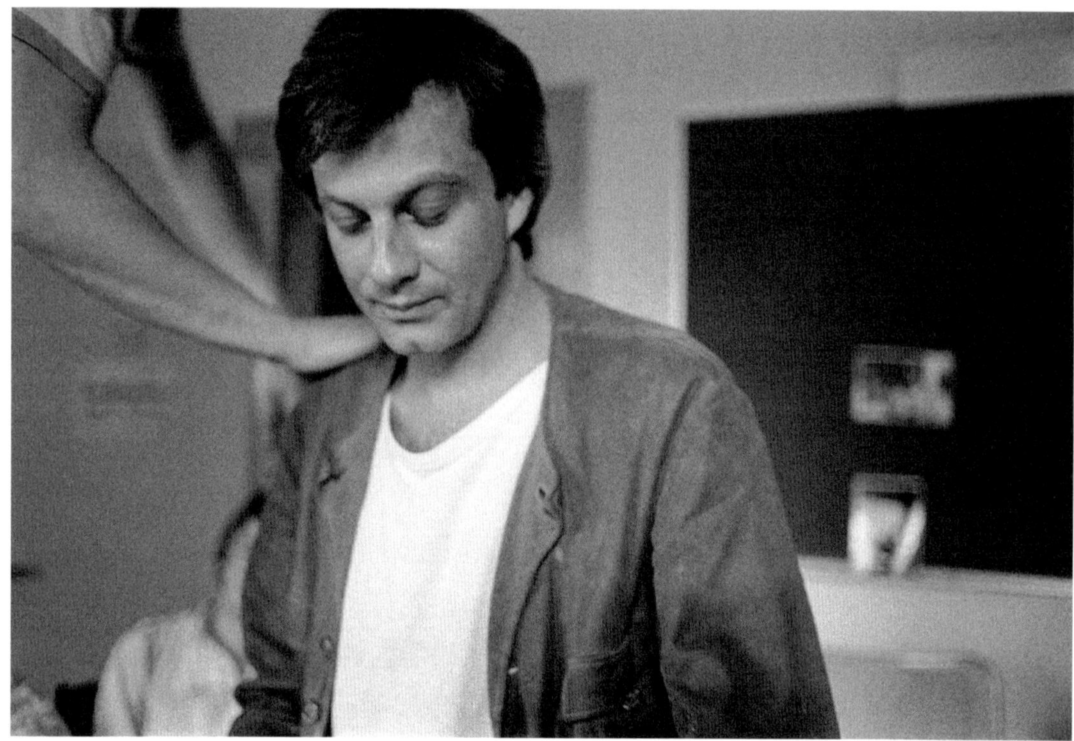

<table>
<tr><td>A C</td><td>Your exhibition *Anna, Inga and Ellen* at Fotogalleriet
also had the theme of memory, of remembering.</td></tr>
<tr><td>B G</td><td>Yes. When I arrived Kirkenes, I visited the culture office in Sør-Varanger municipality to tell them that I was going to photograph the three sisters, and that I intended to exhibit my work in town. Then I was told that the Sámi language was dead, and nobody spoke Sámi anymore in Sør-Varanger. But I knew that my grandmother and the sisters spoke Sámi. I remember as a child, my aunt Inga standing in the window, talking to my grandmother on the road in Sámi. If somebody walked past, they'd start to talk Norwegian. The Sámi language was so hidden. Because of this, I bought a cassette recorder, and I asked them if I could record them when they were talking. We were drinking coffee and speaking Norwegian together, and I asked if they could talk Sámi. But it wasn't possible: it was so built into their minds that if someone couldn't understand Sámi they wouldn't speak it. But as soon as I left the room, closed the door and</td></tr>
</table>

          Memories Return When Least Expected

went into the kitchen, they'd start talking Sámi together. So I put on the recorder, went out, and I heard them
talk in Sámi. I also recorded them singing Sámi psalms.
Yoik wasn't allowed, because it was a sin. They were
Christians, and especially aunt Inga was a very strong
Læstadianer believer. Still today, Lars Levi Læstadius is
very important for many Sámi people.

My friend Kjersti Martinsen helped me to put
together the audio track with the *yoik* and the three
sisters drinking coffee and singing psalms. It was made
for Fotogalleriet as a part of the exhibition. And at that
time they had to turn over the cassette, and put it on
again manually when the exhibition space was open.

A C   Had you seen other exhibitions where there was
sound? Where did this idea come from?

B G   Yes, I remember Anders Petersen used sounds in his exhibition *Cafe Lehmitz*. I decided to use the recordings in
the exhibition because it became an important part of
the story about my ancestors. It wasn't part of my plan
when I went up north to do the project.

For the installation at Fotogalleriet, I got help from
the photographer Guri Dahl. We worked well together.
I didn't use frames, just glass fixed on to the wall with
nails. The images were in three different sizes. I hung
them in series, some high and some low. I used the
whole exhibition space.

A C   Why didn't you frame the images?

B G   I think the photos have a better connection with one
another without the frames. That's what I think today,
but what I thought at the time, I don't know.

A C   It seems quite courageous and uncommon.
Through your decision, you take away the fact
that when photography enters an exhibition space,
it becomes a precious object. When you take away
the frame, it's a more of an everyday object; it
brings the familiar and the unfamiliar together.
It's quite disquieting. Was this your intuition?

   Bente Geving in Conversation with Antonio Cataldo

B G   Yes, I think so.

A C And how did people react? I imagine this was
quite different from what people had seen before.

B G   At that time I was living in Berlin and I came to Oslo
to install the exhibition and to be there for the opening.
The exhibition got attention from the papers, and also
many visitors. I rediscovered lately that it had reached
Kirkenes and the Northern areas through the Sámi
newspaper *Ságat* and *Sør-Varanger Avis*, in addition to
being written about in *Arbeiderbladet, Morgenbladet, Aftenposten*, and *Friheten. Klassekampen* used the headline
'Three women to fall in love with'. This was a pleasant
surprise for me.

A C Why do you think that this project was important
at the time both for you and in general?

B G   I went north and asked questions about our Sámi
ancestors, and I'm glad today that I made these photos. My grandmother and her sisters were proud. My
mother was too, when she came to the exhibition. It did
something to her. She and her family got dignity; we all
got dignity.

A C So it was a statement of your Sámi identity? I can
imagine there was a lot of resistance at the time
towards Sámi people in the south, in the capital,
and 'coming out' as Sámi?

B G   What I didn't know was that our Sámi identity was
still a secret among some family members. So to make
an exhibition about the sisters was to make it official
that my relatives were Sámi, and that was quite hard for
some. To be a Sámi was something to be ashamed of,
it was hidden away. Every time I asked about the Sámi
tradition or the language, I got the answer that it had
no importance.
    The Alta action [protest against the building of a
dam on Sámi land] which took place at the beginning
of the 1980s, began to change things. I was living in
the Netherlands at that time, and it was the first time

          Memories Return When Least Expected

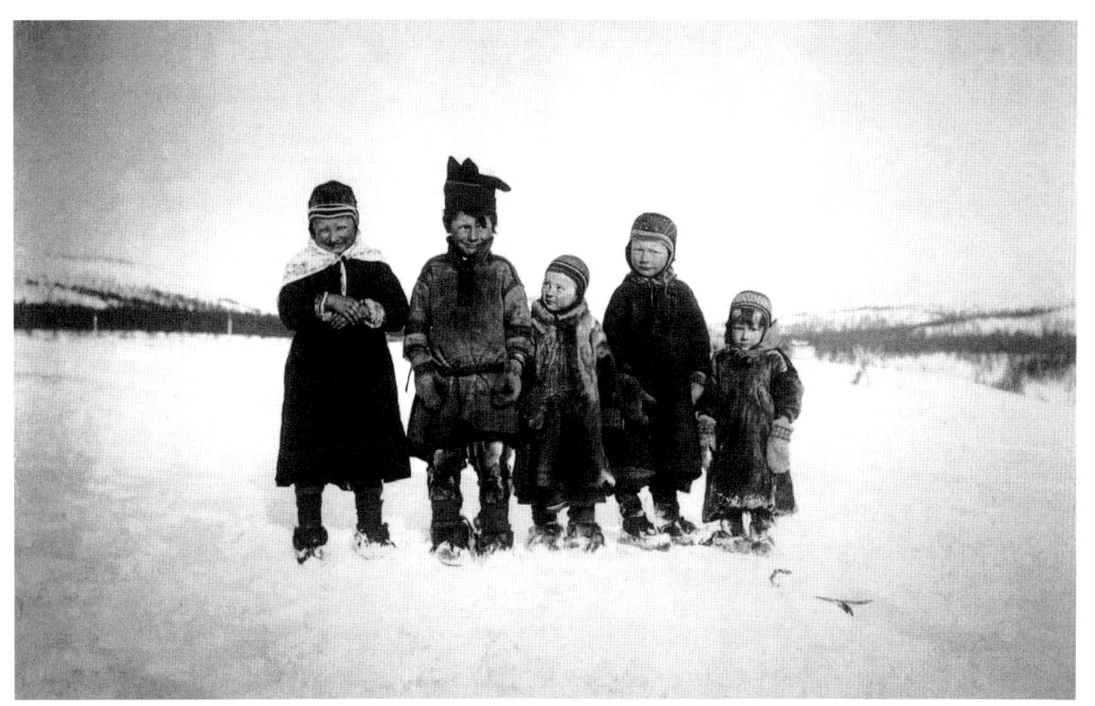

I read anything about Norway in the papers abroad. It
was very difficult to be so far away when this movement
happened. It was so hard to get knowledge about it
from my Sámi relatives.

Ellisif Wessel (1866–1949) photographed people in
Sør-Varanger, and if it hadn't been for her, we wouldn't
have known that there were so many Sámi people in
the area. I think this heritage of shame was passed to
my mother and then passed on to me. But I thought my
children and my nephew should be proud of their background and their history. They are now, but it's taken
a long, long time, and I'm still searching and trying to
figure out these memories. I think the body remembers
– it remembers the repression and the grief of feeling
worthless. And now they've also found out that this is
genetically passed on to the next generation.

AC   Do you think this is made visible in the images?

BG   The project is more a documentation of three old Sámi
                women, of a generation that had been hidden and is
                now disappearing. It's a tribute to my mother, my great

    Bente Geving in Conversation with Antonio Cataldo

grandmother, grandmother and her sisters. It's important to take care of one's heritage, to ask questions, and
not to hide it away. It was also a very personal project.
In a way, it's the documentation of the beginnings of
my travels, my photographic practice, and my life. But
does this come through to the people looking at the
photos? I hope so, but I don't know.

After it opened at Fotogalleriet, the exhibition, was
shown in Kirkenes and at Tromsø Museum. In 2016
the pictures were shown again, in the exhibition *Ringen
– fra Kirkenes til Kirkenes*. I showed the sisters along
with new photos, the *Kosmos* and the *Rosegarden* series.
Anna, Inga and Ellen were in a larger context. I made
the black and white images as a projection on the wall,
together with the sound of the women talking and
singing. It made an impression on me to listen to their
voices again and sees the photos, and it also made an
impression on the audience to see and remember what it
was like over 30 years ago. Now my relatives are happy
with what I did. It's become a circular story in search of
our Sámi identity.

We've Got Pacifiers Instead of Culture in this Country
Robert Meyer in Conversation with Helle Siljeholm

Helle Siljeholm is a choreographer, performer and visual artist, based in Oslo. Her artistic practice involves film, installation, choreography and performance and deals with questions of social imagination in relation to context, in the present and for the future(s), and has been presented nationally and internationally. Robert Meyer is a Norwegian art photographer, professor, photo historian, collector, writer and publicist. In 1989, he executed the project 'The Forgotten Tradition', which included an exhibition at Oslo Kunstforening and a book on the emergence and development of Norwegian landscape photography up to 1914. He first exhibited at Fotogalleriet in 1979. They spoke on 13 March 2020.

Introduction by Helle Siljehom

Currently, I'm working on the development of a choreographic art project called *The Mountain Body* (*TMB*). *TMB* is planned as a series of choreographic interventions on various rockfaces all over the world, and it derives from the interest in examining complex and potential relations between body, nature and culture in the light of today's climate crisis. The work on these interventions will bind the locations together, as in a 'mountain chain'. The project is being developed on the basis of an earlier one, *Notes on Stone and Other Social Landscapes*, curated by Høstscena and the museums Jugendstilsenteret and KUBE in Ålesund, 2017. Central to this work was a choreography based on everyday movements such as lying, sleeping, standing and sitting, carried out by six climbers from Ålesund Klatreklubb on a 200-metre-high rockface outside the town of Ålesund. The positions and movements of the climbers were marked with natural and eco-friendly pigment, which they carried in small containers. The imprint/trace remained there as a temporary 'runic painting' on approximately 100 x 60 metres of the rockface before it was eventually washed away by nature itself – a natural consequence of wind and weather.

These projects relate to my interest in the role that landscape has played in the development of the national identity in Norway, as well as the role of art in the presentation of ideologies linked to the body, nature and culture. In a conversation

   We've Got Pacifiers Instead of Culture in this Country

with Fotogalleriet's director Antonio Cataldo
about these issues, he mentioned the unique work
by Robert Meyer *The Forgotten Tradition* from
1989, which included an exhibition at Oslo Kunstforening and a book on the emergence and development of Norwegian landscape photography
until 1914. The day after Norway locked down to
prevent the spread of Covid 19, I contacted Meyer
on Skype and asked him about this project.

Helle Siljeholm How did *The Forgotten Tradition* come about?

Robert Meyer

The Forgotten Tradition is a small sliver of research that
I worked on for many years. Ever since I started with
photography as a child, I've been fascinated by the history of photography. As early as 1959, I began to write
down various extracts from this history in a notebook.
I actually used it to arrive at ways of taking photos that
weren't those kind of high-gloss black and white pictures on thin paper that were destined to be printed in a
newspaper.

In 1972, I think it was, *Dagbladet* interviewed me and
I was asked what history I'd read that led me to work
in the way I did. I said that I didn't read other people's
books about the history of photography. Instead, I read
original accounts – I collected 'evidence' when developing my research. I had experience from the Norwegian
national crime investigation service (Kripos) and had
learnt a lot about how they worked with credibility
and documentation. The academic system is a lot less
stringent than the legal one. When I met Leif Preus,[50]
he thought this was interesting. He collected too. We
started to share information.

A number of years later, I realised the exhibition and
the book *The Forgotten Tradition* about photography, art
and cultural history. A few years before my exhibition, a
history of art had been written. Called *The Great Tradition*, it was a history of landscape painting from the Romantic period onwards. The most important side-factor
in the history of Norwegian landscape painting was
photography, but that had been forgotten.

In the exhibition at Oslo Kunstforening I showed,
among other things, that the painter Andreas E. Diesen

50
Leif Preus (1928–2013) was a
Norwegian photographer and
founder of the Preus Photo
Museum in his hometown of
Horten in 2005.

                    Robert Meyer in Conversation with Helle Siljeholm

used photographs by the landscape photographer Knud Knudsen as a point of departure. Knudsen had taken a series of photographs that he called 'motifs for painters', photographs that he was unable to sell in the usual way.

H S Were the painters out in nature at the same locations as the photographers had been, or did they paint directly from the photographers' photographs? And if so, what did that mean for the representation of nature in the paintings?

R M I was working on a J.C. Dahl exhibition for the National Gallery on precisely these issues. There, I was given the assignment to visit places that Dahl had painted. I had really good insight into what the various photographers had taken pictures of at these locations. I discovered that the places had changed a lot, especially due to agricultural methods in the nineteenth century up to the mid-twentieth century, which meant that thickets and deciduous trees had almost disappeared. From the interwar period onwards, Western Norway became almost deforested. But the interesting thing is that art isn't contained in the picture. Nor does what you experience lie in the picture. These are important matters that people fail to consider. Photography operates in the realm of one's preferences and experiences. When you see a picture, you assess it and like it in a subconscious way on the basis of your emotional relation to the concepts used. This emotional interpretational basis is closely related to the pre-lingual human being. A painting, however, comes into being over time: the scene is viewed, assessed, adapted and painted. In the original Romantic landscape painting – and not many people talk about this in the history of art – the artistic value lies in the poetry, not in the brushstrokes. In the photograph one can get close to this poetry – almost irrationality – by photographing the experience, not constructing it. It's basic hermeneutics, so to speak.

H S So how does this relate to the development of the national-political project? Did the artists consciously work on how their representations of nature could be incorporated into such a development?

  We've Got Pacifiers Instead of Culture in this Country

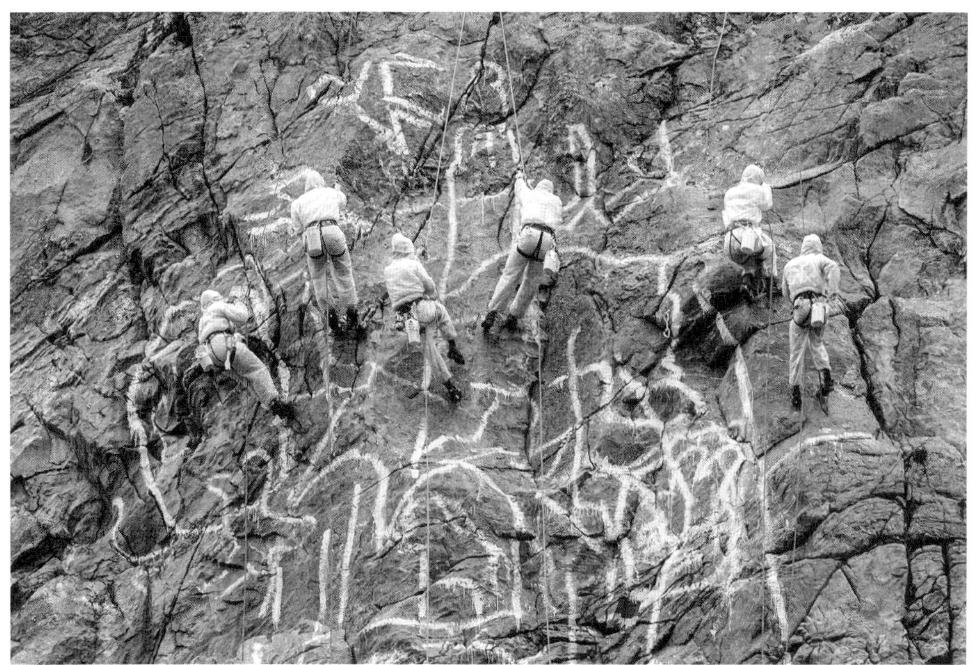

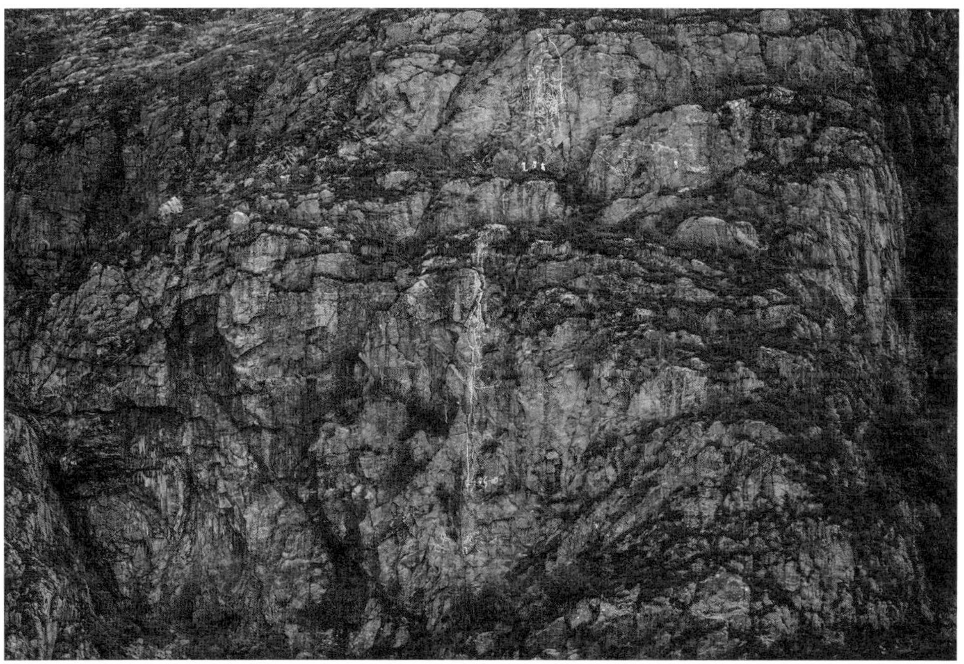

   Robert Meyer in Conversation with Helle Siljeholm

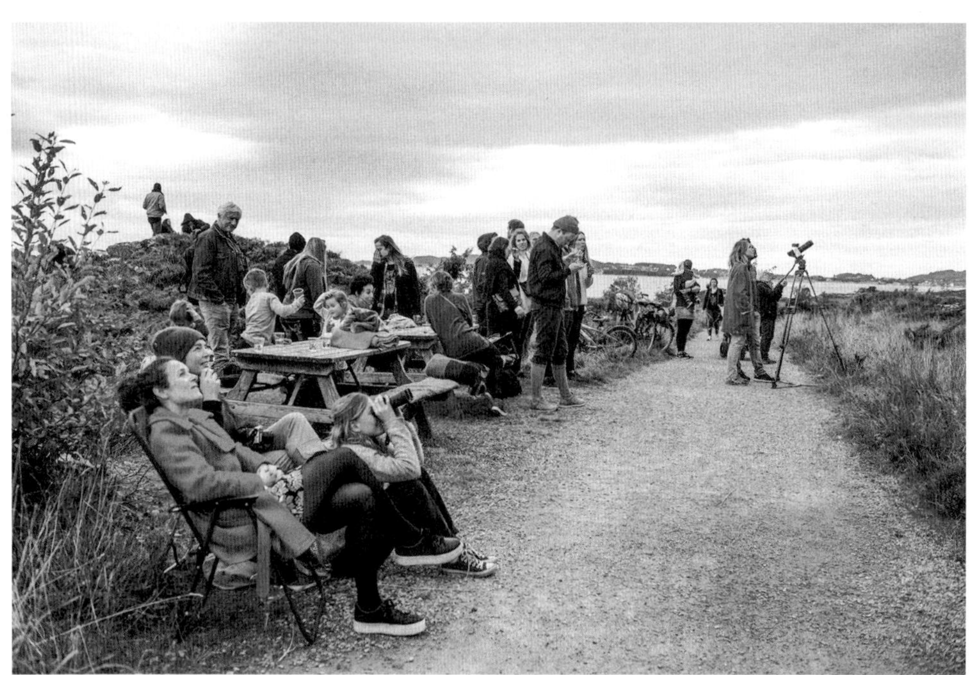

We've Got Pacifiers Instead of Culture in this Country

R M

Ah yes, the national-political dimension! In the US, natural areas were approved by Congress as nationally important, such as the Rocky Mountains – a resolution based on photographs. With regard to Norway, photography came to a country that had this great need of an identity. After the 'Danish rule' period of several centuries, people had to try and work out what it meant to be Norwegian. Being Norwegian was, for a great many people who had a Danish family background, lineage and education, a question of being different from a Dane. One finds the first polarisation there. I've read several times in newspapers from the 1820s and 1830s: 'I don't hate the Danes BUT…', followed by some pretty hefty tirades.

Norwegianness had to be emphasised, accentuated, and this also included the presentation of the landscape. It's not as if the photographer who took the picture of the Vøringsfossen waterfall was the first person who discovered Vøringsfossen – rather that he saw a potential there via the interpretation that this was an attractive and fine national symbol. In that way, concepts are established around what is 'typically Norwegian'.

In the task of establishing itself as a national state, Norway had many possibilities, but also limitations. The establishing of its identity via the landscape had a cultural-political intention. At the same time, it was probably just as much the photographers' search to find the poetry in the landscape. The farmers wouldn't say the same thing about the landscape as the photographer – to them the mountains were simply in the way. They felt that a well-cultivated piece of land was the most beautiful thing. So it also has to do with types of interest. *The Forgotten Tradition* described an attempt to identify oneself with something that was of high quality via the Romantic understanding of poetry. And since foreign countries were so enthusiastic about this, that type of consensus about the landscape arose.

H S

So in that way, art becomes (tourist) industry, politics and consensus all in one – a sort of Holy Trinity?

    Robert Meyer in Conversation with Helle Siljeholm

R M

Yes, definitely. And the photographers found out that when they took a good picture – photographers didn't have any artistic training back then, and artists not much either – it was based on a certain type of presentation of the landscape they were photographing. A presentation where a picture is taken from a certain spot gives the impression that everything is fine and impressive, and it's precisely here that one gets involved in the question of visual art, where a picture acquires a symbolic value – and that of course also lies in the composition, form, depth and such things. The effect is that when you later travel through, let's say, a valley you've seen a picture of, you say 'Oh, here we've got a picture!', because you're seeing precisely the original photographer's point of view: the 'Kodak moment'. This becomes convention and consensus. In other words, the picture that confirms what you know is a good picture, while the picture that doesn't confirm what you know is a bad picture. Such attitudes create a cancer. If you only do what confirms something, you get no development, no curiosity. I've very often experienced, not only among ordinary people but also in institutions, even in schools, that there's a search for certain types of confirmation. This is restrictive and prevents development.

When I talk about 'free photography', I mean that you have the freedom to like things on your own terms. Photography is *not* the transportation of information.

H S

Among all the photographs you've seen of Norwegian landscape, do you have examples of photographs that also create other narratives about it?

R M

Do you know the work of Knud Knudsen?

H S

Yes.

R M

His work deals with what in the eighteenth century people called the 'Sublime', i.e. fear mixed with joy. Knudsen took many pictures of waterfalls. What he so clearly demonstrates here is that when you take a picture – this was at the time of the wet-plate process – the waterfall becomes so soft that there's no risk involved.

   We've Got Pacifiers Instead of Culture in this Country

But Knudsen wanted to evoke the sublime experience, so he composed the image so that the rock, which juts out, creates a counterpoint to the bridge, with which you identify as a human being. The overwhelming aspect recurs in many of his pictures – it lies in the experience of dimensions. Many of the pictures have been taken in such a way that the rockface goes right down into the boatsman's head, for example. It's a matter of using your emotional interpretation, a common technique in the nineteenth century. Knudsen develops and uses it in his own way. He changed to dry plates in 1884, as did most Norwegian photographers, and using dry plates, he gained more nuances and clouds in the sky. But he fostered the wet-plate contrast; he cultivated a slightly graphic-art method in order to create the contrast. When Gustave Courbet launched realism in the 1850s, it was opposites that it was all about, not reality. Knudsen uses this at a sublime level, where he opens up the possibility of your experiencing the emotional dimension: 'Help, I'm afraid of heights – there's a rock there. I might fall!' That sort of thing. I'm simplifying of course, but it *is* that simple to emotionalise: the art of making something personal for the viewer. An awful lot of art is about this. The eye-catching device is the human being. The rock is a natural consequence. If it falls down, it won't be a soft landing.

In Sweden, when I used to teach there, someone told me: 'Knudsen believed that the man is walking through the Styx' – the river between us and the realm of the dead. I didn't know that when I wrote about the picture, but later I took the boat along Geirangerfjord. The skipper pointed to the hole in the rockface, which is visible in the photo, and said: 'That hole over there in the rock was called the Gate of Hell.' The ferryman is Charon, who transports souls across to the realm of the dead. Those who don't manage to get on board become zombies, according to that way of thinking. Such narratives about the landscape are, then, present in the photograph – and in our culture. But we're seldom made aware of it, since, as everyone knows, we have no cultural education in this country. What we learnt in 1814 and in 1905 was that we are not Danes and not Swedes. It's a negative mode of thought – we are not

    Robert Meyer in Conversation with Helle Siljeholm

51
Gro Harlem Brundtland
served three terms as Prime
Minister of Norway (1981,
1986–89, and 1990–96). In
1993, she said: 'It's typically
Norwegian to be good.'

like others. From the nineteenth century we learnt as something self-evident that Norwegians live much closer to nature, so that makes us more original, more genuine. Which is what Gro Harlem Brundtland actually said.[51] But it's not typical to be good in Norway, it's typical to be Norwegian. We have a lack of culture; a lack of understanding. Then these other stories about us disappear. We ought to put much more effort into giving individuals the freedom to see pictures based on themselves and not, for example, on what bureaucrats have decided.

H S   So what you're saying is that the pictures Knudsen took are often reduced to a politically controlled narrative concerning the sovereignty of individuals in their meeting with their surroundings. In this narrative, is too little attention paid to other semantic strata in the picture such as questions related to spirituality and human vulnerability when encountering nature? Perhaps the picture has to do with the extent to which we enclose the rock or the rock encloses us. Where are the real boundaries between body, nature and culture?

R M   Yes, that is what it's about, or can be. One shouldn't be obsessed with what's right and what's wrong, but trust oneself. Art is all about opening up. To take the 'right' picture is a misunderstanding. When people ask me 'Is this a good picture – ought I to buy it?', I get cheeky and say, 'How did you find you wife? Did you ask your friends?' You have to be personally interested in it, not in what's in the catalogue and the price, etc. Money means nothing.

Strindberg writes that when one goes to an exhibition, one should stand in front of a picture and count to ten before moving on to the next, so that people understand that you're looking. He really hits the nail on the head when it comes to vanity.

H S   Do you think it's possible to alter vanity in people?

                                          We've Got Pacifiers Instead of Culture in this Country

R M

Yes, I think it is possible. Vanity isn't included in Catholicism's list of deadly sins. But the deadly sins have to do with things out of which you create an ego, as a protection, a syndrome, a symbol of weakness. Therefore it is a deadly sin. You die from it. I've always been interested in Buddhism, and once when I was in Bhutan, I sat down beside one of the higher-ranking monks. I thought, 'Now I've got the opportunity to ask existential questions', so I asked what he could say about the human ego. He talked without any embarrassment about the problems he'd had with his vanity as a young man. He confirmed that the ego isn't self-awareness but self-protection, and you paint yourself into a corner.

We have so much. The only thing we've lacked until now is a crisis, so in a way it was high time that one happened, because we're so far removed from empathy, and from care and understanding of each other. The only politician who's talked about the individual in recent years comes from the Centre Party (SP), which has grown enormously as a party because of it. When Trygve Vedum[52] talks about the individual and the experience, he gets a lot of votes. But what gets the most reward is the hatred – or whatever you want to call it – that the Progress Party (FRP) has of diversity.

Our national identity is to dislike others. It's so stupid. While we're talking about cultural history, we should remember that Ibsen was the first person to voice deep distrust against Norwegianness – he wrote about it in *Peer Gynt*. It's so wonderfully done. We lack a debate and discussion about these things and our culture. It's a shame, in my opinion. And the solution isn't always that things were much better before, but they would be much better now if we'd had true cultural feelings and understanding, and weren't so obsessed with winning Olympic medals.

H S

Don't you think, though, that there ought to be a fresh start on the national project? Perhaps one dealing with who is to be included in it, one that seeks to define what it ought to be?

[52] Trygve Vedum is a Norwegian politician and has led the Centre Party (Senterpartiet), whose main focus is on decentralised economic development and political decision-making, since 2014.

Robert Meyer in Conversation with Helle Siljeholm

R M   No, because then there's a danger of nationalism, and
that wouldn't be a good thing at all. The absolute most
important thing in Norwegian culture and social life –
everything – is art. If we don't understand that, we're
impoverished. If the state ever administers art, it's to
sell it. They have to have money. What got Oslo to
build the Opera House was that they thought in terms
of money. And even more so in the case of the Munch
Museum, which even FRP supported. They believe that
there's no point in art if one doesn't earn money out of
it. They understood that when Petter Olsen sold *The
Scream* at Sotheby's in New York. It's like a dummy you
give babies to keep their mouths shut, isn't it? Pacifiers
is what they're called in English. We've got pacifiers
instead of culture in this country.

H S   You've said that the history of photography isn't a
ploughed field. Is there perhaps something positive about that?

R M   The question is, what plough has been used? I mean, if
the authorities had understood what power lay in the
medium when it was made, one would never be allowed
to use it. The picture is us, ourselves, not others – it's us.
We create it ourselves. In that way we can use history to
understand the present.

H S   Yes, but understanding the present also has to do
with what canons one uses.

R M   Yes, yes, I know, but what we call ourselves here and
now, that's our present age, and it's this – our awareness
of the world as it is now based on our experience – that
conditions our understanding of history. We haven't got
any other way. We've eaten from the Tree of Knowledge, we've been ejected from our fundamental naivety
and spontaneity. What you can do with photography –
I've talked about this at Fotogalleriet for many years – is
to seek the spontaneous, the intuitive, the immediate.
Not to think about what it will become and how. You
can search for that afterwards. Everything in a picture
has to do with why you're interested in taking it. In that
way you can start to get to know yourself. This isn't

                                We've Got Pacifiers Instead of Culture in this Country

amateur psychology, it's life experience. The best way to interpret photography is without prejudices. We see the world with the same eyes that we see photography with. If we can lay aside existential angst, trauma and everything that's wrong with us – perhaps we look crazy, aren't rich enough, don't wear the right clothes – but if you take the world for what it is, that's where you see yourself. That's where you can use photography. Because photography doesn't do what you want – it *is* what you want. As with fire: a good servant, but a terrible master. But it's always important to be yourself, isn't it?

H S Yes, I understand that, but what if the problem with pictorial representation also lies with us artists, since we're precisely the ones who open up the possibility of an interpretation for an audience, and we ourselves are a result of our education and experience, which we can assume is limited in various ways? How can we think and get beyond our own limitations? What if the problem is us as well?

R M You mean us who work with art?

H S Yes.

R M Aha, yes – well, that's the snag, isn't it!

   Robert Meyer in Conversation with Helle Siljeholm

A Conflicting Image of the North: The Ecology of Kåre Kivijärvi's Photographic Practice
Hanne Hammer Stien

Hanne Hammer Stien holds a Ph.D. in Art History with a focus on photography and photographic theories. She is associate professor at Academy of Fine Arts and Vice-Director for Education and Artistic Research at The Arctic University Museum of Norway and Academy of Fine Arts. Stien has curated numerous exhibitions in addition to art projects in the public space.

Kåre Kivijärvi was a Norwegian photographer born in Hammerfest in Northern Norway, where he worked as a photojournalist before studying photography in Germany under Otto Steinert. Later, he worked locally and internationally as a freelance photojournalist and exhibited widely. Kivijärvi is known for being the first photographer in Norway who in a broad sense was accepted as an artist.

When dealing with conversations on artistic photography in a Norwegian context it is impossible to bypass Kåre Kivijärvi (1938–1991). His black and white landscape photographs *Peregrinations I*, Peregrinations *II* and *Peregrinations III* were accepted by the Annual Autumn Exhibition in Oslo in 1971. With roots going back to 1882 and the radical protest of artists against the bourgeois establishment, the annual Autumn Exhibition has served as an important showcase for contemporary art. After the acceptance of Kivijärvi's photographs to the 1971 exhibition, the event became a symbol for the overall recognition of photography as an artistic medium in a Norwegian context. This moment in time, when Kivijärvi's photographs were categorised as paintings because there existed no category for photography, reminds us of the short and troubled history of artistic photography not only in Norway, but worldwide.

Kivijärvi's subjective and productive approach, and his embodiment of the romantic idea of the artist as a visionary seer, helped to make him a mythological figure in histories of photography in Norway. As I have argued elsewhere, his northern background, which he also made the main motif in his work, connected him both to an idea of the Indigenous, the magical and the sublime, and fed the spectacular anecdotes that surrounded him and that still surround his work.[53]

Kivijärvi was instrumental in the establishment of the Norwegian Association for Fine Art Photographers (FFF) in 1974, whose aim was to 'promote artistic photography as a subjective expression and ensure the political interests of independent photographers'.[54] Here 'Subjective expression' and 'independent photographers' refer to an idea of photo-based

53
See: Hanne Hammer Stien, 'Kunstneren og fotojournalisten Kåre Kivijärvi – konstruksjonen av en myte', in: Anna-Riitta Lindgren et al. (eds.), *Kven i fortid og nåtid. Rapport fra seminaret 'Kvener og skogfinner i fortid og nåtid'* (Tromsø: University of Tromsø, 2009), 113–130.

54
See: https://www.fffotografer. no/om-oss/historikk (accessed 17 October 2019).

A Conflicting Image of the North: The Ecology of Kåre Kivijärvi's Photographic Practice

art as subjective and autonomous, and creates an opposition to commercial photographic practices, perceived as objective, non-expressive and unfree. Kivijärvi, who studied with Otto Steinert in Germany, had a more synthesising approach. Even though he worked as a photojournalist, he insisted on exhibiting his work within an art context and his photographs were always in transition between the field of photojournalism and the field of art, creating an expansion of both.

After his death in 1991, Fotogalleriet presented an exhibition to commemorate both Kivijärvi and his artistic oeuvre, leading to headlines in the press like 'Kivijärvi should get his own museum' and 'Pioneer at Fotogalleriet'.[55] The description of Kivijärvi's work presented in the press release reflects his ability to embrace both artistic and documentary expectations of photography: 'The starting point of Kivijärvi's work is documentary photography or reportage, but he adds his own expression and this makes the photographs transcend normal definitions of the genre.' However, the description also reveals a diametrically opposed point of view that has permeated theoretical discussions where photography's identity have been 'determined as a consequence of *either* nature *or* culture'.[56]

In light of Kivijärvi's pioneering achievements, it comes as no surprise that Fotogalleriet initiated the memorial exhibition. Looking through the space's newly organised archive, however, I do find it surprising that his work was not shown there at an earlier stage. Maybe it was the shifting positions of his photographs, from photojournalism to art and back again, that made his work appear too ambiguous. Perhaps there were other, more pragmatic reasons.

Looking back at Kiviärvi's photographic practice from a contemporary (and post digital) point of view, the ecological character of his practice seems particularly relevant to the theoretical conversations of today. Most importantly, his oeuvre contributes to current discussions within the contemporary art world about our common colonial history, a history that the power structures of today reflects. Focusing on 'the intersection of the three tribes'[57] – the Sámi, the Kven and the Norwegian – and highlighting the resilience of the people living in Northern Norway and in Sápmi, Kivijärvi creates an image of the north that is by no means outdated. By depicting the entanglement of people and places, Kivijärvi makes us aware of the social, historical and political complexity of the colonial situation in the north.

[55] Odd Sønvisen, 'Kivijärvi bør få museum', in: *Nordlys*, 30 September 1992, and 'Pionér i Fotogalleriet', in: *Klassekampen*, 28 August 1992.

[56] Geoffrey Batchen, *Burning with Desire. The Conception of Photography* (Cambridge, Massachusetts: MIT Press, 1997/1999), 21.

[57] In Norwegian, this translates to *de tre stammers møte*. For more information, see: https://no.wikipedia.org/wiki/Tre_stammers_m%C3%B8te (accessed 18 October 2019).

     Hanne Hammer Stien

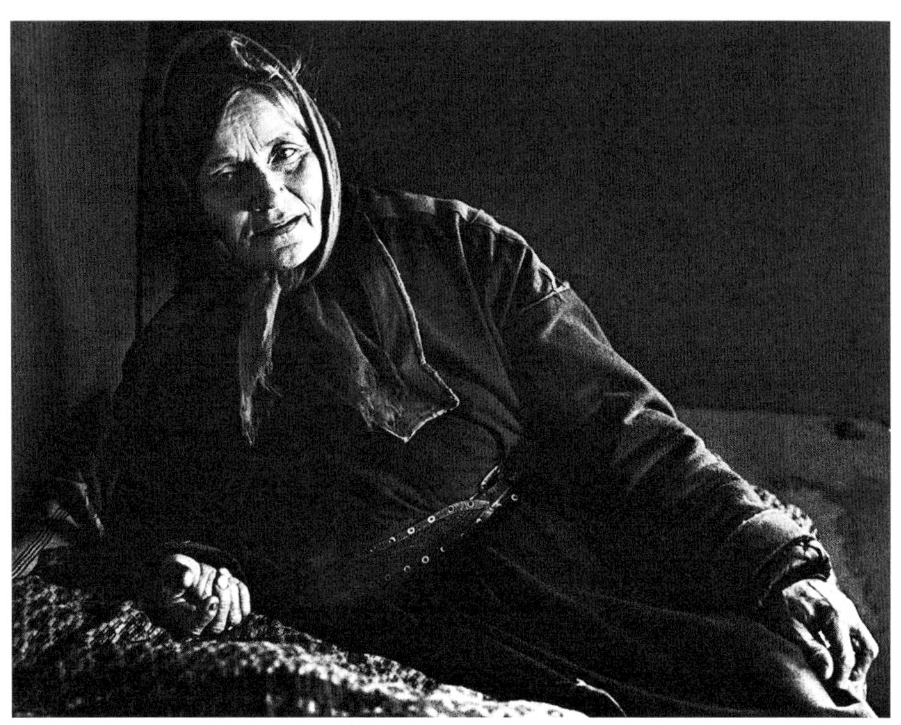

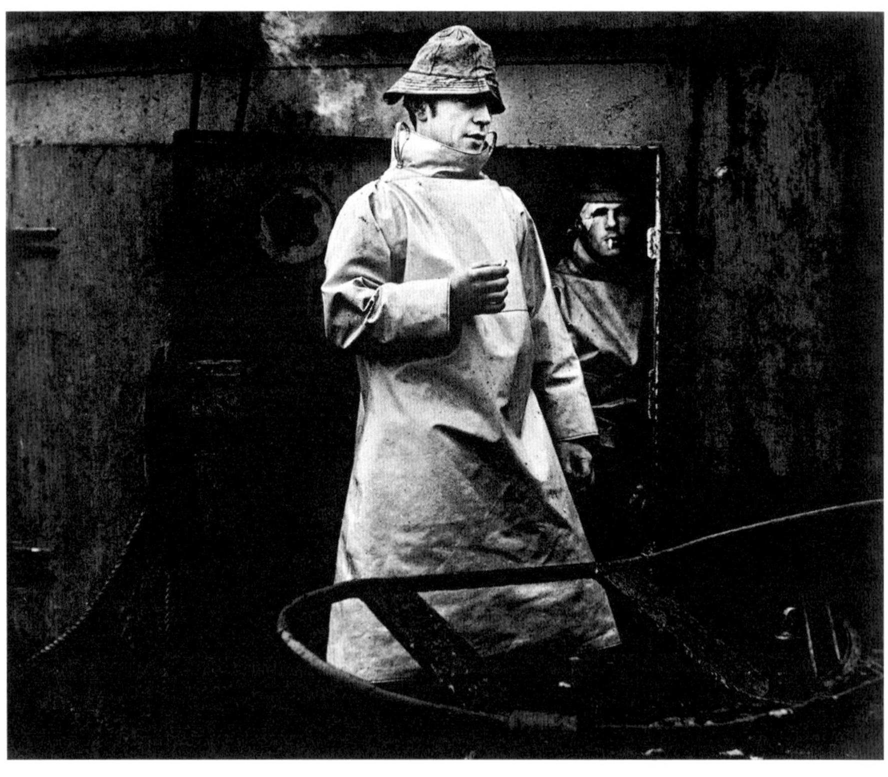

A Conflicting Image of the North: The Ecology
of Kåre Kivijärvi's Photographic Practice

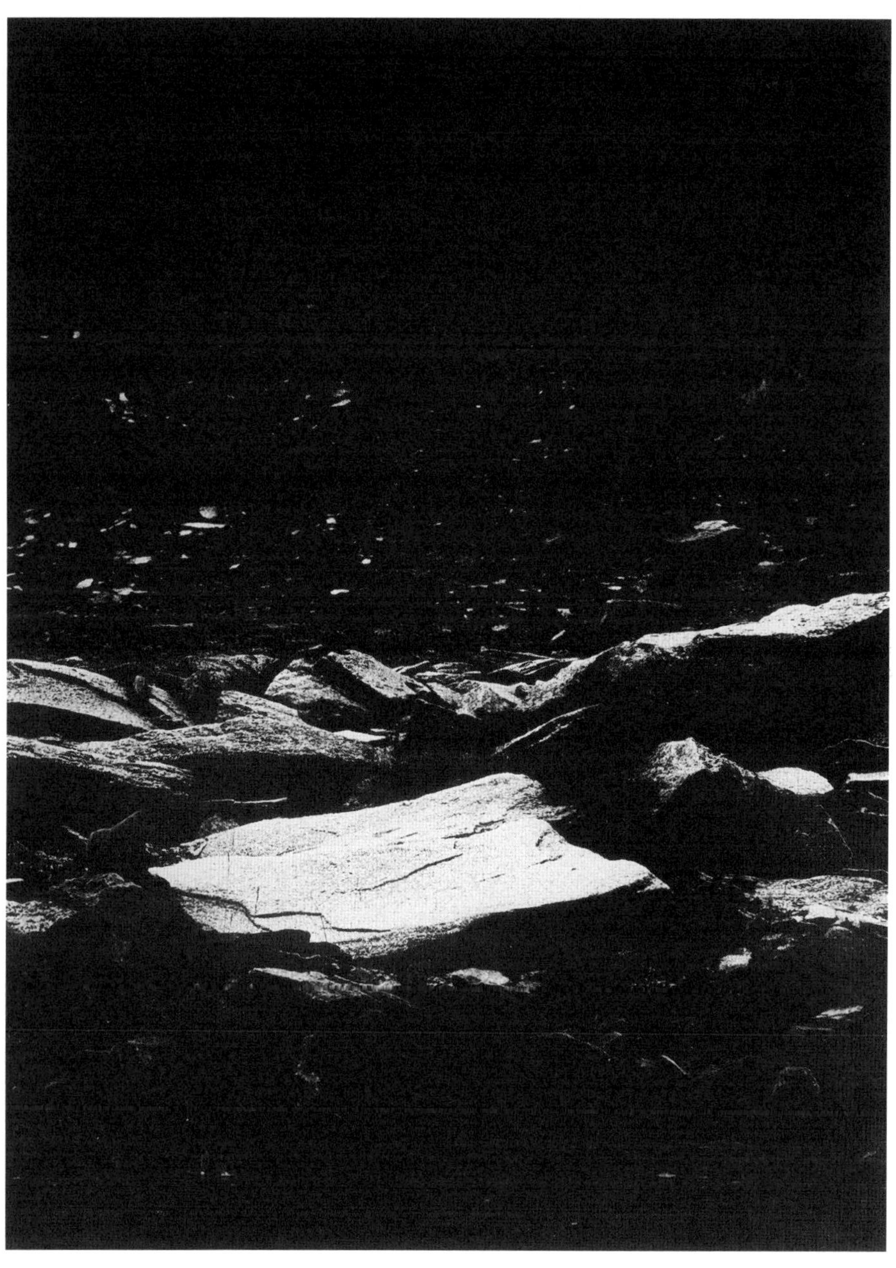

Hanne Hammer Stien

Reflecting upon photographic images in the framework of the digital age, Marco Bohr and Basia Sliwinska, in the introduction to *The Evolution of the Image* (2018), highlight the ecology of photographs.[58] Photographs take part in complex networks of relations and they mean different things to different people. Bohr and Sliwinska argue that this is particularly the case today, when digital culture is rapidly changing the structural integrity of the image as it morphs into a piece of programmable software.[59] However, they argue, if one looks back at history, the radical reconfiguration of the human vision, which dictates how images are constructed, could be said to have started as early as the 1800s, first with the breakdown of the camera obscura and its linear optical system, and second with the arrival of a new mobile observer – the camera. They explain:

> Since the Renaissance and the introduction of different intervening technologies into the visual field, such as *camera obscura*, the perspective and how we look, what we look at and how information is processed, have changed. The camera designates a further point where both seeing and looking and the spectacle become multidirectional and often guided by perspectival illusion. [...] Camera expanded our access to invisible vision and the disembodied.[60]

When modernisation in the 1900s brought signs and images that were easy to reproduce and distribute, vision became deterritorialised and detached from physical space. Industries of the image and of spectacle developed. Photojournalistic practices contributed to the deterritorialisation of vision by enabling wide audiences to experience people and places they were not able to visit themselves, for example through magazines. Later on the deterritorialisation developed even further with digital technologies, in such a way that 'networks have redistributed and expanded the viewing space' of human beings.[61] Bohr and Sliwinska's examples from recent years, where images and the instantaneous sharing of these, had a profound impact on political subjectivity include the Arab Spring, Black Lives Matter and Occupy Wall Street.[62]

58
Marco Bohr and Basia Sliwinska, 'Introduction', in: idem. (eds.), *The Evolution of the Image. Political Action and the Digital Self* (New York: Routledge, 2018), 1–11.

59
Bohr and Sliwinska refer to: Ingrid Hoelzl and Rémi Maries, *Softimage. Towards a New Theory of the Digital Image* (Bristol: Intellect, 2018), 3.

60
Marco Bohr, and Basia Sliwinska, 'Introduction', in: idem. (eds.), *The Evolution of the Image. Political Action and the Digital Self* (New York: Routledge, 2018), 2.

61
Nicholas Mirzoeff, *How to See the World* (London: Penguin Books, 2015), 13.

62
Bohr/Sliwinska 2018 (see note 58), 2.

A Conflicting Image of the North: The Ecology of Kåre Kivijärvi's Photographic Practice

The ecology of photographs and the deterritorialisation of vision was also a precondition for Kivijärvi's photographic practice. He started working as a photojournalist in his hometown Hammerfest at the age of eighteen. After studying photography in Germany, he continued to work as a freelance photojournalist between Norway and Finland, mainly depicting the north and presenting his photographs in papers and photojournalistic magazines such as *Viikkosanomat, Vest-Finnmark Arbeiderblad, Nå* and *Magasinet for alle*. In parallel, he exhibited widely within an art context. The photographs presented in a photojournalistic context immediately seem similar to those shown in an art context. He uses the same motifs and balanced semi-abstract compositions, while black and white contrasts dominate his aesthetic language.

In 1959, Kivijärvi received a commission from the fish fillet factory Findus in Hammerfest to document trawler fisheries in the Barents Sea. In this context, he shot one of his best-known motifs, *Trålergatser, Svalbardbanken* (Trawlers, Svalbard Bank). Two versions of this image exist. The image presented in an art context was printed in 1966. In the forefront of the horizontal photograph, we find a man dressed in oilskins. In the background, a masklike face appears. The contrasts in the print burn out the details in the photograph and isolate the two figures, leaving the surrounding environment in darkness. It is not immediately evident that the two are on the deck of a trawler at sea.

Another, earlier version from 1961 is part of the series made especially for Findus that hung for many decades in the factory. They were shown for the first time outside of Hammerfest, at Henie Onstad in Oslo from 2017–18. In contrast to the print presented in an art context, the Findus version is vertical, and the format is considerably smaller. Since the print highlights the greyscale of the photograph, the details that were lost in the other version are here clearly visible, making the image less ambiguous than in the artwork, which appears more abstracted, even staged. The context is the same, but it has morphed into something else. The formal-aesthetic transformation of the image substantiates the different expectations of documentary and artistic photographic practices. To understand how these different expectations merged in Kivijärvi's practice, it is helpful to place his work within a photo-historical context.

     Hanne Hammer Stien

As mentioned earlier, Kivijärvi studied with Otto Steinert in Germany towards the end of the 1950s and the beginning of the 1960s. Pedagogically and theoretically, Steinert had a huge impact on photography in Europe at the time.[63] He developed the term Subjektive Fotografie (Subjective Photography) in response to contemporary scientific expectations. Inspired by the avant-garde of the interwar period, more specifically the heritage of László Moholy-Nagy and the Bauhaus school, he emphasised creativity, personal engagement and technical and interdisciplinary knowledge. According to Steinert, the photographer is an active agent, similar to the artist. He acknowledged staging and perceived the work in the darkroom as part of the photographic process itself. While, early in his teaching Steinert highlighted an aesthetic-oriented photographic programme, he later opened up towards different approaches to photography. For Steinert, it was not about separating photo-based art from other photographic practices and commissioned work. He saw Subjective Photography as an approach that could influence all kinds of photographic practices.

The two versions of *Trålergatser, Svalbardbanken*[64] challenge an understanding of photography that creates an opposition between the autonomous and the unfree, the expressive and non-expressive, the subjective and the objective, and culture and nature. By synthesising artistic and documentary approaches to the photographic image, Kivijärvi's practice emphasises photography as an expanding field and the always becoming (morphing) of images. On the one hand, his documentary style and his practice as a photojournalist are essential for his choice of motifs and the graphic expression that he developed through contemporary paper printing techniques. On the other hand, the formal aesthetics and productive approach to photography are embedded in his practice as a whole.

Geoffrey Batchen has already argued that any critique of photography should recognise its ambiguous and shifting identity that 'refuses to settle at any of the available poles of identification (nature, culture, the intrinsic characteristics of the medium, the exigencies of context)'.[65] For Batchen, it is crucial that photography operates within an expanded field where different technologies, practices and images interact. When it comes to Kivijärvi's photographic practice, expanding from photojournalism to art and back again confirms

63
Thilo Koenig, "'Ich lasse alles gelten, was Qualität hat." Otto Steinert als Lehrer' / "'I accept everything of quality", Otto Steinert as Teacher', in: Ute Eskildsen and Thilo Koenig (eds.), *Otto Steinert und Schüler. Fotografie und Ausbildung 1948 bis 1978/Otto Steinert and his Students. Photography and Education 1948 to 1978* (Essen: Museum Folkwang, 1991), 8–28.
64
Kristin Aasbø, *Kåre Kivijärvi. Fotografier 1956–1991* (Oslo: Forlaget Press, 2011), 16–17.
65
Batchen 1997/1999 (see note 56), 202.

A Conflicting Image of the North: The Ecology
of Kåre Kivijärvi's Photographic Practice

the necessity of upholding the idea of photography's uncertain and ever-morphing identity, even if it took place in the pre-digital age.

Images of the North

While preparing to write this essay, I found myself driving through the landscapes of Finnmark on my way home to Hammerfest. Reflecting upon Kivijärvi's travels in the region as a young photojournalist towards the end of the 1950s and the 1960s, I was reminded of one of his portraits, the black and white photograph of Katri Jefremoff.[66] Shot in 1966 in Sevettijärvi, a small village in the municipality of Enare in Finland close to Neiden, a village on the Norwegian side of Sápmi, the photograph displays Jefremoff half lying on a couch. While the prints shown in exhibitions burn out most of the details in the photograph, making the contours of her body visible, highlighting her face and her hands, the negative reveals more information and indicates her Sámi identity by making it clear that she is dressed in a *gákti*, a Sámi dress, and wears a monochrome headscarf.[67] By presenting Jefremoff in an intimate way, portraying her close up inside her own kitchen, and at the same time burning out the details in the print, Kivijärvi rejects the deadpan style, the detachment and the lucidness that has signified ethnographic photography of Sámi people and focuses mainly on Jefremoff as a human.

The strong appearance of the woman in the portrait has always intrigued me. She seems to look directly at me. Even if she is photographed half lying down, the image transcends her supine position by focusing on her proud facial expression. Like other photographs by Kivijärvi, the isolation of the subject, whether human or non-human, works as a means of decontextualisation or even alienation, making it difficult to place it within a given time or place. On the one hand, the isolation emphasises the composition and the formal aesthetics of the photograph. On the other hand, it creates a concentration on the subject matter, and the relationship between the one who is being looked at and the one looking.

Arguing that all photographic portraits are performative, Peggy Phelan specifically associates this performativity with the body.[68] Portrait photographs strive at all times to create an inner form that reproduces the body of the portrayed so that it appears as a 'real' body, she argues. In the attempt to create a present and real body, the subject stages herself as an image.

66

For more photographs from the series, see: Aasbø 2011, (see note 64), 168–177.

67

Ibid, 170–171.

68

Peggy Phelan, *Unmarked: The politics of performance* (London: Routledge, 1993/1996), 35–6.

     Hanne Hammer Stien

In accordance with Phelan's observations, the portrait of Jefremoff may be understood as a space where the self-examination of the person portrayed, and the photographer's examination of the person, meet – it becomes a dialogical contact zone, a space where cultures clash and grapple with each other, often in contexts of highly asymmetrical relations of power, such as colonialism, slavery or their aftermaths.[69]

Looking at this portrait of Jefremoff anew, Kivijärvi's often cited words come to mind: 'My world is different. The streets I know. The language I know is something else than – Florence, Rome and Paris.'[70] Revisiting Kivijärvi's statement in the context of the growing global interest in Indigenous art and knowledge, I recognised that I never fully understood the content of these words. The pathos of Kivijärvi's embodied and performative appearance in public might have fooled me into thinking he used these words to enable his mythological and mystical outsider position. Identifying as Kven and growing up in on the Norwegian side of Sápmi, Kivijärvi had a different perspective from many of his colleagues. Knowing that Sevettijärvi was founded when fifty-one Skolt Sámi families were evacuated there from Petsamo after the wars in 1949, the portrait of Jefremoff becomes symbolic. It is not a coincidence that Kivijärvi took interest in Sevettijärvi. Sevettijärvi represents the lived experiences not only of Sámi people, but also the migratory Kven. On a representational level, the different experiences of people living in the north seem to resonate in Kivijärvi's images, which at the same time appear silent and loud, minimalistic and monumental. By opposing a dehumanised and distanced representation of the landscape and people of the north that can be found both in the romantic landscape tradition and in ethnographic records, Kivijärvi creates a subversive image of the north that focuses on the resilience of people, their deep engagement with their surroundings and their spirituality. When asked about his relationship to Lestadianism,[71] a conservative trend in Lutheranism that he repeatedly depicts, for example in *Læstadianere*,[72] Kivijärvi's answer reveals his political situatedness. He argues that Lestadianism was mainly a political movement, supporting the oppressed, the Kven and the Sámi, and opposing everything that had to do with the colonisation of Finnmark – what he describes as 'the decay and the flattening of time'.[73] Even though Kivijärvi claimed not to be a politically engaged artist, his relational commitment to people and places of the

69
Harriet Purkis, 'Making Contact in an exhibition zone. Displaying contemporary cultural diversity in Donegal, Ireland, through an installation of visual and material portraits', in: *Museum and Society*, 11, 50–67.

70
Bjørn Teisrud, 'Hammerfest på kunstkartet', in: Alvin Vaseli et al. (eds.), Årbok 91 *Hammerfest – Sørøysund* (Hammerfest: Hammerfest Historielag, 1991), 41.

71
The teachings of Martin Luther and the Swedish preacher Lars Levi Lestadius (1800–1861), who founded the religious movement when he was a pastor in Northern Sweden in 1840, are fundamental for Lestadianism.

72
Aasbø 2011, (see note 64), 132–3.

73
Teisrud 1991, (see note 70), 38.

A Conflicting Image of the North: The Ecology of Kåre Kivijärvi's Photographic Practice

north makes his photographic practice political in its own right.

I started this text by presenting Kåre Kivijärvi in relation to his position within histories of photography in Norway. I continued by placing his photographic practice within current theoretical conversations in the digital age, the ecology of photography and its ever morphing identity. By the end of the text, I argue that Kivijärvi's deep engagement with people and places of the north, and the complexity of the colonial situation, make his oeuvre more relevant than ever, due to urgent discussions within contemporary art that place the Indigenous at the core of the conversation.

Hanne Hammer Stien

*On the Margins of Feminism, Counterculture
and Anarchy in Oslo in the 1980s*
Lill-Ann Chepstow-Lusty
in Conversation with Liv Brissach

151.

Through her photographic practice Lill-Ann Chepstow-Lusty has come to be known as a relentless agitator around issues of nationalism, identity, sexuality, tourism, ethnicity, kitsch and coins – her most recent craze. She held her first exhibition at Fotogalleriet in 1994, the two-person show Møte *with Børge Kalvig, and returned in 2002 with the solo exhibition* Viking Nouveau, *where she explored the remembrance of the past by travelling for three years across the world to find those obsessed with the Viking period. At the time, she was known for images of fat ladies, cowboys, male pin-ups and random tourists as a counter approach to what she dismissed as 'meaningful' black and white photography that she felt dominated the photographic art scene at the time. Chepstow-Lusty's images were in her own words 'trashy', stereotypical touristic snapshots that could be taken by anyone, in an early exploration of an aesthetic that we see in the works of several contemporary artists today. In 2013, some of her series were contextualised within the women's movement and art production during the 1970s and 1980s, in the exhibition* Hold stenhårdt fast på greia di: Kunst og feminisme i Norge 1968–89. *If we are witnessing a form of canon-expansion to include pivotal and female-driven moments in visual culture of the early 1980s, what does Chepstow-Lusty, a central figure in both the UK and Norway, have to say about it, given that she is, in her own words 'not a joiner'?*

Liv Brissach and Lill-Ann Chepstow-Lusty met in Oslo in September 2019, to share ideas about photography, representation and not joining in.

On the Margins of Feminism, Counterculture
and Anarchy in Oslo in the 1980s

Liv Brissach How did you decide to become a photographer?

Lill-Ann Chepstow-Lusty By accident! In 1977, I'd finished my foundation year at the art school in Eastbourne [Sussex, UK], and I had to specialise in something. I thought I was going to go into graphic design, but I didn't get in. I applied for every other department. The only thing left was photography. My family had a Kodak Instamatic camera, which my mother got us by saving up the coupons that came in packs of cigarettes. I didn't show any particular talent as a youngster. In fact, I wasn't allowed to use the camera at all because I would cut off heads in the photo frames.

LB But you got into the photography department?

CL I put on a show in the interview: selling my family's holiday snapshots as the best photos that had ever been taken. I was one of the eight accepted, from the many who applied. Later, I learnt from someone on the panel that you can train a monkey to take good photos, but you can't train someone to lie that well, and that's how I got in!

LB What were your early impressions when you started portraying male subjects in ways that were unconventional at the time?

CL It was the late 1970s in Britain, and photography was heavily male-dominated. My male co-students got women to pose for them in the thin disguise of making 'art', so I decided to do the same with men. This was before The Chippendales existed and I didn't know about Robert Mappelthorpe, and neither did my male models.

My background doesn't have anything to do with the arts. I grew up in a small seaside town in Southern England and was highly influenced by the legendary Donald McGill's saucy seaside postcards, where everything is, as we would say in English, 'tongue in cheek'.

L B   Is this how the *The Loveable Nuts* photo, which
was included in the seminal exhibition *Women's
Images of Men* at the ICA, London, came about?

C L   I was trying to get one of my male co-students to act
out an idea I had for a parody of an advertisement on
display on the London Underground featuring two
women wearing bras with the slogan 'Underneath They
Are All Loveable'. He was going to be in his under-
pants with a bag of nuts hanging over the waistband.
While photographing, I had to stand behind the backdrop with a cable release and wasn't allowed to see him.
When he saw the image, which wasn't very good, he
at least saw the potential, and I was allowed to have
another go with better lighting. And yes, this photo got
into 'Women's Images of Men' and even became the
cover of the book. I was eighteen years old when I made
this in 1978, and then the exhibition opened a couple
of years later. The show was the sensation of the 1980s:
there was a queue from the ICA to Trafalgar Square,
and nobody had ever seen anything like it. After the
ICA, it travelled across the UK to many of the most
important institutions.

At some point, there was a big conference with art
historians in discussion about the exhibition and its
impact, and I was just this little girl from Eastbourne
hanging around in the audience, knowing nothing
about art history. One art historian was talking up and
down about how my *Loveable Nuts* photograph was 'lo-
botomising the male'. Now, the reason why the head is
cut out like this is because I had a long lens and a very
short studio, so I couldn't get back far enough to fit in
his whole head and legs.

L B   What decisions went into the planning and
shooting of *Bold*?

C L   My family ran a guest house when I grew up, and we
had a little chalet hut in the back garden where I slept.
I've always been fascinated by advertising, and wanted
to make funny comments by subverting its language.
I think this was an easy thing to do in such sexist
times. At the time this photo was shot, a new washing

On the Margins of Feminism, Counterculture
and Anarchy in Oslo in the 1980s

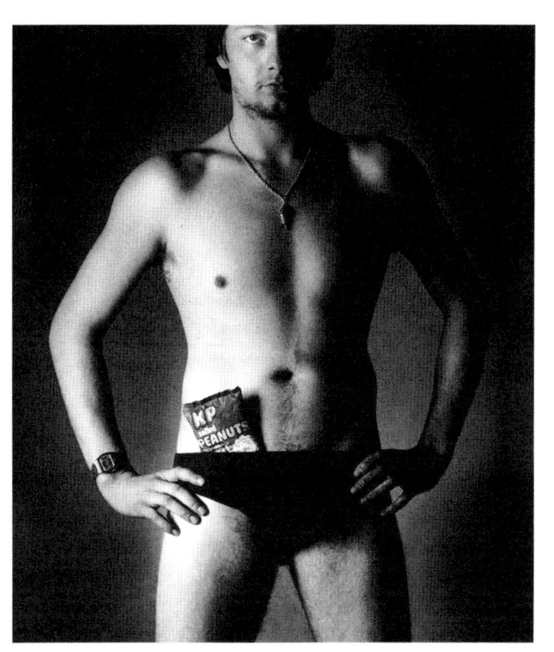

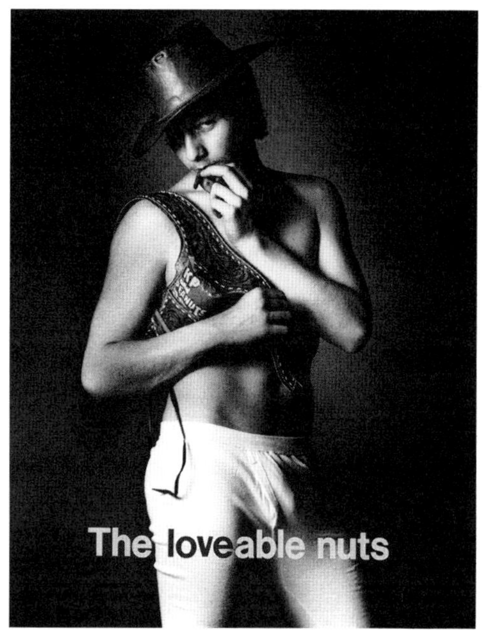

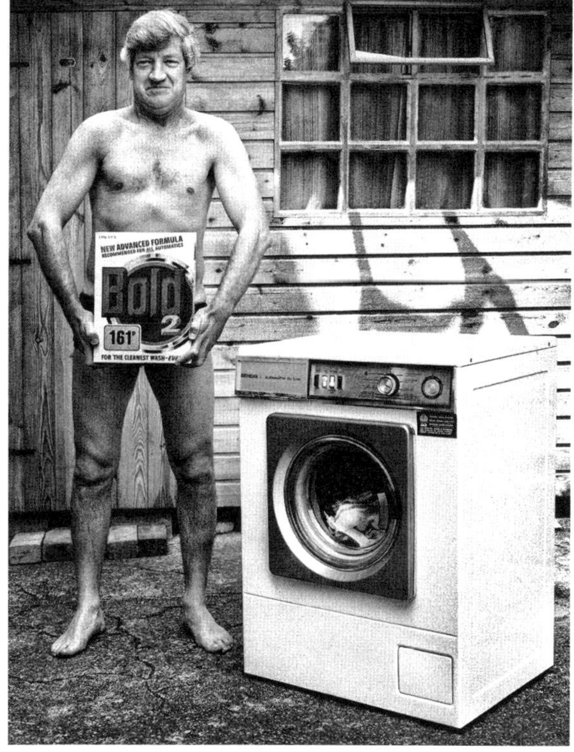

   Lill-Ann Chepstow-Lusty in Conversation with Liv Brissach

machine had just been delivered to our house, and we
had quite a handsome guy living up in room number 5
at the guest house. I said to my dad that I was going to
knock on his door and get him to pose for me. When
my dad wouldn't allow me to plague one of our paying
guests, I said: 'Well, then you'll have to pose!' And in
a way that worked better, as it showed a regular guy as
opposed to a very hunky one. The photograph is called
BOLD after the name of the washing powder called
Bold, which we had lying around by chance.

L B You moved to Oslo in the early 1980s, at a time
when new types of artist and activist run spaces
were redefining the city.

C L There were 4.5 million unemployed people in Britain
in 1980 and in 1981 my parents lured me over here on
a skiing holiday and left me, making sure that I got a
job. I ended up working in an old people's home, Oslo
Lille Indremisjon Sykehjem. Understandably this was a
bit of a shock and I had to start from scratch. I had my
studio, where I also illegally lived in Stenersgata 1. The
building was doomed for demolition, but the municipality of Oslo saw their chance to rent it out to artists
and other cultural-interest groups before it became what
is now Oslo City. On the ground floor was Café Vära,
which was one of the first cafés to sell – believe it or not
– cappuccinos. We're talking 1984. They also used the
walls as a gallery.

L B How did underground publications exist, circulate
and flow in connection to or independently of the
underground exhibitions in these spaces?

C L In the early 1980s, underground publications were fully
independent, and thus had no connection to the underground exhibitions. They were two very different
media – publications and space. I started working for
Gateavisa – a journal rooted in the counterculture and
anarchist movement. The style was very often fresh, innovative and provocative, at times messy and infantile.
The magazine mocked all kinds of authoritarian and
puritanical tendencies, and had a mix of humour and
anarchism.

On the Margins of Feminism, Counterculture
and Anarchy in Oslo in the 1980s

This launched my publication career and artistic practice outside of the space of the photography establishment embodied by Fotogalleriet, which was showcasing predominantly predictable black and white photography. At this time, Oslo had an urban awakening with Cafe De Stilj, Café Vära and Galleri Kameleon at the then anarchistic cultural house Blitz, which offered alternative exhibition spaces. Mikkel McAlinden, Fin Serck-Hanssen and myself would follow each other in the circuit. *Gateavisa* was circulated by subscription and by the contributors who were 'paid' by getting a number of copies to sell. Some brave souls personally approached people in cafés, and others such as myself would stand in front of Stortorvets Gjæstgiveri until I either sold out or died of embarrassment. We weren't so unlike today's =*OSLO* for Oslo's disadvantaged, or the Roma *Folk er Folk* street publications.

L B   Do you consider yourself someone who passes through a lot of places without permanently settling?

C L   I'm not a joiner. If you look at my career, I've been everywhere, but could never commit to only one environment.

L B   Having published books continuously since the 1980s, have you observed any big changes in readership, circulation and interest in artist-made books?

C L   We had serious intentions, no matter how flippant it may have appeared. We didn't get funding, but we still made it. Today, it's largely pseudo-political heavily funded vanity publishing.

L B   As a photographer, artist, book-maker and sometimes curator, would it be fair to say that some of your work is situated at the centre of the art world, like when you exhibited in 'Women's Images of Men', while other projects reach entirely different audiences. I'm thinking in particular of how widely *Gay Kids - Kule barn som også finnes*

      Lill-Ann Chepstow-Lusty in Conversation with Liv Brissach

reached, both as an exhibition [Museum of Cultural History, Oslo, 2008] and as a book [Abstrakt forlag, 2008].

C L   So did all my other books. I'm the rare case of the periphery reshaping the centre, while still remaining the periphery. I've never really been interested in reaching out to the art world – I've been interested in reaching out to the world. The fact that my books made it into libraries may suggest a bit of success there.

L B   When you were making the *Pin Downs* calendar in 1985, were you thinking of it as a feminist project?

C L   When I did this in the 1980s, I did it as a feminist. But the feminists – especially the ones in the UK – couldn't stand me. I don't mean the artists, but the women's movement. They saw me as a traitor, and as being as bad, or even worse, than men. I was fighting sexism with sexism.

L B   They weren't able to see that over-identifying with those power mechanics can be a way of subverting them?

C L   Exactly. Strangely enough, I felt much more at home with the anarchists and the women who were playing in bands in Blitz. I had earlier played in a punk band in England, but we didn't really take off.

L B   I'm very curious to hear your thoughts about the exhibition *FEelMALE*, looking back at it now, many years on. Many masculine-of-centre women and non-binary identified people don't necessarily aspire to look or feel like men or women. It's more about defining completely new sets of beauty and handsomeness that make up categories of their own. However, because non-heteronormative beauty has little visibility in mainstream society, butchness, androgyny and female/non-binary masculinity are often misunderstood in binary terms.

C L I've been there, done that, bought the t-shirt. Putting on more and more of these labels is just increasingly alienating and divisive. I don't attach any of these labels to myself, and nor have I ever perceived any of the people I've photographed through these reductive, divisive, alienating, restrictive and unappealing categories. We're more than pronouns and labels – I refuse this! FTS and the establishment rhetoric!

L B For me, these terms serve two very important needs: firstly, naming the power structures that dictate desire, forge hard gender boundaries and limit imagination. Heteronormativity is one such term that should be named rather than letting it exist as a faceless, invisible force. Patriarchy is another. Secondly, labels like butch, non-binary, etc can be very empowering tools for describing shared realities and common experiences of living in an otherwise heteronormative world, while still providing enough room to be different within those labels. Of course, this is strictly by self-identification. Not subscribing to this language, how do you talk about the *FEelMALE* project?

C L Growing up in a time marked by a fundamental void of lesbian role models, if one didn't fit into a traditional stereotypical female mould, the leap into thinking that one must have male tendencies was always lurking in the background. At the point of making the exhibition *FEelMALE*, this wasn't a theme that was part of the art scene, or that was dealt with anywhere, actually. One of the advantages of not being highly educated in art history, and thus of not following the trends of the day, is that it lessens the chances of plagiarism. Using humour has also been my method of communicating touchy subjects, something that nowadays everyone gets so easily offended by. If I'd been a youngster today, I would have been dragged off for gender assignment therapy. But when it comes to what body one inhabits, I'm just lucky to have a healthy one. So not unlike a popular title used for a work of art, I'd like my future label to be *Untitled*.

   Lill-Ann Chepstow-Lusty in Conversation with Liv Brissach

L B It seems like you've thoroughly immersed yourself
in the projects you've been working on in the past,
often taking an almost participant-observer role,
going to western festivals in Norway or inves-
tigating people who are obsessed with Vikings
outside of Scandinavia. Do you have a current
project that you're developing and would like to
share some thoughts on?

C L   I've always been an amateur anthropologist. Now,
I'm looking into the establishment-tribe of curators
and their attempts to dismantle true artistic practice
through words – and strange words at that!

Fin Serck-Hanssen in Conversation with Michael Andrés Forero Parra

Fin Serck-Hanssen has become known for his 'surgical' portraits of musicians, the first generation of Norwegian punks, AIDS-crisis sufferers, prison inmates, North Sea divers and gay people. Since 1987, he has exhibited his work at Fotogalleriet numerous times. In 1996, he held his first solo exhibition at the institution, titled Gaywatch, *a series of portraits he realised in the Oslo area. He has always been equivocal to 'gay aesthetics' as a term, seeing it as something artificially designed to discriminate and create difference.*

Michael Forero, co-founder of Museo Q in Colombia and a PhD candidate at the Curatorial Research Collective at TU/e, conducted this conversation with Serck-Hanssen by email and telephone from May to November 2019. They discussed homosexuality, collective memory, architecture and queer exhibitions.

Michael Forero In 1996, when *Gaywatch* was exhibited, I was starting high school in Bogotá and I was suffering from bullying, something I had to endure until I graduated in 2001. Homosexuality was only decriminalised in Colombia in 1980, and although the country is now considered one of the most advanced in terms of LGBT rights in the region, discrimination and violence are still part of daily life for many citizens. Can you tell us a little bit about the context for LGBT people in Norway when you took these photographs? What was your own context when growing up?

Fin Serck-Hanssen When I grew up, homosexuality wasn't talked about. As kids, we were told to keep away from some people who were 'different'. I didn't know about gay people, but I was attracted to people who lived life differently from the mainstream. I didn't think of them in terms of sexuality. I was fascinated by gangsters, freaks and artists. In retrospect, I remember family and family friends who were gay, but this was never talked about.

I was in a relationship with a girl in my youth and I also experimented with gay sex, but it wasn't until I went to a meeting about gay liberation that I realised this was an important part of me and there was much more to it than sex. It was a culture and a liberation movement. I became aware of the political aspects and the gay culture, which was liberating, exciting and

   Bogotá-Oslo

also frightening. At the same time, I was entering the punk scene in Oslo and I met gay punks there who became my best friends. Those were important and mind-changing relationships that formed my life and identity. We went to punk gigs and ended up in gay clubs. Neither punks nor homosexuals were appreciated and were often attacked in the street. This can still happen from time to time, but to a much lesser extent. Now we have laws against hate crime. Today, trans people are the most exposed to violence.

MF   Who organised the meeting about gay liberation?

FSH   It was organised by DNF 48, which is now named FRI. They sporadically had meetings in the largest towns, where volunteers talked about being gay or lesbian. Later, as the organisation got bigger and formed local branches, they also had meetings in schools. In the late 1970s, early 80s, there was a big conflict in DNF 48 and it became divided. Left wing members split and formed the new organisation AHF and different local groups.[74]

When I was in my early twenties, a new disease entered the gay community. We didn't know what it was, that it was fatal and ended in a painful death. We didn't know how it was transmitted; was it drugs or sex or sharing drinks? Then, we heard of people dying. It came closer and closer, and we had to go to our close friends' funerals. This, of course, had a big impact on the gay scene and on me as an individual.

74
According to Fin Serck-Hanssen, DNF 48 stands for Det Norske Forbundet av 1948 (The Norwegian Confederation of 1948), the first Norwegian gay organisation, a name chosen because it would not out its members. FRI stands for Foreningen for kjønns- og seksualitetsmangfold (The Association for Gender and Sexual Diversity), and AHF stands for Arbeids gruppe for homofil frigjøring (Homosexual Liberation Working Group).

MF   How was *Gaywatch* conceived? Who are the people portrayed and why did you feel the need to take photographs of them?

FSH   At the time I made *Gaywatch*, I was working as a volunteer for the Norwegian Gay Health Committee. We had seminars and spread safer sex information and condoms to the gay scene. I felt it would be interesting to document the diversity of the scene and see them in their home surroundings rather than in the clubs. I tried to make images that were relaxed, capturing gay men in their homes with partners or friends, with their

Fin Serck-Hanssen in Conversation
with Michael Andrés Forero Parra

children or their AIDS medication. I tried to make a
series about how I experienced the diverse gay scene
in Oslo at that time. I brought my own lighting, used
a high-saturation film, and at the same time tried to
catch a relaxed atmosphere. In a way, it was also meant
as a visual aid to remind me of those to whom we tried
to communicate a safer sex message.

M F   You highlight the relevance of the surroundings
and the home of the people portrayed in *Gaywatch*. What role does architecture (interior or exterior) play in these photographs? Did you choose
the spaces where people were photographed or
was it a common decision?

F S H   The architecture enhances the scene of a photograph,
whether it's a staged or a more random shot. I often
work with semi-staged settings. I can choose a location
or model and improvise from there. I can make changes
to the location and add or remove clothes during the
shoot. I like to have the person I photograph be free to
control their own pose and respond to things that happen during the shoot. I'm mainly aware of the light and
how it's reflected or absorbed, and that the people feel
comfortable in front of the lens. I love the lack of control and element of surprise that photography is full of,
even in staged settings. I guess that's one of the reasons
why I'm still fascinated after all these years of practice.

M F   Was the contrast/matching of the clothes and the
furniture intentional?

F S H   When I photograph someone, I let them wear what
they feel comfortable in. If I feel anything is visually
distracting, I might suggest something else. I rarely
make pre-decisions about clothes and backgrounds,
but instead work with the surroundings to match or
mismatch the colours with the subject. This I mostly
do spontaneously, and it can be consciously or subcon-
sciously, so I discover it later in the editing. I'm not
looking for a perfect match of colours, or repeating
architectural elements etc. Images like that tend to bore
me. The little trembling of almost harmony is more

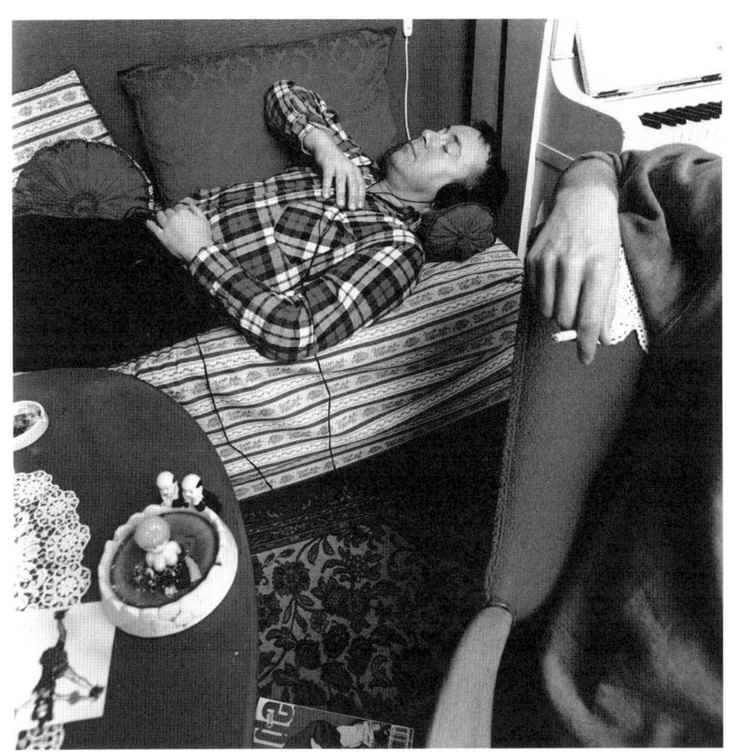

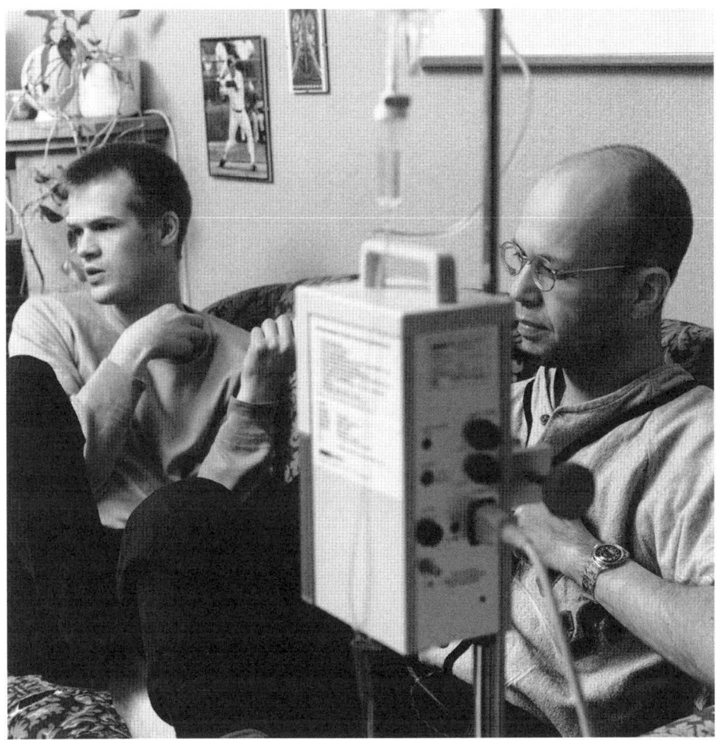

Fin Serck-Hanssen in Conversation
with Michael Andrés Forero Parra

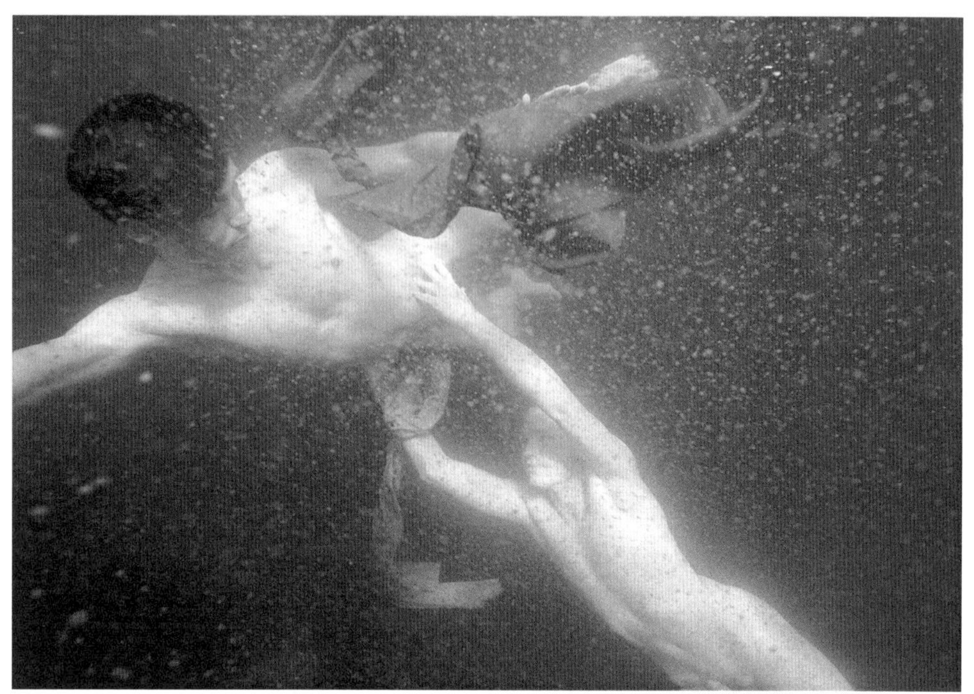

166.   Bogotá-Oslo

interesting. The unrest of trying to make sense of an image fascinates me. I think an image that needs time to be absorbed and still be direct in its language is what I try to achieve.

MF Do you remember how *Gaywatch* was installed at Fotogalleriet back in 1996? Would you have done anything differently, in terms of how your photographs were exhibited in the space?

FSH *Gaywatch* was exhibited at Fotogalleriet when it was located in Kongens gate, so it was a different space. The series was shot with a Rolleiflex camera in a square format. I made all the prints the same size, about 80 x 80 cm in a dark brown wooden frame. As far as I can remember, they were hung at the same height, with some distance between them. If I showed them today, in the new space, it would be interesting to exhibit them in a dialogue with contemporary images. I'm working on a series called *Queer Icons*, where I photograph people who are influential outside the mainstream and are more than fifty years old. Some of them appear in both series, so it would be interesting to show them together in some form. It would also be exciting to exhibit them in dialogue with other artists whose work relates to the series.

MF Do you involve yourself in how your work is exhibited?

FSH Yes, absolutely! I make a plan of how I think the work should be installed and how the walls, colours and light should be and from there I work in the actual space with the curator or designer. Sometimes, the original plan works; at other times it ends up quite different. It's in the room that the exhibition gets its life.

MF Communicating or disclosing your sexual identity is a lifetime process that for some LGBT people can be exhausting but liberating. I vividly remember the cover photograph of TIME magazine in 1997 when comedian Ellen DeGeneres posed with a smile on her face confirming she was gay. Recently, in 2019, US presidential candidate Pete

Fin Serck-Hanssen in Conversation
with Michael Andrés Forero Parra

Buttigieg and his partner posed together, embracing, with matching pants and belts. These images are now part of a larger queer imaginary where, for example, drag and camp are celebrated on prime-time television and fashion shows. Do you remember an image that had an impact on your coming out process or maybe an event that forced you to acknowledge your sexual identity publicly? How were attitudes in Norway during the 1990s, when people (artists, politicians, celebrities) came out of the closet?

FSH

I came out in the late 1970s and at that time it was not much talked about. There were no role models, except for a few activists. When Wenche Lowzow came out as the first openly gay member of parliament in 1979, it was a big issue. My first memories of gay people in the media were from the movies *Death in Venice* (1971), *Car Wash* (1976) and *La cage aux Folles* (1978). I also loved the camp part of popular music that played with androgyny, like Marc Bolan, David Bowie, Roxy Music and the New York Dolls. However, these artists played on androgyny and sexuality, but it wasn't until I heard Tom Robinson's 'Glad to be Gay' (1978) that I saw an angry and proud openly gay artist. I found it very liberating and inspiring to hear him come out so loud, proud and without shame. Other important influences for me at that time were the book *Villskudd* (1979) and movies like *Taxi Zum Klo* (1981), *Querelle* (1982) and Pedro Almodóvar's films.

In the mid-80s, drag shows came out of the gay clubs into the public media. But then drag queens didn't come out of the closet. Jan Tomas, who's now maybe the best-known gay public person in Norway, worked as a female model, and would deny being gay at that time. This was quite typical for the 1980s and 90s. I think the AIDS crisis did force us to talk about sexuality in an open and frank way. This made way for tearing down obstacles for LBGT to come out after the 1990s.

 Many museums, on both sides of the Atlantic, have developed exhibitions recovering a 'queer history' and addressing questions of representation (for example, *Queer British Art* at Tate Britain, *Hide/Seek* at the Smithsonian's National Portrait Gallery, or *Art AIDS America* at the Bronx Museum of the Arts). Do you mind that some of your series, such as *Gaywatch* (1996), *Theme AIDS* (1993) or *Underwater* (1987) might be catalogued as 'gay art'? Do you mind being considered a 'gay artist'? What are your thoughts about these categories like 'queer art', 'queer sensibility' or 'queer (curatorial) interpretations'?

 I see it can be useful to use the term 'gay art' in terms of acknowledging a sort of special memory within. Art can represent a collective memory, true or false, that can have a big influence on our culture. Some of my work deals with gay themes and as a gay artist I can see that my sexuality and desires have an influence on my work. If some of my work gets catalogued as gay art, I'm proud of that.

I find this queer sensibility interesting. In terms of art, it's been there for a long time, but now it's starting to get broader attention. I guess its nature is to communicate on two levels, one to a general audience and one to a subgroup.

I saw the exhibition *Queer British Art 1861–1967* at Tate. It was great to see art in this context. I'm looking forward to Queer British art after 1967!

I think gay art or queer art is important for our culture. Unlike many other subcultures, we don't reproduce ourselves in the same way as heterosexual families do. We don't pass on traditions and culture to the next generation in the same way. We often have gay 'families' – a group of friends who meet on a regular basis. These friendships often include people of different ages, where stories and culture can be passed on. But as a group, we're more dependent on art and culture to maintain a common identity. In this context, I can see the *Gaywatch* series as gay art, since its subject matter is gay people and a documentation of gay life at a certain time. The *Underwater* series deals with the male body seen with a gay eye, so I guess that also qualifies as gay art. *Theme AIDS* has a more general subject matter, even if it applies to gay people. They're portraits of innocent people who received a death sentence, and on top of this, were stigmatised.

M F   Can you tell us more about *Underwater* and *Theme AIDS*?

F S H   The *Underwater* series was mostly a celebration of a hot Norwegian summer, although the earlier black and white images are more existential body studies in water. The black and white images from the mid-80s are an experiment in how the body is transformed by water and light. The body is dissolved and fragmented and was meant to trigger emotions that I experienced at that time. The coloured underwater images are much more playful and celebratory. They were almost like a drag show underwater: vivid colours and wigs together with naked bodies made a good playground to celebrate gay culture.

The *Theme AIDS* series was part of the group exhibition *Theme Aids* at Henie Onstad Kunstsenter. I wanted this to be a series about people, not an abstract approach. I was angry and upset seeing my friends getting sick and dying. I wanted to achieve a very direct portrait and wanted to make portraits of people infected by HIV/AIDS at a time when not many people were open about their disease and there was a big stigma. In addition, just before a medicine that worked was introduced, being infected was regarded as a death sentence. I approached Pluss, an organisation for people living with HIV/AIDS, but no one wanted to participate. I discussed this with my best friend, who'd just been diagnosed and moved back to Oslo from New York. He'd been part of the ACT UP movement in New York and he agreed to be photographed for this project. I made the portraits with a 4 x 5 camera and with a very direct light from both sides using a red backdrop. Friends helped to spread the word and asked around and I got fourteen volunteers to participate. I remember Trine, who was very sick but still came to my studio to be photographed and came to the opening in a wheelchair because she felt this was important. She died just weeks after that. The exhibition was still open, and people put flowers under her portrait. I still get tears in my eyes when I think of her and her struggle.

M F   This reminds me of a thought by Professor Jonathan Katz in his essay included in the catalogue of the exhibition *Hide/Seek* in which he maintains that 'historically, queer art has drawn power from oppression and from the inventiveness, ingenuity, and originality it encouraged as a strategy of survival'.[75] This makes me think about memory and how some artworks and cultural projects can be considered some type of testimony or evidence of a different past. What are your thoughts about photography and memory?

75
Jonathan Katz, 'Hide/Seek: Difference and Desire in American Portraiture', in: Jonathan D. Katz and David C. Ward (eds.), *Hide/Seek: Difference and Desire in American Portraiture* (Washington, DC: Smithsonian Books, 2010), 56, companion volume to the exhibition of the same name which opened at the National Portrait Gallery, Smithsonian Institution, October 2010.

F S H   Photography obviously has had a role as a tool for memory-saving – family albums and press photos are examples of this. The visual impact of an image can be a trigger for memories, just as a smell can provide a strong memory. They can trigger the brain to release past experiences. This is a powerful trait of photography.

M F   Tate curator Clare Barlow, in the catalogue of the *Queer British Art* exhibition, affirms that, 'Queerness is an unstable category and can be rooted in particular contextual frameworks. As those frameworks change or knowledge of them is lost, artworks can acquire or lose a queer significance that was not part of their original conception.'[76] In 100 years, what framework or idea about your work should never be forgotten by curators and audiences?

76
Clare Barlow, 'Introduction', in: idem. (ed.), *Queer British Art 1861–1967* (London: Tate Enterprises, 2017), 16, companion volume to the exhibition of the same name which opened at Tate Britain, April 2017.

F S H   I think the nature of queerness is to change and adapt meaning in different times and cultures. The documented gay culture is relatively new, and is only now receiving appreciation and being documented seriously. I think artwork in public spaces like Elmgreen and Dragset's sculpture *Memorial to Homosexuals Persecuted Under Nazism* in Berlin is important and powerful. If

Fin Serck-Hanssen in Conversation
with Michael Andrés Forero Parra

my work is seen by coming generations as a document
of scenes from a time and culture that were outside
the mainstream, that would be fine. I hope that it adds
history and awareness of past struggles.

M F   Very recently, I came across Skeivt Arkiv, the
Norwegian National Archive for Queer and
LGBT History, created in 2012. In Latin America, there have been similar initiatives founded
like Archivo de la Memoria Trans in Argentina,
Museo Q in Colombia, Museo Memoria LGBTI
in Ecuador, and Museo MIO in Costa Rica. As a
photographer who's documented some gay history in Norway, what would you say are the blind
spots that still need further research and understanding for a comprehensive LGBT history in
Norway?

F S H   It's great that Skeivt Arkiv has started documenting
and collecting LGBT history and I think they have a
big and important job to do. One thing is to research
the political and organised LGBT life. More challenging I guess is the unorganised culture like clubs, street
life, cruising arenas and a history of smaller subcultures,
substitute families.
                            When the AIDS crisis started, people in our com-
munity were engaged and felt the need to do some-
thing. I think this dramatic period of time would be
especially worth further research and exploration.

M F   In the context of the anniversary of the Stonewall
uprising, can I ask you what other gay and lesbian
artists and photographers inspire you and why?

F S H   Many artists have inspired me in different stages of
my life. Among them are John Waters, Francis Bacon,
Oscar Wilde, Genesis P Orridge, Peter Chrisopherson,
Tom of Finland, Kenneth Anger, Nan Goldin, Cindy
Sherman, Baron von Gloeden, Robert Mapplethorpe,
Rainer Fassbinder, George Platt-Lynes, Diane Arbus
and Wolfgang Tillmans. First, they move me on an
emotional level, then they challenge me in the way I
see things, make me feel proud, ashamed, angry, happy,

inspired, provoked or wondering. Their work can take
me off guard and make me see myself and the world
from a slightly different angle.

M F   Is there a Norwegian artist (queer or not) whom
you think is still unacknowledged or not properly
known?

F S H   There are many great Norwegian artists who deserve
to be shown. Personally, I'd like to see new exhibitions
from Thomas Phil, Guri Dahl, Steinar Buholm, Lin-
da Bournane Engelberth and Simen Kjellin, and also
exhibitions from young artists like Bendik Syversætre
Johannessen and Jacob Landvik.

M F   Social and dating apps have brought a massive
widespread use of photography and video. Built-in
cameras in mobile phones allow people to register
every moment of their lives. Cameras in public
spaces capture us everywhere we go. Newborns
now have a complete portfolio that parents make
available through the web. It seems we no longer
have any possibility of existence without a photographic register. Our (good, and sometimes bad)
memories are constantly saved and reproduced.
What are your perceptions of photography today?
In a world with so much visual information, how
do you find a focus?

F S H   I think the widespread use of photography today has
enhanced the interest in photographic art. I still find
photography interesting and challenging. I still feel
insecure, and I question myself about how to approach
the process of making an image. Maybe this is why I
don't get bored.
A meeting with the young generation made me
aware of how the mobile phone camera and apps have
influenced their view. I'm working on a project with
a young trans person, and she never felt the images
looked right. After a while, we found out that her selfies were mirrored and that was the way she saw herself.
She wasn't comfortable with the way my camera captured her in an un-mirrored way.

Fin Serck-Hanssen in Conversation
with Michael Andrés Forero Parra

M F   Can you share details about this new project?
       What are your thoughts about the representation
       of trans people in media or arts, and how will you
       portray this trans person?

F S H   It's a project of portraits of Hedda[77], who's a girl in
                                   her mid-twenties. She was born with a male body. I've
                                   photographed her in the different stages of gender-con-
                                   firming surgery. Often trans people are portrayed as
                                   very extroverted, sexually loaded, streetwise or androg-
                                   ynous and beautiful, or with a strong focus on gender.
                                   My project has a quiet approach, even if some of the
                                   post-operation images can be disturbing in nature. I
                                   don't think I portray a trans person in a different way
                                   from any other person. The only difference is maybe
                                   the fact that some trans persons I've photographed will
                                   be more aware of looking feminine or masculine, which
                                   isn't an issue that I emphasise when I photograph. I
                                   personally find the ambiguity interesting, but I also find
                                   it interesting to cooperate with a person in a transgen-
                                   der stage to find an image that reflects their self image.
77   In this project, Hedda trusted me to document her the
The work in progress   way I see her, although I also hope to include her own
was shown as part of the
programme *Le Book Club* at   selfies. It's been a privilege to be able to work with her
Fotogalleriet in early 2020.   in such a turbulent and vulnerable time of her life.

M F   To end, what do you think will be the future of
       gender?

F S H   I think and hope we'll gradually develop into a non-
                                   binary-gender society and that gender will no longer
                                   be an issue.

Eivind Furnesvik I've written a few questions, so let's just
chat and see where this goes.
        It's wonderfully ironic that your first solo exhi-
bition, which opened on your thirtieth birthday,
was called *Getaway*, but rather than getting away
from the art world it actually brought you into it.
Is there anything you regret now, looking back
after sixteen years?

Matias Faldbakken Yes, well the die was cast! What can I say? In a way, I
already had a sort of career as a writer before that. In
a sense, I debuted quite early on. You could say that in
those years – between twenty-six/seven and thirty, I
was a bit of an 'early bloomer' *and* a 'late bloomer'. My
debut was both early and late.
        Now, I've never tried to remember how that exhibi-
tion came about, but I know that the impulse behind
using that video clip came from a primeval fascination
with all kinds of online and gaming-related things –
and maybe there's some link back to art history. There
was a sort of linear perspective, but in a very new media
format. Those motorcycle and speeding videos were
starting to appear, and there was more and more of that
sort of thing back then. The Internet had been around
for several years, but it was nowhere near as advanced as
it is today, with all the social media formats flooding us
constantly.

E F   Yes, even YouTube – as a sort of library – had
barely begun.

M F   Exactly. It was more that files would pop up here and
there, and you'd see things you'd never seen before.
Anyway, there was this historical fascination with
linear perspective and some cinematographic vanish-
ing-point-related stuff – the whole first-person shooter
perspective, where you have a point of view, or whatever
it's called.

E F   Indeed, it's a subjective position – you see the
actor's field of view.

M F   Yes, you're seeing through the antagonist's eyes. I don't
remember exactly what I was thinking, but when I look
back, I can see that there are so many things I've always
been fascinated by, and it all comes together in one
form, and it sticks. That's often how I work: if there are
enough coordinates of things I'm interested in there,
stuff that can be brought together in a simple format,
you only have to get it into a gallery, point at it and
insist on it.

E F   I was actually thinking about that while I was
trying to put together some questions. You made
your debut quite late, but you did so – or rather
you came onto the scene – just after the 'Nordic
miracle' had given way. The kudos that came
from being a Nordic artist were gone, but the fact
remains, of course, that your trilogy had the sub-
heading *Scandinavian Misanthropy*. There's also
the fact that the motorcyclist is Swedish, though
that's not emphasised the way it is in the title of
your books – it's taken from a Scandinavian political or consumer culture. Without asking whether
it was important to you to make that link – was it
important to you that it came from a Scandinavian context? Or was there something else that's
unique about it?

M F   I remember that it was the former, I think. The *Getaway* video that was doing the rounds online at the
time was from Paris. I think that was the first one I
saw. It featured this madman who managed the whole
motorway around Paris in eleven minutes or something
like that. From start to finish, the video was just around
Paris, and he was driving like a lunatic. Right after
that, the 'Ghost Rider' from Sweden popped up, and in
a way it surpassed the continental version. I think maybe the more domestic perspective also resonated with
the books; the idea that this peaceful part of the world
was also producing a sort of extremism, as I'd touched
on a lot in the books. So I think I picked a slightly
more homemade version of this when I first did it. It
was less well known, but also worse …

                        Matias Faldbakken in Conversation with Eivind Furnesvik

E F   No, because I'm thinking – and this is just my interpretation – that part of what's dynamic about that video is …

M F   It's so bloody quiet and calm around the guy who's driving, basically.

E F   Yes, but just to add a little context – if this text is supposed to be an introduction for someone who hasn't seen the video – from the get-go you have a motorcyclist who is enormously competent, outstandingly talented, but their talent goes way beyond what the speed limit or the law allows. And on top of that, you've got a motorcycle that's so powerful and fast that basically no car – unless you're driving with a modified motor or a Formula 1 car – can catch it.

Also, in the Scandinavian context, it's like you don't think threats like these exist, and the police aren't equipped to deal with it. So there's all this confused distance between what the law and the police are meant to do, and what they're capable of doing, when faced with this new threat. Because the threat – even though there have always been people who want to drive fast – is also pumped up by the fact they can now film it and share it immediately. It's like the sort of media that's cropped up recently actually drives the bike forward.

So, this Scandinavian thing comes about, a bit like in *Seinfeld*, where we don't have any problems, so we have to come up with our own. Better than *Seinfeld*, though: you have this Swedish film[78] about a police station that's going to be shut down because there's no crime, and so a police officer begins to fake crimes to make sure that the police station stays open. You instantly provide the police with something to do. And it sinks into another term where you're really just throwing the classic, social democratic police a curveball, and suddenly it's back to zero and you have to think about what sort of resources we have.

[78] Editor's note: *Kopps* (2003), dir. Josef Fares.

M F

Yeah, that's completely to the point. And also, through-out my trilogy, my trick was to show a kind of desperation to produce friction – that, for want of friction, you have to whip things up yourself. With motorcyclists in the past, I guess they had only their friends as their audience, but in this case you have a kind of show-off with a bigger audience, which means that the extremes get bigger and things get wilder.

Another feature of these videos – which I didn't use, because I just wanted the speed – is that they drive around the city until they find a police car or patrol vehicle, then they position themselves in front of it and burn the tyres and make lots of smoke, then they speed away. Considering they never have a number plate or manage to find out who's behind the visor, they have no chance of catching them, basically.

So they get on their bikes and drive outside of the law, so to speak, where they can stay – as long as they're smart in the way they distribute the film and that kind of thing, so they can't be traced another way.

E F

But at the same time, and we've talked about this before – I think we had it in the press release, and it was met with a bit of criticism: it's a kind of 'from nowhere to nowhere escape'. It starts with an image, and finishes exactly five minutes and fifty-nine seconds later. But as an aside for those who want some context, I was sitting on the other side of the wall we'd built, separating the office from the gallery and making it into a corridor. You had the five minutes and fifty-nine seconds, followed by a second of peace, and then it started all over again. It was awful, like some form of Chinese torture, or maybe it was the opposite of Chinese torture because you knew exactly when it was coming, and you'd then be reminded of the alternative. The sound was actually so loud that every time the phone rang I had to go out into the street, into actual traffic, to answer the call. I couldn't use the phone in the office, that's how bad it was. But what I'm getting at is how, during those five minutes and fifty-nine seconds, you didn't actually get anywhere; you've just been driving.

   Matias Faldbakken in Conversation with Eivind Furnesvik

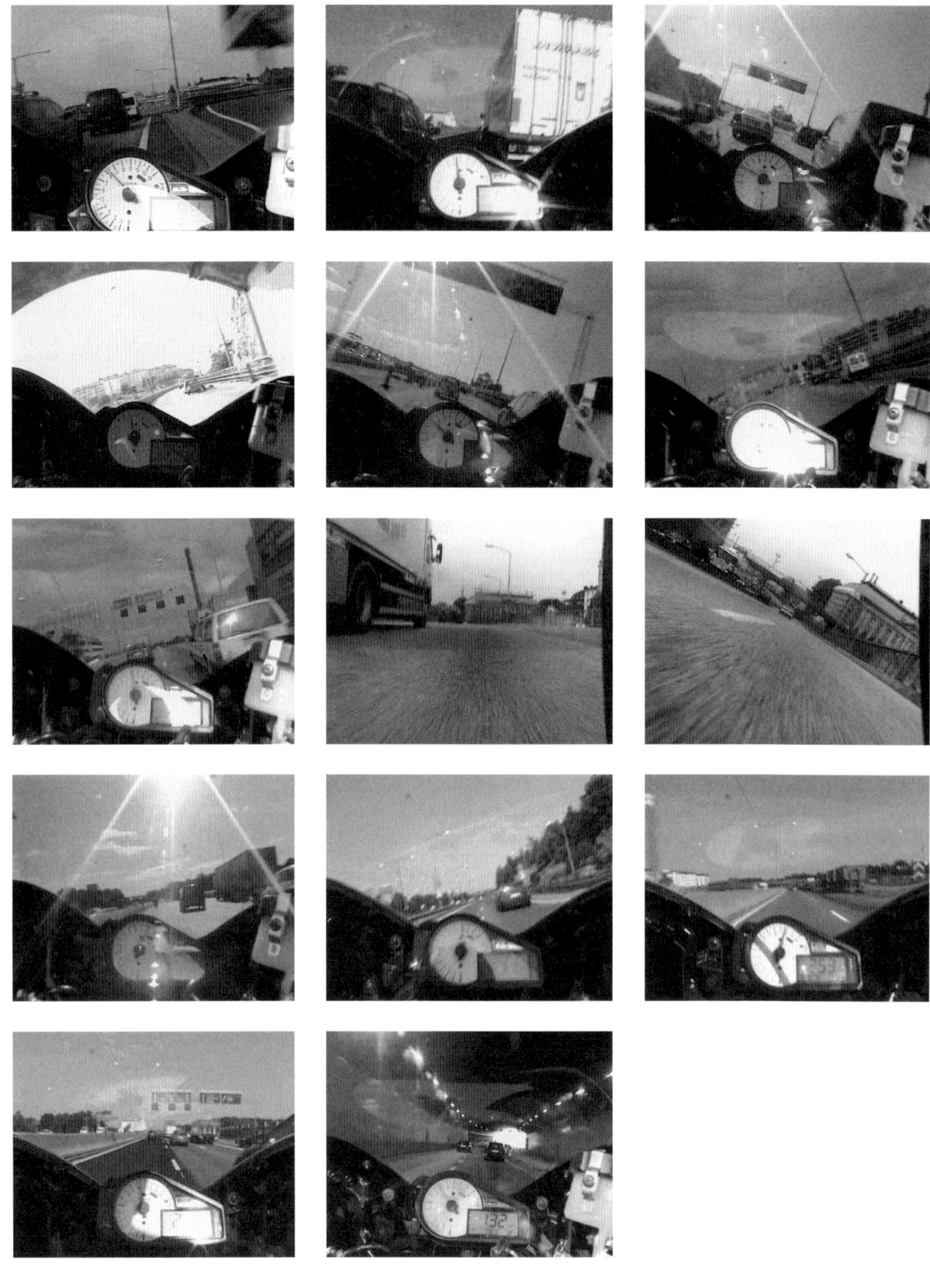

 Getaway

M F Yeah, I actually edited the material because there's a lot of pottering around and accelerating and that kind of thing. I cut out the highlights, I suppose, the parts when they're going the fastest, at the most hysterical speeds.

What I think I thought back then, was that even in a nowhere-to-nowhere type escape – if we can even talk about an escape here – there is, in a sense, a moment of ecstasy at the highest RPM, at the highest speed. So, I really just took those moments and put them together, prolonging the ecstasy somehow. You can almost look at it as a more 'momentary', ecstatic experience than as a lasting solution.

E F The motif, or the method you used there, makes it relevant to talk about escapism, which I think has also become more valid as a category given the sustained development of the media that distributes this type of video, social media, and the increasing roboticisation of society.

We all suffer, both as a Norwegian society and as a global society, with what to do with this vast biomass of people as there's an ever-decreasing number of jobs available. And one of the few ways we can give meaning to people without jobs – well, it's by giving them one form of escapism or another: on-screen entertainment, which is a sort of pastime, after all.

Another motif is looking at the meaningless or the non-productive – things you might call futile, and which I think have been a motif in your earlier work. Looking at things chronologically, you could say that this is a motif you're addressing in an advanced way here. Is this something you think about yourself?

M F Let me take a step back so I can think about this escapist-moment thing. If you look at, let's say, Instagram, compared to the old-fashioned narrative formats, you'll see that people post highlight after highlight after highlight, no? All you see is a series of highlights. And this has become a kind of 'kick', which means you hang on to these things. So regarding this type of narrative,

   Matias Faldbakken in Conversation with Eivind Furnesvik

this represents a completely different way in which you can escape – just like how you could lose yourself in a film or a book where you're looking to exchange this world for another.

E F   Yes, it certainly depends on an activity for the motorcyclist – if nothing else – so you have to do something. If you just sit and stare, you don't need to do anything else but press the YouTube icon before clicking on the Instagram icon.

M F   Yes, I just mean that the way I cut it together is, sort of, a version of it – almost a bunch of highlights.

E F   Yes, 'full throttle' all the way.

M F   Exactly, which also invalidates the narrative, doesn't include the beginning and the end – cutting out how the ghost rider gets up in the morning, decides to do all this, puts on his leathers, that sort of thing. Going home afterwards …

E F   Eating Swedish meatballs with lingonberry jam.

M F   Yeah, ha ha! I was just thinking about a new form of escapism, where one highlight snaps at the heels of the next, and which just goes on and on and on.

E F   But, to expand on what I said earlier about working in that 'office' landscape, there was a real physical discomfort on my part, the noise. And for the viewer, there was a discomfort in standing in front of a pretty big screen, surrounded by that noise, using your body to compensate for the movement in the picture, making the biker's movements, the camera's movements, align with your own. It made a lot of people sea-sick at first. But then the five minutes fifty-nine seconds passed, and you gradually got used to it. There was a critic who noticed that from the moral transgressions at the beginning, you begin to decode it all, and by the time you head out – providing you're not bored – you have at least reconciled

yourself with the situation. In a way, this is also
linked to the ... I can't think of the Norwegian
word for 'futile' – not perishable ...

M F   So, it's not excessive.

E F   Yeah, right, that it serves no purpose, wouldn't
you say? There's something slightly despairing
about it all. If we turn back to the content and
also consider the situation you were in: did you
think about that, or have you since?

M F   I'm just thinking aloud here, but I didn't really have
much experience with exhibitions. Looking back now,
you can see that it was my first chance to use the bright,
white, open gallery space that, in one way or another,
is a chamber of subtlety, a place where you finally have
the opportunity to do something subtle, but I turned
all that on its head and tried to make it as unsubtle as
possible. I made everything inverse in the gallery room.

E F   Yeah, it became a corridor.

M F   Yes, an inversed corridor, I didn't follow any architectural logic. It was also very dark inside, the windows ...

E F   Yes, we made sure that it looked like your typical
sex shop, seeing as there were many of them in
that area back then.

M F   Yeah, that's true. Full of sounds and the most intrusive
imagery. So, in a way, it was completely stripped of all
subtlety, in favour of the kind of brief, experiential type
thing in that box. It was actually my first take at using
the artistic space like that. In a way, it was about twist-
ing and resisting all potential.

E F   I remember that you used an anarchist A on the
invites for *Getaway*. That might be the most
heavy-handed part of it.

M F   Yes, exactly, and I remember you saying that back then,
too.

                        Matias Faldbakken in Conversation with Eivind Furnesvik

E F   I'd say it again now if you did the same today.

M F   It would have been funnier today.

E F   Like you say, it was the first attempt, and in some
respects you've gained other experiences. But
maybe no matter what you choose to do with the
exhibition opening here [STANDARD (OSLO)]
in October, you've also earned the right to do a lot
of strange things. If you decide to use the anarchist A here, in a way you've earned the right to.
But back then, it felt …

M F   Noted, ha ha.

E F   That it was almost …

M F   I'll use two anarchist A's, so it'll be St*A*nd*A*rd.

E F   No, what I was going to say was that it maybe felt
a bit like being a nineteen-year-old who's been to
Greece and come back with a dolphin tattoo on
their ankle or something.

M F   Yes, but I also remember that it was a very deliberate
attitude.

E F   What, so it was supposed to be a little embarrassing?

M F   I knew that it was embarrassing, but at the same time
I really felt like dipping my finger into that – stirring it
up a bit.

E F   Yes, all these different elements you're talking
about somehow came together to make the exhibition a bit like a fist – such a simple layout in the
room and such a – how should I put it? – physical
or experiential installation.

M F   What you need to remember is that when you saw that
       anarchist A, you had a rather extreme exhibition. I al-
       ready had the first two books behind me, and everyone
       on the Norwegian scene who'd read my books – and
       there were many who had – they knew that I didn't
       have a 1:1 relationship with 'So, time for anarchy here',
       no?

E F   No, no, no.

M F   So, in a way it was all put together beforehand. I might
       not have deserved much in terms of installations back
       then, but I think that thematically, I'd already opened
       up certain things, and I had a thematic field that I'd set
       out and prepared quite well in the first two books …
       the dialectics of rebellion, in a way.

E F   OK, and in a way the symbol-juggling, including
       your use of them in *Macht und Rebell*, which …

M F   Symbols that are both too full and too empty, don't you
       think? In a way, it was an attempt to whip things up
       again.

E F   OK, so maybe this would be a good time to zoom
       out a little bit – with *Getaway*, which was your
       first exhibition, and the ones that followed, all
       the way up to the exhibition with the two works
       we passed on the way in, from 2005, your first at
       STANDARD (OSLO). Those works from 2005,
       they were even more antiseptic as appropriations.
       We've talked about it several times with regard to
       the way you did it. You could of course say that
       there's subjectivity in the editing of video mate-
       rials, but then it's also important that the video
       material is found that way – it seems vital for you
       that this stuff is out there, that you can find it
       on other platforms. From that sort of editing in
       2005 you've gone from mild editing to digitally
       enhancing: the perfect, sterile presentation of a
       baseball bat. Then, from there, towards a more
       subjective and actually quite whimsical produc-
       tion today, encompassing far more of your own

    Matias Faldbakken in Conversation with Eivind Furnesvik

inadequacy. Do you ever give much thought to
that development yourself?

M F   Yes, I do, actually. I don't know what more I should say
about that. In the arts, you always have to see. Time is
always looking back, whilst I'm going forward. I started
with a fist and now there's less and less of that, in a way.
I don't know …

E F   Just a load of fingers instead?

M F   Ha ha, an outstretched hand.

E F   Ha ha, yes, no, it's more the opposite, given that
I've also looked back over your shoulders whenever you've been given the opportunity to show
a little bit more of your art … Whenever there's
been a museum invitation and you're either asked
to utilise something the museum already owns
or there's an expectation that you'll cover specific
positionalities in your work. You yourself are incredibly critical with regard to what holds water.
Seeing as it's now sixteen years since *Getaway*,
would you say that it still holds water?

M F   Well, I don't actually think about it very often, but I've
never been embarrassed about that exhibition. I thought
it was completely … considering how I was thematically
consistent … I feel it was a pretty logical starting point.

E F   If you got an invitation now, would you take it
with you into an exhibition?

M F   It's already been installed and run at the Museum of
Contemporary Art.[79] They already have it in their
collection. Now that I've seen it there, I think it's good
enough.

E F   I actually think it's one of your works that has
done the rounds the most. It's been shown fre-
quently, and of course much of this has been at
group exhibitions about counter-culture, underground, speed, or the motor in contemporary art.

[79]
Editor's note: *Getaway*
was presented in the exhibition *PARADOX: Positions in
Norwegian Video Art 1980–
2010* at the National Museum,
Oslo, in 2013.

         Getaway

M F Yes, it's like … not a slice of life but a slice of the Internet, and after a while it becomes like a patina of some kind of historical … or just a slide of something from that time: like a little time capsule. You start to get a little of bit of that feeling maybe.

E F Yeah, Paul Virilio talks about something called the accelerated view. About how we're becoming more and more skilled at reading images. Our visual ability is getting better, and we're adapting increasingly quickly to technology and new media – not just streams of images but also cuts that aren't necessarily logical; we're able to compensate for the missing parts. He talks a lot about Surrealism, where some images are removed from the middle of a sequence and someone moves from right to left, but we still understand what's going on in the images that are missing. Looking at it like that, your video is a document, in a way, of our visual abilities. And it's actually possible that if you fast forward – no pun intended – it no longer has any of the clout that it had in 2003.

M F No, exactly, I agree. There's nothing fundamentally shocking or surprising either. The flow is more rigid now, wouldn't you say? And we're more used to starting the day with all sorts of things hitting our eyeballs. The way I handled the themes at the time – in my books, too – was a way to find various areas or issues that I simply turned the volume up on. It was almost its own form of accelerationism, thematically speaking, like 'This is what it's about' and then you only have to turn up the volume and hit the gas pedal, no?

E F Yes, it's almost a cacophony …

M F Yeah, and just making the content more extreme to see what it's like or whether it'll crack somehow. With that sort of working logic – which I fine-tuned a little here and there via books and the first works of art – I thought the film was a good example and it works pretty well. Even if it doesn't have much surprise or shock value, that sort of thing. But I still think that if you step

   Matias Faldbakken in Conversation with Eivind Furnesvik

into a 'black box' and see it running, it has a certain pull, or at least it's enticing enough for you to stand there a few minutes. But also, on a purely technical level, the speed limit in Norway and Sweden is pretty much the same as it was at that time and 300 km/h is still fast.

E F   Yes, and you'd die pretty quickly if you crashed at that speed.

M F   Yeah, and it's not possible to drive much faster than that on Norwegian and Swedish roads. So there's something about how the upper limit for what is possible on a Swedish highway still stands. I think it probably has a certain effect while you're standing there, watching it. But maybe when it comes to the media, it's not as effective.

E F   It would be interesting to imagine what an artist who was trying to make an equivalent piece of work today would do.

M F   Well, we'll see in October.

                    Getaway

When we look back at institutions and their histories, we look for seeds of change. In the mid-2000s, British curator and writer Susan Bright collaborated with the Norwegian photographic scene through Fotogalleriet. She was involved in its discursive public programming and curated the exhibition Something Out Of Nothing *in 2007. Artist and writer Nina Strand has participated in Fotogalleriet's programming at different points in time as both editor-in-chief of* Objektiv, *when she co-curated the exhibition* Two-Timers *in 2011, and as an artist with the project* Thumbing The Library: Gardening Networks *in 2018. Objektiv interviewed Bright for its third issue, and Bright and Strand have continued a long-term dialogue on the development of photographic art.*

Bright and Strand met in Paris in early September 2019, and again in the summer of 2020 to discuss how institutional change should be redefined. Together they will curate the f/stop photography festival *in Leipzig in 2021.*

Nina Strand Shall we start by talking about our involvement
with Fotogalleriet?

Susan Bright I first worked with Fotogalleriet in 2005. At this time I was doing some adjunct lecturing at the University of Creative Arts in Farnham in the UK. The course leader in photography was Anna Fox and she was very interested in forging relationships with other countries – whether through galleries, museums or artists. There was a Norwegian student on the course at the time, and he organised a trip for us to meet photographers, artists and curators around the country. Through this I met Ida Kierulf, who was then director of Fotogalleriet, and Jonas Ekeberg, who was then Director of the Preus Museum. It was from this meeting that Ida suggested a joint conference with UCA and Fotogalleriet. This became *On Time: The Interplay between Still and Moving Images* held at the Art Academy in Oslo in 2005, in association with Fotogalleriet and the Preus Museum. Memorable speakers were Sophie Howarth, who was then a curator of public programmes at Tate, London, and Victor Burgin.

Then in 2006, Ida asked me to be one of the three curators to create three exhibitions for Fotogalleriet's 30th Anniversary in 2007. The other two curators were Geir Haraldseth and Tom Sandberg. I had pretty much free rein, but I had to select artists through an open call

   The Institutional Reset

of members from the photographic artists' union, the Norwegian Association for Fine Art Photographers. It made my job much easier, as I was really not aware of much Norwegian art and photography. I knew the bigger names of a certain generation that had achieved a more international focus – such as Mette Tronvoll, Vibeke Tandberg and Torbjørn Rødland – but that was about it.

I saw a lot of landscape and I was rather seduced by the romanticism of it and how alien it was to my own relationship to land and 'home'. Initially, I wanted to do something around this, but Ida pleaded with me not to, as it can slip into cliché. This stuck with me and so in the end the centrepiece or fulcrum of the show became Ane Hjort Guttu's concrete sculptures *Smalvollen*.

N S When we made *Nordic Now*, *Objektiv*'s seventh issue, it was a survey of Nordic tendencies, and everyone expected a lot of landscape. We decided not to have that as a tendency because it's what you expect from Nordic photography.

S B Exactly. *Smalvollen* by Ane Hjort Guttu is a group of monolithic sculptures that make an oblique commentary on nature, on the 'non photographable' and the over-photographed as well as the complexities of abstraction. This became central to the thinking for the exhibition. I began to feel that I could only really consider other work in relation to these sculptures and what they represented. The final exhibition ended up being titled *Something Out of Nothing* and looked at photography's relationship to sculpture and still life through the prism of abstraction. The artists featured were Ole John Aandal, Margareta Bergman, Else Marie Hagen, Ane Hjort Guttu and Espen Tveit. This was over ten years ago, and of course, abstraction and photography's expansion into the three-dimensional and more process-based works is commonplace now, but at that time I think we were all grappling with this a bit. From this connection with Fotogalleriet my relationship with Ole John Aandal continued, and I wrote a short essay for his book *Juvenilia*. I think it's worth noting that he made the book in 2008, when we weren't really familiar with the kind of selfies he was working with.

                              Susan Bright in Conversation with Nina Strand

N S   Ole John Aandal was the director of Fotogalleriet
for a while, fresh from the Institute for Photography in Bergen, having studied alongside Torbjørn
Rødland among others, under Robert Meyer.
He brought the gallery closer to the white cube
it is today. He threw out the comfortable sofa
they had, painted everything white and started
programming super debut solo shows with a lot
of artists who are still relevant on the Norwegian
photo scene. He had the idea of these found online images very early on, didn't he?

S B   He did. It's a very compelling, strange and
adventurous book. So, what's your involvement
with Fotogalleriet?

N S   The exhibition space has been super important
for me and a lot of others for a long time. A show
that made an ever lasting impression was *Jeg er
nesten alltid redd* (I Am Almost Always Afraid)
by Kim Hiorthøy in 2003. Hiorthøy asked his
friends to stand in front of a super-8 camera for
as long as they could. For three minutes you can
look at these people and kind of see all their
thoughts, anxiety and self-consciousness seeping
out of them. There was also the exhibition with
Lieko Shiga in 2008 that I'm also still thinking
about. So it was a fun challenge for me to do my
show there, since the library is such a gem.

S B   It seems like some of the directors have taken more of
an interest in collecting books than others. What's the
history of that?

N S   Many of the directors have contributed a lot
of books, some of which, it seems, they got as
presents. I hope they'll re-make their library to
show the best books. I made a selection of these
– books that I think we should all look at – and
laid them out on a big round table. I found a first
edition of Anders Petersen's *Café Lehmitz* lying on
the floor. I also chose some of Torbjørn Rødland's
earlier books, because it seems he's always been
very conscious of the book and book making. I

picked a lot of photography books from the very beginning, and I had a book by Ane Hjort Guttu as well, a beautiful photo-text book that I hadn't seen before.

SB Have you seen the show at Fotogalleriet that's on now as we speak, *Pasenau and the Devil*?

NS Yes, and I loved Maria Pasenau's book *Whit Kind Regrets* that came out last year. Her project of taking back the male gaze on the nude female body is extremely poignant. Ever since the #MeToo revolution, I've wondered if and how the male gaze on the nude woman will survive. She's in complete control over what we see, and it's her own gaze on herself and on her friends' bodies.

SB It's quite a bold start from the director Antonio Cataldo in terms of programming, I must say.

NS Yes. I was wondering, as we're discussing Fotogalleriet, how it stands in comparison to other similar spaces in your opinion?

SB It's been very interesting doing the exhibition *Feast for the Eyes: The Story of Food in Photography*, since it's travelled to similar institutions in Europe, such as FOAM in Amsterdam, C/O Berlin, The Photographers' Gallery in London and the Hasselblad Foundation in Gothenburg, Sweden. They're similar because they're photography-specific, but on the whole, they're bigger in terms of space and profile. What's fascinating is that Fotogalleriet has a similar history to some of them – in that it was started in the 1970s by photographers who felt they didn't have an institutional space to show their work.

All the exhibition spaces I mention have a very strong standing within their community – as with Fotogalleriet. Although linked by medium, they all have very bold identities and stand out from one another. None of them really get enough funding and they're doing an amazing job on very little. In addition, it's an interesting time for them all as major museums are finally showing more photography and as photography

  Susan Bright in Conversation with Nina Strand

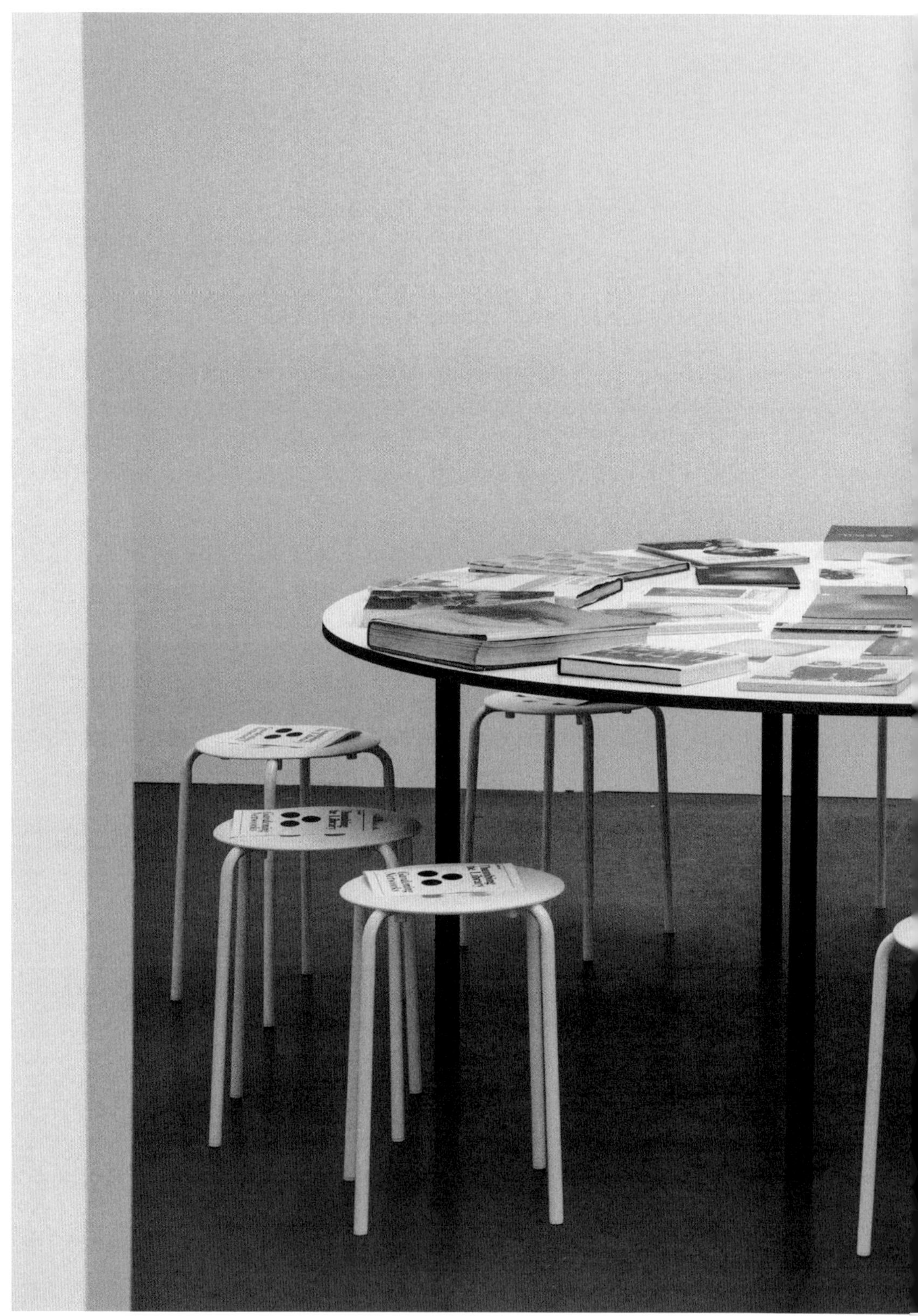

The Institutional Reset

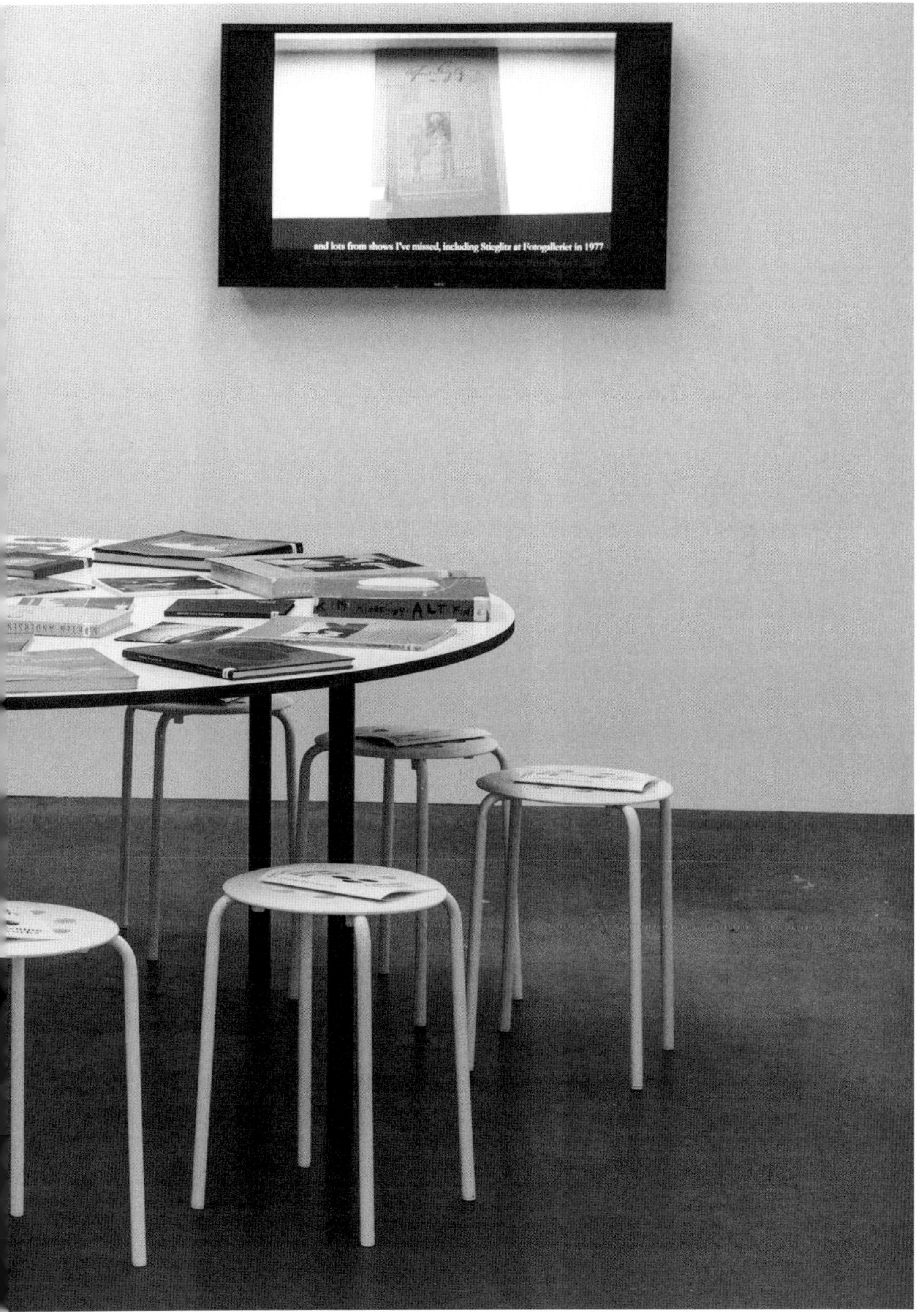

   Susan Bright in Conversation with Nina Strand

expands too – so I guess it's time to reassess their positions again in terms of being medium-specific spaces. What's their role and place in the larger arts ecosystem? What's important about them all is that they're all places for photographers, curators and editors to meet – they're part of a community. It's interesting that Paris doesn't have the same history as the other European cities, as well as Australia and America, where independent spaces started in the 1970s. Rémi Coignet told me that Le Bal was the first one to have a real sense of community in Paris. You don't just go to Le Bal to look at photography – you go to eat and visit the bookshop.

N S   In the country where photography was invented, they established Maison Européenne de la Photographie (MEP) in 1996, Henri Cartier Bresson Foundation in 2003, Jeu de Paume around 2000, and Le Bal in 2010.

S B   They all seem a bit late. I wonder why? But what's so remarkable about Paris is how many photo-specific exhibition spaces there are in comparison with other cities.

N S   We'll see what happens at MEP with the new director Simon Baker, who was the first photography curator at Tate Modern. He opened his tenure with shows by Ren Hang and Coco Capitán – maybe to get a new audience. In addition, this place has one of the very best libraries of photobooks that I know of thanks to Irène Attinger who worked there for thirty years.

S B   Speaking of books, have you seen any good exhibitions of books? What we've experienced in the past ten years in photography is a huge increase in photobooks, but I've yet to see a good exhibition on this expansion – either online or off. It seems that everyone wants to collect them, but when they're displayed you can never really see them. It's frustrating, since you lose all tactility, olfactory experience, intimacy and the personal rhythm of looking, which obviously is such an important part of experiencing books.

    The Institutional Reset

N S Well, here I'll be subjective, because we're making such a show in January – Fotogalleriet, Temple Paris and me. We're developing the thinking from the seminar *Photobook: Reset* that Bruno Cechel and Ann-Christin Bertrand did at C/O Berlin in September 2018. This considered whether the photobook is in crisis, both economically and existentially. We're continuing to reflect on this. Our point of departure for *Le Book Club* is whether the photobook can be the primary exhibition space. And if so, what will that exhibition space be?

S B How do you show this process? That's a rhetorical question – I know you're still thinking it through, so I don't expect an answer. You don't show this journey with any other art form, but somehow it seems so crucial to the making of a photobook that perhaps it needs to be shown somehow? I have a large archive of exhibition installations and design and I recently added an exhibition on Ladybird books. It was a wall – a massive installation – with all the covers. It really expressed the vastness of the series and the continuity of design. But I always want to touch them, feel them and smell them – and this is why I think I ultimately find exhibitions with books disappointing. As somebody who also makes books, how would you display yours?

N S I was happy to show work from my book *Dr. Strand* at a window gallery near the City Hall when I launched it, but since the book, zine and magazine is my 'gallery', it wasn't essential for mc. It was the placement more than anything. The book is about my late mother, who once held a speech there on the International Workers Day. The same year, three zines in my series *Artist Stories* were accepted at the annual Autumn Exhibition in Oslo, and I was happy to install them as an actual art piece on the wall, where people could also read them.

S B I'm very interested in your different areas of work. You curate, edit *Objektiv* magazine and you're also an artist.

                                      Susan Bright in Conversation with Nina Strand

I hate the term 'juggling'. I don't see these things as separate – do you? How do all these things feed into one another for you?

N S   The work with *Objektiv* helps me get my own work done. Interviewing other artists and writing about photography is inspiring and also motivating for me. I see my work with *Objektiv* and my texts on photography as a part of my artistic practice, and many others I know work with multiple hats on, such as being an artist/teacher/writer/curator. As W.J.T. Mitchell says in *Objektiv* #14: 'In art school today the old idea of the artist going to the studio and making something and putting it in a gallery and then remaining silent is long gone. The art schools today tell you that you'd better learn to write, and you have to write about your own art, and you have to learn to talk about it. You have to speak.' This also includes writing about other artist's work, to act as art critics in a way, and many artists state that writing about art challenges their own art.

S B   Gilda Williams – the author of *How to Write About Contemporary Art* – said a similar thing, and mentioned that writers are joining the art department rather than creative-writing departments at Goldsmiths where she teaches in London. Everything is becoming more reliant on everything else. I think this expanding of what's expected of certain roles can only be a good thing, and more inclusive. Because of this, multi-hyphen careers are more common now than ten years ago. It's interesting to me that you mentioned Ole John Aandal earlier. He was a director of Fotogalleriet, but also maintained his career as an artist. Others I know stop one career and switch to another, as both are pretty absorbing – especially when you work full time at an institution. I self-identity as a curator and always have done. The writer bit of my title is part and parcel of that and I've become much more comfortable with it over the span of my career. For me, curating is an art that involves accompanying, sharing and exchanging knowledge, by placing value in dialogue and making it visible through research. I consider the curatorial space a site of collec-

   The Institutional Reset

tive learning, for the artist, the audience and myself. This needs to be based on relations of partnership, solidarity and sharing. This can be done through a myriad of cultural expressions, as well as exhibitions. It's taken me a long time to really understand this.

I can't have one without the other – curating and writing are intertwined. They feed off one another. Both are forms of thinking through research. I'm beginning to write more about other aspects in my life and this is essential to how I curate. Of course, what's happened now is the word 'curator' is so overstretched and I see people use (and misuse) the word in their job title when really they've achieved so little – it's a handy catch-all. The growth of festivals has encouraged this and also social networking – it assumes that curating is putting pictures in an order. As with the line that 'everyone is a photographer now', it can be said that everyone is also a curator and a writer. A lot of it's just extraneous noise. You still have to make sure that what you do stands out as something worth looking at, reading or paying attention to. You have to say something!

What other trends or changes have you noticed over the course of *Objektiv*'s ten years? We've touched on more abstract and sculptural work being the norm, the elasticity of jobs and the increase in the photobook. Anything else?

N S   When we launched our nineteenth issue with Temple Arles Books during the Rencontres d'Arles in 2019 we invited the audience to join us in making mind maps for the future, brainstorming on what tendencies have been strong since 2010. Sculptural photography, the ever-expanding photobook, diary photography and photography as sociology are still very much on the scene. Diary photography is represented today by many artists, including the already mentioned Capitán, and Pasenau. Photography as sociology makes me think of the work of Deana Lawson or Frida Orupabo. Lawson, with her multifaceted representations of black iconography, describes her photographs as negotiating knowledge of selfhood through a corporeal dimension, and Orupabo with her raw collages looks closely at

      Susan Bright in Conversation with Nina Strand

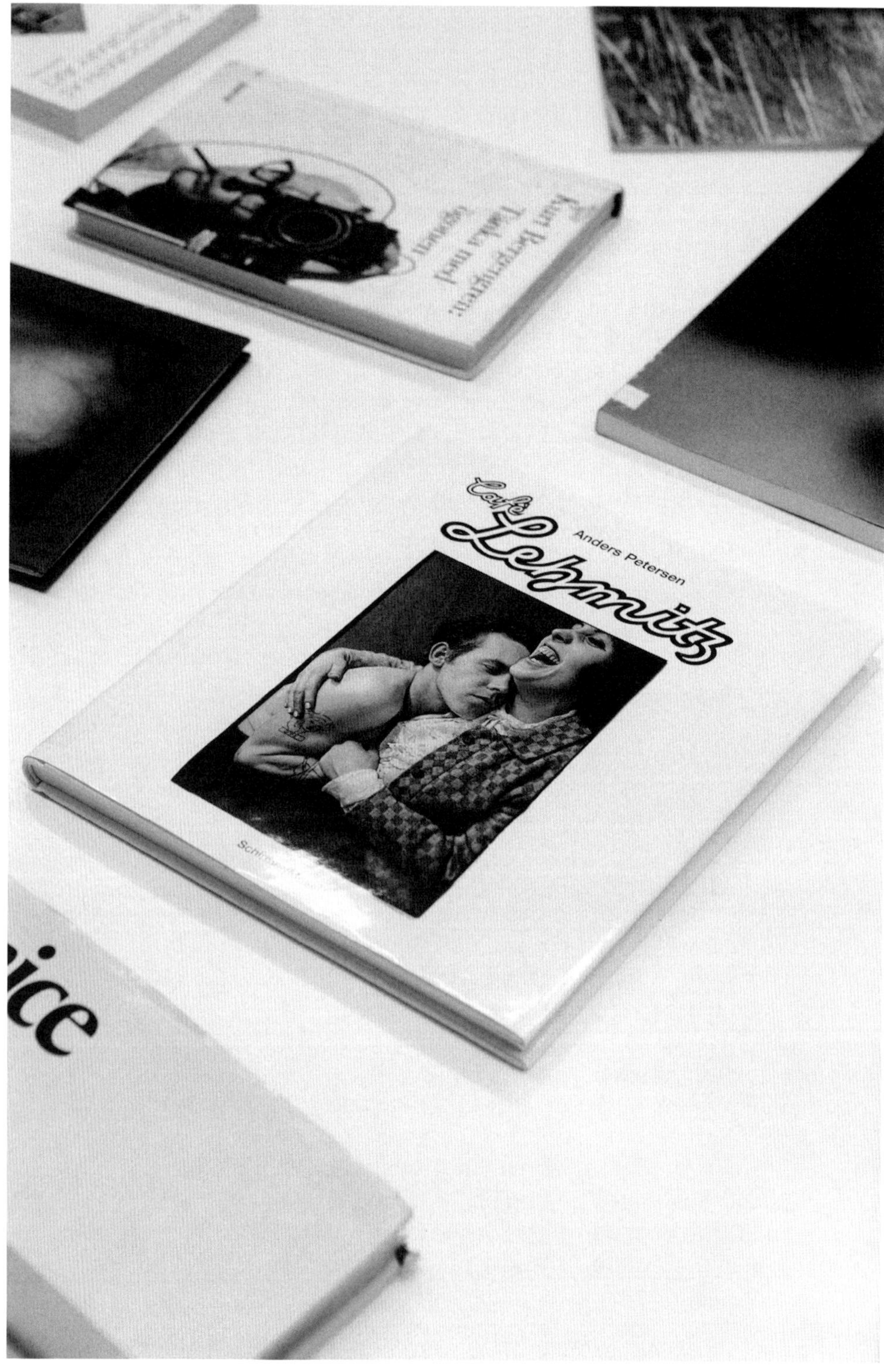

The Institutional Reset

the black body. The portraits of Jakob Landvik
or Elle Pérez, working with their peers from the
LGBTQIA+ community as their subjects, and
visualising the complexities of gender identity,
also fit into this category.

S B

I think *Aperture* has been instrumental in championing this approach to photography in its magazine. And other institutions in NYC such as Red Hook Labs must also be noted for their work with the community. But for all these changes, situations within institutions are less fluid. Overwhelmingly white, male directors with a majority of female staff working underneath them is still the norm across most of the bigger institutions that work with art and photography – from museums to tech creative directors. It's very easy to get disillusioned. I've been saying this for so long – I'm the person everyone rolls their eyes at, thinking 'Here she goes again'. However, I am an optimist, and as much as I want changes to happen overnight, I know that it's a process. I was listening to an interview with veteran tennis player Billy Jean King the other day and she made the very astute point that when you read history it seems to go fast, but when you live it, it's so slow. So it's left up to those who aren't in a situation of privilege and dominance to keep pushing and demanding changes from the groups that still dominate. Things can only change when those dominant groups accept changes and, crucially, implement them. How will they know if changes are even necessary if people don't continue to point it out? I've found it's best to view this as exciting rather than exhausting.

N S

I'm sure Fotogalleriet will be at the forefront of this future change for the photographic institution. And I am excited to be working alongside you to look closer at how we reset the photographic festival. How to make a festival in the middle of a global pandemic when we don't know what the art scene – or the photography scene – will look like after a vaccine is found and confinement is over.

Susan Bright in Conversation with Nina Strand

S B

Yes, it will certainly be a curatorial challenge. And one that's long overdue if I'm honest. Festivals needed a rethink. The structures were beginning to feel very 'samey' from country to country. In addition the arts in general have traditionally been drawn to international line-ups. With the pandemic and environmental concerns this has to be reconsidered. For 'f/stop' we'll all have to look more closely into the local situation as well as internationally when considering the display and dissemination of images. Structurally we've discussed the need for slower rhythms, horizontal structures and more local engagement working alongside the international element of the festival. We really want this festival to be different from past editions. It's about balance and creativity, globalism and locality and an assessment of where we are now. I'm also looking forward to intersecting online and onsite contexts with the continuation of the *Visual Wanderings* series you started on the *Objektiv* site.

N S

It's a tumultuous time, also with the BLM movement in the midst of the pandemic. I hope this will develop into a revolution for people of colour as #MeToo was for women. Both things are addressed in the series, where we're inviting photographers from many different countries to create art that responds to our new situation: what does the lock-down mean for their work, what's important for them to convey, and what are their reflections on the time to come? Each photographer picks another artist to create a work, and in this way, we hope to create a visual dialogue that runs across many different countries, in order to get a bigger picture of how this crisis and its aftermath are playing out for photographers all over the world.

S B

We're committed to trying new processes and experimenting with other ways of imagining and building a common space. In order to do so, we aim to assemble a 'work in progress' in many ways. We'll embrace curating in its most expanded form, and I hope we'll extend the possibilities and reach of a festival. By treating the festival as an ongoing discourse, and mode of reflection, we hope to reach outwards whilst also allowing the festival and ourselves to be challenged by the complex situation of our time.

 The Institutional Reset

Ane Hjort Guttu's work has been shown on several occasions at Fotogalleriet, the most recent being the solo exhibition Furniture Isn't Just Furniture *in 2017. Mike Sperlinger is a professor at Oslo National Academy of the Arts. Ane Hjort Guttu and Mike Sperlinger met in Oslo, November 2019.*

Mike Sperlinger   Could you talk about *Smalvollen* [2004], which is one of your earliest works and was the first thing you showed at Fotogalleriet, as part of the show *Something out of Nothing*?[80] It's an interesting, polemical work about photography.

80
Something Out of Nothing took place at Fotogalleriet in 2007. The group exhibition was curated by Susan Bright and displayed works by Margareta Bergman, Else Marie Hagen, Espen Tveit, and Ole John Aandahl, as well as Ane Hjort Guttu.

Ane Hjort Guttu   Yes, I started out as an art photographer, and that work was a response to the feeling that I couldn't really take photographs any more. I made a project called *Modernistic Journey* [2002], which was about the suburbs of Oslo and the architecture there. Then I realised that there's something very problematic about photography in the sense that it always looks *nice* – or rather you can make everything look nice. You can make the disorderly look orderly, you can romanticise disorder. It's very hard to get out of that romanticism. I realised that I had to stop photographing.

MS   What kind of work were you excited about at the time?

AHG   I was influenced by the whole German tradition, Bernd and Hilla Becher onwards, and Lewis Baltz and the New Topographics, which I addressed in *Smalvollen*. And also Norwegian landscape photographers like Per Berntsen or Tom Sandberg. There was a whole generation of photographers in the 1990s that somehow related to these older photographers from the 1970s and 1980s. Then I found out that I didn't want to do that anymore; it was too easy and too limited, and too patriarchal as well, when I look back at it. *Smalvollen* was a statement about that.

MS   *Smalvollen* is based on this district in east Oslo. What was so special about that site?

                    Stating the Obvious

AHG   It's very pictorial. It has this mix of forgotten nature, which somehow develops by itself, and small industry – heaps of old cars and tyres. It's a typical SLOAP [Space Left Over After Planning]. The river Alna flows through it, which has been covered over in most of the rest of Groruddalen. So there was also a political side to the choice of this place, because it's the east side of Oslo, which was heavily developed for industry, and you can only find this river now if you really search it out. The work included two non-figurative, almost Constructivist or Brutalist sculptures in concrete lying on the floor. They were a bit topographic, you might say, and I stated that they represented – not directly depicted, but represented – two different parts of Smalvollen. Then there was a webpage that contained photographs, snapshots of me and my friends going on a tour, which I arranged in this area. I guess the statement was that this place can't be pictured; it has to be represented in a different way to capture its specific spirit or characteristics.

MS You say those sculptures represent the place, but they're really in the language of abstraction – was this a kind of parody, a negative gesture?

AHG   I don't think it was negative; it was very sincere. I actually felt that we have to find another strategy for representing these areas, because we love these kinds of unruly landscapes, but you can't depict them through photography. The idea was that there would be no pictures of the place in the exhibition space; they were only on the webpage, and not professional photos in any way, just documentation from this tour that I'd made. The point was to state that someone had taken the trip there, and that the place could really only be experienced if you were there.

MS Did you stop working with photography after that and move into film?

AHG   I continued working with photography, but it was in a different way – for example, in my work about the suburbs, *Å bo i drabantby* [2004], where I was referring to other traditions of photography and not trying to express myself through it any more.

            Ane Hjort Guttu in Conversation with Mike Sperlinger

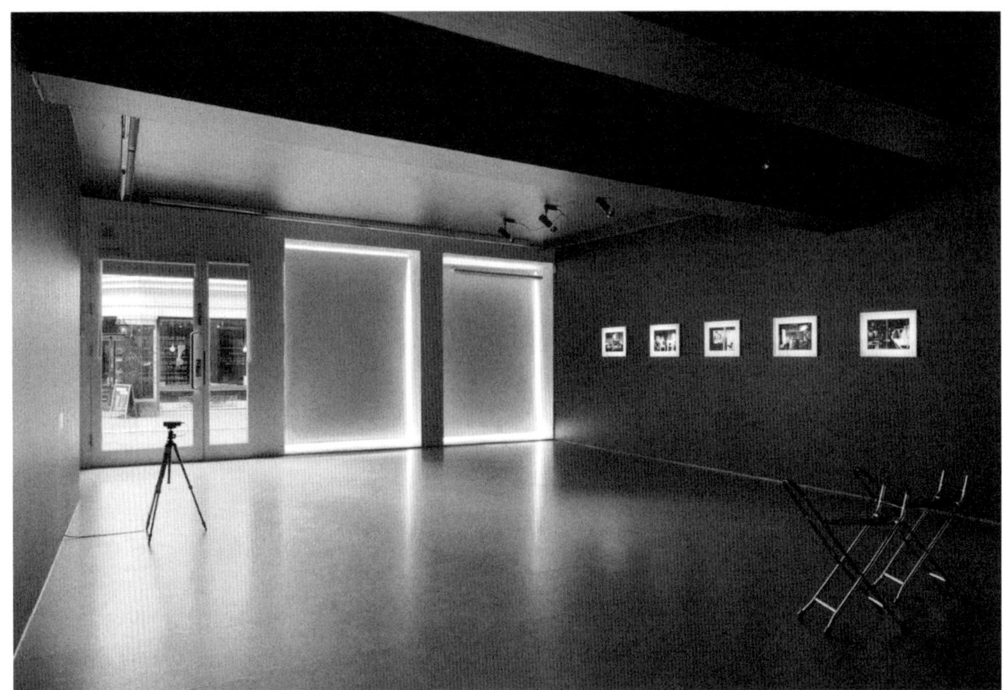

M S   Photography features as subject matter in many
of your films – there are at least two that rely on
still images with narration, for example. But other
works, like *Four Studies of Oslo and New York*
[2012] or *Furniture Isn't Just Furniture* [2017], seem
to start out implicitly from commercial genres of
photography like the property portfolio image or
the IKEA catalogue.

A H G   I went away from trying to reach something new in
photography into examining how photography is used,
and how to disrupt these existing picture schemes.
Maybe that was the only way I could access photography. Then I started working with a cinematographer
and she, of course, believed in her own images, but for
me it's really difficult!

M S Can we jump to the much more recent work you
showed at Fotogalleriet in 2017, *Furniture Isn't Just
Furniture*? It's a very different piece of work from
Smalvollen, but maybe there are some parallels.
There's this sense of being located on the periphery of the city, for example, the exurban space of
IKEA. But if *Smalvollen* was about the challenge
of representing the specificity of this space on the
periphery of the city, *Furniture* seems to be about
the promise, or the threat, of universality.

A H G Yes, or the generic – generic images, and also generic
language of course. It's a banal set-up: two people are
literally trapped in the furniture of an IKEA store, and
they treat it as if it were an artistic project. The idea
they have is to immerse themselves in this commercial
environment, and then come out on the other side with
something real or true – because I'm dealing with this
idea of the true, I think, in all my work. I don't really
know what I think about that film, but the most interesting aspect is that idea: instead of trying to get away
from what's typical or generic all the time, to go *through*
that. Or as Genet says, 'To escape the horror, bury
yourself in it.'[81] In fact, my new film about an art school
has the same idea: you're in the belly of the beast and
from there you can do something subversive, perhaps.

81
From *Our Lady of the Flowers*
by Jean Genet (1943).

M S The characters in *Furniture* are like pierrots, or
figures from a late Beckett play.

A H G They're typical theatrical figures. The idea was to
merge these two stereotypical identities or environments: IKEA and theatre in the tradition of Robert
Wilson or the like. I also had this Beckettian idea of
stating the obvious. I was inspired by a text discussing
the tree in *Waiting for Godot*, where the writer claims
that the tree is a 'symbol of a symbol' – a kind of
pompous prop that's dismantled from within the play.
Vladimir and Estragon comment on this tree throughout the play. And my idea was to go through this banal
set-up, of people stuck in their middle-class lives, and
come out on the other side. So it's the opposite of *Smalvollen*, where I tried to do something non-representa-
tional to represent the place.

  Ane Hjort Guttu in Conversation with Mike Sperlinger

M S But there's another element consistent with a
lot of your work, which is this very ambivalent
relationship to the rhetoric of art making. There's
a moment where one character says, 'We must
keep believing that what we do is important, even
if it just makes a few people think again, see the
world in a new way.' The idea of an artwork not
being universally understandable, but maybe it's
enough if one person understands it – what's your
relationship to that?

A H G That's the rhetoric of the whole of art education, I
think, or the simplified version of it. I guess I was
trying to merge that language, which we use all the
time, with the commercial language of something
like IKEA. Of course, in that context, it just becomes
another cliché and that's what's so sad about the whole
scene. They hate this language, they hate the situation,
so they try to support themselves by repeating this tru-
ism from art, that 'if just one or two people think some
new thoughts because of it …' [Laughter] I think that's
where hope collapses in the film.

M S Can you say something more about the role of
language in your own work?

A H G Mostly, my work is about spoken language and images.
The whole idea of speaking about what's in the image
I find incredibly interesting: this doubleness that appears when you describe an image. I'm not so interested
in the idea that the image is supposed to be alone and
speak for itself. I actually hate this romanticism around
the image, and the big white border around the photograph, the idea of showing not telling, all of that – I
think it's terrible!

M S You're also interested in strategies of representation, but several of your works, like *The Paper is
the Line's World* [2007] or *Untitled (City at Night)*
[2013], depict artists working with different forms
of abstraction. You seem to be fascinated but also
puzzled by the languages of formalism, by the
intensity these artists invest in questions about
particular shapes or forms of mark-making.

                                     Stating the Obvious

AHG   I think that I operate with all these alter egos, which these people represent, because I can't really *be* the person who believes in these squares and circles – I have to go through some other kind of figure to be interested. I'm more interested in their struggle than in their questions, maybe.

MS   And what's their struggle?

AHG   I think it's about *practising* poetry, as the Surrealists put it – accessing a completely different way of approaching the world, or transgressing your own limitations. And it's about investing in these abstract forms – they must represent something that's very deep and personal, and which can't be expressed in another way in that particular time or context.

MS   It seems the flipside of that in your work is the cognitive dissonance of being an artist who's politicised and living in the world, but trying to reckon with it through those formalist or modernist ideas. So the films invoke the figure of homelessness again and again, as a quite raw, literal manifestation of who and what you step over on the way to the studio – which is maybe the sceptical alter ego.

AHG   Yes, the flipside of not being that person who can stand within the fascination of form is that you're always torn between identifying with that person and stepping outside into a social context where the artist becomes pathetic, in a way – the gesture becomes pathetic.

MS   But your work oscillates between those perspectives; it doesn't moralise or settle on one of them.

AHG   Isn't it like that when you see a struggling figure? You identify with that person, but then suddenly you're out of that identification and then you see how helpless they are, or how closed. I have the same feeling when I speak to students: I'm able to go completely into their mindset, their own world that they conjure up, and I can see that in this cup [picks up her coffee cup] there's

    Ane Hjort Guttu in Conversation with Mike Sperlinger

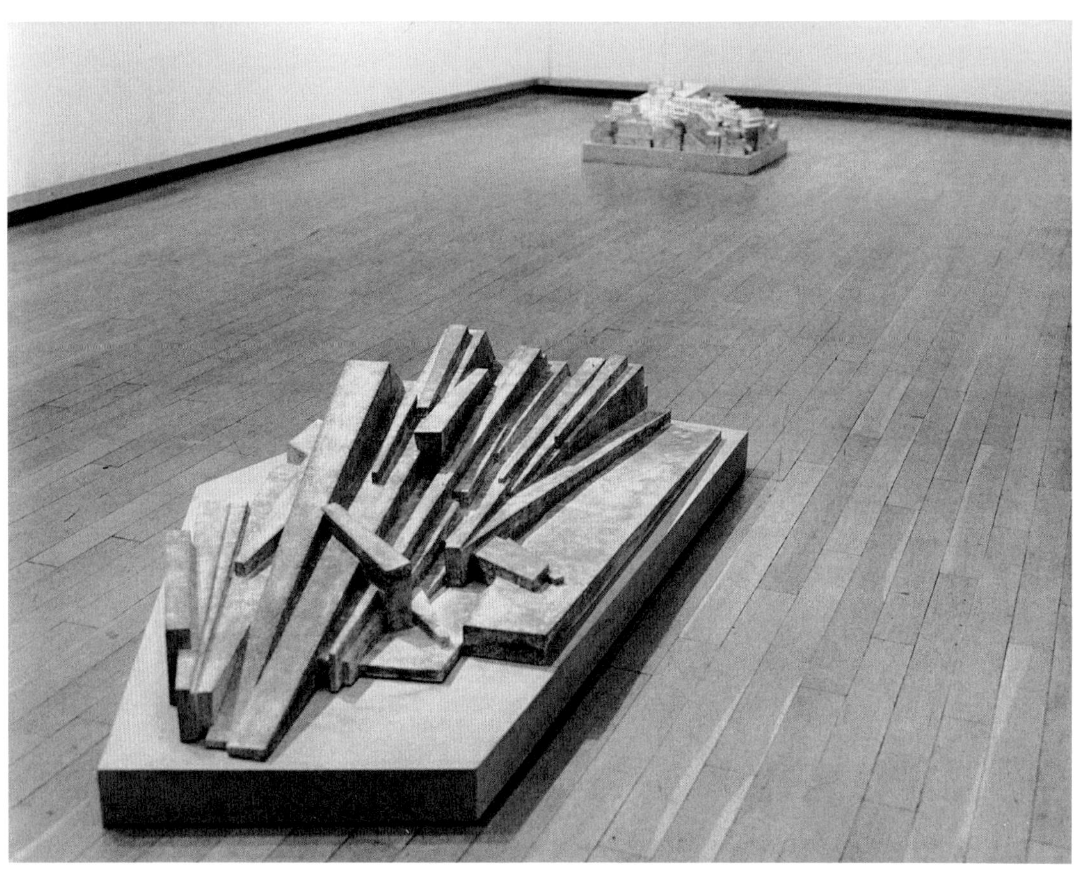

Stating the Obvious

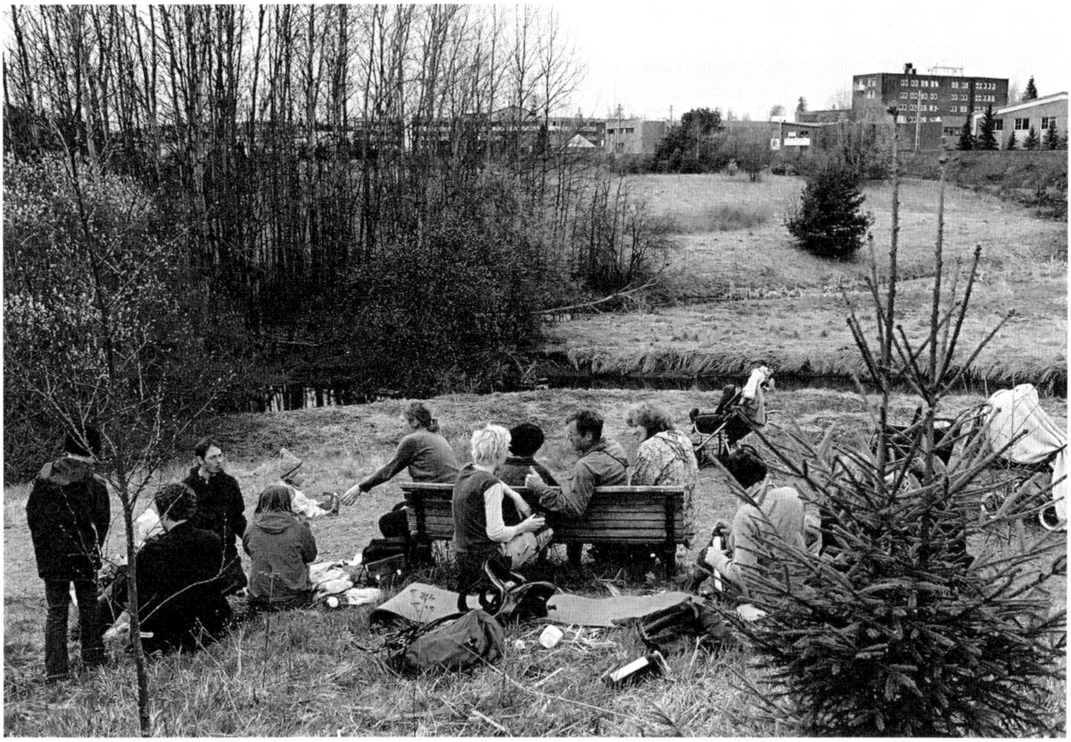

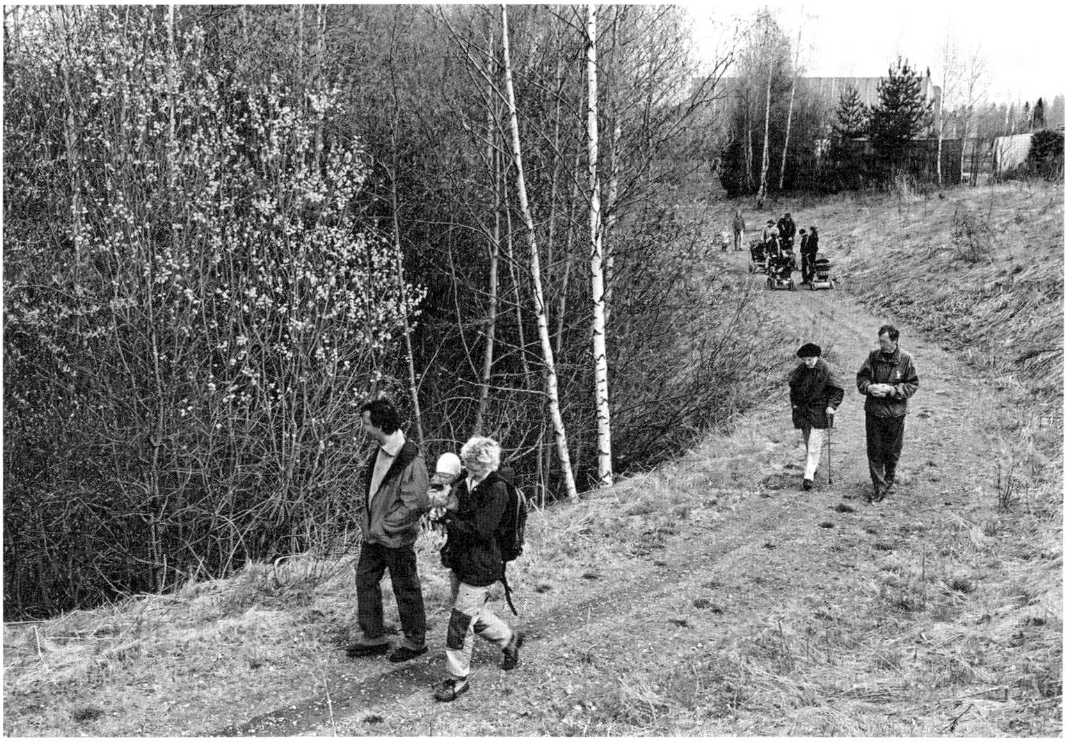

     Ane Hjort Guttu in Conversation with Mike Sperlinger

something more, something enormous, and it's universal and fantastic … And then suddenly, it breaks and you go outside, and it's just a cup and it can never be anything else, and the whole project is – limited. I think that's fascinating, and sad, because a central dream for the avantgardes of the twentieth century was of course that art and life should become one. And you can't really be an artist if you can't believe this cup has enormous possibilities, but at the same time, you can't just stay there.

M S   But what is your relationship to a figure like Lee Lozano, for example? In works like *Untitled (City at Night)* or *Time Passes* [2015], there's this flirtation with the idea that to face that contradiction honestly, as an artist, ultimately might mean to step out of art entirely.

A H G   I'm really fascinated by Lee Lozano, and she's even quoted in *Time Passes*, with a portrait hanging on an art school wall. It's a natural 'parallel' thought for most artists, I think, to leave the art world. It's great that someone actually did it, so we can have this work to refer to.

M S   What about her late work – for example, deciding not to speak to women any more?

A H G   I think that's a super-intelligent work, but I can't really say why. I mean, not speaking to men would be really bad! [Laughter] I think there's this weird contradiction in that work: of course, it's not good, morally, but it's a good work.

M S   Your works often contain fictional narratives about artists – they become like fables about artistic extremes. What would it mean to take abstraction completely seriously, for example, or to make hundreds of drawings and never show them, like the artist in *Untitled (City at Night)*, or to become a beggar as a work, like the character in *Time Passes*, or to be Lee Lozano and not speak to women? What's powerful about these figures isn't necessarily the works they've made, or their art-historical traces, but the human stories.

    Stating the Obvious

A H G   Which is also a bit sad. But my fascination and scepticism also has to do with class, I think, because I
come from this mixed-class background: a west-end
bourgeois family on my mother's side, and a quite
poor working-class background on my father's. So I've
always been oscillating between these cultures. That's
why I think it can be hard for the children of artists
to become artists themselves. Of course, they can be
talented, but they have this sense that art is self-evident,
a natural choice for them. I step outside of art all the
time and see how little it appeals to a lot of people, and
what kind of threshold there is just to walk into an art
space for many people.

M S   In some of the recent works, there seems to be
this interest in not just a more accessible content,
but also a different kind of distribution. These
are works that are hovering on the edge of being
narrative short films, which could potentially be
shown in very different kinds of contexts. How
important is that idea of other contexts to you?

A H G   I'm a little confused about it. There's this possibility
of distribution – film-festival culture, or selling your
work to TV stations etc – which for a long time I didn't
understand because I came from the art field. Then I
was very interested in that for a couple of years, because
it seemed to work, and now I'm a bit sceptical again!
[Laughter] Because I feel that it's very hard to find
contexts for films that are as complex and interesting
as the art field. I find myself explaining in a very simple way, getting very simple questions about the film,
or being curated very literally – for example, a festival
line-up where films about suburbs were all in the same
programme.

M S   So you feel caught between those worlds?

A H G   When I was in the Timisoara Biennial recently, I felt
as if I was coming home.[82] There was a kind of respect
and complexity within the curation and the works of
the other artists. I love being in contact with very different media and aesthetic strategies. At the moment, I

82
The Art Encounters Biennial
2019, held in Timisoara, Ro-
mania.

    Ane Hjort Guttu in Conversation with Mike Sperlinger

don't have any students working with film and it's very inspiring to talk about sculpture or painting – to me it's ultimately the same questions we're dealing with in film.

Maria Pasenau held her first solo institutional show at Fotogalleriet in August–October 2019. Pasenau and the Devil *was a threefold project consisting of an immersive multimedia installation of newly commissioned photographic and sculptural pieces, a nomadic video work and a publication. Bjørn Hatterud is an author, curator, and noise musician who grew up in redneck, blue-collar areas of the Norwegian countryside. He is disabled, queer and deviant in every way. They spoke on 23 February 2020 at Shoddyfabrikken in the infamous suburbs of Groruddalen in Oslo.*

Maria Pasenau

When I was busy on the Fotogalleriet exhibition, it was extremely hard work. I had this urge to do *everything.* I was like: 'I want to do a CD, I want to do a book, I want to do films, I want to do sculpture, I want to do photographs, I want to do poems, I want to redo the whole room.' It drove me completely crazy. What got me through this period was the thought that it could help me buy a house.

Bjørn Hatterud   That's quite a big investment.

M P

I was actually looking at houses in Denmark, but the bank told me that they wouldn't give me a loan to buy something abroad. So I had to look in Norway and then I found one in Odda that suited me best.

B H   So you bought it?

M P

Yes, and it only cost Kr. 500,000 – for half a house – and it costs practically nothing to live there. We can travel wherever we want and make use of residences. That's how it is when you're an artist – it doesn't really matter all that much where one lives. I think it's better to be in a place where you can really work, where you don't have all that much else in the way of input.

B H   Many artists here in Oslo pay around 10,000
a month in rent, along with such heavy fixed
monthly expenditure that it's impossible to take a
chance with anything else.

M P   Yes, the risk is so big. It's quite difficult to be an artist. During the six months I was working on the Fotogalleriet exhibition, my partner Tore was living in Berlin, and I was paying a lot extra for the flat we had in Oslo. I had to work at JapanPhoto to be able to do the exhibition, because you don't get a regular salary from working as an artist.

B H I think there's a big difference between artists who come from families where there's a lot of money and those who come from families where there isn't. If you come from a wealthy background, or marry someone with a lot of money, money is no big hassle. For most of us, money means stress.

M P   True enough, but it can be nice to live without so much expenditure. And to be able to use the money one has on art – that's important for me. That's what I do too. I've recently published a new book with money from the book I launched in connection with the Fotogalleriet exhibition. It's really awesome to be able to do things like that.

B H And it's also great not to have to explain the project to someone so they'll give you money. When did you start photographing?

M P   It was when I was on holiday with my mum and dad. I was so bored I started to take pictures with dad's camera. He found it annoying because there were all these pictures of flowers and other stuff between each family photo. That was why I got my own camera.

B H How old were you then?

M P   I bought my first camera with money from my confirmation, a mirror-reflex camera. That was when I started seriously, and what's funny is that I started to take self-portraits even then. I took photos with a slow shutter – sort of heavenly or ghostlike pictures. And I became a member of Drammen photo club.

                Maria Pasenau in Conversation with Bjørn Hatterud

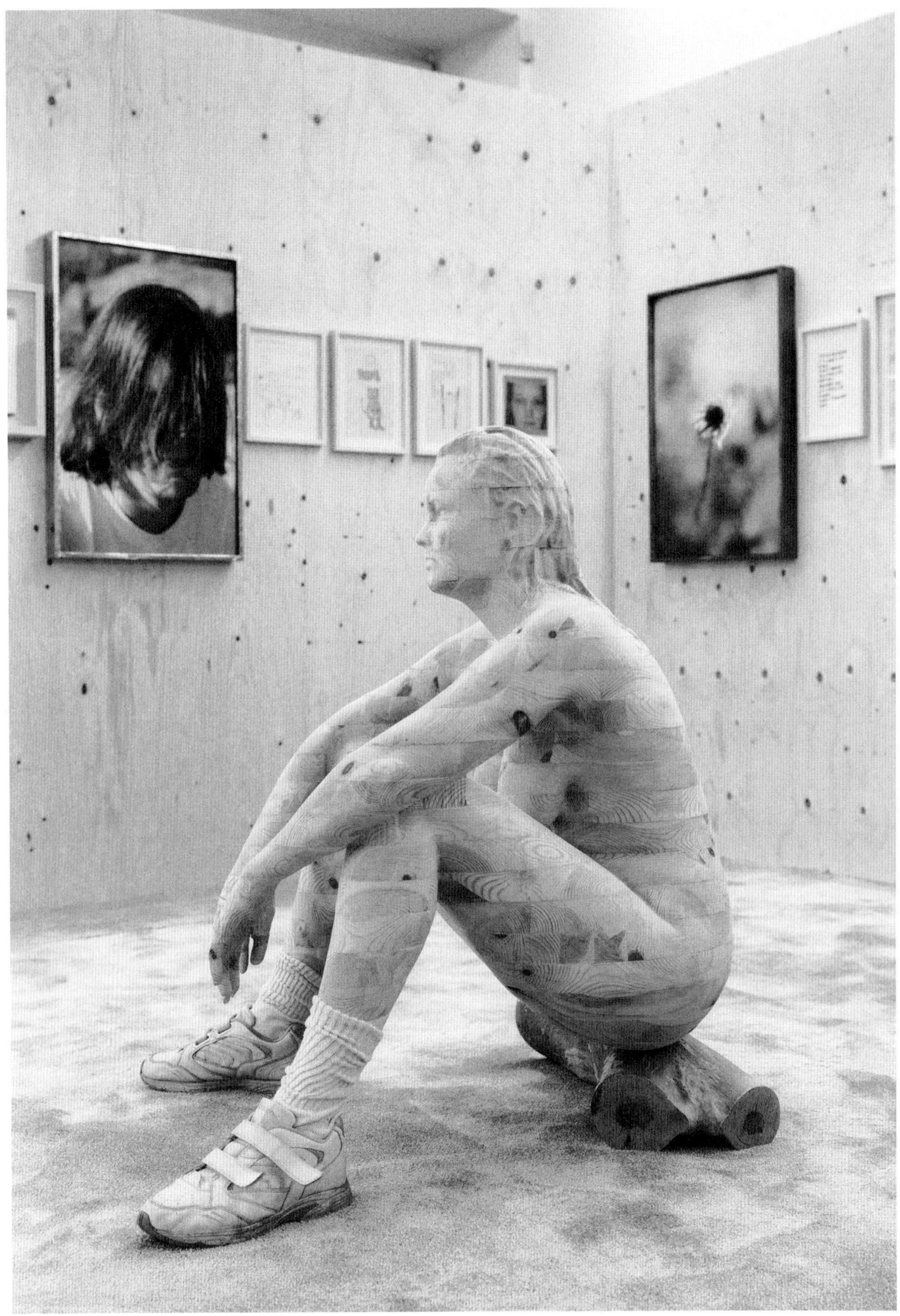

218. Looking for Freedom

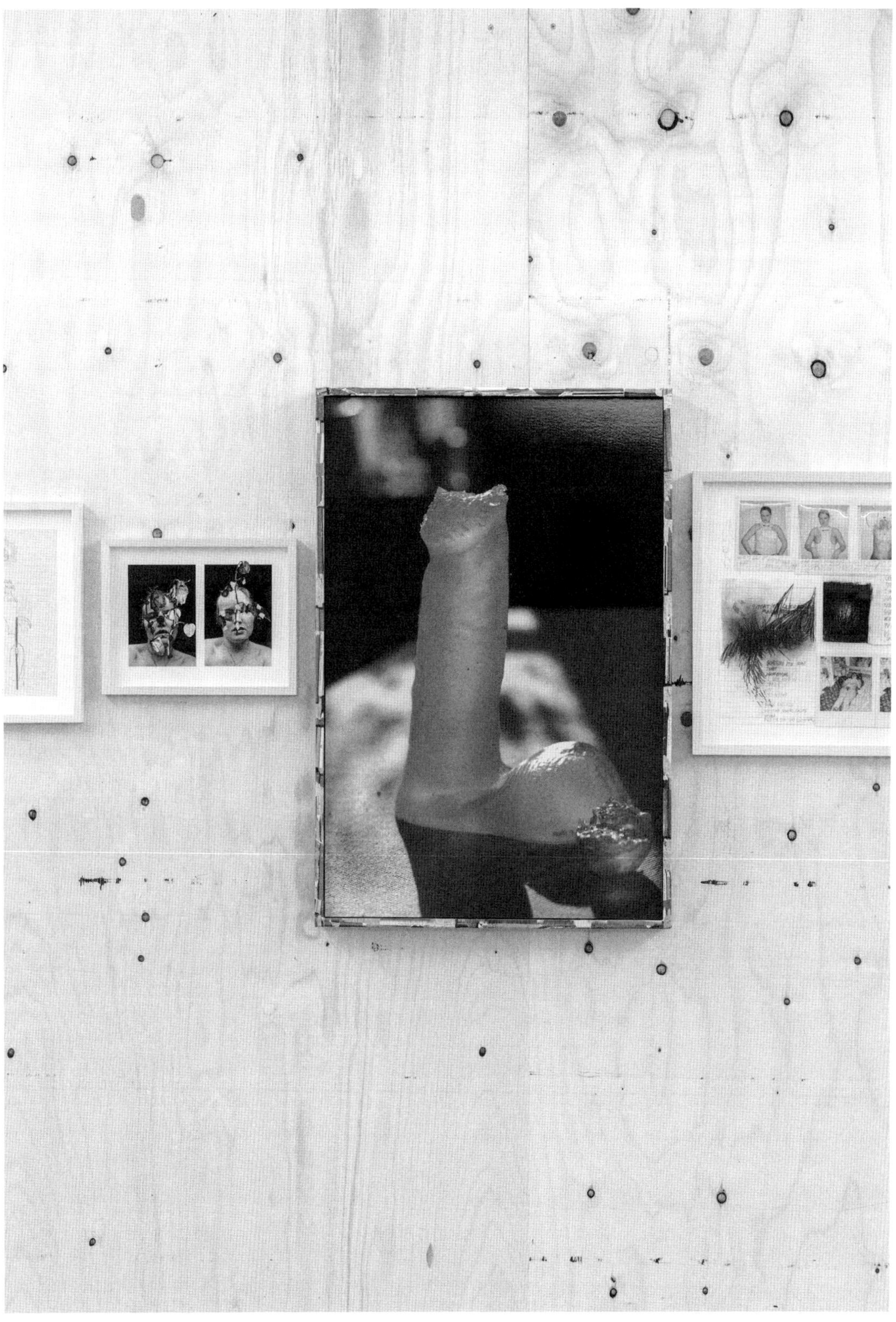

 Maria Pasenau in Conversation with Bjørn Hatterud

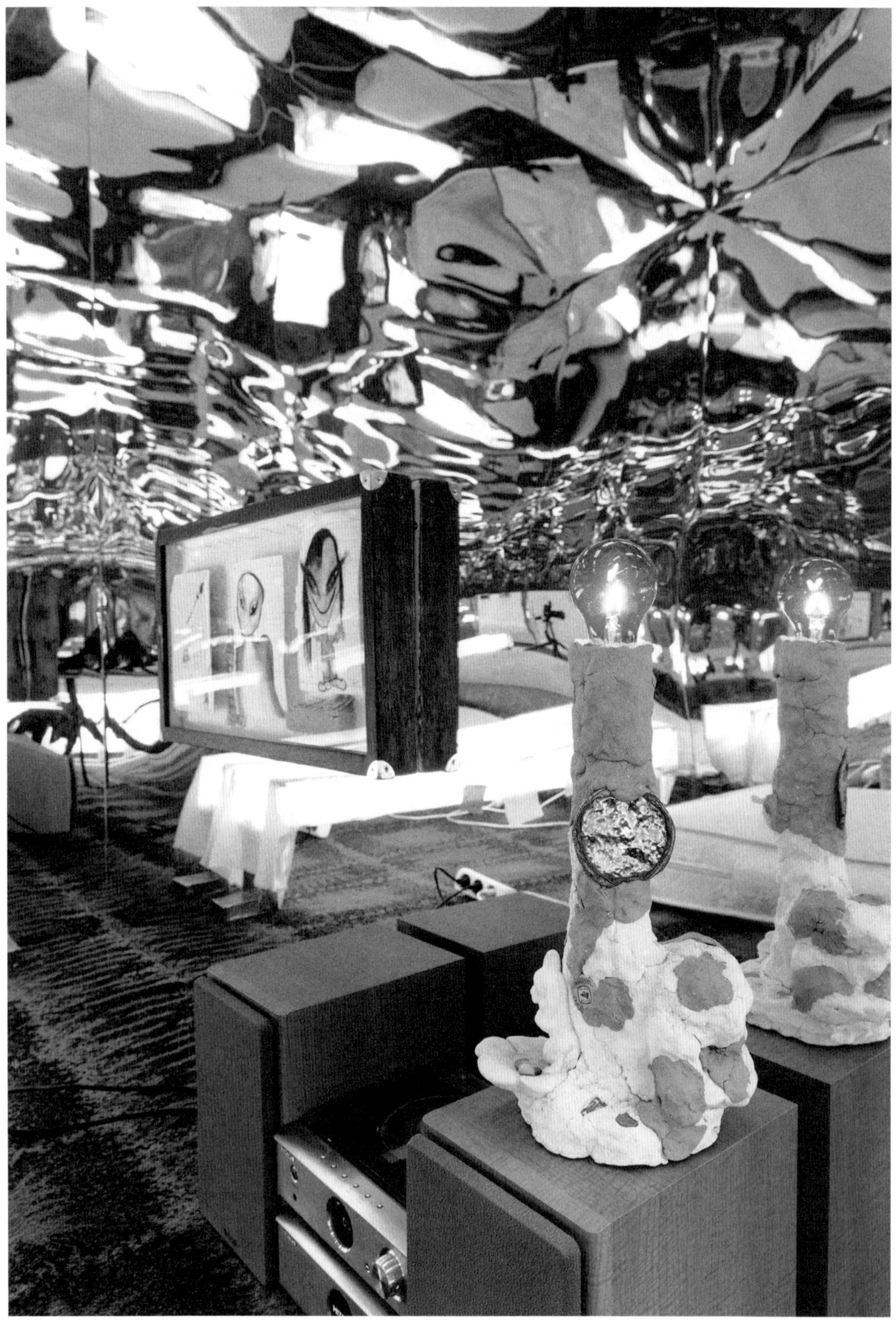

 Looking for Freedom

B H   I was just about to ask if you joined a photo club.

M P   The club was mostly old men. They were very keen
on us learning about shutter and blender, and all that
sort of stuff, so I learnt a bit about it before I started on
media and communication in upper secondary.

B H   When you entered that environment, did you go
along to exhibitions and stuff like that?

M P   I think we perhaps had an exhibition with the youth
group, but there wasn't that sort of thing, no.

B H   How old were you when you left home?

M P   It was just after upper secondary. Then I moved away
as far as possible, away from my parents. Well, people move abroad, but I didn't know any English, so
Trondheim was in a way the furthest I could get. I
moved there and started at the Norwegian School of
Photography. It was important for me that they had a
dark room, because I wanted to work with analogue
photography. At the same time, I gained access to the
rest of my confirmation money, so I never needed to say
no to anything. I was always out with the others, was
completely free and took lots – really lots – of analogue
photographs.

B H   Of people you met and situations you were in?

M P   Yes, just friends really. We partied, had fun, bathed and
took photos.

B H   So you found a milieu at the school?

M P   Yes, there was a group of friends who always hung out
together. I seized chances to talk to people who visited the school. I made contact and sent emails to lots
of people I simply liked, such as Morten Andersen. I
sent him an email and said 'Hi, I really dig what you
do, shall we go out for a coffee when I'm in Oslo?', and

   Maria Pasenau in Conversation with Bjørn Hatterud

we did. Then I sent a message to Bjarne Melgaard. He never answered, but it was worth it later, because he saw the message when we became friends. My mum always told me I shouldn't be afraid of making contact with people.

B H   The worst thing that can possibly happen is a no.

M P   Yes, or that you don't get an answer. Taking the initiative was tremendously important for me. Lots of people think the school should do everything for you, but that's not true at all. You have to seize chances. When I attended the arts' school Prosjektskolen in Oslo, people said, 'I wish I was in an art environment', and I'd think, 'Well, you are. You're at Prosjektskolen, you've got the best teachers, all the coolest artists in Oslo come here and give lectures. Make friends with them!'

B H   When did you start at Prosjektskolen?

M P   After Trondheim, I lived at home for a summer, then I moved to Oslo. I worked on a night watch at Shell, in Bjørnsletta, for half a year. I thought I could do photography and have that job on the side, because it was only every other week. That winter I met Matias Kiil, and he told me about Prosjektskolen, so I quit the job and started there. It was brilliant and cool. At the school in Trondheim I was often criticised because people felt analogue was out. There was a completely different freedom at Prosjektskolen.

B H   When people look at your first book, *Whit Kind Regrets Pasenau*, which has some photos from when you were at Prosjektskolen, they might think 'This girl is simply out on the town' and that this is the most hyper-urban life, since you're always outdoors in the city streets. But a lot of it's been staged, hasn't it?

M P   No, the photos really are from that period. They're pictures from when I moved to Oslo and up to 2018. That's what life was like then. We were out a lot. I couldn't have taken those photos at any other time.

    Looking for Freedom

B H   During the past two or three years, it seems as if
you've gone through a kind of maturing phase.

M P   Yes, a big one. I think it's important that the projects
I undertake show a development of my artistry. I'm
twenty-five years old now. I feel old to be me.

B H   I've noticed that when you photograph men,
they're nearly always sensitive and vulnerable,
but with the women it's as if they're just about to
attack you, like a python or something. Are you
conscious of this?

M P   No, I haven't really thought about it before. I do what
I think is interesting. I pick up the camera if there's
something I think is important.

B H   So you articulate the concepts and thoughts in
your head first?

M P   No, no, no. It's the situation that I think is interesting.
It doesn't have all that much to do with the picture,
really.
      You have to learn to pick up the camera at the right
moment, so that it becomes part of you. So that it won't
feel wrong if you pick it up and the situation becomes
different.

B H   So it becomes more of a tool to capture something.

M P   Yes. It's the same when I write texts or draw – it's the
same thing for me, in a way.

B H   In your latest book there aren't all that many photographs – more drawings and texts.

M P   It starts with a picture of me when I was little and the
text 'My list of organised certified stuff. I don't believe
that everything started with a big bang. Who told you
that?'. The book questions everything we know, that we
accept as facts. Where *Pasenau and the Devil* starts with
a series of photos of me crying, this one starts with a

   Maria Pasenau in Conversation with Bjørn Hatterud

series of drawings of women. After the opening at
Fotogalleriet, we took the boat to Denmark. There I
found a book for young girls, with female silhouettes
that one can draw clothes on. But the silhouette has
been drawn in an insanely sexy way, so I felt so provoked and wanted to draw my own figures.

B H   They're quite Bauhaus-like get-ups, with flared
trousers and …

M P   Yes, I really like that one, with a Jack Daniels T-shirt
and …

B H   A big dick.

M P   Yes. And some emos and aliens.

B H   There are more and more texts and drawings in
your books. What is it that photos are no longer
able to communicate?

M P   I love stories. I've always drawn, but I haven't always
written. I got bad feedback at lower and upper sec-
ondary level, because I had so many spelling mistakes,
and that was why I began with pictures, because then I
could tell stories without using text.

B H   So the fact you have dyslexia was an obstacle?
Maybe the fact that you now write is a showdown
with shame.

M P   Yes, absolutely. When I released the last book at Tronsmo's bookstore, I read from it in English. That's some-
thing I could never have imagined myself doing when
I was younger. But I'd like to get over all these things
– singing, for example. At Fotogalleriet I included a
sound work – there was some singing in it too.

B H   Would you say that to expose things that are a bit
shameful is a recurrent feature of your work?

M P   I think that it's important for me. It feels then as if I've
mastered it. I can be a bit scared, and then I think it's

                        Looking for Freedom

good for me to do it. I was scared stiff before I did the
performance at Tronsmo's, and when in 2018 I had a
performance with clarinet and poem at Fotogalleriet,
I'd never been so scared in my life. At the same time, I
felt that one shouldn't be over-critical and should dare
to open up. If you sing out of tune but it makes you
happy, then you ought to do it. Why should it be so
dangerous?

BH Yes indeed. And if you've got pimples, show
them. If you've got grey hair, don't dye it.

MP Yes, I think it's strange what's seen as being normal.
We're all of us completely different. People have to understand that. People have always dressed up and posed
in front of the camera, but now it's usual to see oneself
as tremendously important and sexy if one has a thou-
sand followers on Instagram. We're so spoilt. I think
one ought to be happy to have a body that functions. I
don't want to be on Instagram anymore.

BH I'm going to say something now that you won't
like me saying, but I must say it even so – you
were one of those who personified the Instagram
wave about five years ago.

MP Someone in upper secondary opened an Instagram
account for me against my will. He put in a password
and user name. If I'd done it, I probably wouldn't
have called myself Pasenau. That was what everybody
called me in upper secondary. I just posted pictures of
things that happened in class and stuff like that. People
thought it was my art, but all I did was to put stuff on it
I thought was great.

BH But was that Instagram account important in
expanding your contact network?

MP Yes. There was a gang of us. That was what the thing
was all about, and then we got known by lots of new
people. What was fun about Instagram was that people
just put out random things. I could see that others liked
the same things as I did and that these people lived in

                    Maria Pasenau in Conversation with Bjørn Hatterud

Oslo. When I moved there, I got in contact with them
and asked if we could go out and have a beer together.

B H   There are lots of different interpretations of what
you do that aren't necessarily rooted in your own
statements – that it's feminist, or Instagram art.
What's it like when people see things in your
works that you didn't intend?

M P   It happens lots and lots of times. People think I'm a
particular sort of person. That's why I get a bit fright-
ened in a way, and shy. I think that they don't really
know what I'm like. I'm tremendously serious about
what I do.

B H   But doesn't that apply to all artists? Sometimes
artistry lives on in different ways from what one
had anticipated.

M P   Yes, you can feel misunderstood. There's also an internal discussion. It'll be great to move away, and then I
won't have to relate to all of this. I can think about what
I feel like doing.

B H   So now it's going to be Odda?

M P   Now it's going to be Odda. It'll be really exciting.
There are buses to Oslo from there, and there's a boat
that goes directly to Flesland International Airport.
Mum and dad have a small homestead that we've used
as a cabin only two hours from there. If we buy a car
we can drive there, fish there and all sorts of stuff. We
shall see!

   Looking for Freedom

*The 'Artist Genius' Doesn't Have to Go Out
and Buy Spaghetti*
Shirana Shahbazi in Conversation with
Stephanie von Spreter

Stephanie von Spreter was Artistic Director of Fotogalleriet between 2011 and 2018, and curated Shirana Shahbazi's solo exhibition Group Show For Oslo *at Fotogalleriet in 2017 as part of the institution's fortieth-anniversary programme. For this salon-style presentation Shahbazi, in collaboration with Fotogalleriet, selected over fifty of her works from the 1990s until today, spanning a period of twenty years. Shahbazi and von Spreter met via Zoom in June 2020 to talk about her work and artistic practice.*

Stephanie von Spreter To my mind, unlike the flood of transient images in the media, and on social media, your works constitute a kind of tranquil space. They have something slow about them, something resolute and clear; they don't have any doubts and stand firm in rocky seas. They're independent objects that resist the ephemeral and create their own timeframe.

Shirana Shahbazi You'd think that photo-friendly media like Instagram would be easily accessible to me, yet the question is whether one wants to move in such a public sphere. It's very foreign to me. And as you say: the flood of images has little to do with me. For me, it has much more to do with an encounter with an image, rather than representation. Representations have become codes. My processes are very slow and boring by comparison – the opposite of momentary. Even if the images sometimes have a fleeting feel to them, they're always calm and concentrated as objects. They invite you to tarry a while, and not to leap from one idea to the next.

SVS This was tangible in *Group Show for Oslo,* where individual works were in dialogue with one another, and each photograph was a window to another world.

SHSH At Fotogalleriet, the various different media were exhibited next to one another and filled the space. That adjacency is a kind of collaging. In the more recent pieces, I've gone a step further and thought about how individual works can combine in a single work. In other words, not exhibiting ten individual works, but technically and physically uniting them; anchoring the spa-

     The 'Artist Genius' Doesn't Have to Go Out and Buy Spaghetti

tiality, the materiality, the different techniques in the image.

Before the Fotogalleriet exhibition, I had a show at Camera Austria. I'd just parted company with the gallery that had represented me before, and therefore I had a lot of pieces in storage. I'd often thought about a salon-style hang, a space crammed full of images. For Camera Austria, there was this huge exhibition hall, but no production budget. It seemed obvious to take it as an occasion to bring all the works together and to claim that, owing to the confluence between them they all speak of the same thing. The exhibition at Fotogalleriet was, consciously, a successor show to that.

SVS Many of your exhibitions include coloured walls, and these not only constitute a highly contrasting background, but also kindle a dialogue with the other works. Your recent works, especially the lithographs, are displayed in combination with handmade ceramic frames consisting of coloured geometric shapes. The superimposition of the themes of the images and the interaction with the coloured surfaces, both in the lithograph and in the frame, give rise to a composition that metaphorically references other, non-Western forms of modernity.

SHSH I am, of course, familiar with the spatial wealth of colours and materials from Iranian culture. I find such opulence fulfilling, inspiring; it keeps you awake rather than being exhausting. The coloured ceramic frames are a miniature version of the coloured walls. However, when you stand physically in front of them, you notice how inexactly the ceramic has been made, and then the levels of the lithographs, the pictorial surfaces. Behind these you can discern a black and white photograph that's also been collaged and reproduced. This superimposition becomes so complex that historical references take a back seat. The wealth of different opportunities innate in different materials and pictorial languages has always accompanied my work, and then coalesces in individual pieces.

Shirana Shahbazi in Conversation
with Stephanie von Spreter

SVS   What gave rise to this use of ceramics?

SHSH   My decision to work with ceramics was connected to
                       my work with architecture. I frequently create art for
                       a specific building, which often opens a door to using
                       new materials, because I can try out new approaches
                       there, endeavour to create art that stands alone against
                       the architecture. Images often play a subordinate role
                       to spaces. For that reason, I usually try to occupy the
                       space, to foster an atmosphere of my own. In these proj-
                       ects, I try to work with the original construction ma-
                       terials and in a certain sense clothe the rooms. During
                       one project, I came across a ceramic factory in Portugal.
                       This new colourful world fascinated me, as did the tac-
                       tile aspect of the colour pattern. There are many mate-
                       rials that interest me and that appear in my work in the
                       form of knotted carpets, silkscreens, venetian blinds or
                       wallpaper, or the floor of Zurich Kantonalbank. Even
                       if I don't produce them myself, I'm still always closely
                       involved with the production processes. And that's the
                       case with the ceramics, too.

SVS   Some of the photographs that you showed at
      Group Show for Oslo are lithographs that reflect
      a personal journey. They arose during a three-
      month trip you made with your family to Iran,
      your parents' home country. However, the images
      don't seem like records of private travel moments.
      They combine, in a very special way, the quality
      of snapshots with an intrinsically coherent com-
      position, precisely cropped, almost hermetic. Was
      this a deliberate method to render the personal as
      something universal?

SHSH   I photograph while experiencing things, almost like
                       making sketches or notes. Originally, I considered
                       this kind of photography to be very private and I kept
                       it quite separate from my exhibition activity. These
                       pieces had a quality of their own. I always bound them
                       in small one-off booklets, which never entered profes-
                       sional channels. But on the occasion of my exhibition
                       at Kunsthalle Bern in 2014, the curator Fabrice Stroun
                       saw these booklets and encouraged me to take the road

                    The 'Artist Genius' Doesn't Have to Go Out and Buy Spaghetti

trip to create work for the exhibition. He was evident-
ly fascinated by the fact that this side to my work had
never been shown in public. So I made a three-month-
long car ride from Zurich to Iran, and along the way
I photographed and photographed and photographed.
Back in Zurich, I made a selection of the images and
then realised them as bi- or tri-colour lithographs. I've
actually always found the notion of a snapshot irritat-
ing, because the momentary nature that's intrinsic to
these images has nothing to do with that anachronistic
process – the action of selecting, of compiling. It's an
immensely slow procedure to infuse the work with life.
Nevertheless, it was important to me that the works
take a step back from photography, because that way
they're stripped of a diary-like, personal, private and
therefore trivial sense. You actually describe it very
accurately: the personal – memories, observations,
the transient – is captured, and yet it has something
collective about it. One gives it a shape that perfectly
manifests this: a specific situation with specific people
and yet, a little further removed from me, an open,
universal, pictorial situation. I also achieve this through
the colours. By reducing things to two or three colours,
you rob the images of their temporality and site-spec-
ificity, and as a result, they're intimate and yet can be
pinpointed neither in time nor place. A poetic space
arises as a consequence, which remains possible through
the extremely pictorial, almost sculptural quality, and
in this way it forges a link between these and my other
works.

S V S   Something similar occurs in your series
      Tehran North.

S H S H   That series also consists of lithographs. They were
                       made at a later date, when driving round Tehran by
                       night in 2015. Now, while it may be possible to identify
                       Tehran – the mood in the streets, the drive round a big
                       city – the photographs nevertheless have something
                       more open about them. These are works that can also
                       be associated with other places.

                       Shirana Shahbazi in Conversation
                       with Stephanie von Spreter

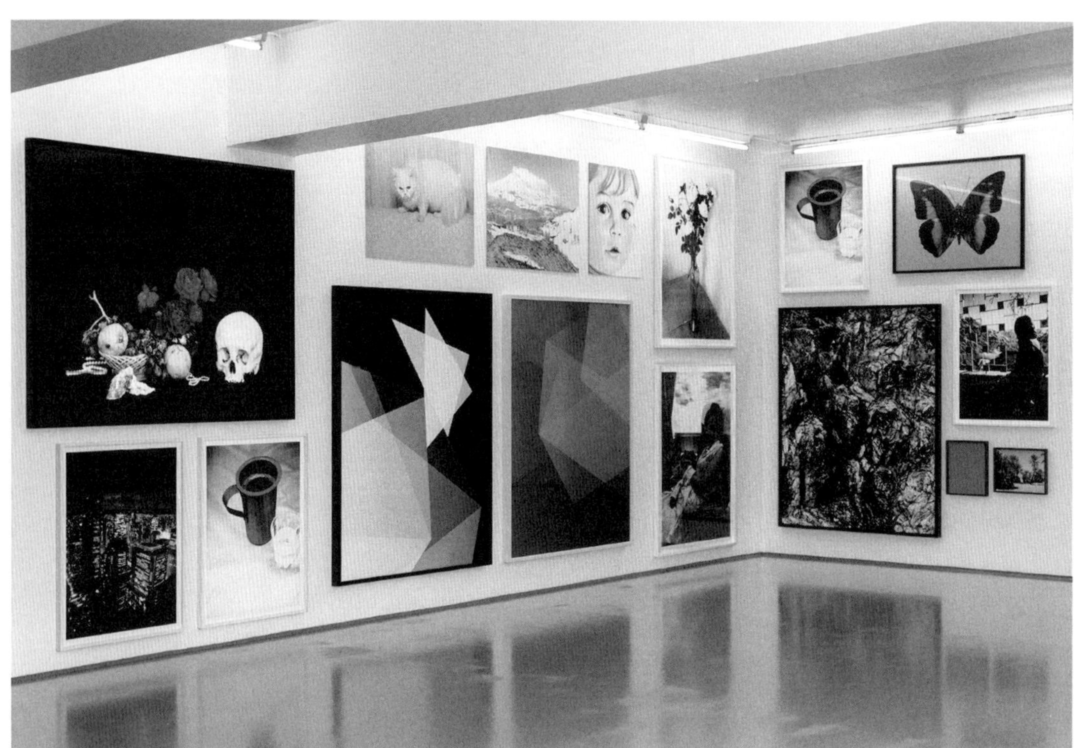

S V S In preparation for our interview, I spent a little
time combing through the literature on your
oeuvre. What struck me was that there are very
few reviews of your publications. Strange, as the
photobook is an important medium. Those of
your photobooks that I know best are *Tehran
North* and *Monstera*, and both stand out for the
fact that the photographs take the foreground,
an image opus, whereas the accompanying text is
secondary (if it even exists). Today, in commercial
and artistic terms, the photobook is experiencing a real renaissance, as can be seen from the
countless trade fairs, festivals and prizes devoted
to photobooks. At the same time, artists' books
and, by extension photobooks, have always constituted a free space for artists, in particular at the
beginning of modernism. What's the relationship
between this format and your photographs, which
are also objects in their own right?

    The 'Artist Genius' Doesn't Have to Go Out and Buy Spaghetti

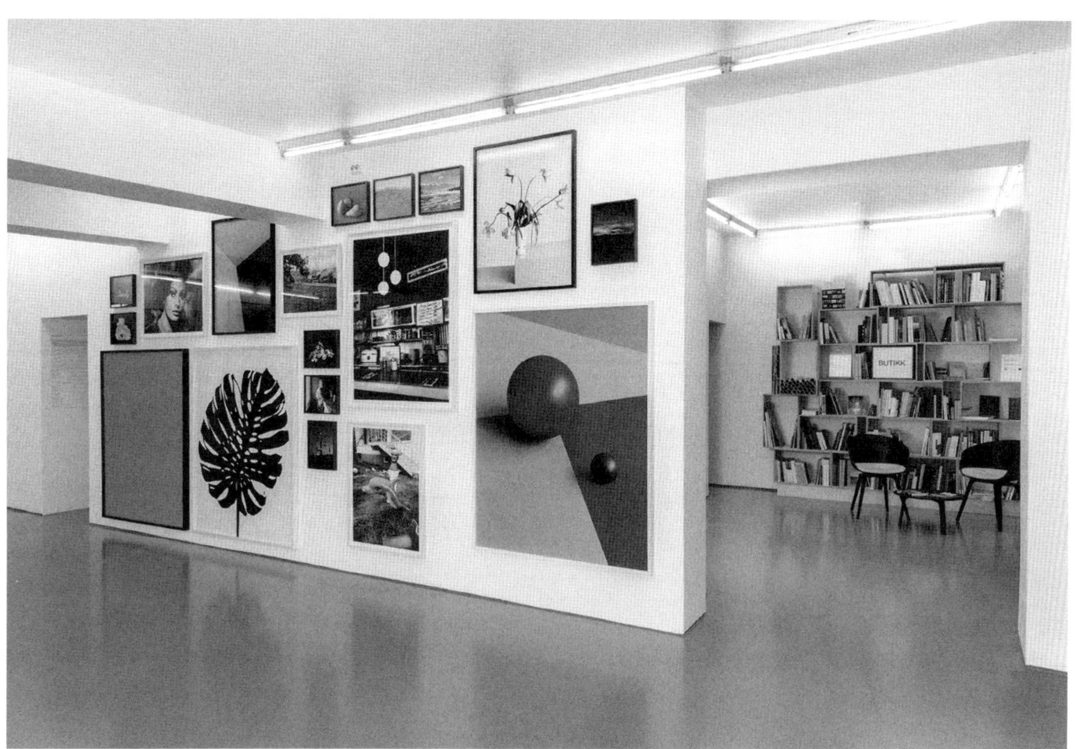

SHSH   The photobook is a marvellous space – not only an
independent medium, but also a space where I'm extremely independent. I work almost exclusively with
Manuel Krebs, my partner and graphic designer. It's
a space that we master well, with parameters that we
know and where no one tries to intervene or tell us to
do something differently. The photobook has something independent, something intrinsically complete,
coherent and enduring about it. The books don't require
exhibitions. Even if many are exhibition catalogues,
they're never illustrations. The books give us the scope
to work independently in space, over and above an
exhibition. And financially speaking, book-printing
has a different frame. Making photobooks is extremely
fulfilling.

One reason why my photobooks don't get reviewed
that much is possibly the lack of texts in them. I'm
constantly being asked whether I feel some animosity
to texts, which isn't the case at all. It's just that with

Shirana Shahbazi in Conversation
with Stephanie von Spreter

the books I've made, there was never a point or place for text. Words can often be stronger than images and can be falsely precise. So I find it better to only create a visual space. This doesn't mean that I don't work with text at all. For example, I've made a few beautiful publications with Judith Kuckart and also with Lukas Bärfuss. However, if you want to work with texts and images, then it has to be a real choice where the one supports the other.

SVS   Do you have any plans for future photobooks?

SHSH   Recently, a graphic designer I know told me that I haven't yet addressed my exploration of spatiality in my books. I'd like to meet that challenge.

SVS   Making a book is very different from working on an exhibition. How do you see you relationship to the curator and the institution?

SHSH   The role of the curators and my own role always depends on the particular project. At Fotogalleriet, for example, as at Camera Austria, we set out to see how many images we could stuff into the space, and that we did [laughs]! I was pretty well prepared, with a plan for the hang. It would have been impossible to have mastered the project without a plan, to simply have gone for trial and error. I think it's best if you're prepared. At the same time, it's all about teamwork. For me, the resulting interaction is key, even if, in your case and at Camera Austria, the works had already been produced.

At Kunsthalle Bern the curator played a greater role in this respect, because he encouraged me to photograph on the trip to and in Iran, even though he didn't know what the result would be and the enterprise might have come to nothing. Not all curators are confident and open-minded enough to say that it can go belly-up, that it can either turn into a trailblazing exhibition or a disaster, and that the institution will live with whatever happens. I've rarely experienced that kind of emotional support. Fabrice completely had my back, irrespective of where I headed. There was no discussion about who would get the credit as the curator.

   The 'Artist Genius' Doesn't Have to Go Out and Buy Spaghetti

There are other curators who feel you're invading their territory and defend their position from the word go. I think they have a problem with authorship.

That said, I've really enjoyed collaborating with curators, particularly the many women among them. It gets interesting when it's not hierarchical, when there hasn't been a power struggle. For me, all interaction pays off, right through to the techniques. That was also the case with you guys at Fotogalleriet. It seems to always be the case when things work out well.

SVS   I encountered not only your works for the first time, but you yourself, at the 4th Berlin Biennale in 2006. Shortly after the opening party you gave birth to your first child. Being a mother and keeping the flag flying in the art world is a permanent tightrope act. Yet it's an issue that affects many people. I remember listening to a lecture by the artist Vibeke Tandberg, who talked about the influence being a mother had on her creative output and also on how her work was received. Her work changed with the birth of her children, when she began focusing on the limits set by other circumstances in life. I've rarely encountered an artist who's repeatedly described this process so openly, publicly and fearlessly. However, the #MeToo movement has demonstrated that it's possible to address themes that, for all too long, have been swept under the carpet. What, in your opinion, needs to change in the art world in order for women to be less stigmatised and not forced to give up their work as artists?

SHSH   It's a shortcoming that we need to address publicly, in order to be able to formulate demands. In Berlin, I'd applied for a scholarship and by the time I got it, I was pregnant. The institution that awarded the scholarship responded quite harshly to my new situation, along the lines of 'Well, that wasn't really the plan.' And I myself thought, 'This is the end of everything. It's the end of the world.' Or of one world at least, and I thought the two worlds weren't mutually compatible. Surprisingly, it was my Iranian grandmother who asked me what on

Shirana Shahbazi in Conversation
with Stephanie von Spreter

earth the scholarship had to do with my pregnancy. Her comment was pretty liberating. It freed me from thinking of stereotypical settings into which a child is born. In Iran, and in many other cultures, people live in larger social structures in which the child doesn't grow up fixated only on one person, and that person needn't even be the mother. In Switzerland, things are harder. Childcare here is a luxury and the dominant idea is that a child's wellbeing depends on it being looked after by its mother, or at least with the father.

As a freelance artist, you need to be very flexible; you're permanently reorganising yourself and establishing a flexible network. There are intense phases, there are quiet phases, there's travel, there are evening events, weekend events. Overall, it's all extremely energy-intensive. But with a certain defiance, it's possible. It's like a mental and emotional state of emergency being an artist and being a mother in parallel. If you're surfing the wave, then you're proud that everything is functioning, and happy about the superpowers that you find when you need them. Sometimes it's great, and young women come up to me and I notice that I'm acting as a role model.

However, at the time of the Berlin Biennale 2006, things were different. There were fewer female artists, gallery-owners and curators with children. It was a bit like the beginning of an era – we were the protagonists of a generation who wanted to define that change. In such a situation, you need to live with a certain strength and resolve. During those moments that aren't so good, it all becomes impossible, and drives you crazy. So I established a certain distance. I withdrew from things and didn't take part in all the social aspects of the art business. Actually, I don't consider it all that necessary, even if I'm not sure whether I'm right or not. Now, I feel that I can talk about the drawbacks of being a woman – overcoming my shyness and saying: 'No, I can't take part in the meeting because of my children.' My ego isn't so all-embracing that I simply trundle through life on my art bulldozer irrespective of what's going on around me.

    The 'Artist Genius' Doesn't Have to Go Out and Buy Spaghetti

Often, institutions have no idea that their set-up
for supporting the arts is geared only to one particular
type of artist, namely the male artist, who's quite simply
not in the situation that I'm in. In such circumstances
you're defined as an individual who only exists through
his (not her) art, meaning not as a person who also has
to go to a school meeting. A child who's sick at home
doesn't fit the myth of the creative artist. Recently I was
invited to take part in a major competition, where we
were all given one month to submit a specific project.
During that time, you of course have other projects
going on, too. Added to which, two of the weeks were
during the school holidays. One daughter was turning ten and I wanted to go on a trip with her, and the
other one had pneumonia. And then I'm supposed to
be able to disappear into my studio, lock myself in there
for a month, and pop out again at the end with a great
project. That simply can't work. The definition of an
artist needs to be updated, because the 'artist genius'
doesn't have to go out and buy spaghetti. I always try to
talk about these things in a matter-of-fact way, without
self-pity. Sometimes, you have the power to be cool and
sometimes you don't. But I at least try not to torment
myself with a bad conscience, and instead tell myself:
'You did good.' At present, during the Coronavirus
pandemic, it's all about keeping the mood upbeat. It'll
be exciting to see how the art scene reinvents itself as a
consequence.

Shirana Shahbazi in Conversation
with Stephanie von Spreter

Magical Works, Grey Ecologies and Affect:
On Complement for Company (skyline and skin)
Susanne M. Winterling in Conversation
with Sara R. Yazdani

To encounter the photographic works of Susanne M. Winterling is to become sensitised to the meditative motifs that flow through her installations. Strange bright green plants, ants, hands, abstract surfaces, skin and perfume bottles – sometimes moving, sometimes still – are surfaces inviting thoughtful encounters. At the same time, they are surfaces that appeal to the sense of touch. One such work is ants and ashes *– an HD video work made by Winterling in 2011. Screened on an iPad – a touch device that has increasingly changed how we interface with and experience surfaces – the video presents ants and ashes slowly moving inside a cold blue surface. It is difficult to differentiate between the living ants, moving in connective communication with one another, and the ash particles, which are moved by a human breath, constantly changing as one becomes immersed in the screen.*

In 2011, ants and ashes *was shown in* Complement for Company (skyline and skin), *a solo exhibition at Fotogalleriet.*[83] *When entering the exhibition space, whose floors and ceiling were painted grey, the viewer encountered small, colourful framed works in-stalled over three of the walls. Another wall – clearly visible from outside the building – was wallpapered with a black-and-white photograph of a skyline – a construction site in the Bjørvika area in Oslo, seen against a cold grey sky. The grey skyline merged with the walls, floor and ceiling, creating an open-ended surface, or, more precisely, the 'skin' or photographic paper of the various motifs and objects presented in the space.*[84] *The framed works are photographs as well as mundane objects – a perfume bottle, a pencil, pepper-mints and a patterned gift-wrapping paper – mounted on colour Kodak photo paper. These were combined with slightly larger and some intimate photographs: a close up of a human neck, a pair of black sunglasses, an open notebook, as well as a 16 mm projector screening two hands of bright colours framing a cache –* untitled (colour cache), *2011.*

Sara R. Yazdani What I find profound about the exhibition *Complement for Company (skyline and skin)*, partic-ularly the work *ants and ashes*, is the analogies it invites between the living and non-living, nature and culture, lived surfaces and mediated surfaces. Many of your works approach photography in processual terms, showing how materiality and the production of nonhuman subjectivity are more important than images as mere representations. I find your approach to rhythm and immersion as a

[83]
The dates of the show were 6 May – 12 June 2011. The show was curated by the then director of Fotogalleriet, Susanne Østby Sæther.

[84]
See: Susanne Østby Sæther, *Complement for Company (sky-line and skin)*, Fotogalleriet Oslo, 6 May — 12 June 2011. Press release, n.p.

Magical Works, Grey Ecologies and Affect
On *Complement for Company (skyline and skin)*

way to deal with the problems of violence very interesting, as well as your critical concern with why
some bodies and lives matter more than others,
and how we must connect through intimacy.

Susanne M. Winterling   These are recurring topics in my work, for sure, and
arranged with a poetic rhyme and rhythm, as you ob-
serve. However, the poetic is grounded and sharpened
in the political dimension of life and nonlife. Sherry
Turkle, in her classic book *Life on Screen*, has made a
cluster of observations – not only on the perceptual but
also on the speculative dimension – which have inspired
me since I was a philosophy student, and these sparkle
through many of my installations. The life of algo-
rithms and the Internet of things is no longer the question. The problem has become, who is allowed to get
ashore on the Italian coast or the Greek island? Which
life can survive climate change? And how do we connect these intimacies and embody these questions in the
space? It must be an immersive space and in the face of
our information overload, the artist's poetry must trigger the senses. Rhythm can help to overcome trauma
and violence – mere concepts not so easily. When I was
working on *ants and ashes*, I was experiencing a heavy
storm. Like Kafka in the story where he meditates on
the world while watching a spinning toy, the ants and
ashes spoke to me. I was reading the signs and focusing
on pattern structures like a code.

SRY   Your work is speculative and poetic, yet highly
political, fraught with, as you underline, concerns with the crises of our world. The scents and
perfumes presented in *Complement for Company
(skyline and skin)* – peppermint and other pecu-
liar smells – combined with the shaded eyes (as
in the sunglasses) further point to this political
dimension of your art, expressed poetically and
affectively. For instance, in the small photographs
on the wall, there are primarily no narratives
or signifiers – but textures and strange affective
forces that, it seems, imply a seriousness. Could
you elaborate on how to read these works and the
objects they present?

                                    Susanne M. Winterling in Conversation with Sara R. Yazdani

S M W

Peppermint for polke and the empty notebook for the poetry to come both manifest a radical refusal of representation, instead favouring the subjective and intimate, places you tune in to. We used to be given these very small peppermint drops – the old-school version of Fisherman's Friend – as children. Sigmar Polke, as well as Joseph Beuys and Martin Kippenberger, were the male artists I respected, even if I criticised them. So this work acknowledges a tradition and a context in which I'm based, but with which I've differed, by taking a sort of radical position as a feminist criticising power structures. Polke, Kippenberger and Beuys were interesting because they reflected on their positions and they were quite humorous and playful when addressing the tragic struggle of daily life. In these plays on the two- and three-dimensional, achieved through the compositions of the photo that include and emphasise the frame, I want to trigger the senses. Can you taste the peppermint if you focus on the texture of this sugary surface?

S R Y The idea of 'tuning in' puts emphasis on how the works push, even create, subjectivity and strange environments where not only human life acts and tunes in. Although your works depict objects – perfume bottles, sunglasses, animals, hands – they work precisely against what you term 'devices of representation'. I read this as a conceptualisation of image surfaces as mediators, as – following the ontologies of Gilbert Simondon – producers of environments where living and technical beings interactively communicate. For him, beings become meaningful and autonomous through dynamic interactions with other beings in their milieu, which can include humans, animals, machines, natural materials such as sand, water, plants and so forth.[85] And as art historian Franziska Brons recently writes on nineteenth-century photographic works depicting the ocean, such as Gustave Le Gray's *Mediterranean Sea, Séte* (1857), photography was already being explored beyond mere visual representation – it was an exploration of how milieus emerge geographically and technically.[86] Environments are not pre-existing

[85]
Gilbert Simondon, 'The Genesis of the Individual', in: Jonathan Crary and Sanford Kwinter (eds.), *Incorporations* (New York: Zone Books, 1992), 304–05.
[86]
Franziska Brons, 'The Sea: Medium and Milieu', in: *Texte Zur Kunst* 29, no. 114, June 2019, 120–44.

Magical Works, Grey Ecologies and Affect
On *Complement for Company (skyline and skin)*

but productive, always in process of mediation, through which objects and subjects (biological or not) are 'individuated'.[87] With *Complement for Company (skyline and skin)*, photography and video, in its various forms and media, magically lead us into milieus of strange material realities, of new unknown realities.

[87]
Simondon 1992 (see note 85),303–06.
[88]
Carolin Wiedemann and Soenke Zehle, *Depletion Design. A Glossary of Network Ecologies* (Amsterdam: Institute of Network Cultures, 2012).

S M W   The question of depletion is the question of the institution,[88] of what it means when subjects and objects join in a refusal of roles in the great game of reification. It's no accident, perhaps, that philosophies of play are back – not quite a renaissance of aesthetic experience, but an affirmation of the openness of objective and subjective constitution. We're so much in interaction with our ecology, symbionts and parasites, breathing what this planet is giving us. The interface of Gaia is where we operate. She's what fuels us and connects us with life.

S R Y   Your art as much as your philosophy, then, underscores the ongoing connections that define bodies and things in terms of their dynamic encounters with other beings. In *After Art*, art historian David Joselit introduces an interesting take on photography in these terms.[89] Discarding the modernist (as in the Formalist) conceptions of medium-specificity and autonomy – terms made explicit in 1962 when Greenberg published the article 'Modernist Painting'[90] – Joselit urges a shift from an object-based aesthetic to a network-based aesthetic, where the capacity of the 'emergence' of images, its ability to create systems and networks despite that it is not living the biological sense, is highlighted.

[89]
David Joselit, *After Art* (Princeton & Oxford: Princeton University Press, 2013).
[90]
Clement Greenberg, 'Modernist Painting', in: Charles Harrison and Paul Wood (eds.) *Art in Theory: 1900–1990. An Anthology of Changing Ideas* (Oxford: Blackwell, 1992), 773–79.

S M W   It's great how you can frame this in art-historical debates and contexts and I'd like to emphasise my practice in terms of the modernist dictum 'A beyond that is a before as well'. It's a window onto another world, tinted and reflected, fragmented, made fractal[91] through devices that work against representation as they complicate and bring in the glitch.

     Susanne M. Winterling in Conversation with Sara R. Yazdani

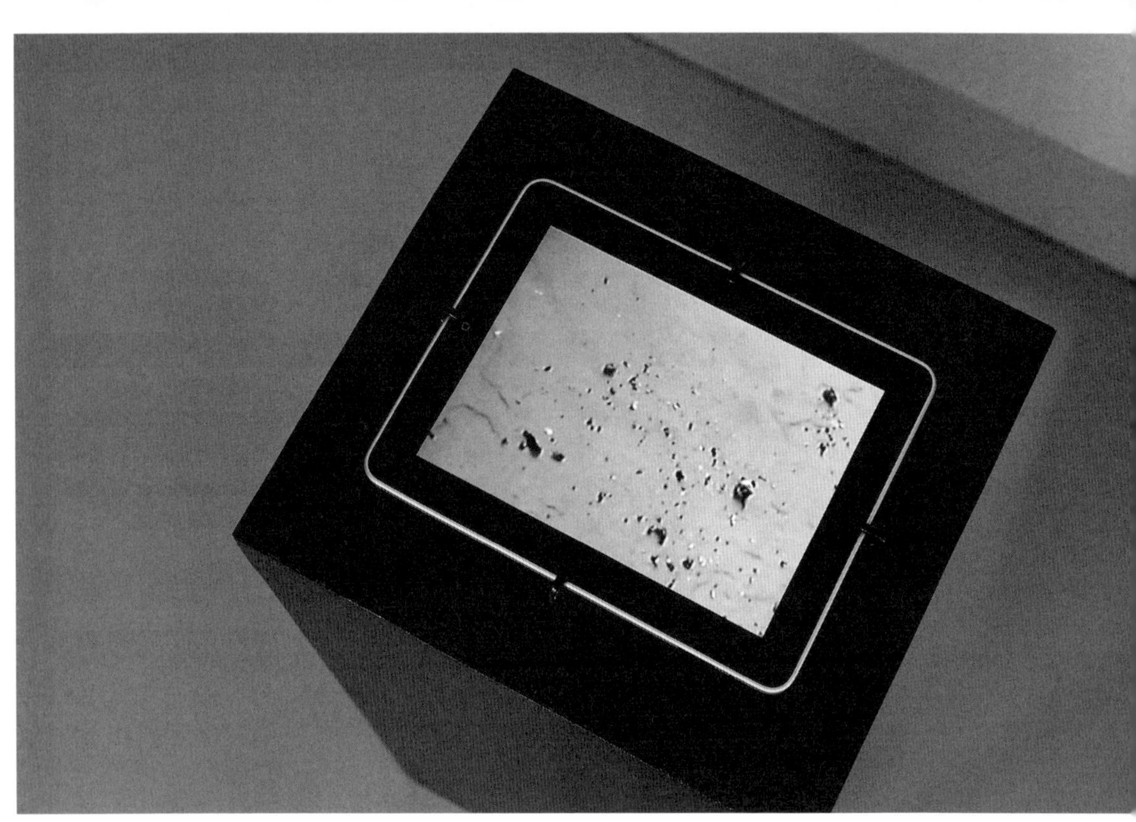

Magical Works, Grey Ecologies and Affect
On *Complement for Company (skyline and skin)*

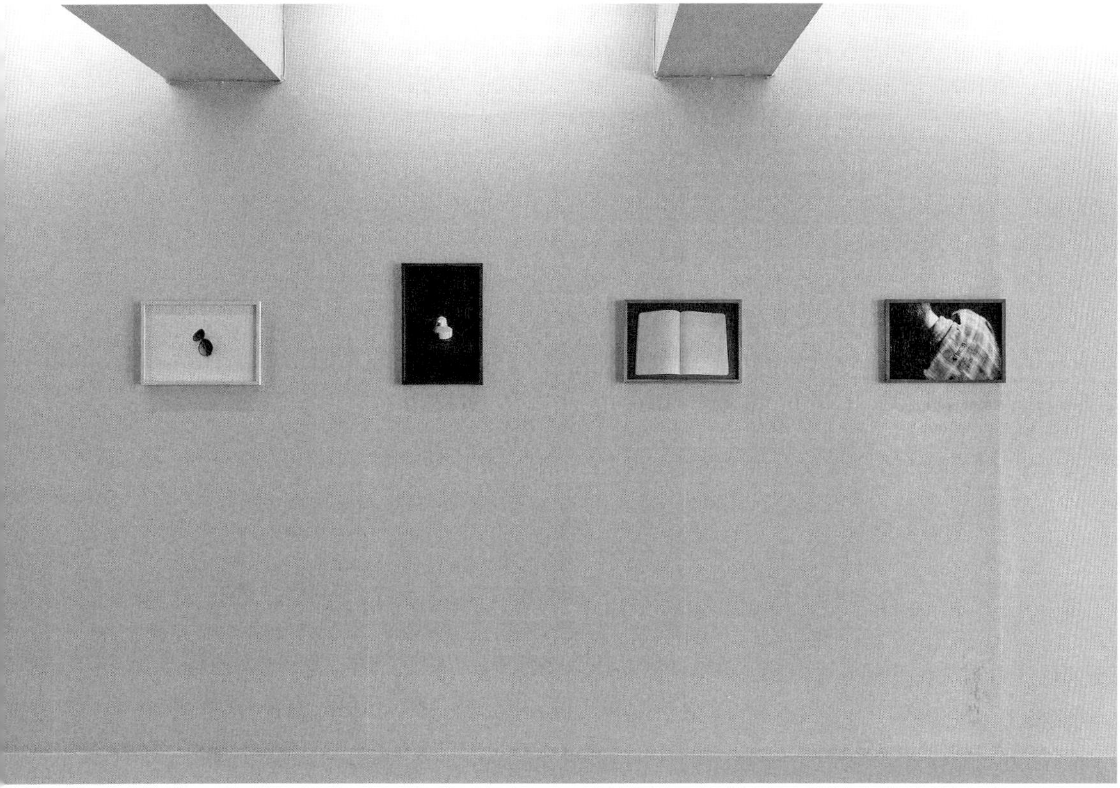

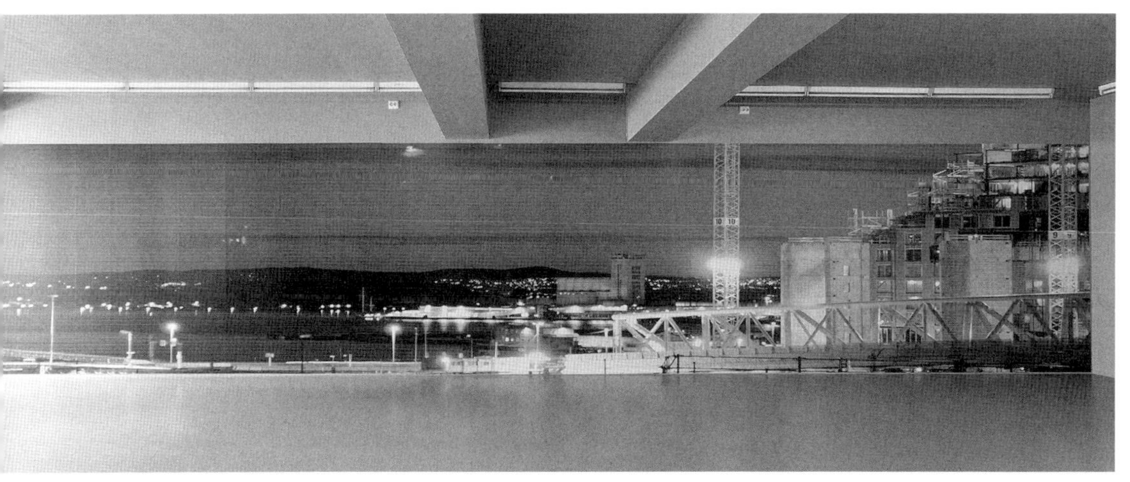

  Susanne M. Winterling in Conversation with Sara R. Yazdani

SRY With another material world in mind, I'd like to return to the sense of touch occurring in *ants and ashes* – the affective aspect I identify in your work, still not yet elaborated. There's a vulnerability to the ants and particles of dust – I'm tempted to touch, feel them with my finger tips. It's almost as if the work evokes some affective force that passes *between* bodies. In *The Affect Theory Reader*, Gregory J. Seigworth and Melissa Gregg define 'affect', 'at its most anthropomorphic', as a 'visceral force' that exists beneath, alongside or beyond our conscious knowing and human emotions.[92] The reason for this, they write, is because this affect is a force that exists and comes into existence *in-between* material and living beings.[93] It's pertinent that their view of affect is a reference to Deleuze and Guattari, who in *What is Philosophy?* write that affects are not feelings or affections: 'They go beyond the strength of those who undergo them. Sensations, percepts and affects are *beings* whose validity lies in themselves and exceeds any lived.'[94] A little touch may seem simple, but the affective forces we face in our everyday encountering with things, materials (such as dust) and surfaces take us back to ecologies and parasites you mentioned earlier. The affective forces of becoming are notably also the 'companies' in your works, as in the title of the exhibition.

SMW Layers of experiences are under the skin; they constitute the skin and the tissue of us. That's why I wanted to have a dedication at that time to my girlfriend in there, as well as to invite people to experience rooms of their own. Layers of dedication are refracted and detracted, untraceable, because the skin is too thin, there's too much information to be completely computed. That's why we can distinguish the ants from the ashes and feel a tip and a breeze on the shoulder so close.

91
See: Karen Barad, *Meeting the Universe Halfway: Quantum Physics and the Entanglement of Matter and Meaning* (London: Duke University Press, 2007) and http://pandorasbox.susannewinterling.com/fractal-sensingthinking-planetary-scale (accessed 1 February 2021).

92
Gregory J. Seigworth and Melissa Gregg, 'An Inventory of Shimmers', in: Gregory J. Seigworth and Melissa Gregg (eds.), *The Affect Theory Reader* (Durham & London: Duke University Press, 2010), 1–29.

93
Ibid., 1.

94
They introduce the concept 'bloc of sensation': a form of sensation that is pre-perceptual, a compound of 'affects' and 'percepts' that transcends any living human being. Gilles Deleuze and Félix Guattari, *What is Philosophy?*, trans. Hugh Tomlinson and Graham Burchell (New York: Columbia University Press, 1994/1991), 164. Emphasis original.

Magical Works, Grey Ecologies and Affect
On *Complement for Company (skyline and skin)*

SRY There's one dimension of photography evolving
in *With Complement for Company (skyline and skin)*
not yet mentioned, namely: the becoming of space
and spatial interrelations.

SMW Dissolving into the image is triggered by an apparatus
of heightened sensibility. You are the apparatus. Your
own senses experience this. But it's not just vision. It's
more space/volume and context that I'm interested in.
Intimacy counters the institutional space and plays with
daily life observations and its conditions: the power
of the frame, gentrified urbanisation (as in skyline) or
the violence of institutions incorporated as infrastruc-
ture and its labour of framing and governing our lives.
We seek company and encounter intimacy in the lived
space: fractal or inconsistent like a glitch, the closeness
of perfume, the taste of peppermint or the bio-acous-
tics of wrapping foil and the fugitive ashes. This is, of
course, a temporary frontier in the network game.
The photograph needs you to be completed. The photo
is nothing if not viewed, framed. The capitalist machine will not stop before the last resource is depleted.
'Since the acceleration of reality leaves little time for
reflection in a world where both the inner and outer
landscapes are perpetually being colonised, we must
begin to have the courage of a grey ecology of instanta-
neity.'[95] The binary is not only the inner and outer but
also the virtual and real. So my greying the exhibition
space not only hints at a grey room in a magazine that
the curator of the show and I were enjoying as artists, as
well as scholars reflecting on media, but also a reference
to network theory and culture.

95
'Today, within a globalized, networked horizon, we all have moved from the "city of lights" to the "city of the instant", where we must begin to think the architecture of a temporality that is no longer night or day, but global and whose architecture is that of the screen. The internet and the globalized circuits do not run on the concept of "open and closed" of a.m. and p.m. They never stop. When we move from night and day, from the past, present, future, to an eternal present of real-time, we must begin to strive to distinguish the "blurring of all the colors into grey". For within this grey landscape, within the digital sphere of acceleration, we have long since seen the effects of a blurring of the virtual and the real.' See: Drew S. Burk referring to Paul Virilio's 'Grey Ecology', in: Carolin Wiedemann and Soenke Zehle (eds.), *Depletion Design: A Glossary of Network Ecologies* (Amsterdam: Institute of Network Cultures, 2012), 90.

SRY A grey ecology serves as an interesting concept
to reveal our contemporary world of crisis, how
it's formed and, as you underline, accelerates into
processes of colonisation. Grey hints at an in-
betweenness, a dispute against nothingness, the
virtual and the real.

SMW An endgame with a strange but sensual surrounding,
the company of intimate strangers you're invited into.

          Susanne M. Winterling in Conversation with Sara R. Yazdani

S R Y   Such an invitation into a virtual yet sensible and
thereby real world—milieu—is an intriguing
place to end this conversation, which centres
around the meditative surfaces we encounter
in your work. Your works of art are magically
leading us into, or, to be more precise, constructing, strange worlds: material and political realities
of the past, present and future, intimately and
affectively bonding different forms and conditions
of life.

Bjarne Bare, an internationally exhibited artist currently based in Los Angeles, worked in Fotogalleriet's archives and library in 2008 prior to founding the artist-run space MELK in Oslo in 2009 with Behzad Farazollahi. In this conversation with the American photographer Catherine Opie, who for more than thirty years has challenged societal norms around gender and sexuality, the artists shed light on artistic concerns in relation to the institution. Opie, who was Bare's teacher at UCLA in 2015-17, opens up a cross-pollination of influences between institutions and artists to make the claim that, contrary to what we are led to believe, there are still not enough images surrounding us today. Opie met Bare at her house in Los Angeles, September 2019.

Bjarne Bare Your wide experience of working in the arts, from community work amongst artists to teaching and positions on various museum boards, is a great basis for a conversation. But I want to start by congratulating you on your Guggenheim Fellowship. Would you like to share something about that project to begin with?

Catherine Opie Yes, it's up in the studio right now. If we were in the studio, you'd be surrounded by it. I applied many times for the Guggenheim Fellowship, each time for different projects. The last one was *The Modernist*, which I didn't get funded, but this one did get funded. It's an exhibition that will be titled *Rhetorical Landscapes*. It's looking at the relationship between landscape and language and how we look at it in terms of community, and what space means to us.

I'm very interested in this kind of positioning of language right now, specifically because of the Trump administration. The pictures in *Rhetorical Landscapes* are all images taken throughout the South, of swamps, but they're really pristine, not out-of-focus landscapes like the previous body of work, not using abstraction. They hover on the edge of the incredibly beautiful landscapes that one would think of in terms of *National Geographic*, but I use depth of field in a certain way, so they're not out of that 8 x 10 large-format school of landscape. So I'm hovering between this place of professional and amateur in these landscapes.

  The Invisible Visible

Then, included along with it is a brand new body of work that's a conversation with my film from *The Modernist*, where the character begins to collage his artwork as he's burning down the utopic, modernist houses of LA. I've now collected a cross-section of different American magazines from *Country Living* to *American Gun* to leftist magazines.

BB   Contemporary ones?

CO   All contemporary, all in the last two years, and I'm collaging them. I've cut images out of many, many magazines, which are all laid out on the tables in the studio. And I've hand-painted these 1 x 1 inch grids on large museum rag board. And I've hired an animator, who just recently graduated from Cal Arts with her masters degree in animation. So instead of revisiting the history of collage from the Bauhaus or John Heartfield, I'm using the process of stop animation, so that a narrative of meaning is seen. It's going to be exhibited on an oversized monitor, like a kind of mall kiosk, so that it becomes human size, and so again, it refers to the body, the relationship of landscape to portraiture. It's a portrait of our time and of our country right now. That will be in a show at Regen Projects at the end of February.

BB   Wow, that's exciting!

CO   So, that's what I'm working on now and that I've used the Guggenheim funding to make this body of work. It's been amazing to be able to have funding to do that.

BB   Of course. And it's a great honour.

CO   Yes. It's a huge honour.

BB   Did you travel to the South to make the pictures?

     Catherine Opie in Conversation with Bjarne Bare

C O   I did. I actually did a residency, which I usually don't do, but it was a teaching residency, where I took the undergrad classes out last winter quarter and went to the Atlantic Center of Arts in New Smyrna Beach, Florida, and that's when I started doing the swamps.

B B   You've taught photography since the 1980s?

C O   Yes, since 1989.

B B   And you hold several board positions: the Museum of Contemporary Art in Los Angeles, the Hammer in Los Angeles, the Mike Kelley Foundation and the Andy Warhol Foundation.

C O   Yes, the Hammer was a three-year term, and was the first board I joined. Then, after my three years on the board, I stepped down and I joined the MOCA board and I've been serving on the Mike Kelley Foundation board for two years. I also serve on the Andy Warhol Foundation board, which has been about three years of service now, I think.

B B   That's great. Do you travel for that one?

C O   I do. The beauty of that is that it's an incredible group of amazing people to talk to. And we get to go to New York four times a year, which then gives me a day of going out and seeing exhibitions. Otherwise, I wouldn't be going to New York four times a year.

B B   How have these various positions that you've held alongside your practice helped shape the community around you, and also your work? Because your practice is a lot about community and a lot about people. Did either come first, do you feel, or has it been a natural growth in that sense?

C O   I think that photography has always lent itself to people. You could be the photographer who goes out and only makes landscapes, but when I moved to San Francisco to study at the Art Institute in the early 1980s, I was looking at the defining period of documentary photography in America, the era of the Farm Security Administration (FSA), and I was looking at John Szarkowski's sensibility from a curatorial standpoint.

BB   Lewis Hine has been mentioned as an influence on you, and Fotogalleriet exhibited his work in 1979, two years after it first opened. I remember he was never included in the FSA project because he refused to give up the rights to his negatives.

CO   It was probably because that he was too old at the point, when Roy Stryker started.

BB   Maybe.

CO   Because if you think of his Ellis Island photographs or even Carolina Mill, those are 1910. So, when the FSA starts, it's a way to reflect on the depression that's happening and what Roy Stryker decided to do, I think, was highly influenced by *Life* and *Look* magazines, what the pictorial document did. But it's interesting what you say about Hine, because Dorothea Lange would shoot two negatives.

BB   I didn't know she circumvented it that way.

CO   Oh, yeah, she was bad. She was bad that way! Stryker would do this horrible thing.

BB   With the holes?

CO   With the holes. Contemporary photographers have riffed on that: the hole punch through the negative.

BB   It's so brutal.

CO   We were also looking at Robert Frank, Garry Winogrand and Diane Arbus, and how the contemporary aspect of photography came from what the FSA did in defining a specific discourse around documentary practices. This was very different from what was happening in New York in the 1980s, in terms of the Pictures generation. And I actually lived in a residence

                    Catherine Opie in Conversation with Bjarne Bare

club, where I worked from 3:00 to 8:00 in the morning
for my room and board, and I started making portraits
of everybody there, as well as still lifes of the residents
club. I was shaped by the different circumstances in
which I lived, and then going through the AIDS crisis,
I couldn't not be part of a queer dialogue at that point.
I was watching a horrible kind of devastation and
homophobia happen within my community and even
though I was photographing master-planned communities and those ideas, it was still always around the
presence of homophobia.

So people and photography have always gone hand
in hand. But with a crisis of photography in terms of
the digital era, I would say that we're seeing much
more studio-based work, much more sculptural-based
photography. But then you have incredible people like
LaToya Ruby Frazier coming out and doing things on
labour. You have Deana Lawson, you have Dawoud
Bey, you have this incredible new movement of documentary again, which often reflects on the idea of
community. And that's really fascinating to me.

BB   And maybe that's the product of the politics we're
seeing now. I'm doing it myself. My work is more
... it's still not a narrative, but it's based on politics
and history and there are no still lifes in my next
show. It's going to be straight photography.

CO   I can't wait to see it. But you've always dealt with the
symbolic. Like when we worked together at UCLA: I
saw your thesis show as a kind of new, symbolic way
of looking at the specificity of a place. It was through
artefacts, so to speak. For me, there was a certain sense
that this was to do with you being from Norway, in the
same way Robert Frank came from Switzerland and did
The Americans.

BB   Yes, it's heavily symbolic. As is my next show.
Each photograph is there to symbolise something,
and I actually have two pictures of people this
time, but they function more as symbols than as
the person they are. I have a photo of a racing car
driver, for instance, and for me, he symbolises

     The Invisible Visible

this drive for capitalism and this forward urge. So
he's sweating in the racing car. I really like this
way of working and I've had a lot of fun with this
project. I think symbolism is important. The way
you deal with the landscapes in your new project
is the same, I guess, because they carry something
beyond just the depicted landscape.

CO   But then they also disappear. I'm really interested in
      how I can still cut images out of a magazine, even
      though most of us are scanning our phones for infor-
      mation. I think it's a really interesting time in terms
      of what photography does. There's a certain nostalgia
      about what the medium can do in creating history,
      but at the same time, print is going to disappear, just
      as swamps will disappear. They'll be underwater, and
      that's why I gave the project the title, *Rhetorical Land-
      scape*. What is a landscape? Is it a place that we inhabit
      symbolically in terms of looking at the politics of our
      time, or is it an actual, physical place? We don't know
      how to deal with space these days. Photography has
      been so much about space, but now we're always nav-
      igating between a screen world and a real, physical
      world, and that's a fascinating state to me.

BB   So fascinating and so abstract. I wanted to ask
      you: since you began teaching in the late 1980s,
      how do you feel the medium has changed? I
      know it's a big question.

CO   That is a big question. One of the things I think is
      so interesting is how art gets framed during different
      periods of time. Especially being part of academia for
      over thirty years now, I'm fascinated when people make
      these declarative statements, like, 'Oh, painting is dead.'
      'Oh, photography is in a crisis.' There are always these
      kinds of declarations that uphold a kind of theoretical
      position on the medium at the time. I remember read-
      ing the obituary after Robert Frank died, where he was
      quoted as saying very much what Cartier Bresson had
      said, which was: 'There are too many images.' But you
      can go back to 1920 and people were saying there were
      too many images even then.

    Catherine Opie in Conversation with Bjarne Bare

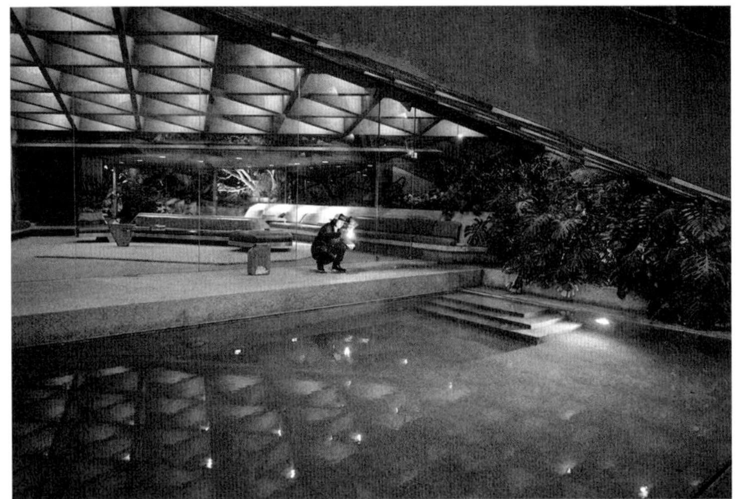

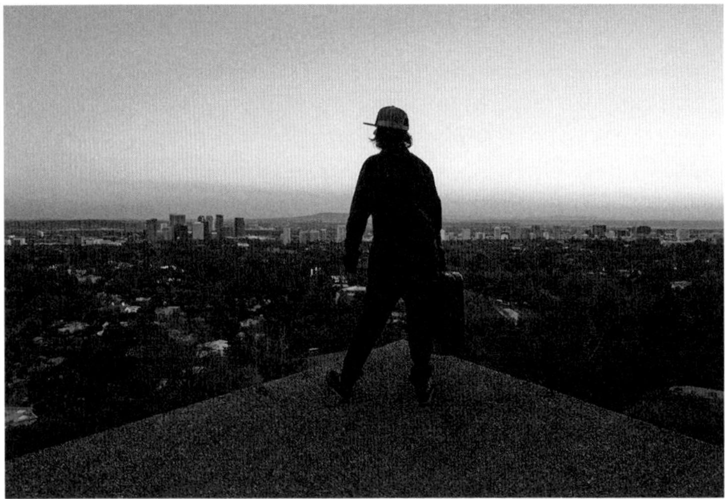

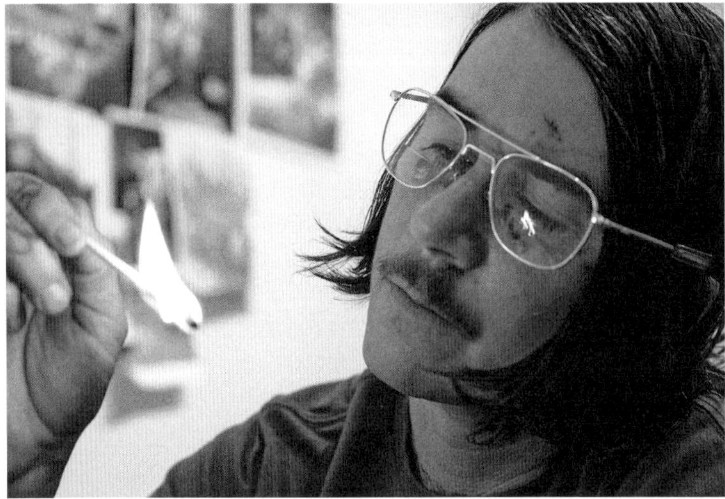

   The Invisible Visible

So, I actually say that we don't have too many images. There's still nothing that serves us in terms of how we create history, in my mind, better than a lens-based practice. That moment when we click the trigger of the camera, and it captures something is forever part of the history of language. And it's the same way that I love digging into the archives at the Los Angeles Public Library or other archives. I wouldn't have wanted to be a photographer if it wasn't for the photographs that Hines made in the Carolina mills.

What I like is that the medium right now is highly discursive without being overwrought in relationship to the examination of the medium, as it was throughout the 1980s and 90s. We had such a rich period of writing on photography during the 1970s, 80s and 90s from Susan Sontag to Allan Sekula to Martha Rossler to Douglas Crimp. I could keep naming the names … And *October* contributed so much. But right now, you have this flux where nobody really wants to make definitive statements about the medium because we're all watching to see how people are manoeuvering through its rich history right now. I feel like that's the state of photography and how I think about it at this moment in time.

BB Yes, that's very interesting. I spoke to Torbjørn Rødland about this. He graduated at the height of postmodern photography, and he said we're in the most incredible time right now, because we're able to cherry pick from all the eras. It's like a post-postmodern time, but you're also able to mix modernism and postmodernism into the medium, and people will relate to it, because we're educated at this level – visually. Instead of just doing an investigation into the medium itself, you can mix narration and conceptualism and you have this amazing freedom within photography right now.

CO That's well said.

   Catherine Opie in Conversation with Bjarne Bare

B B   I think it's a good time, and, as you said earlier,
       I think global politics are necessitating change
       in photography. You do have some responsibility
       politically, I think, as a photographer these days.

C O   I've always felt that. My work can have moments
                           when there's no kind of political agenda, so to speak,
                           but there's always some relationship to history, which
                           encompasses all of that, in terms of critical thought,
                           language, the specificity of identity. All of that is this
                           constant place of exploration for me.

B B   The philosopher Vilém Flusser has been import-
       ant for me. He wrote in 1980 that photography
       basically saved the world because it was invented
       at a time where there was a crisis in France. You
       had the pre-modern working class, the farmers,
       who were largely analphabets, versus the aristoc-
       racy, who in turn were increasingly intellectual,
       and there was this immense gap between the two.
       And then photography came in and it made a
       bridge; it made a communicative tool. I think it's
       a great theory.

C O   I think that's what LaToya Rudy Frazier tries to do
                           with her work. I do too.

B B   And maybe it's stronger now than ever, or more
       important than ever.

C O   It's interesting. Yes. I think that photography bridged
                           this gap, so that the community actually felt proud.

B B   And you've done that, too.

C O   Yes, it's about pride. How do you claim a sense of
                           ownership within your own community, unless there's
                           representation of that community?

B B   You make it seen.

C O   You make the invisible visible.

                         The Invisible Visible

What Remains
Silja Leifsdottir in Conversation
with Håkon Lillegraven

Silja Leifsdottir is a curator and writer who worked as Gallery Coordinator at Fotogalleriet from 2011 to 2017, alongside her curatorial studies, and in 2017 curated the group show What Remains *as part of Fotogalleriet's fortieth anniversary programe. Håkon Lillegraven has been Head of Mediation at Fotogalleriet since spring 2020. During the summer of 2020, they corresponded via telephone and email about Leifsdottir's exhibition and the research that motivated it.*

Håkon Lillegraven Can you tell us something about the background to your curating the exhibition *What Remains* at Fotogalleriet as part of the fortieth anniversary programme of the institution in 2017?

Silja Leifsdottir

In 2015, I applied to take a Master's programme in Curatorial Practice at the University of Bergen.

The programme is collection-based and it was possible to follow it alongside my position as coordinator at Fotogalleriet. I applied with the fortieth anniversary of Fotogalleriet as my curatorial project after conversations with the then artistic director Stephanie von Spreter. In the light of Fotogalleriet's fortieth anniversary, I wished to research issues connected with representation and communication, combined with the capacity of the photograph to transcend time.

In the initial phase of the project, I studied many historical exhibitions and archives, including a generous dose of megalomanic projects curated by Western white males, which eventually led me to NASA's project with Voyager Golden Records. In 1977, NASA launched the unmanned spacecraft Voyager 1 and Voyager 2 to fetch data about the planets Jupiter, Saturn, Uranus and Neptune. Since both craft were to continue into outer space, it was decided to equip them with information about the Earth, in the event of their being found at some point by other intelligent beings in the universe. The information, which was encoded on a gold-plated copper disc, contained greetings in fifty-four different languages, a collection of music by, among others, Bach, Mozart and Chuck Berry, plus samples of folk music. It also contained various sound recordings, such as the humming of an engine and a baby babbling. Finally, 118 images were chosen, which were then encoded with the rest of the material onto the disc, so that it could be reproduced by eventual non-terrestrial beings. Among the

 What Remains

selected images is everything from iconic photographs of new-born children and magnificent natural scenery to such human feats as ascending mountains, killing animals and constructing tall buildings. In addition, there's a series of images that, at first glance, have a less obvious intention, such as a portrait of a woman in a shopping centre, and a man grilling food.

Back then, Golden Records was criticised for only showing humanity from a positive angle, but perhaps the most obvious problem area is the attempt to represent the whole of Earth's civilisation via 118 images (and from an American perspective). What kind of story does this selection tell us, and implicitly what stories do the exclusions tell us about the time when the selection was made? Humans have always felt the need to leave traces behind them, but our language is constantly changing. The oldest cave paintings go back 35,000 years, and the 118 photographs out there in outer space are meant to be able to do the same. If you were to choose just one image to represent the world/humanity today to an unknown audience 40,000 years from now – what would you choose?

The work on finding the images for the disc was led by the well-known astronomer and communicator Carl Sagan, in cooperation with the journalist Jon Lomberg. Golden Records was sent off into outer space in 1977, the same year Fotogalleriet was established. NASA, in other words, was also celebrating the fortieth anniversary of its archive project and thus was the perfect framework for the project. It resulted in a group exhibition, with the artists Liv Bugge, Kristina Bengtsson, Toril Johannessen, Ditte Knus Tønnesen and Tori Wrånes, featuring Clare Milledge, as well as a publication named *GR-09022017* in collaboration with ten co-curators and more than a hundred participating artists. I printed 300 copies of the book and at present have about twenty left. The exhibition was both well-visited and very well received.

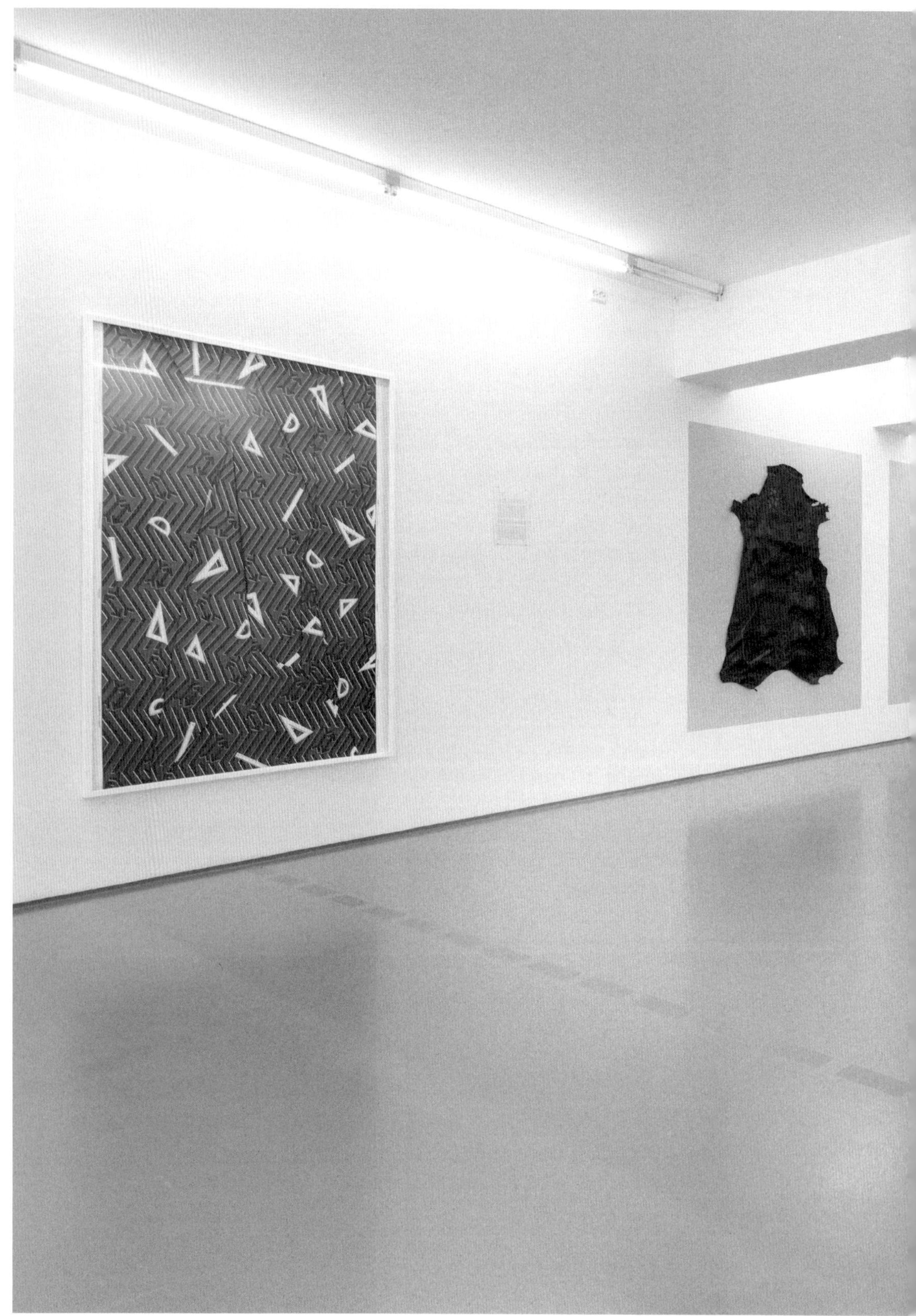

What Remains

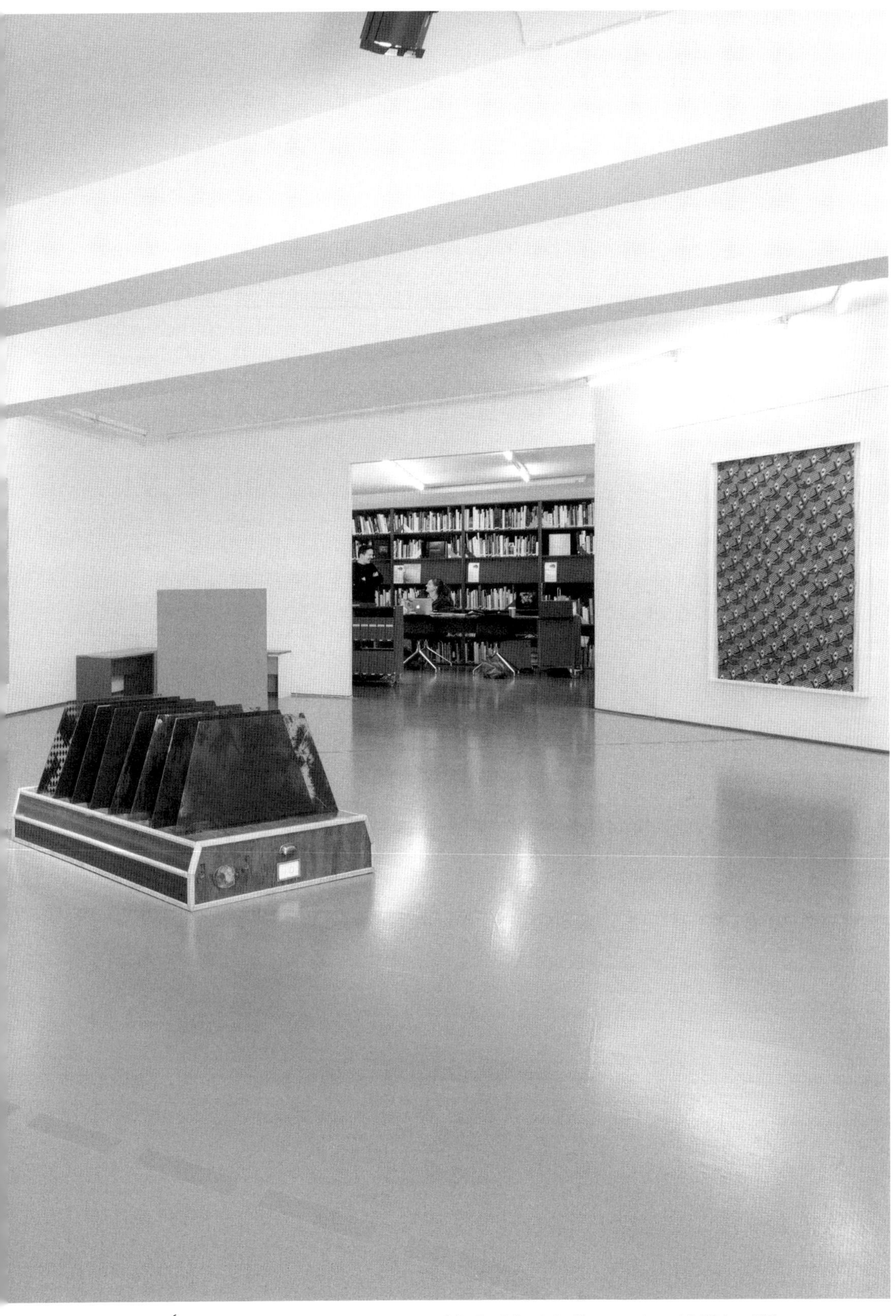

Silja Leifsdottir in Conversation with Håkon Lillegraven

H L   Can you tell us about the publication accompanying the
exhibition? How did it come about?

S L   NASA's archive Golden Records was the starting point
for both the exhibition and the publication. The exhibition included artists who work with photography
indirectly and who explore the issues and thematics of
a universal language, perception, semiotics and image-
awareness. But many limitations exist in a physical
space, so I also wanted to make a linked publication
that could provide more space for exploring the various
issues involved. I decided to do a 're-make' of Golden
Records, with the 118 photographs that were originally
chosen as a point of departure.

    I also wanted to make a book of photographs com-
pletely stripped of any kind of text, something that
– ironically enough – is a rare sight. So all the artists
were asked to choose a picture that could stand without
a title, as part of the investigation into the capacity of
the photograph to communicate as a 'pure' language
without involving any text. Nor were the photographs
credited directly by name beneath the picture. This
was to enable the reader to see the picture in isolation,
without any previous knowledge. A well-known name
like Wolfgang Tillmans beneath a picture would, naturally enough, make you read the work in the light of his
art. A name like Lau Wai would place the picture in a
geographical context. All the information was therefore
collected on the last page, under a cover flap. Behind
these publication choices lies a strong belief that both
the photograph and work of art, generally speaking, are
able to communicate a great deal on their own, and my
job and responsibility as a curator, among other things,
is to be able to see what and how much/little text ought
to accompany the work of the exhibition so that mediation will serve all parties in the best way possible.

H L   As you point out, you already had insight into the
history/archive and activities of the institution via your
position as coordinator. What, in your parallel work on
Fotogalleriet's history and archive and your own curatorial practice, motivated the curatorial framework you
put in place for the project?

           What Remains

Running parallel with my Master's programme, Martina Petrelli was employed to establish an archive for Fotogalleriet. The work on the archive made it possible to gain a better overview of Fotogalleriet's history. This is an impressive history of exhibitions, with major names, but it nevertheless became obvious that the gallery had been run by three men for a quite a long period of time. This mode of operation remained until a fixed-term artistic director was appointed in 1992 – the first female leader, Hanne Holm-Johnsen. Of the approximately 800 artists who exhibited at Fotogalleriet from 1977 to 2016, only 26 percent were women, most of whom exhibited after 1990.

The archive's evident exclusions interested me more than the established history of Fotogalleriet, and when I was given the assignment of opening the anniversary programme at Fotogalleriet with my curatorial project, I wanted to break with the traditional methods of marking anniversaries, such as exhibiting selected works or artists from Fotogalleriet's history in a more or less linear way, from Kåre Kivijärvi to Torbjørn Rødland. Part of the history is that Fotogalleriet began a dialogue and a collaboration in 2015 with Hege Oulie and the Preus Museum, which wished to mark the fortieth anniversary of Fotogalleriet with its own exhibition that would deal with the history of the institution in a more traditional way via a display of works from historical exhibitions, combined with material from the archive. This exhibition *The Young Lions* opened on 2 April 2017 at the Preus Museum.

Although the exhibitions *What Remains* and *The Young Lions* appear to be extremely dissimilar, they have one thing in common: the link between past, present and future. I find this shared time aspect particularly fascinating to work with in a photographic context, since time is inextricably linked to the medium of photography itself. The time aspect of photography is one of its basic components, which drastically changed the history of art and of humanity. The conception of photography as a representation of reality has been discussed by philosophers, psychologists, journalists, documentary photographers and critics for several decades, and its trustworthiness has long since been debunked. Even so, it's still the closest we can get to a depiction of

Silja Leifsdottir in Conversation with Håkon Lillegraven

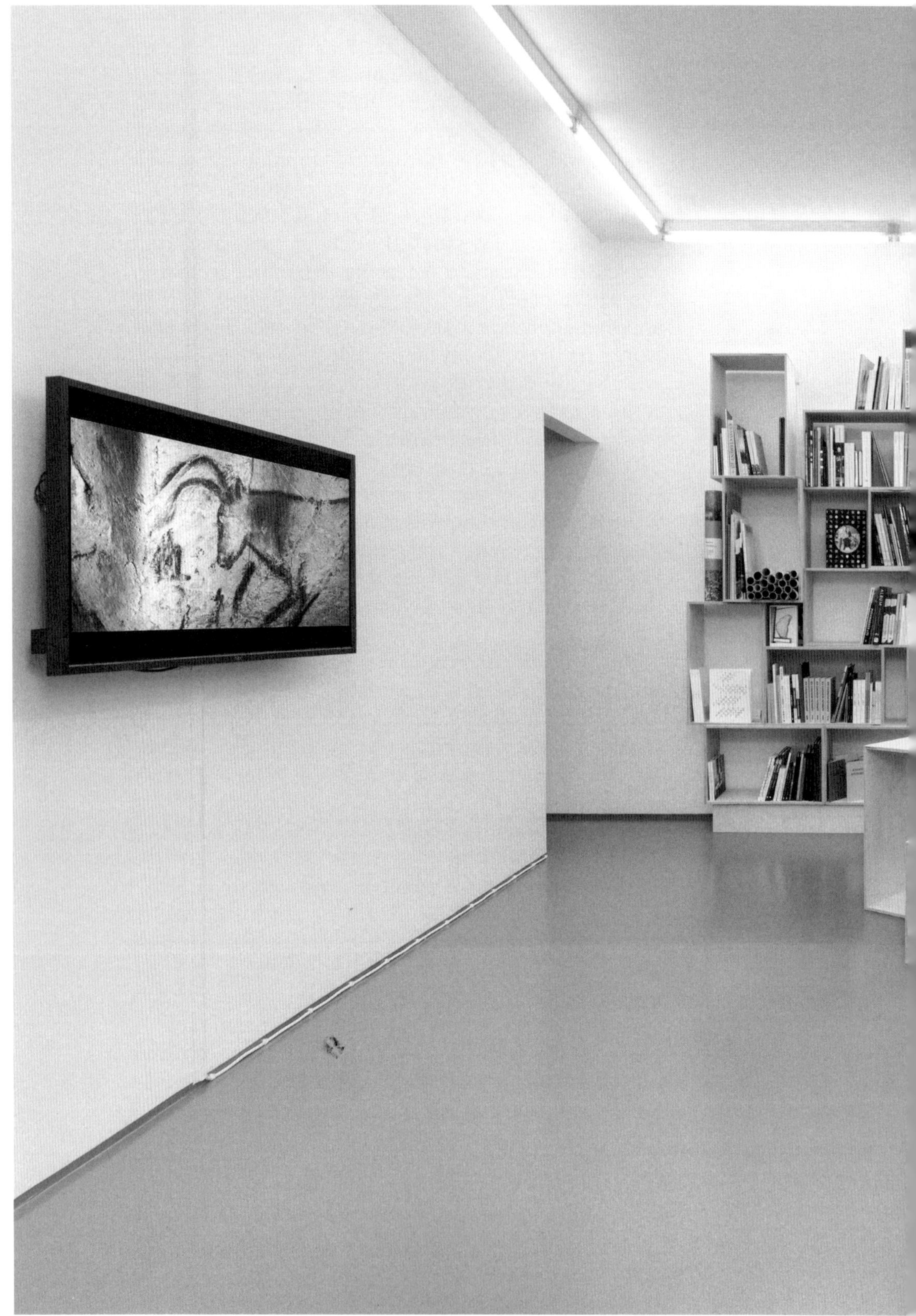

What Remains

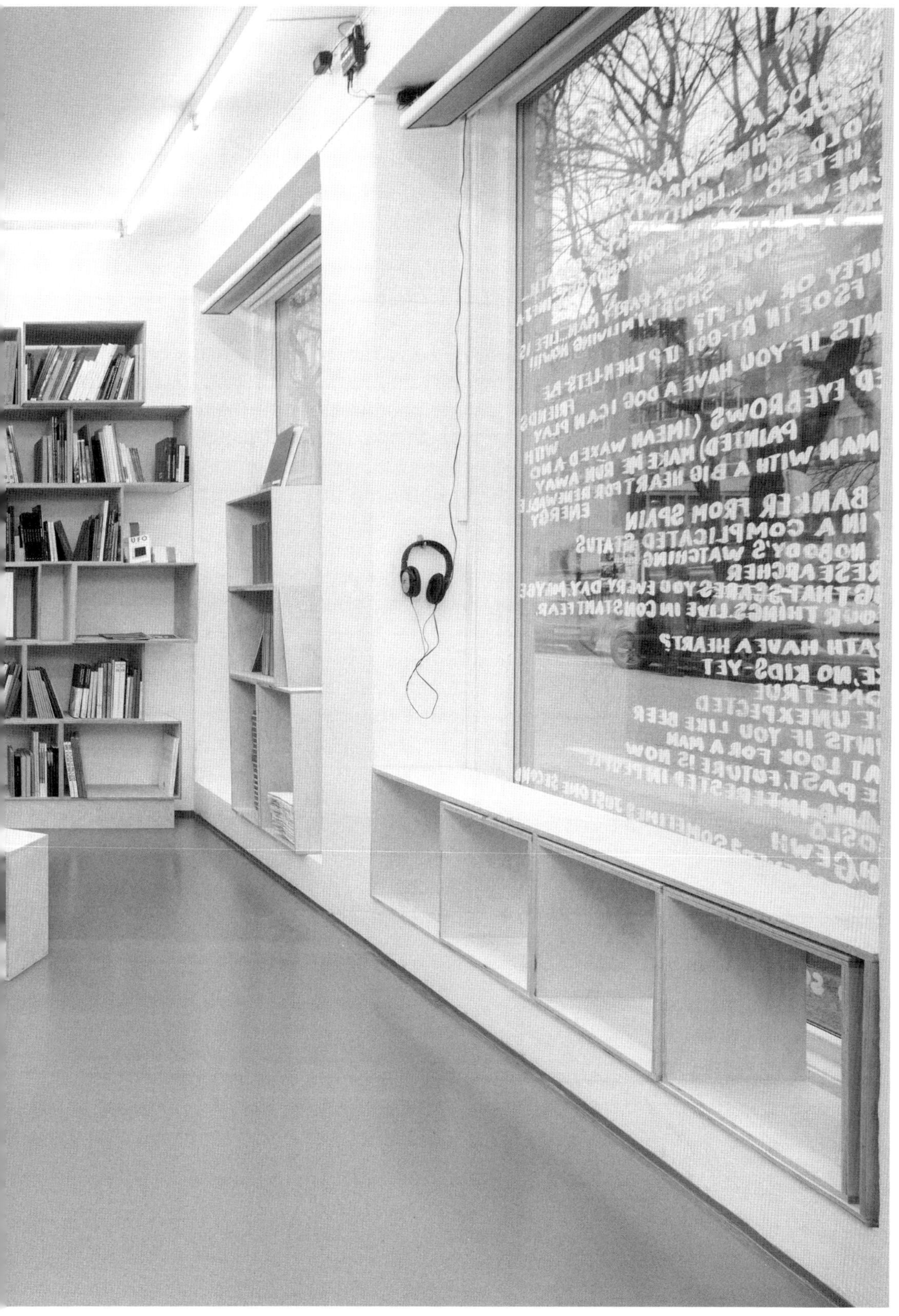

Silja Leifsdottir in Conversation with Håkon Lillegraven

historical events. Despite subjectivity and digital manipulation, we still to a certain extent rely on what we see in a photograph as an authentic representation of reality, even though we're aware that the opposite is true. As such, photography has the magical ability to transcend time with narratives that reflect the past, not necessarily as it was, but as you or others wish it was. Photography, then, makes it possible for our present self to journey into an unknown future and into histories, ensuring that they won't be forgotten. Notwithstanding the fact that photography is perceived as conserving an instant, there is a tension – and a precarious balance – between preserving a memory and reconstructing it. To me, this is part of the core of photography and the reason why my fascination with the medium is apparently endless. Via this project I wanted to investigate how the ability of photography to transcend time is faring at present.

HL   In the press releases for *What Remains*, you chose not to stress the fact that the exhibition consisted entirely of female artists. Can you say something about why?

SL   Being a curator means supplying some form of context for the project and being aware of just how much a context can influence the artistic content – for better or worse. If as curator I'd chosen to emphasise the fact that I invited only female artists, I think this would have affected the way the exhibition and the works were perceived to a very great extent. And a curator's job is also to provide a context within which artists feel comfortable. Most of the female colleagues of my acquaintance prefer to be called 'artist' or 'curator', not 'female artist' or 'female curator'. In this case, the artists would have had a different task from the one I wished to focus on. For that reason, this was an underlying thematic rather than a prominent aspect of the exhibition.

The choice not to include this in the press release also has to do with a general discussion in my entire project, where representation, decontextualisation and text versus form are recurring themes. Can objects/ images speak for themselves, independently of the artists' voices, or are the objects mute and in need of a text with an explanation or information that can speak for them? And, in that case, who is to be the 'voice'?

      What Remains

As a newly qualified curator, I found it particularly
instructive to see that no one noticed the gender of the
artists taking part before I eventually mentioned it myself. This helped me to understand just how important
the context is that one gives an exhibition in text form.
I hope and believe that this was also because the artistic
content and the curatorial concept were solid enough
for there to be no need to look for other threads in the
exhibition.

HL   Your 'statement' as a curator about the inclusion of only
female artists in the exhibition came in the form of the
opening speech, where you read out the names of all
the artists who'd taken part in Fotogalleriet's travelling exhibition *Nyere Norsk Fotografi* (New Norwegian
Photography) of 1979–80, which contained no women.
Can you talk a bit about this performative gesture as a
curator – why you chose to do things in that way?

SL   *New Norwegian Photography* is perhaps the most glaring
example of a lack of female artists, since its title signals
an exhibition featuring tendencies from the whole
country, but without a single woman being included.
The exhibition presented works by: Dag Alveng, Alf
M. Andreassen, Jim Bengston, Per Berntsen, Anders
Bromstad, Alf Edgar, Hans Olav Forsang, Jens Hauge,
Hugo Henriksen, Nils-Jørgen Kjærnet, Morten Krogvold, Morten Løberg, Harald Nervesen, Lavasir Nordrum, Jamie Parslow, Tom Sandberg, Johan Sandborg,
Jørn Sundby, Arvid Sveen and Kjell Sten Tollefsen. The
jury consisted of Tom Martinsen, Robert Meyer, Arne
Walderhaug and Bjørn Winsnes.

In the same way as this exhibition wrote itself into
the history of Fotogalleriet, I wanted to make all those
present aware of the fact that with this new exhibition
including only women, they were part of a new history being made. It's a question of being aware that the
present time will become history tomorrow.

HL   A great deal of work with Fotogalleriet's archive un-
derpins this book, and it's interesting that the press
release for your exhibition (where your motivations for
your choice of artists aren't made explicit) is a part of
our institutional archive, but not your opening speech,

      Silja Leifsdottir in Conversation with Håkon Lillegraven

which is just as important a document/piece of evidence regarding your curatorial approach. Have you subsequently had any thoughts about what it means for the reading of such projects in the future when institutions fail to archive such documents? How can we as institutions and curators become better at thinking of what 'golden records' we're leaving the future?

S L

I completely agree that the speech ought to have been archived. But since the institution wasn't in the habit of archiving anything other than press texts and documentation images, it was forgotten. This is probably because it's not a part of a lot of people's practice to think about what we leave for the future. I can't count how many press releases we found in Fotogalleriet's archive where the title and date of the show and the name of artist were there in black and white, but where the year wasn't mentioned, because it was considered unimportant when the press release was written. And we still think in that way. It's easy to forget that someone may come along ten, twenty, a hundred or even 40,000 years from now, trying to find a meaning in what we're doing today. And since neither you nor I can know what/who/which things will crystallise and prove important to preserve in the future, I think one must accept that it's up to others to write or change the history *en route*, in a similar way to how we now attempt to correct history by emphasising female artists, for example.

I think that both curators and institutions must become better at having two ideas in their heads at the same time: today's public *and* an unknown public at some unknown time. But, when all's said and done, we're only human, with various views, and what should be included/excluded in an archive as part of a future history will always be subjective to a certain extent. And because time, as well as art and photography, is always developing, the archive must of necessity constantly admit its own limitations, strengths and weaknesses. Images can't be translated unchanged between periods of time or between places – or archives, for that matter. Frictions and changes will always arise in the translation process. Time will distort, corrode and store different versions *en route*, like a memory that changes slightly every time you bring it out and examine it.

 What Remains

A key work in the branch of philosophy that investigates the origin, nature, methods and limits of human knowledge is *The Order of Things* (1966) by Michel Foucault. This book shows how different periods of history have been characterised by their own contemporary conditions of discourse and respective areas of knowledge – determining what it is possible or acceptable to affirm – and how these have been subject to change over time. In the chapter 'The Prose of the World', Foucault elaborates on how resemblance played a constructive role in the knowledge of Western culture. He specifies four categories of resemblance: 'convenience', where the extremity of one element is also the beginning of the next, like a chain; 'mirroring/echoing', where elements duplicate infinitely like a series of concentric circles; 'analogy', where an element extends to an endless number of relationships through which everything in the universe can be drawn together; and lastly, 'sympathy', a free state of mobility.

For me, these similitudes resonated when reading the article 'Artistes Iconographes' (Iconographer Artists) by Aurélien Mole and Garance Chabert.[96] This essay highlights different types of 'intra-images' in iconographic practices: 'montage' – bringing items together to create meaning within a collection; 'archiving' – focusing on the systematic accumulation of thematically connected and/or identical items in order to level meaning; 'astronomy' – combining items without common values to create new readings through the singularity of each item.

Such patterns are traceable in both artistic and theoretical practices of 'thought-diaries'. These writings do not recount the passing days, but instead figuratively represent an editing room in which works and the reflections around them are created. The intentions and usages of such diaries span from being written for publishing or public presentation to being annotations on artworks, revealing aspects and lines of thought beyond the works. These latter writings may become an important addition to the artwork, collecting the many levels of 'knowledge-solitude' or research work that constitute an archive in itself, and that are often not visible in the work's final result.

With reference to this, the *Mnemosyne Atlas* assemblage work by art historian Aby Warburg (1866–1929) is exemplary in confronting personal stories with the history of the world, and in presenting the problem of historicisation in regard

96
Published in the magazine *ART21*, no. 25 (winter 2009–10).

On Archives

to any question of intimacy, context and contemporaneity. Warburg's pioneering, experimental art-historical practice has been described as 'constellations' exploring new associations, meanings and (hi)stories within a given collection. It was chosen as a theoretical starting point for the creation of the Fotogalleriet Archives. Inspired by Warburg's notation system,[97] a customised stamp was designed and produced to identify all the elements in the archive within four main categories. In this way, the stamp became a new trace, juxtaposing past and possible future usages, as well as facilitating public access. Additionally – seeing the juxtaposing of documents as a method for the analysis of knowledge – Fotogalleriet's photobook library, video archive, slide archive and exhibition history were added to the archive's catalogue.

Started in a basement in 1977, Fotogalleriet was the first institution of its kind in the region to analyse the rapidly expanding nature of photography. The exhibition space does not intend to grow in size or mandate, but rather to use its established position to continue as an agent for growth, focusing on the contemporary practices and discourses of image making. The experience of the Fotogalleriet Archives was successful for setting in place for the first time public access to the history of the gallery, promoting Fotogalleriet in the role of research agent, and linking exhibition activities with the study and the production of knowledge in the field of contemporary art photography. The project led to experimentation in the exhibition programme, (re-)establishing connections with local and international partners, multiplying links between artistic practices, as well as the levels for experiencing them and the conversations within and around them.

Due to the intrinsic essence of humanity, archives cannot be objective, even if subjected to a system or a protocol. Although there is often a scientific aspect in their set-up and conservation, no collection can escape being influenced by the subjectivity of each one of us, our choices, and our ways of seeing. Sometimes, fictional or artificial archives may therefore be more effective than real or original ones. For this reason, in my work with archives I have progressively moved away from the academic notion from which I had started to approach them. And yet there remain two symmetrically opposed aspects that continue to somehow coexist in my work with archives, since I find that fundamentally an archive can consist of a set of documents, but also of a single one.

[97] Originally in Hamburg, the Warburg Institute was moved, under the shadow of Nazism, to London, where Aby Warburg's photographic collection is still available to the public. The collection is organised iconographically, by subject rather than by artist or by period – including the histories of art and science, and their relationship to superstition, magic and popular beliefs. This unique filing system sprang from the first era of image reproduction, allowing for the 'migration' of images, objects and ideas across geographical and historical contexts. Accordingly, the metaphorical term 'image vehicles' (*Bilderfahrzeuge*) was coined by Warburg in order to trace iconographic developments and the social function of images through cultural history.

Ultimately, archives represent for me a state of in-between, a non-place determining and enabling the transition between different layers of reality. They represent and converge thoughts and meanings, creating new 'images' not through what is collected, but through their gaps and absences.

In the face of urgent social issues of representation and recognition, the gaps one can find when looking at archives between the screaming affirmations of what is there to be seen and the silent statement of what is not there, represent spaces for understanding – as well as being tools for retrospective transparency, for inviting dialogue, and for renewed opportunities of conscious acting. Without losing respect for, nor underestimating the implications of big data and of how necessary scientifically driven archives are, we should also understand an archive as a necessary repository that can be implemented with minor effort across social and cultural establishments. The archive as a contemporary and customisable medium can allow for the creation of new categories that are lacking in classical-system representations, for establishing diversity within the (hi)story of a place by allowing new – or reaffirmed – 'spaces' to become visible. If archives were used as tools in this way, sustainable changes could be created and become established, finding their place within a history of exhibitions and within the history of humankind.

*Zayne Armstrong and Ellinor Aurora Aasgaard's
project* Days *— an experimental serial drama that
questions the social imaginary of the 'soap opera' by
substituting the abstracted Hollywood world of the
long-running TV series* Days of Our Lives *with the
specifics of contemporary Berlin – showed at Fotogalleriet in October/November 2020. The project originated in and moved beyond conversations between
Armstrong and Aasgaard. Through its development,
the artists had many fruitful and inspiring conversations. While the following is a piece of fiction, it points
to conversations that were essential in the development of the project.*

I arrive a bit early to meet him, and stand in the cold damp
night by a tree where I've locked my bike. He texts to say he'll
be 15 mins late, so to meet him inside. Despite having suggested the café-bar, I'm reluctant to go in alone, so with my
extra half-hour I have an espresso in a café on the floor below.

Once upstairs, he seems to also have just arrived. I join
him at an intersection of walkways, at a low coffee table sand-
wiched between two chairs, one crammed into the corner. I
look around for other options, but the whole maze is similarly
occupied with furniture made for spacious lounges. I set my
bag on the nearer chair, he adjusts himself and hesitantly
removes his jacket. I ask if he had wanted *this* chair. Yes, I
wanted this one,' he says as he puts his things onto that chair,
and starts to pull it out from the corner and into the walkway,
forcing the coffee table into my chair, then my chair and me
out into the other walkway.

Holding my breath, I realize why I suggested this place,
as well as why I was reluctant to come in any earlier: it's very
smoky in here. I don't smoke, and he smokes a lot.

I thought you said your colleague would join us?

Yes, she will, but later. Just so you two can meet. So, because this is somehow about moving our ideas about the soap
opera out of being just ideas, I'd like to take notes. Is that
OK?'

Yeah sure, but what I told you about HIV and all – it's not
really something I'd want in like a public biography about
me.' He gazes out of the facing windows that overlook the
busy intersection below.

276.

Of course. I'm mainly interested in finding ways for us to hang out, so meeting now is motivated by that urge, and it really does have to be motivated by something else, something more than just the money, because there barely is any now, and we're just crossing our fingers that we can actually pay you for your time, your contribution. I search his face for some sign of disappointment, but he just looks at me sweetly. I continue: 'We have made some funding applications to do this writing part, and the tricky thing is that while we don't actually know if we'll get the money yet, we – well no, I'll speak for myself – *I'm* eager to get started with the writing, because this first episode will sort of set the stage; it will potentially have long-term consequences.

Expressionless, he takes out his rolling tobacco.

The waitress comes, but I barely look at her.

He tells me that, when asked the question, 'Why did you come here?', he offers one of two answers, depending on who's asking and what the context is. If it's someone he expects to talk to just once, in a bar, on a bad date, an acquaintance whom he wants to remain as such, then he'll tell them that this is just another of his escapes from Cairo, the escapes that used to be routinely funded by jobs on some film or other, but which after the revolution, dissolved. Now it's just an escape derived from habit, a habit revealing itself to him more recently as motivated by a desire to run away from himself. He doesn't want to invest time and energy in casual exchanges, so this version allows him to keep the answer short and impersonal.

With a tall beer sat in front of him, and then me my tea, the waitress asks for the money directly. Three guys sit down opposite us, talking politely in English, like 'how've you been?' chit chat. He's noticed them too, and I watch him instead of the guys, to see how he sees things, but he just exhales smoke and I follow his smoke up, up to the dropped ceiling panels, like in an office building, but each tile covered in decorative felt-tip pen drawings of LSD-trip-like imagery. I think out loud that I always forget to look at the ceiling properly when I'm in here. I look back and lock eyes on him, asking for his second kind of answer.

          Zayne Armstrong

His former lifestyle provided him with an international network of friends, and in all these places he'd go to escape, he had friends, lots of close friends: 'a friend in Lebanon would text me asking if I have any hash for her, while I'm actually in India, but I hook her up with someone in Beirut. It's a casual feeling, but a deeper level of comfort and familiarity than anything I feel here.

The waitress passes again, now catching my eye. Her long black leather skirt is cinched in at the waist, her bobbed hair somehow matching her puffy white sleeves. He also notices her. We agree: great look.

The other answer – which he claims he's already told me – is a different truth. On one of these escapes, three years ago in Lebanon, there was an uprising over a trash problem, so he went to stay with friends to participate in the demonstrations. On this trip, he also went to get tested for HIV, and got positive results. To return to Cairo for proper testing and treatment – where his registration with a clinic would likely result in a confrontation with his various past projects of political resistance – was unappealing.

He rolls his maybe third cigarette – should I ask him to elaborate? – and holds it in his hand, his elbow resting on the short coffee table between us, and leans in close, exhaling casually. No elaboration, just smoke in my face. The waitress passes again, with raised eyebrows to ask if we're OK.

He tells me that a couple of friends – not married, but together, a couple who would separate three months later – invited him to Hamburg to take advantage of a facility for testing which kind of HIV he has and what treatment he'd need, a place this friend had access to. Instead of waiting a week in Hamburg for the test results, a city he was quickly bored by, he came here on the invitation of an ex-lover. He wasn't in love with this city, like people often say they are. He had visited here a number of times before. He likes the city's support of personal freedom, but its sense of vanity and self-centeredness, less so. Apart from his ex-lover, he had a few friends here, Egyptian-Lebanese, Egyptian-mix, Egyptian people, and this provided him with some hook of a social network to start out. Initially, he thought he'd just be able to get the test results and medication and go, but later he realised that, of course, he'll need the meds recurrently, so staying might be in order. But then, how to do that?

  Interview with a Friend

He sees me struggling to position my notebook on the cluttered table, and with the fourth cigarette in hand, takes my not-quite-empty green tea and moves it across to the unused section of the table, and comments that we don't need this lower coffee-table-book shelf. If it wasn't there, we'd be able to sit at it properly, with our legs underneath. I reach over and take back my tea. He apologises and I say that having left the teabag in, these are the most potent sips, which I can't forgo.

He tells me he got married to a friend of a friend of a friend of a friend, a Portuguese man who's been here for over a decade.

Ah, I hadn't really realised you were married.

I wasn't staying here with some plan; it all developed rather organically. A friend at an NGO helping refugees – though I'm not a refugee – was approached by this Portuguese trans person – so it's not 'he' who's my husband, but 'they' – a radical anarchist, who wanted to offer EU citizenship through marriage, if it'd help someone. We met, and the basic chemistry was there, so we did it.

He hates it when people ask 'what do you think of it here?', especially people from here. 'I'm not here because of this place, but rather as a consequence of a series of reactions to small events. A year, and it was all done. I had a five-year visa.' Over the next couple of years, he kept thinking that he somehow needed to 'integrate' in order to renew his visa later, or to get permanent residence – he's been taking German courses, trying to be a good citizen, doing his taxes etc, to be invisible in the system. But then a week ago he found out that it actually doesn't matter what *he* does, but more what his husband does, and that it's not about complying with the German system, but with a whole other set of EU citizenship regulations. Now he doesn't have his international network of friends like he used to. Here, he doesn't have any friends with whom he can just sit in bed and cry.

I glance up from my notebook, where I'm quickly writing my questions for clarification, and realise this is so far the most heartfelt moment of our conversation, but I can't quite follow what he means. I look him in the eye again to see if I can decipher the significance of that statement, but he just looks down, and I watch him lick the rolling paper and glue his fifth, or seventh cigarette together.

     Zayne Armstrong

Another guy joins the group next to us; greeting hugs, a fist bump, the group reshuffles.

The waitress passes again, elegantly evading the mess of male bonding, including my leg, which I didn't realise was also obstructing the walkway.

One of them, a rather handsome guy, finds a chair and adds it to the cramped pathway. I uncross my legs. 'How've you been? Wait, what happened to Bodie? Is he still out there?'

In checking him out, I notice one of the guys who's been there all along, but till now obscured by his friends' faded-denim back. I think I know him. I lean in to tell my friend that one of these guys is, I think, this closeted guy I hooked up with not so long ago. The guy notices me – for the first time? – and I'm sure now that it is him.

Do you want to talk with him?

No, no, I say, 'that'd be messed up.

It seems he's incapable of making new friends here. Everyone is apparently disposable, even if they're staying. The city is full of hedonism, everyone fucking everyone. Now, despite having a husband, ha ha, he meets guys, but nothing amounts to a more than a 2 or 3 week thing. They're always saying that they aren't emotionally available for something, or they're un...

I watch him inhale, and I look over to the guys across from us: ' … or they're closeted, or in an open relationship.' I ask him what came first, the discomfort he has, or the place being uncomfortable?

No, no, this is his own karma. It's not because of the character of the place. A lot of people come here to recreate themselves. He used to think that Cairo was the problem, but you have to confront yourself if you're going to evolve.

Are you somehow optimistic about that?

No, I don't like the word optimistic, I prefer hope – he looks down at my notes – hope comes from faith, to which you actively have to surrender. It's an active positioning … it's not cognitive, but comes from something within you, independent of anything external. Whereas optimism is blind, it's superficial, it's fake and dumb, it's not based on anything. Optimism is a naive expectation of something you think you deserve.

It's also possible to come here not as an act of escape, but as a realistic attempt to deal with your life', I say, surprised by my own misplaced defensiveness.

No, coming here wasn't an escape, like going to Lebanon. The flight there from Cairo was cheap. He'd been going since he was nineteen. He was at this summer camp for the youth of Arab families – the leftist, academic families – but these camps were too fascist, so he escaped, took a bus to Beirut, by contrast a total freedom place, and fell in love with it. Since then, he's been going there regularly, especially since film school, to see friends, and to work on films sometimes. It's his second life. He really does love Beirut ... he had a room in a friend's house where he would always stay.

'But maybe this idea of your karma catching up with you here is a product of testing positive?

'Coming here happened like ... it somehow came out of nowhere. I actually got over the HIV diagnosis very easily. I think that's not the issue, because that was something that I could no longer be in control of. I did it to myself. I remember the night, at a sauna in Amsterdam, and I was out of control. The whole process of coming here has been smooth. He knows it's been smooth because of this realisation ... that this was fine, he'd accepted what he'd done, and that now he's subject to the aftermath. And the universe supported it: the friend with the access to the testing facilities, the marriage, everything just happened effortlessly.

He's now dealing with a different struggle: how to surrender to the things that are out of his control. This is his current project, and it's mainly a love thing.

Ah ... I wasn't expecting that; I didn't think that you were talking about that – about romance.

No, I don't like that word.

OK, so then, your current, like, life project is somehow about a love thing. And perhaps the stigma around HIV, which is more of a cultural problem, surely isn't helping. But wait, what's out of your control? And what's within your control?

The waitress comes and takes my empty teacup, his empty beer glass. 'Big questions', he tells me, and gets up to go to the toilet. She asks if we want another?

                    Zayne Armstrong

He asks if they have any snacks – a big thing of peanuts for 2.50 – do you have any of those pretzel sticks? – No, but you can go buy whatever from downstairs and bring it up – That's not an issue? – No, no, we're fine with that sort of thing – OK, OK. He walks off.

The waitress lingers. Oh sorry, I don't know what he wants actually.

Another guy joins the group. The closeted guy pushes his chair back to make more room. The floor lamp behind him begins to topple over, but seeing me watching this – my face must have communicated the threat; I guess I gestured or pointed a little – he turns as the lamp hits the wall and the bulb pops. The waitress goes over. Quickly assessing the situation, she tells them to leave it. He turns to give me an exaggeratedly impersonal thank you anyway.

My phone rings. My colleague friend asks how late we'll stay. She's not sure if she can make it, and how's the talk going?

'It's OK, but we might have to rethink our approach to writing. I'm having a hard time getting a clear idea of the kind of soapy drama we want … Everyone we're talking with has these stories that are too, like, nuanced and complex. No-one has, like, risen from the dead or escaped a mental institution.'

'But he said he's got lots of stories of these sexual escapades since moving here that he wanted to write about, no?'

Can you imagine writing from your position, bringing your self into it? I'm thinking of how to … make this easy, to reduce the amount of labour you'd have to put in before we know if the project can even pay you for your time.

The waitress returns with a piece of cardboard and a brush to sweep up the broken glass. The faded-denim jacket guy gets up to attempt a forceful take-over of the cleaning. The closeted guy now makes intent eyes at me.

Well, I've literally not left my apartment for the last three, no, four days. I don't see anyone. I'm now doing this work of acceptance – acceptance of my circumstances, and perhaps writing on this with you could even support that process.

I respond that the nature of this kind of work is always slippery; often it feeds on one's own self-discovery. Framing that as valuable labour is great, and also easy to neglect. The last time I was tested for HIV and STIs', I tell him,

                    Interview with a Friend

'my EHICard had expired and I had no other insurance, so I would have needed to pay something. I certainly couldn't have afforded to get tested, but the guy at the clinic informed me that sex workers get free tests, and asked if I was a sex worker.

I look at the closeted guy across from us. With the lamp gone, his dark zone apparently allows him look at me all he wants.

So I thought, well really, if you break it down, am I a sex worker? If I weren't so poor I might not even be confronted with this question.

There's a clear distinction there, he says. You can claim there's ambiguity there, but … I can tell you, for those of us who are sex-workers, that ambiguity can be … unhelpful. He takes a filter between his lips.

I cross my legs, take my note book up onto my knee – *What's going on, did he just tell me he's a sex worker?* But without looking up, I coolly continue – What did you mean before, when you said that I was asking you big questions?

You asked me about the nature of one's control over their life, right?

Sure … I wait for him to respond, forcing my face up from my lap, suddenly self conscious. He confidently packs a pile of tobacco shreds into the frail paper, looks at me, and shrugs.

     Zayne Armstrong

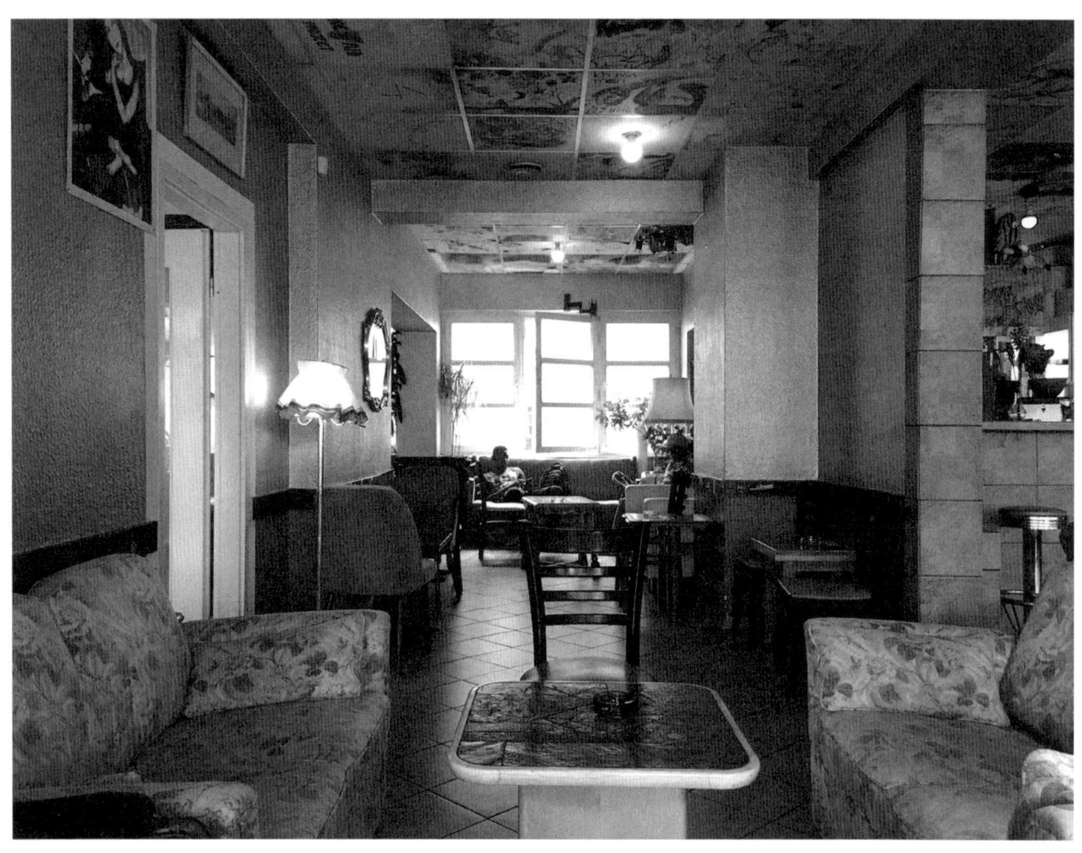

    Interview with a Friend

Politics in the Image of Blackness
Nikhil Vettukattil

98
Edward Said, *Culture and
Imperialism* (London: Chatto
and Windus, 1994), 336.

*Imperialism consolidated the mixture of cultures and identities on
a global scale. But its worst and most paradoxical gift was to allow
people to believe that they were only, mainly, exclusively, white, or
Black, or Western, or Oriental.* − Edward Said[98]

I.

Stock Images

The proliferation of information technology has made large
datasets and information available to individuals, advertisers,
corporations and governments on an unprecedented scale.
Huge amounts of countervailing information are being spun
and cycled through official and unofficial channels, as well
as legal and illegal images, 'alternative facts' and 'fake news',
available to anyone with an Internet connection, anywhere in
the world. It is almost as if, overnight, everyone has gained
the potential to confront what Umberto Eco called 'the an-
ti-library', that vast assortment of knowledge, whether 'legiti-
mate' or 'illegitimate', that we have not yet encountered. Such
a moment would have offered a great opportunity for all of
us to be more aware of our ignorance, to widen our gaze and
unsettle our assumptions, if we had not instead hastily set off
to find justifications and confirmation for biased opinions in
order to exercise the power of 'facts' and 'authority' over one
another.

In 2013, the saturation of photographic surveillance technologies, affordable smartphones and the implementation
of police body cams reached critical mass. This equipment,
combined with official and unofficial media channels, gave
increased visibility to the previously unacknowledged fre-
quency of murders and acts of brutality perpetrated by
law-enforcement officers, dispersing virally across the globe.
These affecting images of death as spectacle migrated with
unprecedented speed through the polity, galvanising respons-
es of solidarity with the grieving, afflicted and vulnerable that
consolidated in the leaderless movement now known as Black
Lives Matter. This growing body of 'empirical' evidence has
led to a wider awareness that questions how the State verifies
and corroborates its monopoly on the social consensus of
truth. This summer has seen the resurgence of BLM in the
midst of a global pandemic.

The relevance of this development for cultural production
should not be underestimated. At the very time when

Politics in the Image of Blackness

neoliberal versions of multiculturalism are the ideology of choice, and art institutions and commercial businesses scramble to implement policies of 'transparency', 'diversity', and 'inclusion', a new global order of policing that condones brutality and surveillance is being implemented. 'Black sites' – saturated regions of unacknowledged racial violence – proliferate with a new intensity through detention centres and torture chambers, international waters and desert borders, Indigenous territories and 'reservations', dark pools (secret trading systems) and the dark web, i.e. the condoned fringes of national sovereignty beyond the field of political, legal and cultural representation. This policing system implements new technologies such as facial recognition and 'big data' to place a renewed focus on establishing and determining identity through documentation, passports, bodies and digital fingerprints. As the art world celebrates its newly expanded identity, it washes its hands of the spreading framework of 'security' that organises its racial and economic borders.

In 2000, Fotogalleriet exhibited Piotr Ulanski's *A Norwegian Photograph*. Continuing Ulanski's inquiry into the clichéd image, this photograph's arrangement of white Norwegian photography students in the shape of a heart presents an image of the country still rooted in a racialised national identity that is deeply alienated from its diverse actuality, in the service of aesthetic ends. As Ina Blom wrote in a review of the show, 'It is only in photographs that communities are unambiguous.'[99] Norway is no exception to the fact that all nation states promote myths of monoculturalism and monolingualism that are reinforced through a fabricated national identity, forged through imperial history, that intentionally misrepresents the variety and interaction of dialects, languages and cultures within the geographical region. This identity is instrumental in the commodification of national exports for the international capitalist market, where cultures are packaged with branding, flags and trademarks, and high prices reward 'authenticity' and origin. All the while, one finds a degree of complacency and blindness to the influence and hegemony of superpowers like America and China to exert their values and perspective on their neighbours, or the unquestioned adoption of English as the *lingua franca* of business, science and the arts. Globalisation superimposes its own varieties of monoculture and monolingualism through international standards in an effort to iron out these

99
Ina Blom, 'Peter Uklanski – A Norwegian Photograph', in: *Nordic Art Review*, vol. II, no. 6, 2000, 83.

     Nikhil Vettukattil

differences in the smooth flow of capital. The global circulation of commodities on the free market stands in contrast to the denial of free movement for people.

2.

Contrast And Exposure

Photography as an artistic practice cannot easily be extricated from its wider practice in society. It has been inherently difficult for it to establish itself as a medium of art, relying on institutions for its context and definition.[100] In this history, Fotogalleriet has been instrumental in establishing photographic-image-based practices as contemporary artistic practice in Norway, providing an institutional form that closely followed the model and self-presentation of the fine art gallery and later of the kunsthalle. One could perhaps also find a light gesture of identification with Alfred Stieglitz's New York venue, Little Galleries of the Photo-Secession (later known as 291), in the decision to exhibit his photographs in the space's second ever exhibition in 1977.

From its inception, the artists exhibited at Fotogalleriet have been those who see their work in opposition to and in conversation with the use of photographic images in the media. A year after the space opened, describing her 1978 Fotogalleriet exhibition in *Morgenbladet*, the photographer Ann Cathrin Eek would state:

> I was starting to get tired of all the superficial images of women in the mass media. Not to mention the superficial, prejudiced and often denigrating images of women in advertising, men's magazines, and photography journals. My responsibility as a photographer was to penetrate this wall of platitudes and prejudices and to portray the reality for women that I saw around me.[101]

Spaces like Fotogalleriet were not produced by a political mandate, but through the work of artists who recognised a need or absence that made it important to set up a place to produce, question and exhibit the possibilities of images related to but not restricted by photography. The exhibition space only began receiving funding from the Royal Norwegian Ministry of Culture in 1986, a role then transferred to

100
We might note here that it was not until 1989 that the Museum of Contemporary Art in Oslo began to acquire photography.
101
Morgenbladet, 4 April 1978 (translation author's own).

   Politics in the Image of Blackness

the Arts Council in 2012. This transformation of Fotogalleriet
from an artist-run space in a basement into a leading institution can be situated within a development across the art
world that Morgan Quaintance has elsewhere characterised
as 'institutional isomorphism': 'the state of inter-institutional
influence in which organisations seeking entry to, or the ele-
vation of status within, a given professional sphere mimic the
formal procedures and structures of established organisations
that set the bar for legitimacy within their sector'.[102]

The deepening professionalisation of the arts field over
these last forty-three years has also seen an increasing isomorphism between the practices of institutions and the artists
they exhibit. This integration has not primarily occurred
through adopting institutional practices that are experimental or deviate from social and economic norms, but through
artists adopting the values of the dominant professional or
corporate culture. Today, in keeping with the normative and
formal procedures of the field, Fotogalleriet has a board, a
council, an intern, mediators, consultants for communication and digital content and biannual programme meetings.
State-funded organisations that deviate from these norms are
few and far between, but they can and do exist.

The dominant paradigm of how to organise at a national,
institutional and increasingly individual level is bureaucratic.
The taxonomic aspect of bureaucracy both structures and
produces the meaning of differences, a pattern reproduced at
educational, institutional and governmental levels that perpetuates structural violence and homogeneity of experience.
Whether an institution defines itself as neutral or not, the
institutional juxtaposition of wildly different artistic practices
has a neutralising effect on the political content of programming. The apparent diversity of programming legitimates the
claim of being unbiased and balanced, but biases can perpetuate through the structure of the programme. If bureaucratic
cultural models outsource the function of being 'critical' or
'radical' to the selection of individual artists and artworks,
they may house them in formal procedures that negate any
such intent. In this way, wide-ranging and often opposing
artistic positions are framed by a process of mediation that
presents any and all such standpoints equally, and therefore
with only barely plausible affirmation. The transparency of
any ostensibly public programme is juxtaposed with the opac-
ity of the relations that produce it and its audience. These

102
Morgan Quaintance, *The
New Conservatism: Complic-
ity and the UK Art Worlds
Performance of Progress*, https://
conversations.e-flux.com/t/
the-new-conservatism-
complicity-and-the-uk-art-
worlds-performance-of-pro-
gression/7200 (accessed 23
August 2020).

Nikhil Vettukattil

procedures are of concern because how can we meaningfully address past biases in the institution's history if we do not in turn connect them with the mechanisms of discrimination as they are deployed in the present?

103
Frantz Fanon, *Black Skin, White Masks* (New York: Grove Press, 1967), 161.

3.
Against the Archival Impulse

Since 2000, less than half of the solo exhibitions at Fotogalleriet have been by women of any background, and less than one in ten by artists of a non-white background. Until two years ago, with Lauren Davis's *Imperialist Nostalgia*, no black artists had been given an exhibition. At the same time, numerous exhibitions throughout Fotogalleriet's history have displayed black and brown photographic subjects through photographs from Haiti, Argentina, the Gambia, Ghana, India, Botswana, Kenya and across many other localities in North America.

Until Bouchra Khalili's exhibition in the summer of 2020, over forty-three years of exhibitions, there has never been a solo exhibition by an artist from the entire African continent. Despite this fact, the history of Fotogalleriet is full of photographs of black bodies, from Per Heimly's *Portrait of Jesus* (1997) (a photo of a black penis with a crown of thorns) to Morten Krogvold's 1993 *Images from Botswana*, the result of an expedition on behalf of the Norwegian Agency for Development (NORAD), or in a more complex sense, in Vibeke Tandberg's 1994 series *Aftermath*, which simultaneously perpetuates and deconstructs colonial discourse in the all-too familiar ways we still call 'critical'. The fascination with racialised forms of seeing and imagining the Other permeates the archive. In the words of Frantz Fanon: 'Only for the white man the Other is perceived on the level of the body image, absolutely as the not-self.'[103]

Maintaining an appearance of neutrality is key to the perceived legitimacy of any cultural institution from the perspective of the State and its mechanisms for funding. I would like to highlight several episodes from Fotogalleriet's history that synchronically and diachronically illustrate the untenable logic of institutional neutrality and demonstrate how its contradictions can produce harmful compound effects. Throughout this text the technical proficiency of the artists I mention is never questioned. In highlighting episodes of systemic violence, I do not wish to ascribe intentional prejudice to the

          Politics in the Image of Blackness

photographers, but rather to emphasise how race is primarily a relation of power, not only a problem of individuated discrimination. The institutional framing of the exhibitions invites comparisons that in turn compound a racial meaning within the system of representation.

In 1979, two years after the foundation of Fotogalleriet, an exhibition by Arne Walderhaug titled *A Journey to the East* presented photographs from his travels in Pakistan, Afghanistan and India. Gro Jarto's catalogue text for the exhibition, states that India is not the homeland of the 'truths we recognize from newspaper headlines and UN reports, not the poverty and beggar's India, not the homeland of hunger.' But she later asks us to: 'Just look at the woman with the shroud and forget everything you know about women suppression and such for a while, look at the woman enveloped in her white shroud until she becomes an image of hidden femininity and obvious mystery.' This double movement of emphasis and then disavowal of racist and sexist interpretation continues to be perpetuated throughout the archive. Such exhibitions paradoxically entrench the European imperial perspective as the subject of histories other than its own, to feature other peoples merely as an object and not as a subject of photography.

However much this tendency of representation has been criticised, its practice continues, most recently in Terje Abusdal's *Indian Interiors* from 2017. Among other images, a series of found X-rays displays the bodily insides of Indians from Tehri. Does this express what Denise Ferreira da Silva calls the 'transparency thesis' by exposing that there is no interiority that can resist exterior determination? What should we make of the exhibition's re-coding of scientific imagery as representing something essential about the subcontinent and its people?

As is the status quo today, all these exhibitions fail to acknowledge the imperial logic of extraction. When the artist extracts images that are then sold, they ignore the role of subaltern subjects in the production of this value. 'Similar to other imperial technologies, photography rendered the communities from which visual wealth was extracted into those who receive almost nothing in return.'[104]

104
Ariella Azoulay, *Potential History: Unlearning Imperialism* (London: Verso, 2019), 368.

Nikhil Vettukattil

In 1986, as part of its frequent practice of double exhibitions, Fotogalleriet presented the work of Espen Tveit
and Oluf Føinum. Tveit's exhibition, called *Z* after the film
journal of the same name, was, as the critic Robert Meyer
noted, a break with the artist's previously abstract formalism to focus on a kind of cinematic realism in representing
scenes from Oslo, Paris and London.[105] By contrast, Føinum's
exhibition *West African Wrestling* presented photographs that
are the result of numerous state-funded trips by the artist to
the Gambia. The contrast between the urban presentations of
Europeans and half-naked Gambian wrestlers is further emphasised by the exhibition poster, which juxtaposes a young
white child innocently gazing into the camera with an image
of two black men engaged in combat. What does this institutional framing achieve except for an imperial logic of difference? As Kuan-Hsing Chen and others have examined in
detail, the identity of the powerful (the imperial subject) can
only be affirmed in its relation and opposition to the dis-em-
powered (colonized): 'Imperialist subjectivity is constituted by
its power relations with the colony.'[106]

Føinum states in a local newspaper: 'It is important for
Africans who come to Norway that we know that they come
from and represent a land with a very rich cultural tradition.'[107] Yet in a review of the exhibition, Robert Meyer
writes: 'Apart from a general competitive spirit, the images
are poor in cultural expression. Despite Basil Davidson's
laudatory words in the catalogue, the pictures are not able to
engage – neither as single pictures nor as a whole.'[108] As in
Walderhaug's exhibition, Føinums's photographs of non-white
peoples and cultures are contextualised by a white author. In
the words of bell hooks, 'To be seen and not known is the
ultimate abandonment.'[109] Even after six trips and many years
of travelling to West Africa, it does not occur to Føinum that
awareness of culture and tradition would be better achieved
by giving space to 'Africans who come to Norway' to represent themselves. If Føinum is impervious to this it is because
acknowledgment would negate his position as the artist, the
owner of the work, and his identity as the mediator, a role
that only serves to insert the European as the subject in the
narration of other histories. The tendency for Westerners to
perceive the plural cultures and ethnicities of Africa as inter-
changeable is revealed when Meyer's review incorrectly claims
that the images are from Ghana, not the Gambia.

105
Robert Meyer, 'Visuell tidtro-
yte', *Aftenposten*, 28 May 1986
(translation author's own).
106
Kuan-Hsing Chen, *Asia as
Method: Toward Deimperi-
alization* (Durham: Duke
University Press, 2010).
107
'Jeg tror også det er viktig for
afrikanere som kommer till
norge at vi vet at de kommer
fra og representer et land
med en veldig rik kulturell
tradisjon', in: *Abeider-Avisa*, 12
May 1986.
108
'Bortsett fra en almindelig
konkurranseand, er bildene
fattige pa kulturelle uttryk.
Tross Basil Davidsons rosende
ord i katalogen evner ikke
bildene å engasjere – hverken
som enkelt bilder elle some
en helhet'. Robert Meyer 1986
(see note 105).
109
bell hooks, *Being the Subject
of Art*, in *Art on My Mind:
Visual Politics* (New York:
W.W. Norton & Company,
1995), 134.

Politics in the Image of Blackness

Three years ago, the exhibition series *Nordic Anthology* included *The History of Botany* by Daniel Hansen, an exhibition marked by colonial nostalgia. Following a decontextualised quote from the journal of colonial scientist Joseph Banks recording his arrival with Captain Cook on Australia's shore, the press release goes on:

> In the introduction to *The Human Condition*, Hannah Arendt describes how she felt militaristic and nationalistic interests overshadowed the moon landing. Therefore, it simply didn't feel quite right to celebrate the occasion. Daniel Hansen believes something similar has happened to our own planet: different interests have come to shape our understanding of places – sometimes whole continents – to a point where we're no longer able to dream of them freely.

This misinterpretation of Arendt's comments cannot make sense except from the viewpoint of the imperial Western subject.

In the period to which Hansen's exhibition refers, botany was crucial to the function of colonisation and empire, as part of a process of discovering crops that could be made economically productive, such as tobacco, cotton, sugar, tea, coffee, rice and potatoes, which had already been great sources of wealth for the empire. Banks's 'scientific' endeavour actively sought to establish the land as a *terra nullius*, an uninhabited 'no-man's land', by denying the humanity of the continent's Indigenous peoples. The comparison to the Moon landing only reinforces this idea of *terra nullius*. The exhibition makes no effort to contextualise or recognise this subtext. Instead, it freely appropriates excerpts from the journal of Captain Cook and Joseph Banks to produce a decidedly one-sided presentation of colonial history, as if it were only a case of the 'history of botany'. This present absence is marked in the exhibition text, which quotes Banks's uncanny formulation: 'In the course of the night many fires were seen.'

We might ask how the programming of this exhibition diachronically impacts on the reception of the work of Lauren Davis some months later, in her exhibition *Imperialist Nostalgia* of 2018. Here, the African American artist presented digital prints 'collaging visual elements that correspond to

   Nikhil Vettukattil

both preconceptions and archaic female and black attributes and that are traditionally associated with fertility and the savage: lavish fruit and exotic plants are combined with elegant limbs of a female black body, or body of colour.' The aesthetics of the work would not be out of place in many of the gentrified bars and cafés of Oslo, and their unconscious invocations of the colonial age. Can Davis's exhibition be seen as a response to Hansen's? Nothing suggests that the work or its framing is capable of encouraging us 'to critically think how these shapes have come into being'.[110] This only serves to reinforce a dehumanising perspective of objectification, even if self-consciously evoked. Neither Davis's work nor Hansen's does anything formally innovative that challenges Western conventions of artistic practice. Davis's work invokes precisely the multicultural paradigm of externally determined difference that I critiqued earlier.

In response to these exhibitions, two simultaneous operations might then be proposed in order to reconstruct image-based practice in a decolonial manner. Firstly, the dismantling and provincialising of what I would like to call 'strategic universality' – dominant forms of abstraction and formalism (Western 'modernist' aesthetics) that claim to express universal, neutral, normative or objective techniques but are in fact particular overextensions of dominant, white, male perspectives and assumptions that erase, negate or integrate others. Such strategic use of universality is also a key element in right-wing discourse on 'freedom of speech'. The possibility of this task is made evident by its opposite: overcoming the need for 'strategic essentialism', by which I mean the way in which abstract, social political characteristics are embodied or localised to individuals as properties of their identity or subjectivity, such as through race, ethnicity, gender or class, and through which they are asked to express an essence that is imposed from without.

For artists of colour to be able to be seen and read in a way that is not reduced to questions of ethnicity and difference on the terms of the dominant white framework[111] will only be possible when white imperial practices are understood as embodying a minority of the world's possible values, knowledge and perspectives. Until then, we might only be invited to express ourselves in relation to questions of our minority status, subjugation, or what we can be made to represent, and not the many other questions in which we also have just as much at stake.

 Politics in the Image of Blackness

110
Press release, http://www.fotogalleriet.no/en/exhibitions/lauren-davis (accessed 23 August 2020).
111
A framework that is equally present in postcolonial states.

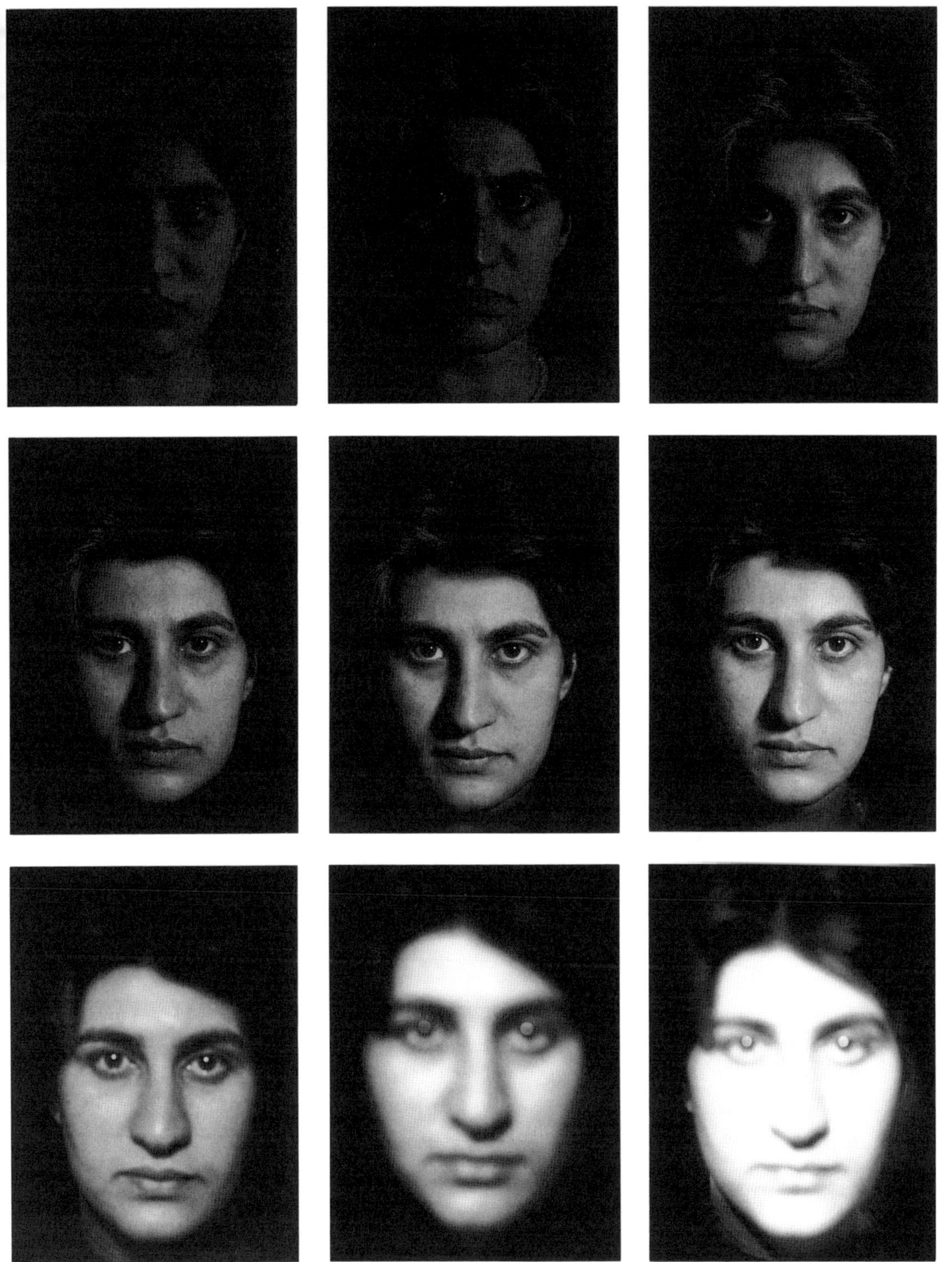

Nikhil Vettukattil

Any significant shift undoubtedly faces great resistance because changing values and histories invariably destabilise the economic value of existing collections wherever they are in the world. A leading survey of global private collections confirms their unsurprising homogeneity, founded on a uniform set of biases, with a consistent focus on male painters of national origin.[112]

If contemporary art can prove itself a place for collectivity in struggle, the work of making a culture that people are really part of, it will require overcoming both socially acceptable, marketable, formalisations as 'painting' or 'photography' and uncontroversial theoretical posturing.

4.
The Political Art of Blackness

I have of course immigrated to Norway, but I'm no longer an immigrant. I'm part of the minority, a woman of the minority. I would really like to call myself a 'black woman'. But I've met with a lot of resistance. 'But you're not black', you know. Black is applied to Africans. That Black could be a political concept has not occurred to the journalists.[113]

In 2004, reflecting on the successes and failures of the Black Arts Movement that first emerged in the 1980s, the artist Rasheed Araeen highlighted the way in which even sympathetic accounts of the movement have a tendency to simplify the significance of the project of Black Art, 'to collapse it into whatever is produced by black artists':

> The allusion to 'race' in this specificity indicates an experience of a particular group of people or a community, which has resulted not necessarily from its own perception of itself but the way white society defines it by invoking its difference. This difference is of course there and is part of the community's identity, but it is not fundamental to what it aspires to.[114]

I want to argue that the communal aspiration to live in a society without systemic forms of oppression, an aspiration that exceeds the integration of cultural identity, finds its reversal in our present multicultural paradigm that promotes the separation of cultural identities at the expense of structural change.

[112] See: *Who Collects Art? An International Empirical Assessment* (Zurich: CREMA, 2014), http://www.crema-research.ch/papers/2014-03.pdf (accessed 23 August 2020).

[113] Anonymous interviewee in: Elisabeth Eide, 'Strategic Essentialism and Ethnification', in: *Nordicom Review*, no. 31, 2010, 70.

[114] Rasheed Araeen, 'The Success and the Failure of Black Art', in: *Third Text*, vol. 18, no. 2, 2004, 135.

For Araeen, Black Art was never about such essentialised difference, but what this difference comes to mean in a society that still has not fully come to terms with colonialism and its imperial logic. Following Aimé Césaire,[115] we might say that without this contextualising of coloniality, it is not possible to understand the resurgence of facism in Europe or elsewhere as it is taking place today. That Black Art was from its beginning anti-colonial and anti-facist should be evident from the early photo collage work by Eddie Chambers *Destruction of the National Front 1979–1980*, which has since become emblematic of the movement.

In the last century, the application of European colonial procedures back onto the nation itself was manifested in Norway through practices like the Norwegianisation policy violently imposed on Sámi peoples, forced sterilisation of native minorities, and the discrimination, expulsion and deportation of Jewish citizens. The logic of these procedures continues to impact the nation, its culture and demography in ways that are still not fully acknowledged.

This period was marked by a general decline of internationalist politics following the civil rights movements of the 1960s, enfolding political struggle back into the national-cultural frame. Whilst this transition has allowed for a more sophisticated development of cultural politics, it has undermined the framework of anti-colonial activism by neutralising some of the political valences of the concept of race as a global idea. The further this repression dissociates the rise of racism, right-wing and authoritarian politics from the colonial, imperial and Cold War logics that are their proper frame, the less comprehensible this rise becomes. And it is in the midst of this transition that we find Araeen's tragic construction of a black modernist avant garde emerging in the very same moment as mainstream acceptance of the 'end of the modern' itself. Modernism as an artistic paradigm, its subsequent deconstruction through postmodernism, and more recently, decolonialism, have not been sufficiently analysed in relation to a broad shift in European immigration policy from a paradigm of resettlement to a politics of foreign intervention – a paradigm shift that neatly tallies with the rise of Non-European immigration after the Cold War.

In Norway, this tendency has been represented in the field of immigration through 'increasingly strict border controls, a decreasing number of asylum applications granted, forced

115
Aimé Césaire, *Discourse on Colonialism* (New York: Monthly Review Press, 2001), 15.

Nikhil Vettukattil

deportations to countries at war and so on'.[116] This post-Cold
War shift in immigration policy and international relations
was signalled by the intention to make Norway a 'humanitarian superpower' in 1994, and the simultaneous identification
of morality with nationality in Prime Minister Gro Harlem
Brundtland's slogan 'It's typically Norwegian to be good!'[117]
This intention to 'do good' no doubt informed the Oslo
Accords and numerous other failed diplomatic projects such
as that in Sri Lanka from the mid-90s until 2007,[118] while still
managing to echo a civilising discourse of the earlier colonial
era. At the same time, 'the percentage of asylum seekers from
all countries granted refugee status, which in 1987 was a modest 7.8 percent, reached an astonishing 0.5 percent'.[119] This is
the expanded context for Vibeke Tandberg's 1994 exhibition at
Fotogalleriet, of the photographic series *Aftermath*, to which I
shall now turn.

Tandberg's series of C-print photographs are digitally
altered versions of Trygve Bølstad's photojournalistic work,
which has been used by NORAD, NGOs, state publications
as well as newspapers. This particular series appears to depict
different forms of 'development' work in Kenya, but the
original photographs have been manipulated to include studio
portraits of Tandberg herself.

Long before the ubiquity of Photoshopping, Tandberg
digitally inserted herself into the humanitarian discourse,
in clichéd scenes such as distributing aid boxes from a heli-
copter, looking lovingly at a child, or offering instruction in
agriculture, always with an exaggerated gesture of sympathy
and innocence. While her simple white frock changes to
signify everything from nurse, scientist, to relief worker, the
red and blue lines on her white socks never cease to represent
her Norwegian nationality. These tableaux invoke a Christian
iconography that superimposes the missionary discourse of
the Good Samaritan onto our neocolonial present. The ease
with which we might first read these images is disrupted as
we come to note their artificality, a strange disjuncture between the white woman in the centre and the Kenyans with
whom she interacts. Though they appear to exchange glances
or touch, there is no literal contact between them. The the-
atricality of Tandberg's exaggerated presence is only heightened by the way in which it places the African subjects in an
imposed context of simplified authenticity. The uncanniness
of the images invites a critical reaction at the same time as

116
Oivind Fuglerud, 'Inside
Out: The Reorganization of
National Identity in Norway',
in: Thomas Blom Hansen and
Finn Stepputat (eds.), *Sover-
eign Bodies: Citizens, Migrants,
and States in the Postcolonial
World* (Princeton: Princeton
University Press, 2005), 296.

117
Ibid, 295.

118
'largely a story of failure',
according to NORAD's own
report 'Pawns of Peace', see:
https://www.oecd.org/coun-
tries/srilanka/49035074.pdf
(accessed 23 August 2020).

119
Fuglerud 2005 (see note 116).

   Politics in the Image of Blackness

undermining this by placing the artist in the foreground. The work is not so much about moral and ethical questions as it is about the narcissistic self-positioning of Tandberg herself. In the same instant as critiquing the position of whiteness, humanitarianism and liberal values, it self-cancels such intentions by re-centering whiteness as the matter of primary concern. As Richard Dyer wrote so eloquently in his work on Whiteness and photography:

> Extreme whiteness thus leaves a residue, a way of being that is not marked as white, in which white people see themselves. This residue is non-particularity, the space of ordinariness. The combination of extreme whiteness with plain, unwhite whiteness means that white people can both lay claim to the spirit that aspires to the heights of humanity and yet supposedly speak and act disinterestedly as humanity's most average and unremarkable representatives.[120]

I have chosen to focus on Tandberg's exhibition because it highlights a kind of limit-experience, a paradox in which the contradictions of the white gaze reach a kind of stasis, an end game. In *Aftermath*, the artist displays a more nuanced self-awareness in relation to race than previous examples I have mentioned, and does so through a more original deployment of formal techniques. By appropriating the contribution of the documentary photographer and erasing it, Tandberg rehearses the gestures of value extraction to which the original photographs lay claim. Yet by maintaining the focus on white feminine subjectivity, the images fail to redistribute the sensible, to inflect Jacques Rancière's turn of phrase: 'Politics revolves around what is seen and what can be said about it, around who has the ability to see and the talent to speak, around the properties of spaces and the possibilities of time.'[121]

Like the movements before it, Black Art did not produce the terms of its enunciation. Just as today, it was collective political unrest that breached the frame of representation in which art could respond. If the conditions for the formation of Black Art in the 1980s emerged through the experience of blackness as a form of discimination, police brutality, and socioeconomic inequality, it exploded in the Brixton Riots, just as it would again and again in the LA riots of 1992, in the

120
Richard Dyer, *White: Essays on Race and Culture* (London: Routledge, 1997), 223.
121
Jacques Rancière, *The Politics of Aesthetics*, (London: Bloomsbury, 2014), 13.

 Nikhil Vettukattil

2011 London Riots, the six years of struggles in the Black Lives Matter movement, to name just a few Western instances.

Without critical reflection on the failures of the Black Arts Movement, it seems unlikely that present demands and complaints against the institutional framework of contemporary art found in Black Lives Matter or Decolonise This Place will go beyond the inclusion and mainstream acceptance of a few individual non-white artists and arts professionals. That is to say, without significantly altering the structure of these institutions, the values they perpetuate, or challenging the present multicultural paradigm of the neoliberal state, the result would only reiterate what happened to the Black Arts Movement in the late 90s and early 2000s. Institutions now complying with the demands of multicultural diversification might only produce an expanded middle class of BIPoC professionals, artists, curators, an artistic elite to buffer and inoculate. If these BIPoC professionals prove unable to maintain a radical agenda, this will not challenge either the structures of oppression or central issues of economic dispossession and radical inequality.

5.

Aperture

It did not take long for the people to discover that all that had been changed was the color of their masters… independence brought little change and they remained chained to the same British-style institutions which the ruling elites manipulated and controlled to perpetuate their own advantages … the end of their struggle was also the end of their dreams. When … truly national consciousness failed to evolve, people began to revert to the security of their traditional parochial and class identities. The seeds of disintegration … were all sown in the colonial period. They are now coming to bitter fruition.[122]

If Araeen locates this failure in the ease with which Black Art disintegrated into divided problems of ethnicity, minority groups and their traditions, he is also specifying a variant of the wider shift from the problematisation of race to the problematisation of culture that was also being diagnosed at the time.[123] As Denise Fereira da Silva has argued 'in the late twentieth century the cultural seems to have displaced the nation and the racial to become the governing political signifier'.[124] Race has been substituted for more indirect forms

[122]
Altaf Gauhar (1987) as cited in: Kuan-Hsing Chen, *Asia as Method: Toward Deimperialization* (Durham: Duke University Press, 2010), 83-84.
[123]
See: Kenan Malik, *The Meaning of Race: Race, History and Culture in Western Society* (London: Macmillan, 1998).
[124]
Denise Ferreira da Silva, *Toward a Global Idea of Race* (Minneapolis: University of Minnesota Press, 2007), xxxii.

   Politics in the Image of Blackness

of systemic racism through questions of 'shared values' and 'culture', which are biased towards the majority that globally perpetuates stereotypical essences of other cultures as a social problem.[125] Minorities themselves mobilising strategic essentialism to claim a place in the existing framework cannot avoid inadvertently reinforcing a false essentialising ethnic identity that also undergirds the ideologies of national socialism and the extreme right. Araeen is keen to emphasise that the importance of the artists in exhibitions like *Essential Black Art* or *The Other Story* had much less to do with their diasporic backgrounds than with the way in which their works articulated a powerful new visual language that radically challenged white European norms of what art was and what it could be. This political and artistic critique has subsequently been erased in and through later institutional recognition of these artists, including Araeen, whose retrospectives and group shows largely ignore his more explicit questioning of race, instead choosing to integrate the work in ways that reform, revise and further the dominant narratives of modernism and culture.

As a lack of historical understanding allows the repetition of the 'infantile egoistic self-importance'[126] that Araeen identified as causing the demise of the Black Arts Movement, politics is again being hijacked by 'performative activism'. Revolutionary changes will not be implemented by shouting at and reforming liberal institutions if this is not backed up by strategies to collectively withhold labour and at the same time rebuild art through new communal forms of intervention. How can this be achieved if there is not also a raising of awareness in the majority of non-white communities to work together to reconstruct society rather than compete for an allotted share of its privileges through diversity politics? To enter the system on these terms is to accept an externally determined form of cultural difference.

Desires for inclusion and assimilation into the mainstream of art are a function of exclusionary discrimination, a distinction that no amount of dissimulation or mimesis will resolve. How, then, to avoid what Denise Ferreira da Silva has described as: 'another doomed strategy of emancipation, namely, the project of producing and interpreting crafts that communicate their particular socio-historical trajectories as subaltern travelers on the road to transparency'?[127] Is Araeen's 'hope for the day when the contingent "Black" of Black Art is no longer needed'[128] not also a case of such doomed aspiration?

125
Explanations of individual violence and criminality (eg. terrorism) are primarily grounded in an idea of ethnicity and culture when concerning people of minority backgrounds rather than, for example, individual psychology, to the extent where people of these backgrounds are asked to take responsibility, to explain or take representative roles regarding these issues. Conversely, white acts of terror are seen as exceptional and personal deviations from the norms of the white majority and disassociated from any implications of a more general responsibility for racist, sexist or economic tendencies in society and mainstream culture. Whether these issues are tackled individually or socially, such inconsistency is a marker of social hypocrisy within the frame of the nation.

126
Araeen 2004 (see note 114), 148.

127
Ferreira da Silva 2007 (see note 124), xxxiii.

128
Araeen 2004 (see note 114), 152.

Nikhil Vettukattil

Critiques of globalisation are at risk of inadvertently fostering such a romantic national sensibility that can deploy the illusory promise to extricate itself from the fateful entanglement of this world, a world in which we cannot but find ourselves. If national institutions in Norway such as Fotogalleriet cannot sufficiently articulate the international stories of which they form a part, they will end up mobilising a retrograde notion of culture that can only bolster a national sense of identity that perpetuates ethnic divisions. Exhibitions like Bouchra Khalili's and the forthcoming exhibition of Maryam Jafri offer some hope of this being achieved, but there is so much work still to be done.

What critics of the politics of difference like Araeen and Kenan Malik fail to appreciate is that these movements emerged in response to the forms of oppression internal to the politics of blackness itself: the sexism, racism, homophobia and anti-semitism that could continue unacknowledged within it, and the patriarchal essentialised subjectivities that could co-opt it. Practices of intersectionality emerged in opposition to these in order to complicate, but also enrich, the terms of solidarity. Such a blind spot is acknowledged in Supata Biswas's review of Araeen's *The Other Story*: 'Given that the bulk of the most exciting work produced in the past ten years has been the work of younger generation Afro-Asian artists, Araeen jeopardises this by his "hang-ups" about modernism, neglecting what would have been the show's major strengths, particularly the contribution of black women.'[129]

Today, if it is no longer possible to organise widely different minority groups under the umbrella of blackness, it is precisely because such a label does not allow for the articulation of the specific forms of discrimination now headed under 'anti-black racism', a racism to which Asian and other communities of colour have not been immune. In light of Poland's integration into the EU in 2004, Polish immigrants now make up the largest growing immigrant group in Norway, whose experience of being policed and discriminated against will not be expressed in binaries of black and white. Nor for that matter will the continuing struggles of Norway's Indigenous Sámi community. Intersectionality is present not only in relations of class, gender and race, but also in the entanglements of race, nationality and ethnicity. While we might speculate under what terms we can today mobilise and assemble, the validity of such categories will only prove themselves through

129
'The Wrong Story', in: *New Statesman*, 15 December 1989, 40–42.

 Politics in the Image of Blackness

a work of collective practice. Acknowledging the problems of Black Art does not, however, negate the possibility to revive the political potential for the present, as a counter-discourse that has been forgotten by a cultural logic of integration ignorant of the asymmetries of power that now envelop it. Recovering its political project of what was once Black Art could instead begin with a collective undertaking to examine and problematise its history in relation to our current moment.

Conversations on Photography

Biographies

Dag Alveng (b.1953) is regarded as a central voice and catalyst within Norwegian photographic art. His photographs are in the permanent collections of major museums in the US and abroad, including The Metropolitan Museum of Art, and The Museum of Modern Art, New York; Museum Folkwang, Essen; Sprengel Museum, Hannover; Stedeijk Museum, Amsterdam; Moderna Museet, Stockholm; the National Museum, Oslo; and Henie Onstad, Bærum. Alveng was one of the initiators and co-founders of Fotogalleriet in 1977 and first exhibited there as part of the Spring Exhibition in 1978, and most recently in 1999.

Zayne Armstrong (b.1986) is an artist based in Berlin. In the autumn of 2020, Fotogalleriet presented his collaboration with Norwegian artist Ellinor Aurora Aasgaard, 'Days', an experimental serial drama that questions the social imaginary of the soap opera by substituting the abstracted Hollywood world of the long-running US TV series Days of Our Lives, with the specifics of contemporary Berlin.

Bjarne Bare (b.1985) lives and works between Oslo and Los Angeles. In 2009, he co-founded MELK, of which he is director, as well as of Cornerkiosk Press since 2011. He was editorial advisor of *Objektiv* from 2010–15. Educated at Oslo Fotokunstskole, Academy of Fine Art – Oslo National Academy of the Arts, and UCLA Los Angeles, he was a gallery assistant at Fotogalleriet from 2008–09 and teaching assistant at the UCLA Art Department to Catherine Opie, Chelsea Mosher and James Welling between 2015 and 2017. Bare participated in Fotogalleriet's first digital exercise 'Let's Talk About Images 2.1.0' in Spring 2020.

Liv Brissach (b.1991) is an Oslo-based art historian. They received their MA from the University of Oslo and their BA from University College London (UCL). As a freelance writer Brissach has written for, amongst others, *Kunstkritikk, Billedkunst* and *Munchmuseet on the Move.* They are one of the co-founding editors of the soon-to-launch online platform for art and technology, *The Grey Box*

(with Vilde M. Horvei and Nicholas Norton). Brissach works for Office for Contemporary Art Norway (OCA) on programme and publication activities.

Dr Susan Bright (b.1969) is an Australian/British curator and writer currently based in London. She has a specialisation in lens-based arts and contemporary visual culture with an emphasis on cross-disciplinary and international programming. She was a curator at the National Portrait Gallery in London before deciding to work independently in the early 2000s. Bright holds a PhD in Curating from Goldsmiths, University of London, and has been a mentor to artists on large-scale long-term projects originated by le Fondation d'entreprise Hermès, Paris, and the organisation Women in Photography, based in New York. She curated the exhibition *Something Out of Nothing* at Fotogalleriet in 2007, featuring the artists Margareta Bergman, Ane Hjort Guttu, Else Marie Hagen, Espen Tveit, and Ole John Aandal. In 2021 she will curate, together with Nina Strand, 'f/stop' photography festival in Leipzig.

Antonio Cataldo (b.1981) has been Artistic Director of Fotogalleriet, since 2018. Here, he is envisioning a research-based programme questioning the social role of images in today's society. Throughout his career, Cataldo has actively sought out novel institutional practices and questioned the economic and technological contradictions underpinning institutional formats. He has worked in different capacities for a number of large-scale exhibitions and symposia, especially through his employment at OCA (Office for Contemporary Art Norway, 2010–18) where he was the co-curator of Camille Norment's *Rapture* at the 56th Venice Biennale, and *Let the River Flow. The Sovereign Will and the Making of a New Worldliness* (both with Curator Katya Garcia-Antón). Cataldo serves on the board of directors of Kunsthallene i Norge, and on the jury of Sandefjord Kunstforening's Art Award.

Lill-Ann Chepstow-Lusty (b.1960) is a Norwegian-British photographer, curator and artist based in Oslo. Her artistic production spans many themes, from nationalism, identity, sexuality, tourism, ethnic kitsch, big women, Norwegian cowboys, modern Vikings, gay kids, transvestites, faeces and coins. Chepstow-Lusty's work has been internationally recognised, and her books published in England, Norway and Sweden. Her photographs have been presented at the National Museum in Oslo, Preus Museum, The Robert Meyer Collection, Arts Council Norway and numerous other cities, from London to New York, Ottawa, Vienna and Bratislava. At Fotogalleriet, she participated in the Spring Exhibition in 1986, and in 1994 held a two-person show with Børge Kalvig called *Møte* (Meeting). In 2002 she presented the solo exhibition *Viking Nouveau*, where she explored the remembrance of the past by travelling for three years across the world to find people obsessed with the Viking period.

Ann Christine Eek (b.1948) is a Swedish photographer living in Norway, with life-long experience in photojournalism, landscape and artistic photography. She is also an art critic, photo-historian and writer. In Stockholm she was educated at the School of Photography (Fotoskolan), and studied art history at Stockholm University, and from 1969–79 was a member of the collective SAFTRA. She moved to Oslo in 1980, and from 1982 until her retirement in 2015 she worked at the Museum of Cultural History, University of Oslo. Besides work with photography, picture archives and digitisation she undertook, and published photo-historic studies. Her main projects include *Arbeta – inte slita ut sig!* (exhibited in Stockholm, Malmö, Oslo etc.), *Albanian Village Life – Isniq, Kosovo 1976* and *The photographs of Explorer Carl Lumholtz.* She has written numerous reviews and articles on photography, while illustrating magazines, and books, and participating in solo and group exhibitions in major institutions in Sweden, Norway etc. Her photographs are in the collections of the Museum of Modern Art, Stockholm (SE),

Hasselblad Foundation, Gothenburg (SE), Preus Museum, Horten (NO), Biblioteque Nationale, Paris (FR) and private collectors.

Matias Faldbakken (b.1973) is an artist and writer based in Oslo, Norway, with an education from the Bergen Academy of Art and Design (1994–1998) and Staatliche Hochschule für Bildende Künste, Städelschule, Frankfurt am Main (1996–1997). In the form of sculpture, readymade, video and drawing, Faldbakken has since the late 1990s posed the question: What is antagonism? The open social critique in his writing is counterbalanced by the deliberate hermeticism of his art, in which found materials are worked into what the artist calls 'negativistic gestures'. He has exhibited at Documenta 13 (2012) and represented Norway at the Venice Biennale in 2005. His five novels are translated into more that fifteen languages. He is represented by STANDARD, Oslo and its Director Eivind Furnesvik. He first showed at Fotogalleriet as part of the annual Spring Exhibition in 2000, and held his solo show *Getaway* in 2003.

Marthe Ramm Fortun (b.1978) is an artist based in Oslo, Norway. Departing from site-specific texts, Fortun's performances use body, language and elusive sculptural boundaries to inscribe closed off institutional spaces with persistent and poetic feminisms. Since completing her studies at the New York University in 2008, Fortun has shown work in a variety of institutions and contexts throughout Norway and abroad, including BOZAR and Gladstone Gallery, Brussels; the Munch Museum, UKS, Kunsthall Oslo, Kunstnernes Hus and the National Museum, Oslo; Henie Onstad, Bærum; Bruce High Quality Foundation, Sculpture Center and Performa, New York, and KW Institute of Contemporary Art, Berlin. She is Associate Professor at the Academy of Fine Art – the Oslo National Academy of the Arts, where she also served as the Acting Dean. She participated in the exhibition *Women in Three Acts*, curated by Kati Simons, at Fotogalleriet in 2019.

Eivind Furnesvik (b.1973) is an art historian with degrees from the University in Bergen and University College of Dublin. Furnesvik was artistic director of Fotogalleriet from 2002–05 and is the founder and proprietor of the gallery STANDARD (OSLO), founded in 2005.

Bente Geving (b.1953) is a Norwegian Sámi photographer and artist, born in the northern town of Kirkenes, but raised in the southern city of Asker. After living for many years in Maastricht, Berlin and Hamburg, she exhibited the project *Anna, Inga and Ellen* at Fotogalleriet in 1988. The exhibition was a result of her investigation of her Sámi identity and roots, through time spent with her family in Kirkenes. Geving's work is represented in several collections, including the Preus Museum – the National Museum of Photography, the Northern Norway Art Museum, the Sámi Art Collection, the Berlinische Galerie and numerous private collections.

Ane Hjort Guttu (b.1971) is a Norwegian artist and filmmaker based in Oslo. She works in a variety of media, but has in recent years mainly concentrated on film and video works, ranging from investigative documentary to poetic fiction. Among recurrent themes in her work are the relationship between freedom and power, economy and the public space, social change and limits of action. Guttu is also a writer and curator, and a professor at the Academy of Fine Art – Oslo National Academy of the Arts. Since 1998 she has held solo exhibitions at Young Artists Society (UKS) and Kunstnerforbundet, and Bergen Kunsthall in Norway, Tensta konsthall in Sweden, South London Gallery, Centre d'Art Contemporain de Quimper in France and participated in group exhibitions in Australia, Poland, Austria, Switzerland, South Africa, South Korea and Ukraine. She participated in group exhibitions at Fotogalleriet in 2003, 2006, 2007, and held the solo exhibition *Møbler er ikke bare møbler* (Furniture Isn't Just Furniture) in 2017.

Bjørn Hatterud (b.1977) is a Norwegian cultural and art critic, author, curator and musician. He was raised in Veldre and currently lives and works in Oslo. In 2018, he published the book *Mot normalt* (Against Normality), and in 2020, the novel *Mjøsa rundt med mor: ei livsreise* (Around Mjøsa with My Mother: a Life Journey). He is also a frequent contributor to *Billedkunst* magazine. In 2019, Hatterud was appointed deputy member of the Advisory Board nominated by the Ministry of Culture for the Arts Council Norway.

Marianne Heske (b.1946) is a Norwegian visual artist, born in Ålesund. She participated for the first time in the annual Autumn Exhibition (Høstutstillingen) in Oslo in 1970 with graphic works. In 1974 she exhibited her first multimedia work at the Autumn Exhibition, and in 1976 she started using video for the first time, introducing the use of the medium into the arts in Norway. In 1980 she moved a small cabin (*løe*) from the countryside of Tafjord to the Centre Pompidou in Paris and back again through *Project Gjerdeløa*. Her work is represented in various public and private collections, including the National Museum in Oslo, the Henie Onstad Kunstsenter, the Bonnenfanten Museum, the Bibliothèque nationale de France, and the National Museum of Contemporary Art in Seoul, amongst others. In addition, she has represented Norway at the Venice Biennale (1986), the São Paolo Biennale (1996) and at the World Exhibition in Hanover (2000).

Paul Hill (b.1941) was amongst the first artists to exhibit at Fotogalleriet in 1977, in a joint exhibition with Raymond Moore. In the 1970s, Hill was a teacher at Trent Polytechnic, of which he became director in 1978. Two of his students were amongst the principal founders of Fotogalleriet. Hill was also the founder and director of The Photographers Place in Derbyshire, where he became renowned for his workshops. He was invited by Fotogalleriet to hold a workshop at Henie Onstad Kunstsenter outside of Oslo in 1978.

Kåre Kivijärvi (b.1938 –d.1991) was born into a Kven family in Northern Norway. After working as a photographer's apprentice in *Finnmark Dagblad*, he was in 1959 accepted at Folkwangschule für Gestaltung in Essen, Germany, where he studied with Otto Steinert. After having served in the Royal Norwegian Air Force as an aerial photographer, he accepted a position as staff photographer for *Helsingin Sanomat*'s weekly news magazine *Viikkosanomat*, which brought him on assignment to Greenland, the Soviet Union, Afghanistan, India, and Nepal. Kivijärvi's work was the first to be accepted by the main yearly art exhibition in Norway, the annual Autumn Exhibition (Høstutstilling). In this respect it can be said that he contributed to the establishment of photography as a distinct art form in Norway.

Silja Leifsdottir (b.1984) is currently curator for the Norwegian Sculptors Society (Norsk Billedhoggerforening). She studied at the Fine Art Photography department at The Glasgow School of Art (2005-08) and Curatorial Practice at Bergen Academy of Art and Design (2015-17) and was Gallery Coordinator at Fotogalleriet between 2011 and 2017. She is currently chairing the board of The Norwegian Association of Curators and is the co-founder of SKREID publishing, an independent publisher of Nordic photobooks. She was a co-curator at the artist-run gallery Holodeck in Oslo for two years (2012-13) together with Lina Norell and Kjersti Solbakken and is the co-founder and director of Oslo Art Guide.

Håkon Lillegraven (b.1992) is a curator, writer, producer, and has been Head of Mediation at Fotogalleriet since March 2020. With a degree in Culture, Criticism and Curation from Central Saint Martins (2014-17) he has participated in art research, mediation and curatorial projects at institutions such as Institute of Contemporary Arts ('In Formation' programme, 2017), *Art Night Open* (2018), *Off Site Project* (2018), Kunstburo (2018), and *Venice Fellowship Programme by British Council* (2018). In 2019 he was coordinating editor for the publication *And Their Spirits Live On* by artist Marianne Heier.

Lotte Konow Lund (b.1967) is a Norwegian artist who lives and works in Oslo. In 1997, Konow Lund started the gallery G.I., which she ran until 2007. Her work is in many private and public collections, including the National Museum in Oslo and KODE in Bergen. Konow Lund won honourable mention for her film *Babyface Assassin* (1991) at the short film festival in Grimstad, where she later sat on the jury. Recently, Konow Lund completed her tenure in one of the artist studios in Oslo City Hall for a two-year period. She has been a board member of UKS, and is currently a board member of the Artists' Association (NBK). She is also Professor at Oslo National Academy of the Arts.

Gry Martinsen (b.1943) was a co-founder of Fotogalleriet. Martinsen is educated as a gestalt therapist and a a child welfare pedagogue, and has worked as a project manager and therapist in the Norwegian Directorate for Children, Youth and Family Affairs services for over thirty years, among other things as project manager for the nationwide education program 'PRIDE', aimed at foster parents and social work. Martinsen published the book *Produkter* (Cappelen Damm) in 1972 and was editor of the trade magazine *Fosterhjemskontakt* from 1991-96.

Robert Meyer (b.1945) is a Norwegian art photographer, professor, photo historian, collector, writer and publicist. In 1989, he executed the project 'The Forgotten Tradition', which included an exhibition at Oslo Kunstforening and a book on the emergence and development of Norwegian landscape photography up to 1914. He first exhibited at Fotogalleriet in 1979, and curated the exhibition *Simulo – norsk samtidsfotografi* in 1987. Fotogalleriet became a foundation in 1979, and Meyer was its first chairman.

Eline Mugaas (b.1969) currently lives and works in Oslo, after spending a decade in New York, where she received her artistic education from The Cooper Union for the Advancement of Science and Art. Having garnered various photographic and scenographic commissions, Mugaas returned to Norway in 2000, where the public was first introduced to her work in the exhibition *Let me be your one way street* at Fotogalleriet in 1998. Mugaas concentrates on photographing urban, everyday motifs, allowing the beholder to discover novelty even in everyday scenarios. She also works with film, collage and curating, receiving praise for *Hold stenhårdt fast på greia di*, an exhibition of activist and feminist art that she co-curated with Elise Storsveen and Kunsthall Oslo in 2013. With Storsveen she has since 2008 published the fanzine *ALBUM*. In 2016, Mugaas published the book *Siri Aurdal by Eline Mugaas*, which recontextualises Aurdal's artistry and led to reconstructions of previous works along with extensive exhibitions. In 2019, Mugaas received the prestigious Lorck Schive Art Prize from the Trondheim kunstmuseum.

Catherine Opie (b.1961) lives and works in Los Angeles. Since undertaking a BFA at the San Francisco Art Institute 1985 and a MFA at CalArts in 1988 she has captured in her photographs gay and lesbian communities, mixing portraiture with less traditional subjects, as well as exploring contemporary landscapes such as highways around her Los Angeles home, the New York financial district, and unpeopled urban sites around Chicago. She has received great critical acclaim, including retrospectives at the Guggenheim Museum in New York in 2008 and the Institute of Contemporary Art, Boston in 2011. She was awarded a Guggenheim Fellowship in 2019. Through photography, Opie documents the relationship between the individual and the space inhabited, and connections between mainstream and infrequent society. Opie has taught at Yale University and is the Lynda and Stewart Resnick endowed Chair in Art and Professor of Photography at UCLA.

Michael Andrés Forero Parra (b.1984) is a Colombian architect working with museums and cultural heritage. He is the co-founder of Museo Q, an awarded non-profit initiative that brings queer cultures to museums, galleries and botanical gardens in Colombia, and is a PhD student at the Curatorial Research Collective at TU/e. Forero has coordinated the development of the Museum of Memory in Bogotá, a project of symbolic reparation for the victims of the internal armed conflict. He has published in Colombia (*Premio Nacional de Crítica*, 2012), Mexico (*Revista Intervención*, 2014 and 2016), the Netherlands (OASE Journal, 2017), and the UK (*Museum Activism*, 2019), and was an invited speaker at the International Symposium: Women in Architecture (Colombia, 2017), at the 44th ICAMT Annual Conference (Finland, 2018), at Sites Queer Conference (Puerto Rico, 2019), at ALMS Conference: Queering Memory (Germany, 2019), and at the ICOM General Conference (Japan, 2019).

Maria Pasenau (b.1994) is a contemporary artist who lives and works in Oslo. She studied at the Norwegian School of Photography in Trondheim and has participated in multiple group and solo shows curated by practitioners such as Elise By Olsen, Julia Peyton-Jones, Stina Högkvist and Bjørn Hatterud. She is one of the youngest artists to have had work acquired by the Norwegian National Museum for its permanent collection. Her first solo exhibition, *Pasenau and the Devil* took place at Fotogalleriet in autumn 2019.

Martina Petrelli (b.1989) is a curator, writer and editorial designer working in Norway since 2014. She is currently curator for NITJA Centre for Contemporary Art in Lillestrøm, coordinator for the Oslo Art Weekend international critics visits organised by Oslo Art Guide, and researcher for The Norwegian Association of Curators. In Norway, Petrelli was project and gallery-coordinator at Fotogalleriet in Oslo (2016–18) while creating the gallery's archive system on the occasion of the forty-year anniversary programme; and worked as assistant curator at Tromsø Kunstforening as well as for the multilingual public outreach at Nordnorsk Kunstmusem (2014–15). Petrelli holds an MA from Sandberg Instituut (Amsterdam, NL, 2011– 13) and a BA from Ècole Nationale Supérieure des Beaux-Arts de Lyon (Lyon, FR, 2008–11), both of which included a strong interest in archives, while her previous education includes studies of philosophy, literature and linguistics.

Karen Fosse Rosness (b.1991) lives in Oslo and graduated with a Master of Art in Society at Oslo Metropolitan University. Rosness has worked for, among others, *Kunstkritikk*, Norwegian Sculptors Society (Norsk Billedhoggerforening) and Fotogalleriet. At Fotogalleriet, Rosness was responsible for the development of the anniversary publication and archiving. She now works for *Morgenbladet* and as a freelance writer.

Aaron Schuman (b.1977) is an American artist, writer and curator based in the UK. He is the author of several acclaimed monographsm, including *Slant* (MACK, 2019) and *FOLK* (NB, 2016), and his work is held in a number of public and private collections. He has curated several international festivals and major exhibitions, and has published texts and essays with Aperture, MACK, *Frieze*, *FOAM*, University of California Press, the *British Journal of Photography*, and others. Schuman was also the founder and editor of *SeeSaw Magazine* (2004–14), and is currently Programme Leader of MA Photography at the University of West England (UWE Bristol).

Fin Serck-Hanssen (b.1958) has become known for his 'surgical' portraits of musicians, the first generation of Norwegian punks, AIDS-crisis sufferers, prison inmates, North Sea divers and gay people. Since 1987, he has exhibited his work at Fotogalleriet numerous times. In 1996, he held *Gaywatch*, his first solo exhibition at the institution, a series of portraits realised in the Oslo area. He has always been reluctant to relate to 'gay aesthetics' as a term, seeing it as something artificially designed to discriminate and create difference. At Fotogalleriet, he has been part of group exhibitions, including three annual Spring Exhibitions (Vårutstillingen) in 1986, 1987, 1988, 1993, and 2017. Most recently, he took part in the exhibition *Le Book Club* with his ongoing project *Hedda* in early 2020.

Shirana Shahbazi (b.1975) is an Iranian-born photographer known for her large-scale installations, living and working in Zurich, Switzerland. Born in 1974 in Tehran, Iran, Shahbazi received her formal training at the Fachhochschule Dortmund and the Hochschule für Gestaltung und Kunst in Zurich. The artist's works have been exhibited at the Hammer Museum in Los Angeles, The Museum of Modern Art in New York, and the Museum of Contemporary Photography in Chicago. Often manipulating her medium as a conceptual gesture, Shahbazi makes photographs in classical art-historical genres, including portraiture, still life and landscape, translating and repeating her images in different media, for instance hand-knotted carpets, or photorealistic billboards painted by artisans hired in her native Iran.

Helle Siljeholm (b.1981) is a choreographer, performer and visual artist, based in Oslo. She was awarded a BA (hons) from London Contemporary Dance School in 2003. In 2016 she graduated with an MA in Visual Arts from the Oslo National Academy of the Arts. Her artistic practice involves film, installation, choreography and performance and deals with questions of social imagination in relation to context, in the present and for the future. Her work has been presented nationally and internationally. Siljeholm occasionally works as a curator, and recent curatorial projects include conceptual development and artistic direction of 'The World's Northernmost Chinatown', the 2019 edition of Barents Spektakel, an international art festival in Kirkenes, Norway.

Mike Sperlinger (b.1977) is a writer and curator based in Oslo, and currently Professor of Writing & Theory at the Oslo Academy of Fine Art. Previously he was assistant director of LUX, a London-based agency for artists working with the moving image. He has written many catalogue texts, including recently for exhibitions by Ed Atkins, Gerard Byrne and Mari Slaatelid, and contributed to a variety of publications including *Afterall*, *Dot Dot Dot*, *Radical Philosophy* and *Texte zur Kunst*.

Stephanie von Spreter (b.1977) is currently a PhD fellow in art history at UiT The Arctic University of Norway in Tromsø. She also works as a freelance curator and writer. In this position she has curated a large number of exhibitions and seminars with a focus on contemporary camera-based art. Von Spreter is also the co-founder and co-owner of the first exhibition guide for contemporary art in Oslo, U.F.O. (ufoguide.no). Before moving to Norway, von Spreter worked for various large exhibitions and projects, including the 3rd, 4th and 5th Berlin

Biennale for Contemporary Art, the 50th Biennale di Venezia and Documenta II. Von Spreter served as the director of Fotogalleriet, Oslo, between 2011 and 2018.

Hanne Hammer Stien (b.1977) is a Norwegian curator based in Tromsø, where she holds a position as associate professor at the Academy of Arts, UiT The Arctic University of Norway. In her curatorial work, she has mainly focused on art in public space and site-specific art projects that relate to the north, either as physical or discursive sites. From an art-historical and museological perspective, her interest lies within tendencies in contemporary art and exhibition making. In one of Stien's last curatorial projects Inger Sitter's monumental painting *Composition in Yellow* (1961–62), commissioned for Findus factory in Hammerfest, was relocated to a newly built primary school in Hammerfest. In her academic work, Stien has been concerned with photo history and photo theory, museological questions and contemporary art.

Nina Strand (b.1973) works as an artist, writer and is the founder and editor in chief of the art journal *Objektiv*. In 2017 *Objektiv* went from page to space, and the editorial board of *Objektiv* curated their first exhibition, *Subjektiv* at Malmö Konsthall. Strand is also co-editor of *STAFETT* (Relay), a Scandinavian photography fanzine. She is a regular contributor of essays on photography to several Norwegian and international publications, including *Dagbladet*, *Camera Austria* and *The PhotoBook Review* by Aperture. Strand has participated in and organised several exhibitions all over Scandinavia, the latest being *Le Book Club* at Fotogalleriet in January-February 2020. In 2021 she will curate the 'f/stop' photography festival in Leipzig together with Dr Susan Bright.

Susanne Østby Sæther (b.1972) is currently Curator of Photography and New Media at Henie Onstad Kunstsenter in Høvikodden, Norway. Sæther holds a doctorate in media science from the University of Oslo, and from 2005 to 2006, she participated in the Whitney Museum of American Art's New York-based Independent Study Program. She serves on the advisory board for *Objektiv*, a biannual

Norwegian journal devoted to film and photography that she co-founded in 2009 with Ida Kierulf and Nina Strand. Sæther has worked as a curator at the Preus Museum in Horten, Norway, co-curated a group exhibition at Malmö Konsthall in Sweden titled *Subjektiv* in 2017, and in 2008, the exhibition *Ghost in the Machine* at Kunsternes Hus in Oslo. Østby Sæther was Artistic Director of Fotogalleriet from 2008–09, and in 2008 curated the exhibition *Comme au cinema: The Cinematic as Method and Metaphor*.

Anna Tellgren (b.1964), PhD, is Curator of Photography and Research leader at Moderna Museet in Stockholm. She has curated numerous exhibitions including *Arbus, Model, Strömholm* (2005), *Lars Tunbjörk. Winter/Home* (2007), *Now: Inta Ruka* (2008) and *Francesca Woodman. On Being an Angel* (2015), which is touring internationally. In 2011 she was responsible for the project *Another Story. Photography from the Moderna Museet Collection*, a major presentation of photography presented across the entire museum. Previously, she has worked as a researcher and lecturer at the Department of Art History at Stockholm University. She was the editor of *The History Book. On Moderna Museet 1958–2008* (2008) and she is Associate Editor of *Konsthistorisk tidskrift/Journal of Art History*.

Nikhil Vettukattil (b.1990) is an artist and writer based in Oslo. Using sound, moving image, sculpture, text, and installation, his works often explore the ways cultural forms such as contemporary art and cinema mediate the relations between everyday experiences and historical time. Forthcoming exhibitions include *Og lenge gikk vi uten lys* at Kristiansand Kunsthall, *The Hum* at Tegel, Stockholm, and *Jeg kaller det kunst* at the National Museum, Oslo. Recent exhibitions and projects include *A is A Guess and A Piece* at Louise Dany, Oslo, *The Vapours*, at Kunstverein Bamberg, *Housewarming* at Le Bourgeois, London, *An Analog for Listening* for flatness.eu, *Extended Hours* for Struktura.time, *Words Fail Me* at Auto Italia, London, and *Cosmopolitan Universal Cinema* at Arnolfini, Bristol, and Close-Up, London.

Ellisif Wessel (b.1866 –d.1949) played a significant role in the Norwegian labour movement in the first decades

of the twentieth century, as a writer, magazine publisher and political agitator. She was an accomplished photographer, who left behind valuable cultural-historical photo material from the Sør-Varanger area. She also published several collections of poems before her death in 1949. The majority of her photographic works can be found in the collection of Grenselandmuseet and the Varanger Museum in Kirkenes, Norway.

Susanne M. Winterling lives and works in Rehau, Berlin and Trondheim. She works with a range of media to explore the sentient economy, digital cultures and the social life of materials across our built environment. Winterling's recent practice reflects upon political as well as aesthetic solidarity among human and animal species in today's challenging geopolitical context. She also remains focused on historical feminist practices and the commons. Winterling is Professor of Fine Art at the NTNU in Trondheim. She held a solo exhibition at Fotogalleriet in 2011 titled *Complement for Company (skyline and skin)*.

Sara R. Yazdani (b.1984) is an art historian and art critic, holding a PhD in History of Art and Media Studies from the University of Oslo ('Self-Sufficient Images: Art Media, and Ecologies in the Works of Wolfgang Tillmans', 2019). Her fields of research and teaching are modern and contemporary art with a particular focus on the history and theory of photography, the relationship between art, media and technologies, theories of the Anthropocene and process philosophy. She is currently working on her first monograph, *Self-Sufficient Images* – a critical history of Wolfgang Tillmans's oeuvre, and the re-emergence of an ecological, processual approach to art photography. As an art critic she has contributed to *Flash Art*, *Artforum*, *Mousse Magazine*, *Kunstkritikk*, *Art & Education*, and *Objektiv*, and her academic writing has been published in a number of academic journals and anthologies on modern and contemporary art. Yazdani lives and works in Oslo and is currently a guest teacher in art theory at the Oslo National Academy of the Arts. At Fotogalleriet, she has contributed to programmes such as 'Let's Talk About Images' (2018–19) and *Le Book Club* (2020).

Biographies

Exhibiting Artists (& Contributors) at Fotogalleriet 1977–2020

1977

Vidar Askland, Per Berntsen, Nils Jørgen Kjærnet, Tom Martinsen; Alfred Stieglitz; Paul Hill, Raymond Moore

1978

Edward Weston; Ann Christine Eek; Diane Arbus; Arvid J. Albertsen, Dag Alveng, Alf Magne Andreassen, Per Berntsen, Anders Bromstad, Karoly Buday, Ole A. Buenget, Kaare Bøe, Torstein Dalemark, Signe Drevsjø, Alf Edgar, Bjørn Eigvad, Svein-Erik Engebretsen, Tormod Flobak, Terje Foss, Oluf Føinum, Randi Solheim Ghilzai, Kai Gjelseth, Borger H. Granli, Espen Grønli, Jens O.Hagen, Olav M. Hammerø, Imre Hancz, Roald E. Hansen, Jens Hauge, Leif Hauge, Hugo Henriksen, Pål Hermansen, Curt Ingemar Hjerstedt, Bjørn Høgrann, Børge Kalvig, Nils Jørgen Kjærnet, Øyvind Kristoffersen, Finn Krog, Reidun Krog, Morten Krogvold, Yngvar Lande, Inger Johanne K. Lundgren, Morten Løberg, Lars Oddvar Løvdahl, Tom Martinsen, Peter Meusburger, Gunnar Misund, Gunnar J. Moe, Turid Kvalvåg Moe, Torbjørn Moen, Annecke Aas Mortensen, Ivar Mølskned, Harald Narvesen, Lavasir Nordrum, Erling Olsen, Petter Olsen, Jamie Parslow, Jan R. Ravnestad, Kristian Rishøi, Sjur Roald, Bjørn Saastad, Tom Sandberg, Sidsel Jakhelln Semb, Herdis Maria Siegert, Annar Skevik, Tor Michael Skillestad, Hanne Smedsaas, Karen E. Solstad, Erik Steen, Siggen Stinessen, Ragge Strand, Jørn Sunby, Helge Sunde, Arvid Sveen, Lars Sørli, Petter Thorsrud, Per Torgersen, Steinar Torvbråthen, Espen Tveit, Jan Ung, Bernt Vatland, Raymond Wardenær, Bjørn Winsnes; Gustavson Myhre; Ellisif Wessel; Harald Narvesen; Marianne Heske

1979

Dag Alveng; Arne Walderhaug; Jim Bengtson; Tom Martinsen, Robert Meyer, Arne Walderhaug, Bjørn Winsnes, Dag Alveng, Alf M. Andreassen, Jim Bengston, Per Berntsen, Anders Bromstad, Alf Edgar, Hans Olav Forsang, Jens Hauge, Hugo Henriksen, Nils-Jørgen Kjærnet, Morten Krogvold, Morten Løberg, Harald Nervesen, Lavasir Nordrum, Jamie Parslow, Tom Sandberg, Johan Sandborg, Jørn Sundby, Arvid Sveen, Kjell Sten Tollefsen; Lewis W. Hine; Siggen Stenersen, Bill Owens; Christer Strömholm

1980

Tom Martinsen; Nadar, Morten Krogvold, Jamie Parslow, Lavasir Nordrum, Jørn Sundby, KjARTan Slettemark; Gro Jartro, Ann Christine Eek; Hugo Henriksen; Weegee, Kjell Sten Tollefsen; Kjell Sten Tollefsen; Aagaard; Jim Bengtson; Per Berntsen, Johan Sandborg; Johan Sandborg; Robert Meyer; Thormod Flodbak; Terje Agnalt, Dag Alveng, Petter Andersen, Carsten Arnholm, Eva Arnholm, Randi Bakke, Kjell Bjørgengen, Helle Borg, Marius Borgen, Ole Andreas Buenget, Trygve Bølstad, Svein Erik Dahl, Ann Christine Eek, Sigurd Eidsøren, Terje Enge, Bjørn Engvik, Bjørn Falch Andersen, Arne J Furseth, Jan Gauguin, Kai H Gjelseth, MonaGundersen, Imre Hancz, Morten Haug, Jiri Havran, Bjørn Høgrann, Gro Jarto, Mark Mattison, Harald Medbøe, Bjørn Melbye, Robert Meyer, Gunnar Misund, Anne Lise Mjaaland, Arild Normann, Ketil Plassgård, Kristian Rishøi, Pål Rødahl, Johan Sandborg, Herdis Maria Siegert, Tone Brække Skramstad, Hans Petter Smeby, John Stenersen, Ragge Strand, Jørn Sundby, Asle Svarverud, Leif M Sørlund, Petter Thorsrud, Kjell Sten Tollefsen, Per Torgersen, Steinar Torvbråten, Erik Wassum, Bjørn Winsnes, Jim Bengtson, Morten Krogvold, Lavasir Nordrum, Alf Magne Andreassen, Karoly Buday, Nils-Jørgen Kjærnet, Morten Løberg, Harry Nilssen, Petter Olsen, Kjell Hansen Stoa, Rolf Støa, Arne Walderhaug, Yngvar Lande, Espen Tveit, Johannes Hagen, Alf Edgar, Børge Kalvig, Harald Narvesen, Solverig Greve, Henny Lie, Åsne Nilsen, Per Nybø, Jan Ravnestad, Leif Hauge, Gunnar Moe, Thor Bjaarstad, Tore Davidsen, Signe Drevsjø, Halvard Kjærvik, Ola Røe, Siggen Stinessen, Arvid Sveen; Rolf Ødegård; Alf Magne Andreassen, Tom Sandberg; Ralph Nyquist, Anders Petersen; Joel Meyerowitz; Dag Alveng, Eva Arnholm, Randi Bakke, Jim Bengston, Ann Christine Eek, Tom Martinsen, Johan Sandborg, John Stenersen, Jørn Sundby, Rolf M. Aagard, Alf Edgar, Jens Hauge, Halvard Kjærvik, Morten Løberg, Kjell Hansen Stoa, Arvid Sveen

1981

John Stenersen, Jens Hauge; August Sander; Sir Cecil Beaton; Henny Lie; Halvard Kjærvik

1982

Dag Alveng, Bjørn Falch Andersen, Petter H. Andersen, Alf Magne Andreassen, Eva Arnholm, Randi Bakke, Per Berntsen, Kjell Bjørgeengen, Marius Borgen, Marianne Brantsæter, Per Brække, Ole A. Buenget, Steinar Buholm, Johanna Butler, Trygve Bølstad, Hans Bøvre, Guri Dahl, Svein Erik Dahl, Alf Edgar, Ann Christine Eek, Bent Endresen, Bjørn Engvik, Knut Harald Evensen, Annette Faltin, Oluf Føinum, Kai Gjelseth, Solveig Greve, Wenche Gulbrandsen, Jens Hauge, Leif Hauge, Jiri Havran, Hugo Henriksen, Kjell Karlsson, Zdenek Kejr, Halvard Kjærvik, Finn Krog, Morten Krogvold, Helene Leland, Henny Lie, Nils P. Lotherington, Tom Martinsen, Mark Mattison, Karen McFarlane, Gunnar Mislund, Thera Mjaaland, Raymond Mosken, Helge Nareid, Dag Nystuen, Jamie Parslow, Nina Reistad, Kristian Rishøi, Ola Røe, Johan Sandborg, Ulf W. Skuli, Arnt H. Sneve, Jon Stenersen, Siggen Stinessen, Rolf Støa, Petter Thorsrud, Kjell Sten Tollefsen, Espen Tveit, Inge Ove Tysnes, Arne Walderhaug, Erik Wassum, Ole John Aandal, Mimi Aanesen

1983

Christer Strömholm; Jiri Havran, Kjell Bjørgeengen; Albert Renger-Patzsch; Harald Medbøe, Thera Mjaaland, Herdis Maria Sieger; Morten Børresen

1984

Øystein Klakegg; Bill Brandt; Alf
Edgar; Eugene Smith; Chargesheimer
(Karl-Heinz Hargesheimer); Toto
Frima; Jamie Parslow; Olivia Parker;
Per Berntsen, Ole A. Buenget, Johs
Bøe, Lill-Ann Chepstow-Lusty, Torill
Ek, Annette Faltin, Leif Gabrielsen,
Solbjørg Gjertsen, Jiri Havran, Anne
Lise Jackbo, Ingar Johansen, Ole J.
Kaland, Helene Levand, Merete Lien,
Tom Martinsen, Karen McFarlane,
Helge Nareid, Lavasir Nordrum,
Sølvi Pettersen, Johan Sandborg,
Espen Tveit, Inge Ove Tysnes, Arne
Walderhaug, Ole John Aandal;
Stuart Klipper; Neil Goldstein, Mark
Mattison

1985

Dag Alveng, Jim Bengston,
Harald Kjærvik, Jamie Parslow,
Tom Sandberg, John Stenersen;
Karen McFarlane, Atle Aas; Johan
Sandborg; Raffael Rheinsberg;
Eugéne Atget; Arthur Rothstein,
Theo Jung, Ben Shahn, Walker
Evans, Jack Delano, Carl Mydans,
Russell Lee, John Collier, John
Vachon, Marion Post-Wolcott,
Dorothea Lange; Arnt Sneve; Bertil
Nordahl, Roland Schröter, Lars G
Safström, Nisse Degerman, Hans
Cogne, Lennart Durehed, Bruno
Ehrs, Tuija Lindström; Lavasir
Nordrum

1986

Bent Egil Johansen; Ron Haselden,
Sharon Kivland; Eadweard
Muybridge; Jens Hauge; Espen Tveit,
Oluf Føinum; Per Balch-Barth, Per
Berntsen, Morten Brun, Sigfrid
Carlsson, Lill-Ann Chepstow-Lusty,
Alf Edgar, Annette Faltin, Erik
Flyen, Karl Gorwitz, Randi Solheim
Ghilzai, Pentti Gregersen, Solveig
Greve, Wenche Gulbrandsen, Imre
Hancz, Morten Haug, Leif Hauge,
Jiri Havran, Bjørn Høgrann, Nils
Johannesen, Bertil Egil Johansen,
Ingar Johansen, Rune Johansen,
Helge Bjørn Johnnysen, Øystein
Klakegg, Ellen S.Lande, Harald A.
Lekang, Merete Lien, Thera Anne
Lise Mjaaland, Raymond Mosken,
Lavasir Nordrum, Mark Orrall, Are
Thune Paulsen, Svein Plukkerud,
Fin Serck-Hansen, Siggen Stinessen,
Billie Thackwell, Ellen Thrap-

Meyer, Espen Tveit, Jan Ung, Garrett
Williams; Anne Noggle; Harald
Kjærvik; Imogen Cunninngham; Guri
Dahl; Rafael Navarro

1987

André Gelpke; Robert Meyer; Robert
Doisneau; David Hurn, Martin Parr,
Peter Marlowe, Chris Steel Perkins,
John Davies, Marketa Luskacova;
Siggen Stinessen; Richard Benson;
Ole John Aandal, Kjell Bjørgeengen,
Marius Borgen, Guri Dahl, Alf
Edgar, Jan Gjessing, Per Maning,
Michael Max, Mikkel Mc, Raymond
Mosken, Sven Påhlsson, John
Erling Riise, Tom Sandberg, Johan
Sandborg, Fin Serck-Hanssen, Dan
Young, Line Wælgaard

1988

Larry Fink; Per Maning; Morten
Andersen, Per Berntsen, Marius
Borgen, Morten Brun, Geir M.
Brungot, Ole A. Buenget, Sigfrid
Carlsson, Hermann Desmeules,
Kristin Døvle, Alf Edgar, Jonas
Ekeberg, Annette Faltin, Eva Klerck
Gange, Bente Geving, Randi Solheim
Ghilzai, Solveig Greve, Wenche
Gulbrandsen, Clas T. Hansen,
Tommy Normann Hansen, Idun
Hauga, Kjetil Haugstveit, Kristina
Hofsø, Gro Jarto, Nils Johannsen,
Bertil Egil Johansen, Ingar Johansen,
Rune Johansen, Sidsel Jørgensen,
Tormod Jørgensen, Ole J. Kaland,
Enok Harry Karlsen, Grete Kvaal,
Helene Levand, Henny Lie, Merete
Lien, Harald Østgaard Lund, Mikkel
McAlinden, Karen McFarlane, Jo
Michael, Thera A.L. Mjaaland,
Raymond Mosken, Lavasir Nordrum,
Pia Pedersen, John Erling Riise,
Hellik Råen, Christine E. Schønberg,
Fin Serck-Hanssen, Arnt H. Sneve,
Petter Strømsted, Arne Svalastog,
Lars Sørli, Billie Thackwell, Espen
Tveit, Inge Ove Tysnes, Øystein
Ustvedt, Øystein Wangen, Garrett
Williams, Line Wælgaard, Ole John
Aandal, Hans Jan Aarsund, Kjetil
Maria Aase; Alf Edgar, Øystein
Klakegg, Jens Hauge, Helge Nareid,
Halvard Kjærvik, Dag Alveng,
Jim Bengston, Fin Serck-Hanssen,
Raymond Mosken, Per Berntsen,
Jiri Havran, Leif Gabrielsen; Bente
Geving; Per Berntsen

1989

Mikkel McAlinden; Ole John
Aandal; Per Berntsen, Geir M.
Brungot, Sigfrid Carlsson, Edgar Alf,
Per Eide, Marit Anna Evanger, Leif
Gabrielsen, Kari Gorwitz, Solveig
Greve, Clas T. Hansen, Nina Hansen,
Jiri Havran, Håvard Houen, Gro
Jarto, Finn Arne Johannessen, Nils
Johannsen, Tormod Jørgensen, Ole
J. Kaland, Henny Lie, Merete Lien,
Thera A.L. Mjaaland, Ole J. Mofoss,
Raymond Mosken, Johan Sandborg,
Sigbjørn Sigbjørnsen, Rolf Starup,
Siggen Stinessen, Espen Tveit, Arne
Valen, Arne Walderhaug, Garrett
Williams, Hans Jan Aarsund, Ole
John Aandal; Morten Andersen,
Jonas Ekeberg, Trine Gjøsund, Maya
Glaser, Finn Arne Johannessen,
Eirik Vandvik Johnsen, Leif Harald
Njølstad, Paul Ivar Paiewonsky,
Annica Thomsson, Margit Solveig
Thon, Anders Aabel, Ketil Åsatun;
Per Berntsen, Alf Edgar, Jiri Havran,
Morten Haug, Jens Hauge, Regin
Solli-Hjertholm, Halvard Kjærvik,
Mark Mattison, Mikkel McAlinden,
Raymond Mosken, Helge Nareid,
Lavasir Nordrum, Johan Sandborg,
John Stenersen, Per Vangsnes, Arne
Walderhaug & Ole John Aandal; Ole
Buenget, Trygve Bølstad, Annette
Faltin, Leif Gabrielsen, Jiri Havran,
Finn Arne Johannessen, Raymond
Mosken, Arild Normann & Jamie
Parslow

1990

Jiri Havran, Henny Lie, Thera
Mjaaland, Fin Serck Hansen; Tuija
Lindstrøm; Lavasir Nordrum;
Jiri Havran; Lotte Jacobi, Laszlo
Moholy-Nagy, Hans Finsler, Fred
Koch, Ralph Steiner, Hans Bellmer,
Georgy Kepes, August Kreyenkamp,
T. Lux Feininger, Lucia Moholy,
Willy Zielke, Werner Rohde, Max
Burchartz, Albert Renger Patsch,
Florence Henri, Grete Stern, Ellen
Auerbach, Ernst Fuhrman

1991

Dag Alveng; Espen Tveit; Bill Brandt;
Josef Sudek; Alf Edgar; Catherine
Cardarelli, Alf Edgar, Bård Ole Ek,
Leif Gabrielsen, Bente Geving, Randi
Solheim Ghilzai, Trine Gjøsund,
Maya Glaser, Nina R. Hansen, Galina
Manikova, Mikkel McAlinden,

Exhibiting Artists (& Contributors)
at Fotogalleriet 1977–2020

Thera-Annelise Mjaaland, Raymond Mosken, Mark Orrall, Per Sølvberg, Vibeke Tandberg, Tore Øygarden, Kjetil Maria Aase; Jiri Havran; Joakim Gemicke; Irving Penn; Keith Arnatt, Martin Parr, Paul Graham, Peter Fraser, Ron O`Donell, Boyd Webb, Richard Wentworth, Jem Southam; Lotta Antonsson, Paulina Olsson

1992

Bente Geving; Dag Alveng, Arne Nordheim; Ulf Celander; BHK Gutman; Morten Andersen; Arne Ronny Berg, Truls Borch, Helga Bu, Ole Buenget, Dag-Arve Forbergskog, Espen Gaarder, Mona Haug, Jiri Havran, Regin Hjertholm, Finn Arne Johannesen, Håvard Gimmestad Johansen, Per Fronth Nygaard, Siggen Stinessen, Annica Thomsson, Mette Tronvoll, Jan Walaker; Kåre Kivijärvi; Robert F. Hammerstiel; Bruce Gilden

1993

Edward J. Steichen; Johan Sandborg; Per Berntsen, Ole Gunnar Dokka, Bente Geving, Astri W. Goksøyr, Rune Johansen, Cecilie Lønne, Henny Lie, Galina Manikova, Hans Hamid Rasmussen, Tore Sandahl, Fin Serck-Hansen, Siggen Stinessen, Vibeke Tandberg, Ole Østen Tokle, Per O. Torgnesskar, Stephan Quassowski, Jan Walaker, Hilde Aagaard, Marte Aas; Fin Serck-Hanssen, Espen Tveit, Leif Gabrielsen, Per Berntsen, Halvard Kjærvik, Øystein Klakegg, Tom Sandberg, Siggen Stinessen, Jens Hauge, Henny Lie, Marit-Anna Evanger, Jim Bengston, Dag Alveng, Tom Martinsen & Jamie Parslow; Ole Buenget, Guri Dahl, Ole Gunnar Dokka, Bård Ole Ek, Jonas Ekeberg, Eva Klerck Gange, Bente Geving, Morten Haug, Leif Lindberg, Hilde Maisey, Mikkel McAlinden, Lavasir Nordrum, Vibeke Tandberg, Ole John Aandal; Karl H. Nymo, Vidar Andresen, Jonas Ekeberg, Kristi Fiske, Jens P. Thuland; Morten Krogvold; Tom Sandberg

1994

Ingvild Jyngen, Mikkel McAlindern, Vibeke Tandberg, Ole John Aandal; Annica Karlsson Rixon; Børge Kalvik, Lill-Ann Chepstow-Lusty; Martin Sjöberg, Hans Hedberg; Tore

Sandhal, Margareta Bergman; Torhild Aukan, Henriette Berg Thomassen, Ketil Born, Lill-Ann Chepstow-Lusty, Alf Edgar, Bård Ole Ek, Kristoffer Eliassen, Mette Eriksen, Marit Anna Evanger, Bente Geving, Trine Gjøsund, Morten Haug, Marius Holth, Finn-Arne Johannesen, Henny Lie, Hilde B. Maisey, Per Maning, Jo Michael, Raymond Mosken, Lavasir Nordrum, Per Olav Torgnesskar; John Riise, Wilhelm Piro; Solveig Greve; Tom Martinsen

1995

Bereket Ben Yaakov, Yossi Breger, Yosaif Cohain, Morel Derfler, Avi ganor, Pesi Girsch, Judith Guetta, Judy Orgel Lester, Simcha Shirman; Trine Gjøsund, Mikkel McAlindern, Vibeke Tandberg, Finn-Arne Johannessen, Morten Andersen, Per Olav Torgensskar, Ole Buenget, Kristin Witberg, Hildy Maisey, Ch. Fr. D. Wesenberg, Anette Sletnes, Rune Johanssen; Michael O´Donnel; Jaroslav Krejci; Hans Ekelund, Marcus Hansson, Torben Madsen, Peter Ohlander, Patrik Elgström, Lars Lindqvist and Robert Nilsson; Arno Rafael Minkkinen; Payram; Jorma Puranen

1996

Geir M. Brungot, Lewis Baltz; Henny Lie; Even Attramadal, Heidi Wexelsen Goksøry, Eva Klerck Gange, Cecilie Lønne, Dag Nordbrenden, Nina Svane-Mikkelsen, Marte Aas; Jaroslav Krejci; Hilde Ågaard; Hilde Maisey; Arne Ronny Berg; Fin Serck-Hanssen; Henrik Duncker, Yrjö Tuunanen

1997

Tommy Olsson; Kirsti Fiske; Vibeke Tandberg; Margareta Bergman, Kristoffer Eliassen, Jenny Rydhagen; Børre Sæthre; Geir Tore Holm; Jonas Ekeberg, Heini Hölttä, Per Olav Torgnesskar; Marte Aas; Erik Steffensen

1998

Jenny Rydhagen; Christine Hansen, Kjetil Haugstveit, Katja H. Høst, Josephine Lindstrøm, Line B.Løkken, Vibeke J. Sjøvoll; Morten Andersen, Hilde Andorsen, Geir Egil Bergjord;

Arne Valen; Pavol Sochan, Karrol Plicka, Robo Kochan; Helmut Newton; Eline Mugaas; Marcelo Krasilcic; Lars Botten, Victor Boullet, Ragnar Hartvig, Per Heimly, Nils Vik

1999

Anders Edström; Martin Parr; Geir Egil Bergjord, Margareta Bergmann, Annar Bjørgli, Inger Lise Hansen, Line B. Løkken, Tom Groves, Anne Lise Stenseth, Heidi Sundby, Talleiv Taro Manum, Arne Skaug Olsen, Merethe Solberg; Ulf Ludin; Dag Alveng, Ingrid Book, Carina Hedén, Marianne Heske, Per Manning, Mikkel McAlinden, Tommy Olsson, Kjartan Slettemark; Bridget Smith; Elise Storsveen

2000

Luisa Lambri; Mattias Härenstam; Per Christian Brown, Matias Faldbakken, Ketil Haugstveit, Heini Hölta, Line Olaisen, Annette Sletnes; Even Attramadal; Piotr Uklanski; Ingrid Book & Carina Hedén; Heli Rekula

2001

Talleiv Taro Manum; Anne-Grethe Thoresen; Morten Andersen, Susanna Hesselberg, Marte Johnslien, Line Løkken, Katinka Maraz, Anna Widén; Hilde Maisey; Inger Lise Hansen; Annar Bjørgli

2002

Doris Frohnapfel; Endre Aalrust, Frank Benjamin Finger, Edvard Gran, Bjørn Hegardt , Aksel Høgenhaug, Tinna Ludviksdottir, Aage Langhelle, Alejandro Pérez, Merethe Solberg Ødland; Lill-Ann Chepstow-Lusty; Charlotte Thiis-Evensen; Frans Jacobi; Janne Solgaard; Signe Marie Andersen, Ina Eriksen, Mette K. Hellenes, Vanessa Baird, Jon Løvøen, Talleiv Taro Manum, Eline Mugaas, Børre Sæthre

2003

Kim Hiorthøy; Hedevig Anker, Ane Hjort Guttu & Per Olav Torgnesskar; Lene Ask, Kjersti Bergersen, Bodil Furu, Andreas Heuch, Martin Skulstad, Morten Torgersrud, Gry Ulrichsen; Gardar Eide Einarsson; Marius Engh; Toril Goksøyr, Camilla Martens; Matias Faldbakken

Exhibiting Artists (& Contributors)
at Fotogalleriet 1977–2020

2004

Dag Nordbrenden; Lene Ask, Maria
Bustnes, Brakkebygrenda Velforening,
Thomas Eriksson, Håkki TM, Kine
Lillestrøm, Arild Mehn-Andersen,
Olga Robayo, Marius Wang, Spis
de Rike, Helge Sunde; Gardar Eide
Einarsson; Lene Ask; Collier Schorr;
Jacob Kolding

2005

Edvard Gran; Anders Bojen,
Kristoffer Ørum, Klara Lidén,
Kenneth A. Balfelt, Antonia Low;
Bård Ask, Mai Hofstad Gunnes,
Victor Lind; Amar Kanwar; (Susan
Bright), Victor Burgin, Jonas Ekeberg,
Anna Fox, Sophie Howarth, Amar
Kanwar, (Ida Kierulf), Uriel Orlow,
(Eivind Røssak); Bodil Furu

2006

Benjamin Alexander Huseby; Birgir
Andresson, Morten Andersen, Sofie
Berntsen, Tiril Schrøder & Andreas
Heuch, Hildigunnur Birgisdóttir,
Bjørn Bjarre, Jacob Dahlgren, Gardar
Eide Einarsson, Jonas Ekeberg,
Leif Elggren, Elis Ernst Eriksson,
Christian Falch & Joachim Cossais,
Jesper Fabricius, Matias Faldbakken,
Sebastian Franzén, Gabriela
Fridriksdottir, Kristjan Gudmundsson,
Wenche Gulbransen, Ane Hjort
Guttu, Hallgerdur Hallgrímsdóttir,
Trond Hugo Haugen, Marianne
Heier, Hallgrimdur Helgason, Mette
Hellenes, Kim Hiorthøy, Geir Tore
Holm, Karl Holmqvist, Torgeir
Husevaag, Leif Inge, Anna B. Jenssen,
Kurt Johannessen, Søssa Jørgensen,
Lars Laumann & Lena Ulven, Karl
Larsson & Andreas Mangione, Per
Oskar Leu, Maria Lindberg, Per
Jonas Lindström, Elisabeth Mathisen,
Pierre Lionel Matte, Bjarne Melgaard,
Terje Nicolaisen, Guttorm Nordø,
Olga Robayo & Marius Wang, Kalle
Runeson, Geir Harald Samuelsen,
Pia Sandström, Maja Lena Sillanpää,
Anders Smebye & Marius Engh,
Jasper Sebastian Stürüp, Dea D.
Svensson, Sten Ove Toft & Andreas
Gjerde, Morten Torgersrud, Pär
Törn, Johan Urban Bergquist, Mikkel
Wettre, Øystein Aasan; Ellen S.
Holtskog, Debora Elgeholm, Carl
Johan Erikson; Mette Tronvoll; Geir
Harald Samuelsen; Stian Ådlandsvik,
Lutz-Rainer Müller

2007

Tone Hansen, Marianne Heier,
Beathe C. Rønning, Lene Berg,
Terje Nicolaisen, Ane Hjort Guttu,
Thomas Hervard, Helga-Marie
Nordby; Ole Martin Lund Bø;
Gudrun Benonysdottir, Ida Ekblad,
Marius Engh, Beata Fransson, Karl
Holmquist, Karl Larsson, Lars
Laumann, Camilla Løw, Bo Melin,
Bella Rune; Eline McGeorge;
Napoleon Habeica, Benjamin
Alexander Huseby, Heinz Peter Knes,
Sølve Sundsbø; Morten Andenæs,
Ola Rindal; Margareta Bergman,
Ane Hjort Guttu, Else Marie Hagen,
Espen Tveit, Ole John Aandal; Larry
Fink

2008

Bård Ask; Lieko Shiga; Lars
Laumann, Per Christian Brown,
Felix Gmelin, Tova Mozard; Sverre
Strandberg; Ida Ekblad; Lene Berg;
Carter, Christian Jankowski, Johan
Grimonprez, Salla Tykkä, Clemens
von Wedemeyer, Knut Åsdam; André
Larsen Avelin, Bjørn Erik Haugen

2009

Patterson Beckwith, Marcus
Hansson, Ulf Lundin, Noguchi
Rika, Christopher Williams; Katja
Høst; Ane Lan; Yamile Calderon,
Ingrid Eggen, Marius Ektvedt, Elna
Hagemann, Christina Leithe Hansen,
Marianne Hurum, Sverre Strandberg,
Roghie Asgari Torvun; Cato Løland,
Alette Schei Rørvik, David Rios,
Kirsti van Hoegee, Birger Åseson
Storaas, Jet Pascua; Sveinn Fannar
Jóhannsson; Line Bøhmer Løkken

2010

Tor Børresen; Helga Bu, Jan Hakon
Erichsen, Else Marie Hagen,
Katarina Marthinsen, Trine Lise
Nedreaas, Randi Nygård, Tammo
Rist, Elise Storsveen, Eline Mugaas;
Espen Tveit; Jason Havneraas; Johan
Bergström, Mårten Lange, Signe Vad;
Kristin Tårnesvik; Helene Sommer,
Alexander Vaindorf

2011

Øystein Wyller Odden; Trine Lise
Nedreaas; Morten Andenæs, Mattias
Härenstam, Line Bøhmer Løkken,
Dag Nordbrenden, Ulla Schildt,

Carrie Schneider, Morten Torgersrud,
Verena Winkelmann; Susanne M.
Winterling; Beate Gütschow, Thomas
Ramberg; Marte Vold, Martin de
Turah, Aida Ruilova, Inger Lise
Hansen, Duane Hopkins, Robert
Todd; Nina Toft, Hilde Honerud

2012

Andreas Bunte, Melvin Moti; Hilde
Aagaard, Azar Alsharif, Ole Martin
Lund Bø, Jan Freuchen, Jason
Havneraas, Cathrine Ruud; Hannu
Karjalainen; Antoinette Aurell, Anne
Daems, Cecilia Edefalk, Icelandic
Love Corporation, Anna Kleberg,
Jenny Källman, Kaja Leijon; Runa
Carlsen

2013

Katja Mater; Ravi Agarwal, Said
Atabekov, Sofia Burchardi, Plamen
Bontchev, Gohar Dashti, Fouad
Elkoury, Hasan & Husain Essop,
Jacob Holdt, Pieter Hugo, Barbara
Metselaar Berthold, Paolo Woods;
Espen Gleditsch, Linn Pedersen,
Sverre Strandberg, Gunnhild
Torgersen, Arne Vinnem; Eivind
Lentz; David Molander; Eivind
Lentz, Maiken Havårstein, Heidi
Mork Lomell, Marika Lüders, Tarjei
Tvedte, Kari Gjerde, Kaja Hegg, Eva
Løveid Mølster; Angelica Teuta;
Andreas Bennin; Jan Freuchen;
Kristine Dragland

2014

Riitta Ikonen, Karoline Hjorth;
Morten Andersen, Line Bøhmer
Løkken, Ole Hagen, Saman Kamyab,
Vilde Salhus Røed, Sandra Vaka
Olsen, Kristine Øksendal; Marte
Elise Stramrud; Synnøve Anker
Aurdal, Victor Boullet; Mladen
Bizumic, Ulla Jokisalo, Ketuta Alexi-
Meskhishvili; Bull.Miletic, Kristina
Norman, Nicu Ilfoveanu

2015

Timo Kelaranta; Henrik Lund
Jørgensen; Sophy Rickett, Bettina
von Zwehl; Damir Avdagic, Jeanette
Christensen, Pål Henrik Ekern,
Bjørn Erik Haugen, Vegar Moen,
Randi Nygård; Christian Tunge, Sara
Skorgan Teigen, Vilde J. Rolfsen,
Johan Rosenmunthe, Petter Berg;
Alec Soth; Øystein Aasan

Trollkrem, Peter Clough, Trine Falch, Sverre Gullesen, Geir Haraldseth, Simon Skredderne HAiK; Richard Alexandersson, Marius Moldvær, Eline Mugaas, Anne-Lise Stenseth; Katharina Barbosa Blad, Grethe Irene Einarsen, Katinka Goldberg, Marie Helgesen, Kamilla Langeland; Adel Abidin; Katja Algert, Janet Biggs, Tonje Bøe Birkeland, Jacob Kirkegaard, Lasse Lecklin, Ulla Schildt, Helene Sommer, Mette Tronvol; Greg Pope, Kristian Pedersen, Marie Kølbæk Ivers; Gary Hill, Ingrid Eggen, Johnsen & Nielsen, Una Hunderi

Gruppe 11, Helle Siljeholm, Daniel Hansen, Anna Ihle, Tonje Alice Madsen, Pete Fleming, Geiste Kincinaityte, Tine Bek, Martinka Bobrikova & Oscar de Carmen, Hanna Fauske, Steffen Kloster Poulsen, Terje Abusdal, Itonje Søimer Guttormsen, Hanne Lillee, Agnieszka Kozlowska; (Silja Leifsdóttir), Werner Herzog, (Martina Petrelli), Coco Fusco & Paula Heredia, Michael Madsen, Pan Lu & Bo Wang, (Bull. Miletic), Andreas Bunte, (Farhad Kalantary), Catrine Thorstensen, (Helga-Marie Nordby), Agnès Varda, (Geir Haraldseth), Robert Ashley, (Iselin Linstad Hauge), Nikolaus Geyrhalter, (Greg Pope), Andrew Kotting, (Per Platou), Owen Land [George Landow], K U K & P A R F Y M E (Ingrid Forland & Vebjørn Guttormsgaard Møllberg), Stine Omar and Max Boss, (Leif Magne Tangen & Sarah Schipschack), Danny Snelson, (Nina Toft), Morten Børresen, (Kjersti Solbakken), Kristin Bergaust, (Ida Lykken Ghosh), Brit Bøhme & Inger Haugen, (Sara R. Yazdani), Susanne M. Winterling, (Jeremy Welsh), Kaia Hugin, (Stephanie von Spreter), Laure Prouvost, (Toft I Honerud), James Bridle, Doug Hall, Elastic Offsprings [Sigrid Bendz & Daniel Peder Askeland], (Ingrid Erstad), Arjuna Neuman, (Caroline Ugelstad), Lene Berg, Eleonora Danco, (Christina Leithe Hansen), George Kuchar, (Susanne Sæther), Victoria Fu, (Marte Aas), Stephen Broomer, (Rhea Dall), Adrian Piper; Liv Bugge, Kristina Bengtsson, Toril Johannessen,

Ditte Knus Tønnesen; Tori Wrånes Featuring Clare Milledge; (Camilla Johansen), (Haldis Hognestad Hasler), (Iris Slazak Løken), (Maud Dedichen), (Sigurd Skeidsvoll), Herman Engdahl, William Weng, Sigurd Skeidsvoll, Sunniva K. Hestenes, Haldis Hognestad Hasler, Joachim Michelsen Kvaleng, Camilla Johansen, Iris Slazak Løken, Ingrid Selte, Ali Arshad, Maud Dedichen, Juni Olav; Ane Hjort Guttu; (Ole John Aandal), (Dag Alveng), (Bjørn Falch Andersen), (Hanne Holm-Johnson), (Hilde Maisey), (Hege Oulie), (Olav Ragnar Rennie Loekke), (Espen Tveit), (Arne Walderhaug); Thomas Hirschhorn; Shirana Shahbazi

Felix Gmelin; Lauren Davis; Morten Andenæs, Kaja Leijon, Solveig Lønseth, Ingrid Torvund; Petrine Vinje; Khaled Barakeh, Terje Abusdal, (Sara R. Yazdani), Bouchra Khalili, (Marianne Hultmann), Eline Mugaas, Delphine Bedel, (Tine Semb), Heba Y. Amin, Maria Pasenau, Knut Åsdam, (Simon Sheikh); Nina Strand; Øystein Agerlie, Celeste Arnstedt, Sanne Vils Axelsen, Simon Berg, Theo Elias, August Eriksson, Christina Leithe Hansen, Damian Heinisch, Anna Hyvärinen, Karina-Sirkku Kurz, Ole Nesset, Steffen Kloster Poulsen, Karolina Paatos, Matilde Søes Rasmussen, Maija Annikki Savolainen, Katarina Skjønsberg, Iikka Tolonen, Tina Umer, and Peter Wessel

Lindsay Seers; Paz Errázuriz, Gluklya & Tsaplya / Factory of Found Clothes, Anastasia Khoroshilova, Ditte Lyngkaer Pedersen, Maya Schweizer, Lilla Szász, Marthe Ramm Fortun; Petter Buhagen, Ingrid Eggen, Silje Lovise Gjertsen, Jon Gorospe, Preben Holst, Hilde Honerud, Mariken Kramer, Klara Sofie Ludvigsen, Bjørn Henrik Lybeck, Gabrielle Paré, Kristian Skylstad, Siri Ekker Svendsen, Synnøve Sizou G. Wetten, Maya Økland; Maria Pasenau; Carolina Saquel; Daisuke Kosugi

(Guilhem All), (Julie Hascoët), Zines of the Zone, Wolfgang Tillmans, Christophe Daviet-Théry, (Sara R. Yazdani), Fin Serck-Hanssen, Juliàn Barón, Marie Sjøvold, (Nadine Wietlisbach), Carmen Winant, (Librairie Yvon Lambert), David Horvitz, (Nina Strand), (Anna Planas), (Pierre Hourquet); Hedevig Anker, Tanya Busse, Yamile Calderon, Edward Cunniffe, Ove Kvavik, Tobias Liljedahl, Tor-Finn Malum Fitje, Giulia Mangione, Vegar Moen; Manuel Pelmuş, (Katalin Erdödi), (Anushka Rajendran), Bjarne Barre, Salvatore Vitale, (Philip Di Salvo), (Vilde M. Horvei), the Society of the Friends of the Virus, Anahita Alebouyeh, Håkon Hoffart, Anders Eiebakke; Marin Håskjold, (Mina Alette Høvik), (Tominga Hope O'Donnell); (Adrià Julià), Terje Abusdal, Abdul Halik Azeez, (Heidi Bale Amundsen), (Delphine Bedel), (Bruno Ceschel), (Paul Gangloff), (Erik Gant), (Roberto Figliulo), Cosmo Großbach, Sohrab Hura, (Kay Jun), Aglaia Konrad, (Moritz Kung), (Silja Leifsdottir), (Hailey Loman), (Catalina Lozano), Vijai Patchineelam, (Bonaventure Soh Bejeng Ndikung), (Anna-Kaisa Rastenberger), (Mette Sandbye), Ursula Schulz-Dornburg, Ahlam Shibli, (Æsa Sigurjónsdóttir), (Ina Steiner), (Niclas Östlind), Stanley Wolukau-Wanambwa, (Antonio Zúñiga); (Anne Lise Stenseth), (Tom Klev), (Henri Terho), (Annika Thörn Legzdins), (Klara Þórhallsdóttir), (Tine Vindfeld); Bouchra Khalili; Ellinor Aurora Aasgaard, Zayne Armstrong; (Siri Hjorth), (Sebastian Makonnen Kjølaas), (Emanuele Guidi), (Fan Popo); (Yony Leyser), (Andrea Lissoni), (Carolina Saquel), (Kita Updike); Anne-Stine Johnsbråten, (Reiko Abe Audestad), (Tara Ishizuka Hassel), (Brian Cliff Olguin), Azumaru; Alaa Hamameh, Ammar Hatem, Ammar Khattab, Diala Brisly, Fadi Aljabour, Fahed Halabi, Michaele Daoud, Nada Ali, Nagham Hamoush, Nour Safadi, Razan Sabbagh, Ruba Salameh, Tamer Mallak, Yaser Kassab, Yerevan Hassan, Zena El Abdalla

Exhibiting Artists (& Contributors)
at Fotogalleriet 1977–2020

List of Images

Acknowledgments

First of all, a thank you is due to Fotogalleriet's board, past and present, for their constant guidance to the institution. In particular, invaluable supervision and support for this book has been provided by Morten Andenæs (Chair, 2019–), Anne Szefer Karlsen (2019–), Andreas Bennin (2019–), Thora Dolven Balke (2020–), Jason Havneraas (2017–20), Tominga O'Donnell (2018–19), Espen Gleditsch (Chair, 2016–19), Kristine K. Wessel (2014–18), Guro Voss Gabrielsen (2015–18), Knut Åsdam (2016–17), and Marte Aas (Chair, 2012–16).

The work on the publication in its current form started in August of 2018 under the newly appointed artistic director Antonio Cataldo. The aim of the publication was to further investigate histories and stories that appeared not to have found the light they deserved. During the period of 2015–17, fundraising efforts were made for a publication to be produced. Since books are long in the making, and archives are perhaps less telling in what they record than in the gaps they leave, it is hard to credit the many people who have contributed directly and indirectly to this incredible work of attempting to recount the history of photography from a situated perspective during the previous five decades. We can only continue to restlessly mend and amend. The scope of this publication was also to supplement the archives with newly commissioned research.

Work on the systematisation of the archive started under the directorship of Stephanie von Spreter with Silja Leifsdottir. Between 2016 and 2018, Martina Petrelli researched, systematised and developed an archival system for Fotogalleriet based on both scientific and artistic principles; the process was supported by the Barcelona Museum of Contemporary Art (MACBA)'s Study Centre (CED), and approved by The National Archives of Norway (Arkivverket).

MACBA, through Marta Vega, Head of Library, Ruben Faneca, Institutional Archive, Paloma Gueilburt, Repository, Cristina Bonet, Exhibition Coordinator, and Maite Muñoz, former head of the MACBA Archive, made an important contribution on best international practises.

The work on guidelines and best practices was enthusiastically supported by The National Archives of Norway through Per Kristian Ottersland, Archivist, Section for Private Archives, Svein Warberg, Senior Advisor, Department for Digitalisation and Conservation, Lars Schanke Aamodt, Photographer, Hugo Johansen, Photographer and Executive Officer, and Synne Stavheim, Assistant Director. A special thanks goes to Arts Council Norway's trainee scheme, which was in its pilot phase at the time, and made Fotogalleriet one of the first institutions to benefit from such a programme. This allowed Petrelli to work on systematising the institution's records and research both in Norway and abroad on such itemisation, opening the path for other small-sized institutions to take care of their historical holdings. The process was further enriched through support by Arts Council Norway's Fund for

Cultural Heritage and work on digitisation of the archive. At Fotogalleriet, additional assistance in working on the physical archives was given by Jóhannes Kjartansson, Frida Edlund, Stephanie Stadler, Charlotte Bouchard-Lafond, Anastasia Lejneva and Arja Horn. Petrelli subsequently coordinated the anniversary programme, taking over responsibilities from Leifsdottir.

The Fotogalleriet's archives were made available to public consultation for research for the first time on the occasion of the opening of the exhibition *What Remains,* curated by Silja Leifsdottir, marking the opening of Fotogalleriet's anniversary programme, running from 9 February to 17 December 2017. A dedicated exhibition titled *Looking into (our) Archives,* was held as an open laboratory publicly inviting key figures of Fotogalleriet's history to contribute and discuss the systematised troves. In addition, in June 2017 a number of key figures were actively invited to participate in the archival work; here, a thank you goes to Ole John Aandal, Dag Alveng, Bjørn Falch Andersen, Hanne Holm-Johnson, Hilde Maisey, Hege Oulie, Olav Ragnar Rennie Loekke, Espen Tveit and Arne Walderhaug.

The Young Lions. Norwegian Camera-Based Art 1977–2017, held at the Preus Museum and curated by Hege Oulie, was held from April to September 2017, consisting of a historical review and the presentation of nine young artists, in a long term collaboration with Fotogalleriet and in particular for the exhibition

with Kristian Skylstad. The Preus exhibition included interviews with witnesses, currently available on the museum's website.

At the beginning of 2018, artists Dag Alveng, Tonje Bøe Birkeland and Terje Abusdal donated exclusive prints to Fotogalleriet to contribute to the realisation of this book, for which we thank them.

Fotogalleriet would also like to thank Ingrid Nilsson, Director, Hanne Holm-Johnsen, Senior Curator, at the Preus Museum for continuing to safeguard Fotogalleriet history through holding parts of its archive, as well as FFF (Norwegian Association for Fine Art Photographers) through Thale Fastvold (Chair of the Board) and Kjersti Solberg Monsen (Managing Director), Katinka Maraz (former Chair of the Board), Matti Lucie Arentz (former Vice Chair) for continuous discussions on the project, since our histories are highly complex and intertwined. We would also like to thank everyone who in any small or large way helped the photographs make it into this book, including Ana María Bresciani at Henie Onstad Kunstsenter, and Vidar Ibenfeldt at Nasjonalmuseet.

In order to formulate the book, a number of informal and formal conversations were held with Bjørnar Pedersen, Liv Bugge, Sille Storihle, Amar Kanwar, Ute Meta Bauer, Trude Schjelderup Iversen, Thomas Hirschhorn, Elise Storsveen, Ingrid Book & Carina Hedén, Beate Gütschow, Dag Nordbrenden,

Acknowledgments

Jan Freuchen, Katja Mater, Melvin Moti,
Morten Andersen, Stian Ådlandsvik &
Lutz-Rainer Müller, Vibeke Tandberg,
Dieter Roelstraete, Florian Ebner,
Katia Mazzucco, David Campany, and
Simon Baker. At Fotogalleriet, a special
acknowledgment goes to Una Mathiesen
Gjerde and Annika Hagstrøm for crucial
editorial discussions around the scope of
the book and for having thoroughly read
the first drafts of the conversations and
given precious feedback.

This book would have not been possible
without the dedication of managing
editors Karen Fosse Rosness and Håkon
Lillegraven.

We would also like to thank Knut Olav
Åmås, Director, and Oskar Kvasnes,
Senior Advisor, Fritt Ord Foundation;
and Hege Imerslund, Director, The
Relief Fund for Visual Artists.

Our thanks go especially to you, the
reader and the artists from within the
field. As an institution striving to
maintain active discussions around
photographic productions, we hope we
are providing all the food for thought
you could wish for.

     Acknowledgments

Conversations on Photography

© 2021 Kehrer Verlag Heidelberg, Fotogalleriet Oslo, artists and authors

Editor
Antonio Cataldo

Managing Editors
Håkon Lillegraven;
Karen Fosse Rosness

Copy editing and proofreading
Melissa Larner

Proofreading
Gérard A. Goodrow

Translations
Texts and conversations by Marthe Ramm Fortun, Dag Alveng and Susanne Østby Sæther, Marianne Heske and Lotte Konow Lund, Anna Tellgren and Ann Christine Eek, Karen Fosse Rosness and Gry Martinsen, Helle Siljeholm and Robert Meyer, Hanne Hammer Stien, Matias Faldbakken and Eivind Furnesvik, Maria Pasenau and Bjørn Hatterud, Silja Leifsdottir and Håkon Lillegraven were translated from Norwegian to English by John Irons.

The conversation between Stephanie von Spreter and Shirana Shahbazi was translated from German to English by Dr. Jeremy Gaines.

Design and cover
Hans Gremmen

Image processing
Kehrer Design (René Henoch)

Production management
Kehrer Design (Tom Streicher)

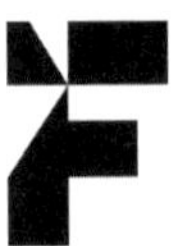

Fotogalleriet
Møllergata 34
NO-0179 Oslo
www.fotogalleriet.no
post@fotogalleriet.no

Printed and bound in Germany
ISBN 978-3-96900-008-3

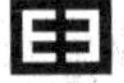

Kehrer Heidelberg
www.kehrerverlag.com

The overview of exhibiting artists (& contributors) at Fotogalleriet is a working file largely based on the Fotogalleriet Archives 1977-2017.

Errors or omissions will be corrected in subsequent editions.

The conversation between Matias Faldbakken and Eivind Furnesvik is an unedited translation by Alice Menzies from a transcription of an original in Norwegian.

Zayne Armstrong's text doesn't comply with the standards of the copy-editing of the rest of the book as part of an intention of the author to resist the norms of publishing and in on-going research related to questioning and confounding standardized rules concerning established power relations in literature, including but not limited to the narrator and the subject of the interview.

Fotogalleriet is the first Nordic institution solely dedicated to photography as a critical art practice, located in central Oslo.

Fotogalleriet's principal funding comes from the Royal Norwegian Ministry of Culture. Additional funding is provided by the Norwegian Photographic Fund (Nofofo). Partial funding comes from the Oslo Municipality.

Major support for this publication has been provided by The Arts Council Norway, BKH – The Relief Fund for Visual Artists and the Fritt Ord Foundation, Oslo.

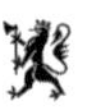

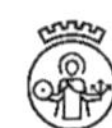

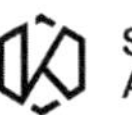

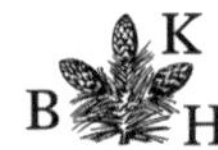